Creative Management

Creative Management

Second Edition

Edited by

Jane Henry

in association with

SAGE Publications
London • Thousand Oaks • New Delhi

This publication is the prescribed MBA Course Reader for the Creativity, Innovation and Change Module (B822) at The Open University Business School. Details of this and other Open University courses can be obtained from the Call Centre, PO Box 724, The Open University, Milton Keynes MK7 6ZS, United Kingdom: tel. +44 (0)1908 653231; e-mail ces-gen@open.ac.uk

Alternatively, you may visit The Open University Business School website at http://oubs.open.ac.uk or The Open University website at http://www.open.ac.uk

SAGE Publications Ltd
6 Bonhill Street
London EC2A 4PU

SAGE Publications Inc
2455 Teller Road
Thousand Oaks, California 91320

SAGE Publications India Pvt Ltd
32, M-Block Market
Greater Kailash - I
New Delhi 110 048

British Library Cataloguing in Publication data

A catalogue record for this book is available from the British Library.

ISBN 0 7619 6610 2
ISBN 0 7619 6611 0 pbk

Library of Congress catalog card number available from the publisher

Printed in Great Britain by Cromwell Press Ltd

Contents

The authors

Professor Teresa M. Amabile, Harvard Business School, Boston, USA.

Professor Chris Argyris, Organizational Behavior, Harvard University, Cambridge, Massachusetts, USA.

Dr Rowan Bayne, Psychology Department, University of East London, London UK.

Professor Geert Broekstra, Management and Systems Science, Nijenrode University, Netherlands.

Professor Guy Claxton, Graduate School of Education, University of Bristol, Bristol, UK.

Professor Mihaly Csikszentmihalyi, Drucker School of Management, Claremont Graduate University, Claremont, California, USA.

Professor Francis Fukuyama, George Mason University, Washington, USA.

Professor Yiannis Gabriel, Organizational Behaviour, Imperial College, University of London, London, UK.

Daniel Goleman, Graduate School of Applied and Professional Psychology, Rutgers University, Piscataway, New Jersey, USA.

Professor Sarah Hampson, Psychology Department, University of Surrey, UK.

Professor Charles Handy, London Business School, UK.

Jeffrey R Hansen, President, J R Hanson Company, New York, USA.

Paul Hawken, Smith and Hawken and Datafusion, USA.

Professor Rosabeth Moss Kanter, Professor of Business Administration, Harvard Business School, Boston, Massachusetts, USA.

Professor Geir Kaufmann, University of Bergen, Norway.

Professor Michael Kirton, previously University of Hertfordshire, UK.

Professor David Krackhardt, Carnegie Mellon University, USA.

Amory Lovins, Research Director, Rocky Mountain Institute, Colorado, USA.

L Hunter Lovins, CEO, Rocky Mountain Institute, Colorado, USA.

Professor Henry Mintzberg, McGill University, Canada and INSEAD, France.

Professor Gareth Morgan, York University, Toronto, Canada.

Professor Ikujiro Nonaka, Hitotsubashi University, Japan.

Dr Peter Reason, Organizational Behaviour, Bath University, Bath, Avon, UK.

Ricardo Semler, CEO Semco, Brazil.

Dr Vandana Shiva, Director, Research Foundation for Science, Technology and Ecology, Delhi, India.

Professor Hirotaka Takeuchi, Hitotsubashi University, Japan.

Preface

The rapid rate of technological development has led to an increase in the pace of change, while globalization and deregulation have led to increased competition. To survive organizations need to be continuously creative and innovative, especially in high wage economies. This has led to talk of the entrepreneurial society and increased interest in ways of developing and sustaining creativity and innovation at work. We now have a better idea of how creativity emerges in organizations and a more developed idea of the principles that lay behind creative management than when the first edition of this book was published nine years ago.

The main thrust of the book is about the processes that underpin creative management. How creative perception develops out of experience, is mediated via intuitive modes of thinking, and elaborated in a social field. How creative thought and action is expressed according to your cognitive style, easier if you are interested in what you are doing, and facilitated by emotional maturity at both the individual and organization levels. Creative management often entails a shift towards greater self-organization, seems to work best where social capital is plentiful, and can lead to new forms of relationship between workers, organization and the community. The book concludes by illustrating how reframing ideas about business and development can affect organizational approaches to social responsibility and sustainable development.

This edition is divided into three parts – perception, style and development, each of which has three sections. Perception includes chapters on creativity, cognition and values and charts the shift to a more systemic view of creativity, the greater attention now paid to the role of tacit knowledge and the paradigm shift in management thinking. Style elaborates on the hitherto neglected role of emotion in management, the way in which cognitive style and personality type affect how we set about problem solving, decision making and change, and the role of action learning and defensive routines in organizational learning. Development takes a wider perspective, looking at new forms of organization, along with moves to more socially responsible management and some state of the art perspectives on sustainable development.

The chapters chosen attempt to outline some of the significant changes in thinking that have occurred in this area and are written mainly by prominent researchers in the field.

In terms of creativity (section A) two key changes in our understanding are the increased emphasis now placed on the role of intrinsic motivation and the importance of the social field or community of practice in which the endeavour arises. Amabile has drawn attention to the key role of intrinsic motivation in creative endeavour. Csikszentmihalyi has shown how creativity emerges from a social field and not solely from an individual.

Our understanding of human cognition (section B) has been revolutionized in the last twenty years, in particular our understanding about the importance of unconscious information processing and the limitations of rational thought. Claxton highlights why innovative thinking benefits from drawing on tacit thought processes. Kaufmann points out the parallels and differences between creativity, problem finding, and problem solving. Nonaka has drawn the management world's attention to the important role of tacit knowledge in knowledge creation and pointed out the extent to which this is recognized in Eastern but not Western organizations.

Some people are speculating that management is in the process of a paradigm shift in which the old organizational ideals of hierarchy and control are being replaced with a looser, networked organization based on commitment (section C). Based on extensive empirical work Mintzberg has been documenting the mismatch between management rhetoric and reality for the last quarter century. Here, in a light piece, he itemized his ten favourite bug bears. Morgan is famed for his excellent book Images of Organization in which he subsumed just about all of management and organization theory under eight metaphors. The idea of different metaphors and their paradigmatic roots has helped open people to alternative ways of seeing organizations. Here he gives a brief more philosophically oriented background to his ideas on the use of metaphor. Boekstra charts three major ways of thinking about organizations.

Emotion (section D) has traditionally been neglected and ignored in management theory (and in fairness, in academia generally). However the new rhetoric of trust, bonding, commitment and buddies means it is getting harder to set aside. Restoring emotion to its rightful place centre stage, Gabriel explains from a psychodynamic perspective why managers can be tempted to repress and displace emotion and, through recourse to his catchy phrase emotional intelligence, Goleman argues that it is primarily emotional wisdom that differentiates between the good and bad leader.

Another factor that affects both what we attend to and the way we set about tasks are our cognitive preferences and personality type (section E). Hampson provides a brief overview of what personality theory and testing can and cannot tell us. Bayne discusses the Big Five, five key personality traits that appear to be genetically underpinned and their relationship to the dimensions in the most commonly used personality inventory, the Jungian based MBTI. Kirton expounds upon the implications of a natural preference for adaption as opposed to innovation and the consequence for problem solving, creativity and decision making and change management style.

Learning (section F) has been a hot topic with managers in the late twentieth century. Here Reason explains the background, varieties and principles of action learning. Argyris explains how many change programmes have the seeds of their own destruction designed within them and how defensive behaviour can worsen the situation. Krackhardt and Hanson illustrate the benefits of trust network maps as an aid to personnel selection.

Culture (section G) can have a big impact on creativity and organization. Semler describes the extent to which it is possible to transform a traditional organization into an entrepreneurial self-organizing network of loosely related businesses. Building on his earlier work on social capital, Fukuyama argues that networks are held together by social capital derived from common informal values, and that the trust derived from social capital is a necessary prerequisite for sharing intellectual property.

The question of organizational responsibility (section H) is taken up by Handy and Kanter. Handy argues that the changed business environment necessitates a new relationship between management and workers, one he likens to the idea of citizenship. Kanter argues that partnerships between industry and social organizations can lead to social innovation that benefits both the business organization and community.

Finally the book addresses the question of sustainability (section I) Lovins argues that a shift in values would allow business to operate profitably in much more sustainable ways. Shiva points out that much modern agriculture and forestry is inherently unsustainable.

Readers of the first edition will notice some continuity of theme, if updated content, in that the first three sections of this book, on creativity, cognition and perception, address many of the same topics as the first three sections of the first edition, likewise the sections on style, responsibility and sustainability address issues raised in sections 4 and 5 of the first edition. However the current edition expands material on culture, learning and emotion.

The readings in this edition of *Creative Management* are designed to complement and extend the text on Creativity and Perception in Management I have written. *Managing Innovation and Change*, co-edited with David Mayle, also acts as a complement to *Creative Management*; while the latter explains some of the processes behind creative management, the former takes a practical look at ways of managing innovation and change in organizations; both books are also co-published by Sage in 2001.

The editor would particularly like to thank Ros Bell and Ian Williams for their comments on an earlier draft of *Creative Management* and Pam Cook and John Olney for help in preparing the manuscript.

Jane Henry
j.a.henry@open.ac.uk
March 2001

Acknowledgements

The publishers are grateful to the following for permission to reprint:

Harvard Business Review for*:* Amabile, T., 'How to kill creativity'; Mintzberg, H., 'Musings on management: ten ideas designed to rile everyone who cares about management'; Goleman, D., 'What makes a leader?'; Argyris, C., 'Empowerment: the Emperor's new clothes'; Krackhardt, D. and Hanson, J., 'Informal networks: the company behind the chart'; Semler, R., 'Why my former employees still work for me'; Kanter, R., 'From spare change to real change'; and Lovins, A., Lovins, H. and Hawken, P., 'A road map for natural capitalism'.

Maggie Pickard for Elwood H. Smith, for five illustrations in Mintzberg, H., 'Musings on management: ten ideas designed to rile everyone who cares about management'.

The British Psychological Association for: Hampson, S., 'State of the art: personality'; and Bayne, R., 'The Big Five versus the Myers-Briggs'.

Pergamon Press, Elsevier Science for: Kirton, M.J., 'Adaptors and innovators'.

Sage Inc for: Morgan, G., 'The theory behind the Practice'.

Cambridge University Press for: Csikszentmihalyi, M., 'Implications of a systems view of creativity'.

Norwegian University Press for: Kaufmann, G. and Gronhaug, G., 'Problem solving and creativity'.

Oxford University Press for: Nonaka, I. and Takeuchi, H., 'The knowledge-creating company: how Japanese companies create the dynamics of innovation'.

Profile Books Ltd and Rogers, Coleridge & White for: Fukuyama, F., 'Technology, networks and social capital'.

Random House for: Handy, C., 'The Citizen Company'.

Zed Books Ltd for: Shiva, V. 'Monocultures of the mind'.

Part 1

Perception

Section A   Creativity

This section contains chapters by two giants of recent creativity research, Teresa Amabile and Mihaly Csikszentmihalyi. Both emphasize how the community in which a person operates affects creative outcomes.

Teresa Amabile, an American academic, has drawn attention to the importance of intrinsic motivation in creative endeavour. Business has traditionally rewarded people extrinsically with pay and promotion but creative actions often arise out of a long-standing commitment to and interest in a particular area. She appreciates this is only one part of the equation, and that expertise in the domain concerned, and sufficient mental flexibility to question assumptions and play with ideas, are also important. Here she summarizes some of the implications of her studies among scientists, researchers and managers in organizations for creativity and innovation. She points out the critical importance of challenge, for example, matching people to tasks they are interested in and have expertise in, allowing people freedom as to how they achieve innovation, setting a sufficiently diverse team the task of innovation, along with sufficient resources, encouragement and support.

Mihaly Csikszentmihalyi has drawn attention to the social context out of which creativity and innovation emerge. For example he has demonstrated the beneficial role of working at a place and time in which other individuals are engaged in related creative activities: such as painting and sculpture in Florence in the 14th century, the development of computers in Northern California in the 1960s and 1970s, and industrialization in SE Asia in the last quarter of the 20th century. Studies of innovation in organizations show the importance of product champions and business sponsors in bringing innovative products through to market. Here Csikszentmihalyi outlines his systems theory of creativity, relating creative effort by individuals to the state of the domain they are working in and the characteristics of those who assess the worth of the creative endeavour in the field concerned. This offers a penetrating analysis of how creative endeavour emerges within a social field. Drawing on years of research in the field, Csikszentmihalyi hypothesizes about the interplay between knowledge about the domain, gatekeepers in the field and creative individuals. Many of the points made here in relation to other domains apply equally well to creativity and innovation in organizational settings.

1 How to Kill Creativity

Teresa Amabile

When I consider all the organizations I have studied and worked with over the past 22 years, there can be no doubt: creativity gets killed much more often than it gets supported. For the most part, this isn't because managers have a vendetta against creativity. On the contrary, most believe in the value of new and useful ideas. However, creativity is undermined unintentionally every day in work environments that were established – for entirely good reasons – to maximize business imperatives such as co-ordination, productivity, and control.

Managers cannot be expected to ignore business imperatives, of course. But in working toward these imperatives, they may be inadvertently designing organizations that systematically crush creativity. My research shows that it is possible to develop the best of both worlds: organizations in which business imperatives are attended to and creativity flourishes. Building such organizations, however, requires us to understand precisely what kinds of managerial practices foster creativity – and which kill it.

The Three Components of Creativity

Within every individual, creativity is a function of three components: expertise, creative-thinking skills, and motivation (see Figure 1.1). Can managers influence these components? The answer is an emphatic yes – for better and for worse – through workplace practices and conditions.

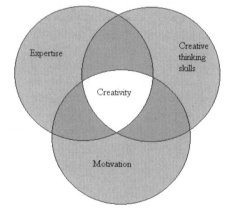

Figure 1.1 The three components of creativity.

Expertise is, in a word, knowledge – technical, procedural and intellectual.
Creative-thinking skills determine how flexibly and imaginatively people approach problems. Do their solutions up-end the status quo? Do they persevere through dry spells.

Not all *motivation* is created equal. An inner passion to solve the problem at hand leads to solutions far more creative than external rewards, such as money. This component – called intrinsic motivation – is the one that can most immediately be influenced by the work environment.

Managing creativity

[Amabile's research has identified six general categories of managerial practice that affect creativity. These are challenge, freedom, resources, work-group features, supervisory encouragement, and organizational support.] Taking these six categories that have emerged from our research in turn, let's explore what managers can do to enhance creativity – and what often happens instead. It is important to note that creativity-killing practices are seldom the work of lone managers. Such practices usually are systemic – so widespread that they are rarely questioned.

Challenge

Of all the things managers can do to stimulate creativity, perhaps the most efficacious is the deceptively simple task of matching people with the right assignments. Managers can match people with jobs that play to their expertise and their skills in creative thinking, *and* ignite intrinsic motivation. Perfect matches stretch employees' abilities. The amount of stretch, however, is crucial: not so little that they feel bored but not so much that they feel overwhelmed and threatened by a loss of control.

Making a good match requires that managers possess rich and detailed information about their employees and the available assignments. Such information is often difficult and time consuming to gather. Perhaps that's why good matches are so rarely made. In fact, one of the most common ways managers kill creativity is by not trying to obtain the information necessary to make good connections between people and jobs. Instead, something of a shotgun wedding occurs. The most eligible employee is wed to the most eligible – that is, the most urgent and open – assignment. Often, the results are predictably unsatisfactory for all involved.

Freedom

When it comes to granting freedom, the key to creativity is giving people autonomy concerning the means – that is, concerning process – but not necessarily the ends. People will be more creative, in other words, if you give them freedom to decide how to climb a particular mountain. You needn't let them choose which mountain to climb. In fact, clearly specified strategic goals often enhance people's creativity.

I'm not making the case that managers should leave their subordinates entirely out of goal- or agenda-setting discussions. But they should understand that inclusion in those discussions will not necessarily enhance creative output and certainly will not be sufficient to do so. It is far more important that whoever sets the goals also makes them clear to the organization and that these goals remain stable for a meaningful period of time. It is difficult, if not impossible, to work creatively toward a target if it keeps moving.

Autonomy around process fosters creativity because giving people freedom in how they approach their work heightens their intrinsic motivation and sense of ownership. Freedom about process also allows people to approach problems in ways that make the most of their expertise and their creative-thinking skills. The task may end up being a stretch for them, but they can use their strengths to meet the challenge.

How do executives mismanage freedom? There are two common ways. First, managers tend to change goals frequently or fail to define them clearly. Employees may have freedom around process, but if they don't know where they are headed, such freedom is pointless. And second, some managers fall short on this dimension by granting autonomy in name only. They claim that employees are 'empowered' to explore the maze as they search for solutions but, in fact, the process is proscribed. Employees diverge at their own risk.

Resources

The two main resources that affect creativity are time and money. Managers need to allot these resources carefully. Like matching people with the right assignments, deciding how much time and money to give to a team or project is a sophisticated judgement call that can either support or kill creativity.

Consider time. Under some circumstances, time pressure can heighten creativity. Say, for instance, that a competitor is about to launch a great product at a lower price than your offering or that society faces a serious problem and desperately needs a solution – such as an AIDS vaccine. In such situations, both the time crunch and the importance of the work legitimately make people feel that they must rush. Indeed, cases like these would be apt to increase intrinsic motivation by increasing the sense of challenge.

Organizations routinely kill creativity with fake deadlines or impossibly tight ones. The former create distrust and the latter cause burnout. In either case, people feel overcontrolled and unfulfilled – which invariably damages motivation. Moreover, creativity often takes time. It can be slow going to explore new concepts, put together unique solutions, and wander through the maze. Managers who do not allow time for exploration or do not schedule in incubation periods are unwittingly standing in the way of the creative process.

When it comes to project resources, again managers must make a fit. They must determine the funding, people, and other resources that a team legitimately needs to complete an assignment – and they must know how much the organization can legitimately afford to allocate to the assignment. Then they must strike a compromise. Interestingly, adding more resources above a 'threshold of sufficiency' does not boost creativity. Below the threshold, however, a restriction of resources can dampen creativity. Unfortunately, many managers don't realize this and therefore often make another mistake. They keep resources tight, which pushes people to channel their creativity into finding additional resources, not in actually developing new products or services.

Another resource that is misunderstood when it comes to creativity is physical space. It is almost conventional wisdom that creative teams need open, comfortable offices. Such an atmosphere won't hurt creativity, and it may even help, but it is not nearly as important as other managerial initiatives that influence creativity. Indeed, a problem we have seen time and time again is managers paying attention to creating the 'right' physical space at the expense of more high-impact actions, such as matching people to the right assignments and granting freedom around work processes.

Work-group features

If you want to build teams that come up with creative ideas, you must pay careful attention to the design of such teams. That is, you must create mutually supportive groups with a diversity of perspectives and backgrounds. Why? Because when teams comprise people with various intellectual foundations and approaches to work – that is, different expertise and creative thinking styles – ideas often combine and combust in exciting and useful ways.

Diversity, however, is only a starting point. Managers must also make sure that the teams they put together have three other features. First, the members must share excitement over the team's goal. Second, members must display a willingness to help their teammates through difficult periods and setbacks. And third, every member must recognize the unique knowledge and perspective that other members bring to the table. These factors enhance not only intrinsic motivation but also expertise and creative-thinking skills.

Again, creating such teams requires managers to have a deep understanding of their people. They must be able to assess them not just for their knowledge but for their attitudes about potential fellow team members and the collaborative process, for their problem-solving styles, and for their motivational hot buttons. Putting together a team with just the right chemistry – just the right level of diversity and supportiveness – can be difficult, but our research shows how powerful it can be.

It follows, then, that one common way managers kill creativity is by assembling homogeneous teams. The lure to do so is great. Homogeneous teams often reach 'solutions' more quickly and with less friction along the way. These teams often report high morale, too. But homogeneous teams do little to enhance expertise and creative thinking. Everyone comes to the table with a similar mind-set. They leave with the same.

Supervisory encouragement

Most managers are extremely busy. They are under pressure for results. It is therefore easy for them to let praise for creative efforts – not just creative successes but unsuccessful efforts, too – fall by the wayside. One very simple step managers can take to foster creativity is to not let that happen.

The connection to intrinsic motivation here is clear. Certainly, people can find their work interesting or exciting without a cheering section – for some period of time. But to *sustain* such passion, most people need to feel as if their work matters to the organization or to some important group of people. Otherwise, they might as well do their work at home and for their own personal gain.

Managers in successful, creative organizations rarely offer specific extrinsic rewards for particular outcomes. However, they freely and generously recognize creative work by individuals and teams – often before the ultimate commercial impact of those efforts is known. By contrast, managers who kill creativity do so either by failing to acknowledge innovative efforts or by greeting them with skepticism. In many companies, for instance, new ideas are met not with open minds but with time-consuming layers of evaluation – or even with harsh criticism. When someone suggests a new product or process, senior managers take weeks to respond. Or they put that person through an excruciating critique.

Not every new idea is worthy of consideration, of course, but in many organizations, managers habitually demonstrate a reaction that damages creativity. They look for reasons to not use a new idea instead of searching for reasons to explore it further. An interesting psychological dynamic underlies this phenomenon. Our research shows that people believe that they will appear smarter to their bosses if they are more critical – and it often works. In many organizations, it is professionally rewarding to react critically to new ideas.

Unfortunately, this sort of negativity bias can have severe consequences for the creativity of those being evaluated. How? First, a culture of evaluation leads people to focus on the external rewards and punishments associated with their output, thus increasing the presence of extrinsic motivation and its potentially negative effects on intrinsic motivation. Second, such a culture creates a climate of fear, which again undermines intrinsic motivation.

Finally, negativity also shows up in how managers treat people whose ideas don't pan out: often, they are terminated or otherwise warehoused within the organization. Of course, ultimately, ideas do need to work; remember that creative ideas in business must be new *and* useful. The dilemma is that you can't possibly know beforehand which ideas will pan out. Furthermore, dead ends can sometimes be very enlightening. In many business situations, knowing what doesn't work can be as useful as knowing what does. But if people do not perceive any 'failure value' for projects that ultimately do not achieve commercial success, they'll become less and less likely to experiment, explore, and connect with their work on a personal level. Their intrinsic motivation will evaporate.

Supervisory encouragement comes in other forms besides rewards and punishment. Another way managers can support creativity is to serve as role models, persevering through tough problems as well as encouraging collaboration and communication within the team. Such behaviour enhances all three components of the creative process, and it has the added virtue of being a high-impact practice that a single manager can take on his or her own. It is better still when all managers in an organization serve as role models for the attitudes and behaviours that encourage and nurture creativity.

Organizational support

Encouragement from supervisors certainly fosters creativity, but creativity is truly enhanced when the entire organization supports it. Such support is the job of an organization's leaders, who must put in place appropriate systems or procedures and emphasize values that make it clear that creative efforts are a top priority. For example, creativity-supporting organizations consistently reward creativity, but they avoid using money to 'bribe' people to come up with innovative ideas. Because monetary rewards make people feel as if they are being controlled, such a tactic probably won't work. At the same time, not providing sufficient recognition and rewards for creativity can spawn negative feelings within an organization. People can feel used, or at least under-appreciated, for their creative efforts. And it is rare to find the energy and passion of intrinsic motivation coupled with resentment.

Most important, an organization's leaders can support creativity by mandating information sharing and collaboration and by ensuring that political problems do not fester. Information sharing and collaboration support all three components of creativity. Take expertise. The more often people exchange ideas and data by working together, the more knowledge they will have. The same dynamic can be said for creative thinking. In fact, one way to enhance the creative thinking of employees is to expose them to various approaches to problem solving. With the exception of hardened misanthropes, information sharing and collaboration heighten people's enjoyment of work and thus their intrinsic motivation.

Whether or not you are seeking to enhance creativity, it is probably never a good idea to let political problems fester in an organizational setting. Infighting, politicking, and gossip are particularly damaging to creativity because they take peoples' attention away from work. That sense of mutual purpose and excitement so central to intrinsic motivation invariably lessens when people are cliquish or at war with one another. Indeed, our research suggests that intrinsic motivation increases when people are aware that those around them are excited by their jobs. When political problems abound, people feel that their work is threatened by others' agendas.

Finally, politicking also undermines expertise. The reason? Politics get in the way of open communication, obstructing the flow of information from point A to point B. Knowledge stays put and expertise suffers.

Source: Extracted from 'How to Kill Creativity', *Harvard Business Review*, 1998, September, pp. 77–87.

2   A Systems Perspective on Creativity

Mihaly Csikszentmihalyi

Psychologists tend to see creativity exclusively as a mental process [but] creativity is as much a cultural and social as it is a psychological event. Therefore what we call creativity is not the product of single individuals, but of social systems making judgements about individual's products. Any definition of creativity that aspires to objectivity, and therefore requires an intersubjective dimension, will have to recognize the fact that the audience is as important to its constitution as the individual to whom it is credited.

An outline of the systems model

This environment has two salient aspects: a cultural, or symbolic, aspect which here is called the domain; and a social aspect called the field. Creativity is a process that can be observed only at the intersection where individuals, domains, and fields interact (Figure 2.1).

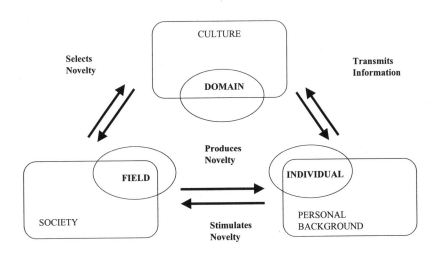

Figure 2.1 The systems view of creativity

For creativity to occur, a set of rules and practices must be transmitted from the domain to the individual. The individual must then produce a novel variation in the content of the domain. The variation then must be selected by the field for inclusion in the domain.

Creativity occurs when a person makes a change in a domain, a change that will be transmitted through time. Some individuals are more likely to make such changes, either because of personal qualities or because they have the good fortune to be well positioned with respect to the domain – they have better access to it, or their social circumstances allow them free time to experiment. For example, until quite recently the majority of scientific advances were made by men who had the means and the leisure: clergymen like Copernicus, tax collectors like Lavoisier, or physicians like Galvani could afford to build their own laboratories and to concentrate on their thoughts. And, of course, all of these individuals lived in cultures with a tradition of systematic observation of nature and a tradition of record keeping and mathematical symbolization that made it possible for their insights to be shared and evaluated by others who had equivalent training.

But most novel ideas will be quickly forgotten. Changes are not adopted unless they are sanctioned by some group entitled to make decisions as to what should or should not be included in the domain. These gatekeepers are what we call here the field. Here field refers only to the social organization of the domain – to the teachers, critics, journal editors, museum curators, agency directors, and foundation officers who decide what belongs to a domain and what does not. In physics, the opinion of a very small number of leading university professors was enough to certify that Einstein's ideas were creative. Hundreds of millions of people accepted the judgement of this tiny field and marvelled at Einstein's creativity without understanding what it was all about. It has been said that in the United States 10,000 people in Manhattan constitute the field in modern art. They decide which new paintings or sculptures deserve to be seen, bought, included in collections, and therefore added to the domain.

The cultural context

Creativity presupposes a community of people who share ways of thinking and acting, who learn from each other and imitate each other's actions. It is useful to think about creativity as involving a change in memes – the units of imitation that Dawkins (1976) suggested were the building blocks of culture. Memes are similar to genes in that they carry instructions for action. The notes of a song tell us what to sing, the recipe for a cake tells us what ingredients to mix and how long to bake it. But whereas genetic instructions are transmitted in the chemical codes that we inherit on our chromosomes, the instructions contained in memes are transmitted through learning. By and large we can learn memes and reproduce them without change; when a new song or a new recipe is invented, then we have creativity.

Cultures as a set of domains

It is useful to think about cultures as systems of interrelated domains. Cultures differ in the way that memes (i.e. technical procedures, kinds of knowledge, styles of art, belief systems) are stored. As long as they are recorded orally and can be transmitted only from the mind of one person to another, traditions must be strictly observed so as not to lose information. Therefore, creativity is not likely to be prized, and it would be difficult to determine in any case. Development of new media of storage and transmission (e.g. books, computers) will have an impact on rates of novelty production and its acceptance.

Another dimension of cultural difference is the accessibility of information. With time, people who benefit from the ability to control memes develop protective boundaries around their knowledge, so that only a few initiates at any given time will have access to it. Priestly castes around the world have evolved to keep their knowledge esoteric and out of reach of the masses. Even in the times of Egyptian civilization, craft guilds kept much of their technical knowledge secret. Until recently in the West, knowledge of Latin and Greek was used as a barrier to prevent the admittance of the masses to professional training. The more such barriers, the less likely it becomes that potentially creative individuals will be able to contribute to a domain.

Similarly, how available memes are also bears on the rate of creativity. When knowledge is concentrated in a few centres, libraries, or laboratories, or when books and schools are rare, most potentially creative individuals will be effectively prevented from learning enough to make a contribution to existing knowledge.

Cultures differ in the number of domains they recognize and in the hierarchical relationship among them. New memes most often arise in cultures that, either because of geographical location or economic practices, are exposed to different ideas and beliefs. The Greek traders collected information from Egypt, the Middle East, the north coast of Africa, the Black Sea, Persia and even Scandinavia, and this disparate information was amalgamated in the crucible of the Ionian and Attic city-states. In the Middle Ages, the Sicilian court welcomed techniques and knowledge from China and Arabia, as well as from Normandy, Florence in the Renaissance was a centre of trade and manufacture, and so was Venice; later the maritime trade of the Iberian Peninsula, the Netherlands, and Great Britain moved the center of information exchange to those regions. Even now, when the diffusion of information is almost instantaneous, useful new ideas are likely to arise from centres where people from different cultural backgrounds are able to interact and exchange ideas.

The role of the domain in the creative process

Cultures are made up of a variety of domains: music, mathematics, religion, various technologies, and so on. Innovations that result in creative contributions do not take place directly in the culture, but in one of such domains.

There are times when the symbolic system of a domain is so diffuse and loosely integrated that it is almost impossible to determine whether a novelty is or is not an improvement on the status quo. Chemistry was in such a state before the adoption of the periodic table, which integrated and rationalized knowledge about the elements. Earlier centuries may have had many potentially creative chemical scientists, but their work was too idiosyncratic to be evaluated against a common standard. Or, conversely, the symbolic systems may be so tightly organized that no new development seems possible: this resembles the situation in physics at the end of the preceding century, before the revolution in thinking brought about by quantum theory. Both of these examples suggest that creativity is likely to be more difficult before a paradigmatic revolution. On the other hand, the need for a new paradigm makes it more likely that if a new viable contribution does occur despite the difficulty, it will be hailed as a major creative accomplishment.

At any historical period, certain domains will attract more gifted young people than at other times, thus increasing the likelihood of creativity. The attraction of a domain depends on several variables: its centrality in the culture, the promise of new discoveries and opportunities that it presents, the intrinsic rewards accruing from working in the domain. For instance, the Renaissance in early-fifteenth-century Florence would have not happened without the discovery of Roman ruins, which yielded a great amount of new knowledge about construction techniques and sculptural models and motivated many young people who otherwise would have gone into the professions, to become architects and artists instead. The quantum revolution in physics at the beginning of this century was so intellectually exciting that, for several generations, some of the best minds flocked to physics or applied its principles to neighbouring disciplines such as chemistry, biology, medicine, and astronomy. Nowadays similar excitement surrounds the domains of molecular biology and computer science.

As Thomas Kuhn (1962) remarked, potentially creative young people will not be drawn to domains where all the basic questions have been solved and which, therefore, appear to be boring – that is, offer few opportunities to obtain the intrinsic and extrinsic rewards that follow from solving important problems.

Domains also vary in terms of their accessibility. Sometimes rules and knowledge become the monopoly of a protective class or caste, and others are not admitted to it. Creative thought in Christianity was renewed by the Reformation, which placed the bible and its commentaries in reach of a much larger population, which earlier had been excluded by an entrenched priestly caste from perusing it directly. The enormously increased accessibility of information on the Internet might also bring about a new peak in creativity across many different domains, just as the printing press did over four centuries ago.

Finally, some domains are easier to change than others. This depends in part on how autonomous a domain is from the rest of the culture or social system that supports it. Until the seventeenth century in Europe it was difficult to be creative in the many branches of science that the Church had a vested interest in protecting – as the case of Galileo illustrates. In Soviet Russia, the Marxist-Leninist dogma took precedence over scientific domains, and many new ideas that conflicted with it were not accepted. Even in our time, some topics in the social (and even in the physical and biological) sciences are considered less politically correct than others and are given scant research support as a consequence.

Creativity is the engine that drives cultural evolution. The notion of evolution does not imply that cultural changes necessarily follow some single direction or that cultures are getting any better as a result of the changes brought about by creativity. Evolution in this context means increasing complexity over time. Complexity means that cultures tend to become differentiated over time, that is, they develop increasingly independent and autonomous domains [and that] the domains within a culture become increasingly integrated, that is, related to each other and mutually supportive of each others' goals. Creativity contributes to differentiation, but it can easily work against integration, [as] new ideas, technologies, or forms of expression often break down the existing harmony between different domains.

The social context

In order to be called creative, a new meme must be socially valued. Without some form of social valuation it would be impossible to distinguish ideas that are simply bizarre from those that are genuinely creative. But this social validation is usually seen as something that follows the individual's creative act and can be – at least conceptually – separated from it. The stronger claim made here is that there is no way, even in principle, to separate the reaction of society from the person's contribution. The two are inseparable. As long as the idea or product has not been validated, we might have originality, but not creativity.

Nowadays everyone agrees that van Gogh's paintings show that he was a very creative artist. It is also fashionable to sneer at the ignorant bourgeoisie of his period for failing to recognize van Gogh's genius and letting him die alone and penniless. But we should remember that a hundred years ago those canvases were just the hallucinatory original works of a sociopathic recluse. They became creative only after a number of other artists, critics, and collectors interpreted them in terms of new aesthetic criteria and transformed them from substandard efforts into masterpieces.

Without this change in the climate of evaluation, Van Gogh would not be considered creative even now. In the sciences as well as in the arts, creativity is as much the result of changing standards and new criteria of assessment, as it is of novel individual achievements.

Societal conditions relevant to creativity

The second main element of the systems model is society, or the sum of all fields. Fields are made up of individuals who practise a given domain and have the power to change it. For example, all the accountants who practise by the same rules comprise the field of accountancy, and it is they who have to endorse a new way of keeping accounts if it is to be accepted as a creative improvement.

Other things being equal, a society that enjoys a material surplus is in better position to help the creative process. A wealthier society is able to make information more readily available, allows for a greater rate of specialization and experimentation, and is better equipped to reward and implement new ideas. Subsistence societies have fewer opportunities to encourage and reward novelty, especially if it is expensive to produce. Only societies with ample material reserves can afford to build great cathedrals, universities, scientific laboratories. But it seems that there is often a lag between social affluence and creativity: the impact of wealth may take several generations to manifest itself. So the material surplus of the nineteenth-century United States was first needed to build a material infrastructure for society (canals, railroads, factories), before it was invested in supporting novel ideas such as the telephone or the mass production of cars and planes.

Whether a society is open to novelty or not depends in part on its social organization. A farming society with a stable feudal structure, for instance, would be one where tradition counts more than novelty. Societies based on commerce, with a strong bourgeois class trying to be accepted by the aristocracy, have on the other hand been usually favourable to novelty. Whenever the central authority tends toward absolutism, it is less likely that experimentation will be encouraged (Therivel 1995). Ancient Chinese society is a good example of a central authority supported by a powerful bureaucracy that was able to resist for centuries the spread of new ideas.

Rentier societies, where the ruling classes lived off the profits of land rent, pensions, or stable investments, have been historically reluctant to change because any novelty was seen to potentially threaten the status quo that provided the livelihood of the oligarchy. This condition might become relevant again as the United States moved more toward an economy where pensions and retirement plans are a major source of income for an increasing number of people.

A different and more controversial suggestion is that egalitarian societies are less likely to support the creative process than those where relatively few people control a disproportionate amount of the resources. Aristocracies or oligarchies may be better able to support creativity than democracies or social regimes, simply because when wealth and power are concentrated in a few hands, it is easier to use part of it for risky or 'unnecessary' experiments. Also, the development of a leisure class often results in a refinement of connoiseurship that in turn provides more demanding criteria by which a field evaluates new contributions.

Societies located at the confluence of diverse cultural streams can benefit more easily from that synergy of different ideas that is so important for the creative process. It is for this reason that some of the greatest art, and the earliest science, developed in cities that were centres of trade. The Italian Renaissance was in part due to the Arab and Middle Eastern influences that businessmen and their retinues brought into Florence and the seaports of Venice, Genoa, and Naples. The fact that periods of social unrest often coincide with creativity (Simonton 1991) is probably due to the synergy resulting when the interests and perspectives of usually segregated classes are brought to bear on each other. The Tuscan cities supported creativity best during a period in which noblemen, merchants, and craftsmen fought each other bitterly and when every few years, as a different political party came to power, a good portion of the citizenry was banished into exile.

External threats also often mobilize society to recognize creative ideas that otherwise might not have attracted much attention. Florence in the fifteenth century spent so many resources on the arts in part because the leaders of the city were competing against their enemies in Sienna, Lucca, and Pisa and tried to outdo them in the beauty of their churches and public squares (Heydenreich 1974). The reason that high-energy physics became such an important field after World War II is that practically every nation wished to have the technology to build its own nuclear arsenal.

Finally, the complexity of a society also bears on the rates of innovation it can tolerate. Too much divisiveness, as well as its opposite, too much uniformity, are unlikely to generate novelty that will be accepted and preserved. Ideal conditions for creativity would be a social system that is highly differentiated into specialized fields and roles, yet is held together by what Durkheim (1912/1967) called the bonds of 'organic solidarity'.

The role of the field

What does it take for a new meme to be accepted into the domain? Who has the right to decide whether a new meme is actually an improvement, or simply a mistake to be discarded? In the systems model, the gatekeepers who have the right to add memes to a domain are collectively designated the field. Some domains may have a very small field consisting of a dozen or so scholars across the world. Others, such as electronic engineering, may include many thousands of specialists whose opinion would count in recognizing a viable novelty. For mass-market products such as soft drinks or motion pictures, the field might include not only the small coterie of product developers and critics, but the public at large. For instance, if New Coke is not a part of the culture, it is because although it passed the evaluation of the small field of beverage specialists, it failed to pass the test of public taste.

Some of the ways in which fields influence creativity follow. The first issue to be considered is the field's access to economic resources. In some domains it is almost impossible to do novel work without access to capital. To build a cathedral or to make a movie required the collaboration of people and materials, and these must be made available to the would-be creative artists. The masterpieces of Florence were built with the profits that the city's bankers made throughout Europe: the masterpieces of Venice were the fruit of that city's seagoing trade. Dutch painters and scientists blossomed after Dutch merchants began to dominate the sea-lanes: then it was the turn of France, England, Germany, and, finally, the United States. As resources accumulate in one place, they lay down the conditions that make innovation possible.

A field is likely to attract original minds to the extent that it can offer scope for a person's experimentations and promises rewards in case of success. Even though individuals who try to change domains are in general intrinsically motivated – that is, they enjoy working in the domain for its own sake – the attraction of extrinsic awards such as money and fame are not to be discounted.

Leonardo da Vinci, one of the most creative persons on record in terms of his contributions to the arts and the sciences, constantly moved during his lifetime from one city to another, in response to changing market conditions. The leaders of Florence, the dukes of Milan, the popes of Rome, and the king of France waxed and waned in terms of how much money they had to devote to new paintings, sculptures, or cutting-edge scholarship: and as their fortunes changed, Leonardo moved to wherever he could pursue his work with the least hindrance.

The centrality of a field in terms of societal values will also determine how likely it is to attract new persons with an innovative bent. In this particular historical period, bright young men and women are attracted to the field on computer sciences because it provides the most exciting new intellectual challenges: others to oceanography because it might help to save the planetary ecosystem: some to currency trading because it provides access to financial power: and some to family medicine, because it is the medical specialty most responsive to societal needs. Any field that is able to attract a disproportionate number of bright young persons is more likely to witness creative breakthroughs.

In the domains of movies or popular music, which are much more accessible to the general public, the specialized field is notoriously unable to enforce a decision as to which works will be creative. It is instructive to compare the list of Nobel Prize-winners in literature with those in the sciences: few of the writers from years past are now recognized as creative compared with the scientists.

In order to establish and preserve criteria, a field must have a minimum of organization. However, it is often the case that instead of serving the domain, members of the field devote most of their energies to serving themselves, making it difficult for new ideas to be evaluated on their merits. It is not only the Church that has hindered the spread of new ideas for fear of losing its privileges. Every industry faces the problem that better ideas that require changing the status quo will be ignored, because so much effort and capital has been invested in existing production methods.

Another important dimension along which fields vary is the extent to which they are ideologically open or closed to new memes. The openness of a field depends in part on its internal organization, in part on its relation to the wider society. Highly hierarchical institutions, where knowledge of the past is greatly valued, generally see novelty as a threat. For this reason churches, academies, and certain businesses based on tradition seek to promote older individuals to leadership positions as a way of warding off excessive change. Also, creativity is not welcome in fields whose self-interest requires keeping a small cadre of initiates performing the same routines, regardless of efficiency: some of the trade unions come to mind in this context.

It requires an adroit balancing act for those responsible for evaluating novelty to decide which new ideas are worth preserving. If a historical period is stagnant, it is probably not because there were no potentially creative individuals around, but because of the ineptitude of the relevant fields.

It might be objected that some of the most influential new ideas or processes seem to occur even though there is no existing domain or field to received them. For instance, Freud's ideas had a wide impact even before there was a domain of psychoanalysis or a field of analysts to evaluate them. Personal computers were widely adopted before there was a tradition and a group of experts to judge which were good, which were not. But the lack of a social context in such cases is more apparent than real. Freud, who was immersed in the already-existing domain of psychiatry; he simply expanded its limits until his conceptual contributions could stand on their own as a separate domain. Without peers and without disciples, Freud's ideas might have been original, but they would not have had an impact on the culture, and thus would have failed to be creative. Similarly, personal computers would not have been accepted had there not been a domain – computer languages that allowed the writing of software and therefore, various applications – and an embryonic field – people who had experience with mainframe computers, with video games, and so on who could become 'experts' in this emerging technology.

In any case, the point is that how much creativity there is at any given time is not determined just by how many original individuals are trying to change domains, but also by how receptive the fields are to innovation. It follows that if one wishes to increase the frequency of creativity, it may be more advantageous to work at the levels of fields than at the level of individuals. For example, some large organizations such as Motorola, where new technological interventions are essential, spend a large quantity of resources in trying to make engineers think more creatively. This is a good strategy as far as it goes, but it will not result in any increase in creativity unless the field – in this case, management – is able to recognize which of the new ideas are good and has ways for implementing them, that is, including them in the domain. Whereas engineers and managers are the field who judge the creativity of new ideas within an organization such as Motorola, the entire market for electronics becomes the field that evaluates the organization's products once these have been implemented within the organization. Thus, at one level of analysis the system comprises the organization, with innovators, managers, and production engineers as its parts; but at a higher level of analysis the organization becomes just one element of a broader system that includes the entire industry.

The individual in the creative process

The great majority of psychological research assumes that creativity is an individual trait, to be understood by studying individuals. The systems model makes it possible to see that before a person can introduce a creative variation, he or she must have access to a domain and must want to learn to perform according to its rules. This implies that motivation is important. But it also suggests a number of additional factors that are usually ignored, for instance, that cognitive and motivational factors interact with the state of the domain and the field.

Second, persons who are likely to innovate tend to have personality traits that favour breaking rules and early experiences that make them want to do so. Divergent thinking, problem finding, and all the other factors that psychologists have studied are relevant in this context.

Finally, the ability to convince the field about the virtue of the novelty one has produced is an important aspect of personal creativity. The opportunities that one has to get access to the field, the network of contacts, the personality traits that make it possible for one to be taken seriously, the ability to express oneself in such a way as to be understood, are all part of the individual traits that make it easier for someone to make a creative contribution.

But none of these personal characteristics are sufficient, and probably they are not even necessary. Conservative and unimaginative scientists have made important contributions to science by stumbling on important new phenomena. At the same time, it is probably true that persons who master a domain, and then want to change it, will have a higher proportion of their efforts recognized as creative.

The background of creative individuals

One of the first issues to consider is whether an individual is born in an environment that has enough surplus energy to encourage the development of curiosity and interest for its own sake. The following personal background factors can affect the incidence of creativity:

- A child is likely to be discouraged from expressing curiosity and interest if the material conditions of existence are too precarious.
- Ethnic and family traditions can have a very important role in directing the child's interest toward specific domains.
- Cultural capital (i.e. home learning, schooling) is essential for a child to develop expertise in a domain.
- Tutors, mentors, and connections are often indispensable for advancing far enough to have one's ideas recognized.
- Marginality (social, ethnic, economic, religious) seems to be more conducive to wanting to break out of the norm than a conventional, middle-class background.

Even though it is said that necessity is the mother of invention, too much deprivation does not seem to lead to innovative thinking. When survival is precarious – as it has been and still is in most of the world – there is little energy left for learning and experimenting. It is not impossible for a talented person to emerge from a ghetto or a third-world country, but much potential is lost for lack of access to the basic tools of a domain.

Ethnic groups, and families within them, differ in the amount of importance they place on different domains. Jewish tradition has emphasized the importance of learning, and Asian-American families have instilled strong academic and artistic motivation in their children (Kao 1995). Some cultural groups emphasize musical abilities, others focus on engineering or technology. Such traditions help to focus a child's interest on a particular domain, thus providing the preconditions for further innovation.

It has been observed that many creative individuals grew up in atypical conditions, on the margins of the community. Many of them were orphaned early, had to struggle against relative poverty and prejudice, or were otherwise singled out as different from their peers (Csikszentmihalyi and Csikszentmihalyi, 1993). For example, all seven of the creative geniuses of this century described by Gardner (1993) were outsiders to the societies in which they worked: Einstein moved from Germany to Switzerland, Italy, and the United States; Gandhi grew up in South Africa; Stravinsky left Russia: Eliot settled in England; Martha Graham as a child moved from the South to California, where she became exposed to and influenced by Asian art; Freud was Jewish in Catholic Vienna; and Picasso left Spain for France. It seems that a person who is comfortably settled in the bosom of society has fewer incentives to change the status quo.

Personal qualities

Having the right background conditions is indispensable but certainly not sufficient for a person to make a creative contribution. He or she must also have the ability and inclination to introduce novelty into the domain.

The following individual qualities seem to affect the incidence of creativity:

- In certain domains (e.g. music, mathematics) genetic inheritance may play an important role in directing interest to the domain and in helping to master it.
- A great deal of intrinsic motivation is needed to energize the person to absorb the relevant memes and to persevere in the risky process of innovation.
- Cognitive ability such as fluency, flexibility, and discovery orientation seem necessary to engage successfully in the process of generating novelty.
- To be able to innovate successfully, a person needs to have appropriate traits – which may vary depending on the field and the historical period. In

general, one must persevere and be open to experience, as well as adopt apparently contradictory behaviours.

Talent, or innate ability, refers to the fact that it is easier to be creative if one is born with a physical endowment that helps to master the skills required by the domain. Great musicians seem to be unusually sensitive to sounds even in their earliest years. It would not be surprising, however, to find that interest or skill in certain domains can be inherited. Howard Gardner's (1993) postulate of seven or more separate forms on intelligence also seems to support the notion that each of us might be born with a propensity to respond to a different slice of reality, and hence to operate more effectively in one domain rather than another. Many creative individuals display unusual early abilities that are almost at the level of child prodigies described by Feldman (1986). On the other hand, a roughly equal number who have achieved comparable creative contributions appear to have had rather undistinguished childhoods and were not recognized as exceptional until early adulthood.

Cerebral lateralization research has led many people to claim that left-handers or ambidextrous individuals, who are presumed to be using the right side of their brains more than right-handers, are more likely to be creative. Left-handers are apparently over-represented in such fields as art, architecture, and music: many exceptional individuals from Alexander the Great to Leonardo, Michelangelo, Raphael, Picasso, Einstein, and the three presidential candidates of the 1992 election – Clinton, Bush, Perot – were all left-handers (Coren 1992; Paul 1993).

Perhaps the most salient characteristic of creative individuals is a constant curiosity, an ever-renewed interest in whatever happens around them. This enthusiasm for experience is often seen as part of the 'childishness' attributed to creative individuals (Csikszentmihalyi 1996; Gardner 1993). Without this interest, a person would be unlikely to become immersed deeply enough in a domain to be able to change it. Another way of describing this trait is that creative people are intrinsically motivated. They find their reward in the activity itself, without having to wait for external rewards or recognition. A recurring refrain among them goes something like this: 'You could say that I worked every day of my life, or with equal justice you could say that I never did any work in my life.' Such an attitude greatly helps a person to persevere during the long stretches of the creative process when no external recognition is forthcoming.

The importance of motivation for creativity has long been recognized. Cox (1926) advised that if one had to bet on who is more likely to achieve a creative breakthrough, a highly intelligent but not very motivated person, or one less intelligent but more motivated, one should always bet on the second. Because introducing novelty in a system is always a risky and usually an unrewarded affair, it takes a great deal of motivation to persevere in the effort. One recent formulation of the creative person's willingness to take risks is the 'economic' model of Sternberg and Lubart (1995).

Probably the most extensively studied attributes of the creative cognitive style are divergent thinking (Guilford 1967) and discovery orientation (Getzels and Csikszentmihalyi 1976). Divergent thinking is usually indexed by fluency, flexibility, and originality of mental operations. Whether divergent thinking tests also relate to creativity in 'real' adult settings is not clear, although some claims to that effect have been made (Milgram 1990; Torrance 1988). Discovery orientation, or the tendency to find and formulate problems where others have not seen any, has also been measured in selected situations, with some encouraging results (Baer 1993; Runco 1995). As Einstein and many others have observed the solution of problems is a much simpler affair than their formulation. Anyone who is technically proficient can solve a problem that is already formulated; but it takes true originality to formulate a problem in the first place (Einstein and Infeld, 1938).

Some scholars dispute the notion that problem finding and problem solving involve different thought processes: for example, the Nobel Prize-winning economist and psychologist Herbert Simon (1985, 1989) has claimed that all creative achievements are the result of normal problem solving.

The personality of creative persons has also been exhaustively investigated (Barron 1969, 1988). Psychoanalytic theory has stressed the ability to regress into the unconscious while still maintaining conscious ego controls as one of the hallmarks of creativity (Kris, 1952). The widespread use of multifactor personality inventories suggest that creative individuals tend to be strong on certain traits, such as introversion and self-reliance, and low on others, such as conformity and moral certainty (Csikszentmihalyi and Getzels 1973; Getzels and Csikszentmihalyi 1976; Russ 1993).

One view I have developed on the basis of my studies is that creative persons are characterized not so much by single traits, as by their ability to operate through the entire spectrum of personality dimensions. So they are not just introverted, but can be both extroverted and introverted, depending on the phase of the process they happen to be involved in at the moment. When gathering ideas, a creative scientists is gregarious and sociable; when starting to work, he or she might become a secluded hermit for weeks on end. Creative individuals are sensitive and aloof, dominant and humble, masculine and feminine, as the occasion demands (Csikszentmihalyi 1996). What dictates their behaviour is not a rigid inner structure, but the demands of the interaction between them and the domain in which they are working.

In order to want to introduce novelty into a domain, a person should first of all be dissatisfied with the status quo. It has been said that Einstein explained why he spent so much time developing a new physics by saying that he could not understand the old physics. Greater sensitivity, naivety, arrogance, impatience, and higher intellectual standards have all been adduced as reasons why some people are unable to accept the conventional wisdom in a domain and feel the need to break out of it.

Values also play a role in developing a creative career. There are indications that if a person holds financial and social goals in high esteem, it is less likely that he or she will continue for long to brave the insecurities involved in the production of novelty, and will tend to settle instead for a more conventional career (Csikszentmihalyi et al. 1984; Getzels and Csikszentmihalyi 1976). A person who is attracted to the solution of abstract problems (theoretical value) and to order and beauty (aesthetic value) is more likely to persevere.

In order to function well within the creative system, one must internalize the rules of the domain and the opinions of the field, so that one can choose the most promising ideas to work on, and do so in a way that will be acceptable to one's peers. Practically all creative individuals say that one advantage they have is that they are confident that they can tell which of their own ideas is bad, and thus they can forget the bad ones without investing too much energy in them. For example Linus Pauling, who won the Nobel Prize twice, was asked at his 60th birthday party how he had been able to come up with so many epochal discoveries. 'It's easy,' he is said to have answered. 'You can think of a lot of ideas, and throw away the bad ones'. To be able to do so, however, implies that one has a very strong internal representation of which ideas are good and which are bad, a representation that matches closely the one accepted by the field.

Conclusion

Creativity cannot be recognized except as it operates within a system of cultural rules, and it cannot bring forth anything new unless it can enlist the support of peers. It follows that the occurrence of creativity is not simply a function of how many gifted individuals there are, but also of how accessible the various symbolic systems are and how responsive the social system is to novel ideas. Instead of focusing exclusively on individuals, it will make more sense to focus on communities that may or may not nurture genius. In the last analysis, it is the community and not the individual who makes creativity manifest.

References

Baer, J. (1993). *Creativity and Divergent Thinking*. Hillsdale, NJ: Lawrecne Erlbaum.

Barron, F. (1969). *Creative Person and Creative Process*. New York: Holt, Rinehardt & Winston.

Barron, F. (1988) 'Putting creativity to work', in R.J.Sternberg (Ed.), *The Nature of Creativity*. Cambridge: Cambridge University Press. pp. 76–98.

Coren, S. (1992) *The Left-handed Syndrome: The Causes and Consequences of Left-handedness*. New York: Free Press.

Cox, C. (1926) *The Early Mental Traits of Three Hundred Geniuses*. Stanford, CA: Stanford University Press.

Csikszentmihalyi, M. (1988a) 'Motivation and creativity: toward a synthesis of structural and energistic approaches to cognition', *New Ideas in Psychology* 6(2): 159–76.

Csikszentmihalyi, M. (1988b) 'Society, culture, person: a systems view of creativity', in R.J.Sternberg (Ed.) *The Nature of Creativity*. Cambridge: Cambridge University Press. pp. 325–39.

Csikszentmihalyi, M. (1988c) 'Solving a problem is not finding a new one: a reply to Simon', *New Ideas in Psychology* 6(2): 183–6.

Csikszentmihalyi, M. (1990) 'The domain of creativity', in M.A. Runco and R.S. Albert (Eds) *Theories of Creativity*. Newbury Park, C.A: Sage. pp. 190–212.

Csikszentmihalyi, M. (1993) *The Evolving Self: A Psychology for the Third Millennium*. New York: HarperCollins.

Csikszentmihalyi, M. (1996) *Creativity: Flow and the Psychology of Discovery and Invention*. New York: HarperCollins.

Csikszentmihalyi, M. and Csikszentmihalyi, I.S. (1993) 'Family influences on the development of giftedness', iIn *The Origins and Development of High Ability* (Ciba Foundation Symposium 178). Chichester: Wiley. pp. 18–206.

Csikszentmihalyi, M. and Getzels, J.W. (1973) 'The personality of young artists: an empirical and theoretical exploration', *British Journal of Psychology* 64(1): 91–104.

Csikszentmihalyi, M. and Getzels, J.W. (1988) 'Creativity and problem finding', in F.G. Farley and R.W. Heperud (Eds) *The Foundations of Aesthetics, Art, and Art Education*. New York: Praeger. pp. 91–106.

Csikszentmihalyi, M., Getzels, J.W., and Kahn, S.P. (1984) *Talent and Achievement: A Longitudinal Study of Artists*. (A report to the Spencer Foundation.). Chicago: University of Chicago.

Csikszentmihalyi, M., Rathunde, K., and Whalen, S. (1993) *Talented Teenagers: The Roots of Success and Failure*. Cambridge: Cambridge University Press.

Csikszentmihalyi, M. and Sawyer, K. (1995) 'Shifting the focus from the organizational creativity', in G.M. Ford and D.A. Gioia (Eds) *Creative Action in Organizations* Thousand Oaks, CA: Sage. pp. 167–72.

Dawkins, R. (1976) *The Selfish Gene*. Oxford: Oxford University Press.

Durkheim, E. (1912/1967) *The Elementary Forms of Religious Life*. New York: Free Press.

Einstein, A. and Infield, L. (1938) *The Evolution of Physics*. New York: Simon & Schuster.

Feldman D. (1986) *Nature's Gambit: Child Prodigies and the Development of Human Potential*. New York: Basic Books.

Feldman, D., Csikszentmihalyi, M., and Gardner, H (1994) *Changing the World: A Framework for the Study of Creativity*. Westport, CT: Praeger.

Gardner, H. (1993) *Creating Minds*. New York: Basic Books.

Getzels, J.W. and Csikszentmihalyi, M. (1976) *The Creative Vision: A Longitudinal Study of Problem Finding in Art*. New York: Wiley.

Gruber, H. (1988) 'The evolving systems approach to creative work', *Creativity Research Journal*. 1(1): 27–51.

Guilford, J.P. (1967) *The Nature of Human Intelligence*. New York: McGraw-Hill.

Heydenreich, L.H. (1974) *Il primo rinascimento*. Milan: Rizzoli.

Kao, G. (1995) 'Asian Americans as model minorities? A look at their academic performance', *American Journal of Education*. 103: 121–59.

Kasof, J. (1995) 'Explaining creativity: The attributional perspective', *Creativity Research Journal* 8(4): 311–66.

Kris, E. (1952) *Psychoanalytic Explorations in Art*. New York: International Universities Press.

Kuhn, T.S. (1962) *The Structure of Scientific Revolutions*. Chicago: University of Chicago Press.

Maslow, A. H. (1963) 'The creative attitude', *Structuralist* 3: 4–10.

Milgram, R.N. (1990) 'Creativity: an idea whose time has come and gone?', in M.A. Runco and R.S. Albert (Eds) *Theories of Creativity*. Newbury Park, CA: Sage. pp. 215–33.

Paul, D. (1993) *Left-handed Helpline*. Manchester: Dextral.

Runco, M.A. (1991) *Divergent Thinking*. Norwood, NJ: Ablex.

Runco, M.A. (Ed.) (1995) *Problem Finding*. Norwood, NJ: Ablex.

Russ, S.W. (1993) *Affect and Creativity*. Hillsdale, NJ: Lawrence Erlbaum.

Simon, H.A, (1985) *Psychology of Scientific Discovery*. Keynote presentation at the 93rd Annual meeting of the American Psychological Association. Los Angeles, CA.

Simon, H.A. (1989) 'Creativity and motivation: a response to Csikszentmihalyi', *New Ideas in Psychology* 6(2): 177–81.

Simonton, D.K. (1988) *Scientific Genius*. Cambridge: Cambridge University Press.

Simonton, D.K. (1990) 'Political pathology and societal creativity', *Creativity Research Journal* 3(2): 85–99.

Simonton, D.K. (1991) 'Personality correlates of exceptional personal influence', *Creative Research Journal* 4: 67–8.

Simonton, D.K. (1994) *Greatness: Who Makes History and Why*. New York: Guilford.

Sternberg, R.J. and Lubart, T.I. (1995) *Defying the Crowd: Cultivating Creativity in a Culture of Conformity*. New York: Free Press.

Therivel, W.A. (1995) 'Long-term effect of power on creativity', *Creativity Research Journal* 8: 73–92.

Torrance, E.P. (1988) 'The nature of creativity as manifest in its testing', in R.J. Sternberg (Ed.) *The Nature of Creativity*. Cambridge: Cambridge University Press. pp. 43–75.

Source: Edited extract from Chapter in R. Sternberg, *Handbook of Creativity*, 1999, Cambridge: Cambridge University Press, pp. 313–35.

Section B Cognition

The authors in this section show that if organizations wish to capitalize on creativity, innovation and knowledge they are well advised to allow space for implicit, analogical and other non-formal ways of thinking.

Guy Claxton is a psychologist, who has been championing the importance of non-standard ways of thinking for some years. In this chapter he outlines the reasons why creativity and innovation may benefit from a less hasty form of thinking which tends to be marginalized in the rationally dominated West. Studies of what managers actually do (Mintzberg 1975; Isenberg 1984) have shown that managers, like the rest of the population, rely heavily on hunches and intuitive thinking to make decisions and guide action, but they normally feel obliged to justify their thinking explicitly and rationally. Cognitive psychologists used to think that rational thinking was paramount, however much to their surprise it is now clear that intuition is often superior in many respects, and that the brain's prime information processor, learner and decision maker operates out of conscious awareness. Rational thought follows, often long behind intuitive wisdom. This chapter seeks to illustrate why we need to allow for different styles of thinking in different circumstances and in particular why innovative thinking needs to draw on non-rational tacit thought processes. These themes and further empirical justification for them are taken up in Claxton's 1997 book, *Hare Brain – Tortoise Mind.*

In his review of the relationship between problem solving and creativity Kaufmann explains how creative thinking has a lot to do with being sensitive to important problems that are worth addressing. He distinguishes between well-structured and ill-structured problems and explains how the latter can be differentiated in terms of their novelty, ambiguity and complexity. He points out that creativity often concerns novel problems and that cognitive biases such as the tendency to search in too narrow a problem space are detrimental with this type of problem. He goes on to suggest that an extensive knowledge base plays a large part in intuitive thinking and that selective forgetting may account for the usefulness of periods of incubation.

Ijuro Nonaka and Hirotaka Takeuchi are Japanese Professors who have studied knowledge creation in innovative Japanese companies. This chapter is taken from their seminal 1995 book, *The Knowledge Creating Company,* in which they present a very cogent account of the deficiency of Western conceptualizations of innovation and knowledge, locating the information processing bias found in the West firmly within its long-standing tradition of rational and dualistic thinking. The emphasis on explicit doing in the West contrasts with the East, where tacit knowledge has long been recognized as an important counterpart to rational ways of knowing. There are a number of reasons for this, perhaps partly because of their pictographic language, the Japanese have a less atomistic and dualistic way of thinking than in the West, so the split between subject and object is less cavernous, and the concept of knowledge is less separated from its development. Nonaka charges that Westerners tend to ignore the process of knowledge creation, and emphasize explicit thought processes at the expense of implicit ways of knowing, which, as Claxton points out, are especially important in the early phase of problem formulation. Nonaka goes on to show how organizations in Japan make space for implicit ways of knowing during organizational innovation processes. The West has already benefited from copying many Japanese approaches to product development and manufacturing. Nonaka's explication of the knowledge creation process offers lessons that are probably just as critical.

References

Isenberg, D.J. (1984) 'How seniors managers think', *Harvard Business Review* Nov–Dec, 81–90.

Mintzberg, H. (1975) 'The Manager's Job: Folklore or fact', *Harvard Business Review* July–Aug, 49–61.

3 The Innovative Mind: Becoming Smarter by Thinking Less

Guy Claxton

Woolworth's, the pyramids and the Internet have one thing in common: they started out as nothing but an idea. As B.C. Forbes, founder of *Forbes* magazine, succinctly put it, thinking is the fundamental material out of which physical structures and real organizations are made. Successful ventures are the embodiments of good ideas. The most precious commodity in every company is not the body of knowledge it already possesses, nor the skill with which this knowledge is 'managed'; it is the quality of thinking which its members routinely and spontaneously display, as they go about their jobs and encounter new challenges.

The successful company needs both innovation and implementation. Innovation without effective implementation can easily lead to a succession of bright ideas that never somehow take off, and which easily leave behind a trail of 'innovation fatigue' and even cynicism. 'Don't worry; it's just the MD's latest brainwave. It'll blow over.' On the other hand, implementation without innovation produces a kind of bureaucratic and stereotyped 'management by numbers' which may be obsessed with the need for accountability, while remaining oblivious to mounting pressures for change (and to opportunities to do so) (West 1999).

In stable times, the risks of faulty implementation may be greater than those of the failure to innovate. If a product has a safe market niche, with consistent demand and no emerging competitors, it may well be smarter to ensure that you keep doing well what you are good at. To try and keep fixing something that ain't broke may entail unnecessary risks and waste valuable time.

But there are a shrinking number of companies left which live in such a world. The runaway speed of change, the increase in complexity, the failure of long-term planning and the need to replace it with shorter-term responsiveness are all well documented. 'The learning organization' has become a cliché, but only because it accurately reflects the demands under which most managers now operate. In such conditions, for managers to leave the creative thinking to the chief executive, and remain preoccupied with routine matters of implementation, is somewhere between myopic and suicidal. As change quickens, and as companies delayer and re-engineer, thinking about and questioning what they are doing, at both tactical and strategic levels, have to become managers' second nature.

Inquiring minds are fast becoming *de rigeur*, and the art of management, in uncertain times, involves a much more delicate and dynamic balance between implementation and innovation than heretofore. It is therefore important to know:

- what the differences are between the innovative and the implementing mind-sets;
- how they interact;
- what are the inner, psychological, conditions which encourage the emergence and the development of the innovative mind-set;
- what are the outer, physical and cultural, conditions which do they same;
- how a dynamic balance between the two can be fostered.

This chapter explores these questions in the light especially of recent work in cognitive science about the nature of creativity and intuition, and the value of kinds of thinking that are 'slow' and 'soft' (Claxton 1997/1999).

The implementation mind-set

There are a number of assumptions that are commonly made about the nature of thinking and learning which are at odds with the view of the mind that is emerging from the laboratories of psychologists and neuroscientists. These assumptions, or 'mind myths' as I shall call them, are embedded both in the way individuals relate to their own mental processes, and in the structures, attitudes and languages of corporate cultures. Even when a company professes to value creativity in its middle and junior managers, its good intentions may be undercut by these old habits of mind and of 'common practice'. It is not that these 'myths' are completely false; rather that they over-emphasize just one aspect of the mind, thereby eclipsing others. In particular, they foreground and highlight mental attitudes and processes that are often conducive to good implementation, but neglect, or even suppress, those that are more relevant to innovation. A first step towards liberating the innovative mind is, therefore, to expose what some of the mind myths might be, and to demonstrate how they both inhibit creativity, and how they conflict with current research. I shall focus on just four of these tacit beliefs, ones that seem to me to be particularly prevalent, and pernicious, in the business world.

The first may be encapsulated in the slogan: 'Being decisive means never having to say you're stumped.' This myth tends to equate decisiveness with a continual absence of confusion, hesitation or uncertainty. A decisive person is able to take in the essentials of a predicament quickly and is either able to produce a rapid response, or at least is able to know exactly what more she or he needs to know in order to decide what ought to be done – and this ability is to be admired. In public settings and private mentalities which act as if they believe this, uncertainty and confusion are seen as aversive conditions. Their presence, or even their imminence, thus tends to generate a degree of personal (or collective) discomfort or even shame, and makes people prone to accept quickly and uncritically plausible-sounding solutions which may later turn out to be superficial or flawed.

The second myth says simply: 'Time is (always) short.' Under this belief, people tend to act as if there were a war on, and therefore to suppose that everything, from production to decision making, has to be done as fast as possible. Speed becomes a universal 'good', regardless of the real exigencies of the situation. Thinking always occurs in an atmosphere of pressure and urgency, and it is presumed that such pressure does not materially alter the quality of the thinking. Indeed it may even be believed that the pressure to deliver has, if anything, a positive effect, in that it 'motivates' people, and forces them to 'focus' and concentrate. Without that sense of urgency, it is assumed, people would be more likely to drift 'off task', and to waste valuable time. Under this belief, faster processing – whether it be in the form of 'quick wits' or the latest upgrade from Intel – is to be preferred to anything more leisurely; and 'slow' tends to become a euphemism for 'stupid' (as it has, for example, throughout the educational system). Being 'slow on the uptake' becomes, like being uncertain or confused, a source of private or public shame, which renders the discovery of solutions urgent (even when in reality they are not), and opens up the same traps as the myth of decisiveness.

The third myth says: 'Information is the most important resource'. If you do not know what to do, get more data. The systematic, comprehensive, up-to-the-minute database is the busy manager's most precious asset, and her or his spreadsheet, laptop and modem are her or his most trustworthy friends. Under this assumption, continual briefings and updates are essential. To be deprived of hourly access to email, voice mail and the Web places you in serious jeopardy – and one of the greatest dangers to good decision making is not to be 'up with the play'. Information is understood to be composed of 'facts' that are clearly expressed and, for preference, unequivocally true. If it can't be programmed, it's probably not good information.

And the fourth myth tells the manager: 'Always (be prepared to) show you're working.' No proposal or conclusion can be taken seriously unless it comes accompanied by a trail of reasoning, which shows how you got there and why it is a good idea. Ideas that lack such an analytical pedigree are not worth very much. Under this assumption, thinking that is intuitive, metaphorical, hazy or half-baked should not be exposed to public gaze, and may even be treated privately as if it were primitive and childish, to be neatened up and explicated as quickly as possible. The best kind of thinking is explicit and clear: articulate, analytical, logical and conscious. Any other kind is at best a sloppy approximation to this cognitive ideal.

The collective effect of these mind myths is to promote a certain mental attitude, and certain kinds of thinking processes, as being the best or the most powerful, regardless of the precise nature of the predicament being tackled. Being quick-witted, clear-headed, well-informed, rational and decisive are valued. Being slow, fuzzy, ignorant, metaphorical or indecisive is not. And also on this view, the mind itself appears to be a kind of rather old-fashioned, slow and faulty computer, liable to suffer from ignorance, confusion and lapses of logic, but (thankfully) capable of being networked with other human minds, as well as with faster and less fallible machines that make up for some of its deficiencies.

I call this the 'Hare Brain' view of thinking, because it values the speed with which the hare is traditionally associated – it likes to 'hare about' – but also to suggest that there may be a downside to the preoccupation with fast, articulate thinking. Such thinking may not be all that it is cracked up to be or, more moderately, we might wonder whether there are situations in which it may be prone to come up with 'hare brained' schemes that might have been avoided or improved upon in a different mental mode: the one I shall call 'Tortoise Mind'.

Before turning to a more systematic look at the shortcomings of Hare Brain, and a fuller consideration of the virtues of the Tortoise Mind, we might note just how much the Hare Brain view has come to dominate corporate culture. To take one example, consider the extent to which managers are selected for their Hare Brained abilities and tendencies, and trained to develop them still further, while their more Tortoise Minded peers are being weeded out. At virtually every management school in the US, and increasingly worldwide, applicants are required to take the GMAT: the Graduate Management Admission Test. Anyone who thinks slowly, who does not always see problems in terms of right and wrong solutions, and who likes to ponder and contemplate, is unlikely to be offered a place on an MBA. Any possible virtues that Tortoise Mind thinking may have are simply given no opportunity to reveal themselves. The GMAT assumes that all good management thinking is of the hare brain type.

Misgivings about the mind myths

When these assumptions about how we think are presented in this stark form, it is clear that they do not represent 'the truth, the whole truth, and nothing but the truth', about the human mind and the way it works. We know, for example, that decisiveness can be shallow and premature, masking a failure to take the time to think more deeply about an issue. John Keats, the poet, described such an acquaintance who could not 'feel he had a personal identity unless he had made up his mind about everything', and he would 'never come at a truth so long as he lives, because he is always trying at it'. In terms of a more familiar aphorism, 'all work and no play makes Jack a dull – and therefore uncreative and underachieving – boy.' Remember the old IBM maxim: 'don't confuse activity with achievement'.

We know that the current obsession with saving time is not always productive. We have proverbs to remind us, such as 'More haste, less speed' or 'Look before you leap.' John Cleese, who amongst his many accomplishments founded the highly successful management training company Video Arts, said in a keynote address at the Training '99 conference:

> Let me tell you the most important lesson I have ever learnt in my 26 years with Video Arts. It is this. When there is a decision to be taken, the first question to ask is 'when does this decision need to be made?' And that's when you take it. Don't take it until then, as new information, unexpected developments, and better ideas may occur. So although taking decisions very fast looks impressive, it is in fact not only show-off behaviour, but actually a bit cowardly. It shows that you'd rather create the impression of decisiveness than wait to substantially improve the chances of coming up with the right decision.

It does not take a lot of thought to realize that there are many predicaments that are not caused by a lack of information. If crime terrorizes a city, it is not because people do not have enough facts at their fingertips. And if a firm goes out of business because a competitor has come up with a fresh and original idea, it is probably more to do with its complacency or its inertia than its lack of information (Postman 1992).

We know that verbal fluency and rhetorical skill are not the same as genuine creativity. There are many in the business world who have grave misgivings about the skewed orientation to thinking encouraged by the management schools. Robert Bernstein, once chairman of publishing giant Random House, confessed: 'That's what frightens me about the business schools. They train their students to sound wonderful. But it's necessary to find out if there's any judgement behind their language.' Roy Rowan, author of *The Intuitive Manager*, talks about a similar business type which he refers to as the 'articulate incompetent' (Rowan 1986).

And we also know, in our day-to-day lives, that many problems are not solved by earnest, rational discussion, or by drawing up long lists of pros and cons for different courses of action. Ideas and solutions often just 'pop into our heads', sometimes in the middle of doing something completely different. Informally, we know the value of 'sleeping on it', and of allowing thoughts to drift, and possibilities to 'come to us'. (In a telling exchange in *Winnie-the-Pooh,* Rabbit asks Pooh how he came to think up a new ditty. 'I don't know', said Pooh, 'It just sort of came to me.' 'Ah', said Rabbit, who never let things come to him, but always went and fetched them.) When we are off-duty, we think like Pooh much of the time. But somehow, as we go into a meeting or sit down to prepare a report, we feel obliged to switch into Hare Brain mode, and become, like Rabbit, purposeful seekers after solutions and busy manufacturers of arguments.

How Hare Brain suppresses innovation

Such informal bits of testimony hardly amount to a strong case against the hegemony of Hare Brain, and in favour of a renewed appreciation of the merits of slower, softer, forms of thinking. There is, however, a growing body of evidence from laboratory studies of cognition which helps to clarify what exactly the downside of clever hare-brained thinking is, and when it needs to be supplemented with a more reflective or intuitive frame of mind. This research is demonstrating the extent to which innovation is suppressed when the Hare is allowed to bully the Tortoise into silence. Some examples follow.

Tunnel vision

The fact that thinking under pressure tends to be more focused than leisurely thinking can be either a benefit or a curse, depending on the nature of the problem. For a greater degree of focus represents a tighter set of preconscious decisions about what is likely to be relevant and what is not. We can make our thinking more concentrated by excluding a whole lot of *possible* considerations that are *probably* not to the point. To do this, we make intuitive judgements about what kind of problem this is likely to be, and what kinds of precedents are likely to be relevant, and then make our thinking more streamlined by basing it on these assumptions. We use these hunches to narrow the 'cone of attention': the range of factors which we take into account.

Where the assumptions are valid, and the situation we are facing turns out to be a variant of one of the familiar scenarios we have selected, the gamble pays off, and our problem solving does indeed become more efficient. But where such analogies, though plausible, are in fact misleading, then the cone of attention may have become narrowed too much, or pointed in the wrong direction, committing us to a fallacious interpretation of the problem, and preventing us from seeing the relevance of other perspectives or sources of information which have been prematurely discarded. And the greater the effort with which we try to solve the problem from within the erroneous view, the more locked in to that view we are likely to become. Hare Brain gets stuck in a groove and (to mix metaphors), the harder it tries, the more it spins its wheels and the deeper it gets embedded in ruts of its own making.

This kind of tunnel vision may be either perceptual or conceptual. Perceptually, we are all familiar with the experience of 'not being able to see for looking', and this phenomenon has been replicated in the laboratory. If you ask people to watch a screen and spot faint flashes of light that may occur either in the middle or on the periphery, the more you increase the rewards for a correct detection, the more they concentrate their efforts on the middle (Bahrick et al. 1952).

But pressure – whether it is induced by rewards, penalties or all-round stress – also makes our sense of possible solutions more restricted and rigid. In a classic study by Abraham and Edith Luchins in the 1950s, people were set puzzles in which they had to use three measuring jars of different sizes to produce a designated volume of water (see Rokeach 1950). For example, you might be given hypothetical jars of 17, 37 and 6 pint capacity, and asked to end up with 8 pints. After a bit of trial-and-error, most people figured out that you could do it by filling the 37 pint jar, and then, from that, filling the 17 pint jar once and the 6 pint jar twice – leaving you with 8 pints in the big jar. They were then given three or four more problems in which, though the actual sizes of the jars were different, the same procedure – subtracting the middle-sized jar once and the small one twice from the biggest – would be successful. Then, on the critical trial, they were given jars of 23, 49 and 3 pints, and required to end up with 20 pints. Many people persisted 'mindlessly' with the same method – even though there is now a much simpler solution: you just take 3 pints out of the 23 pint jar. And the prevalence of this myopic approach increased dramatically the more pressure people were put under. As the stakes get higher, so the cone of attention narrows and problem solving becomes stereotyped and uncreative. It is not hard to see the relevance of this result to real-life trouble-shooting and decision making.

The converse is also true: that if you want people to be able to 'think outside the box' – to question conventional assumptions and generate innovative ideas – then you have to allow them time to relax and meander. And you have to create a culture within which it is seen as being OK to do that. Harriman, the US railroad wizard, once declared that he liked to drop in unannounced and find one of his executives with his feet on the desk. Harriman assumed that the man was taking time to think. B.C. Forbes comments on this: 'But isn't it true that nine out of ten executives would hesitate, would be almost ashamed, to be seen sitting at a desk apparently completely idle? Has it not become fashionable to appear busy every moment of the day?' (Krass 1997).

The research shows that people who are good at accessing a state of gentle reverie, in which they can allow their minds to drift and play with images and ideas, are also more creative (Lynn and Rhue 1986). People who can allow themselves to guess, generate and express possible solutions even when they are very unsure, arrive at creative solutions sooner than those who are unwilling to 'think' until they have a much higher degree of confidence in what they are thinking (Baker-Sennett and Ceci 1996). When a test of creative problem solving is preceded by an exercise that makes people feel relaxed and happy – a clip from a comedy show, for example – their performance improves (Isen et al. 1987). When tests of analytical intelligence and creativity are carried out in either 'serious' or 'playful' conditions, creativity is better in the playful state, while analytical problem solving shows no difference (Boersma and O'Bryan 1968).

Tunnel vision can be induced by anything that increases the sense of pressure or stress. Offering large incentives will do it, just as well as imposing penalties for failure. Putting people under time pressure reduces creativity. Making them work in adverse physical conditions, such as a hot and stuffy room, has the same effect. And, perhaps most pervasively of all, a culture that is critical and competitive, in which there are real social costs involved in voicing ideas that are unusual or which sound half-baked, is a powerful suppressor of innovation. George Prince, the co-founder of the creativity-enhancing programme called 'Synectics', concluded that: 'any action that results in the offerer of an idea feeling defensive tends to reduce not only his speculation but that of others in the group ... The victim of the win-lose or competitive posture is always speculation, and therefore idea production and problem solving. When one speculates he becomes vulnerable. It is easy to make him look like a loser' (Prince 1975).

This is not to say that pressure or criticism are always inappropriate: far from it. In the phase of management planning and decision making in which ideas are being tested, elaborated and implemented, the Hare Brain is of vital importance. Tortoise Mind comes up with all sorts of ideas, if it is allowed – but not all of them are good ideas, by any means. The wheat has to be sorted from the chaff, and implications worked through in detail. The ethos in the most productive and successful scientific laboratories, for example, is one of 'agonistic support' (Dunbar 1996), in which periods of solitary creativity – individuals musing over the meaning of their results in a leisurely or even playful manner – are interspersed with vigorous critical discussions in which teams will submit each others' ideas to the most searching examinations. The crucial feature of these debates, however, is that criticism is neither directed nor taken personally. Everyone understands, even when their latest theory has taken a severe mauling, that the goal of such critical appraisal, to which all subscribe, is the production of the highest quality research.

Analytical paralysis

As well as causing the cone of attention to become narrow and over-conventional, an habitually hare-brained attitude can also be over-analytical. Some problems, especially those of a technical or logistical nature, succumb to the logical, methodical approach of Hare Brain. Where the problem space can be accurately characterized in terms of a relatively small number of well-known, clearly defined and independent variables, then hard analytical thinking may well be the best tool for the job. 'Brain-teasers' are often of this sort. For example: 'the police have four suspects for a crime, Alan, Bob, Chris and Dave. Each has made a statement, but only one of their statements is true. Alan said "I didn't do it". Bob said "Alan is lying". Chris said "Bob is lying". Dave said "Bob did it". Who is telling the truth, and who did the crime?' Intuition and reverie will not help you here; only a methodical exploration of the possibilities.

However, most real-life management (and indeed personal) problems are not of this type. They are more messy, holistic and ill-defined. You may not be able to 'see the wood for the trees' if you insist on focusing exclusively on the details using an analytical approach. Even some stylized puzzles may be like this. For example: 'a conniving moneylender offers to cancel a merchant's debt if he will gamble with his daughter. The three of them are standing on a path composed of black and white pebbles, and the moneylender proposes putting one of each colour in a small bag and letting the girl choose. If she picks black, she has to marry the moneylender. If she picks white, the debt is cancelled and she is free. However, she sees that the moneylender has actually placed two black pebbles in the bag. What should she do?' No amount of logical thinking will get you to the smart solution: she picks one stone out of the bag, but as she does so she fumbles and drops it on the path before its colour can be seen. 'Oh dear', she says. 'Never mind: we can tell what colour it was, because it must be the opposite of the one that remains in the bag.'

Several studies by Jonathan Schooler at the University of Pittsburgh have shown that analytical thinking actually interferes with solving what he refers to as 'insight' problems. When people are asked to think aloud, their performance on insight problems suffers, whilst their ability to solve analytical problems is

n unimpaired. What is more, those who maintain a stream of rational thought are less likely to come up with creative solutions than those whose minds go blank from time to time (Schooler et al. 1993).

Premature articulation

Hare Brain thinking is articulate. For it to work, all the relevant aspects of a situation have to be capable of being talked about. There has to be an adequate vocabulary. If the person or the group involved do not have such a vocabulary, then insisting on the use of articulate speech or writing as the sole medium of thinking means neglecting any information that cannot be put into words, and therefore operating with only an impoverished model of the predicament. Forcing people to articulate and justify their reasons for making a decision may be tantamount to forcing them to neglect more of this non-verbal data – and thus to invite them to make bad choices. Again, this possibility has been demonstrated in the laboratory. Students at the University of Virginia were asked to choose their next year's courses either intuitively or by 'thinking methodically and carefully weighing up the pros and cons so you can explain and justify your choices to someone else'. A different group of students were asked to choose on of a number of art prints to hang on their study wall, again either intuitively or methodically. When all these were followed up some time later, those who had been encouraged to think most systematically and explicitly turned out to be less satisfied with their choices that those who had been more intuitive (Wilson and Schooler 1991). As Donald Schon (1983) has persuasively argued, most of the situations with which professionals are faced on a daily basis contain significant facets that are hard to articulate, and they should thus be wary of insisting on clear analyses and expositions, especially during the early stages on problem solving when the parameters and the vocabulary are likely to be at their most hazy.

Other studies have shown that our softer, quieter thoughts often have greater validity than we think. When people are learning to manage a complex environment, their intuitive grasp – their 'know how' – develops much faster than their ability to describe what they are doing. Expertise precedes explanation. However, during the pre-articulate phase, people often dramatically underestimate their own level of performance. They make perfectly good decisions and actions on the basis of hunches, yet may believe that they are merely guessing (Berry and Dienes 1993). Their 'feelings' are reliable, yet their confidence in those feelings is weak.

Interestingly, when people's learning does not involve the intuitive stage, their conscious knowledge seems unable to guide their actions. Patients with damage to certain parts of the frontal lobes of the brain are as good as normal people at eventually being able to explain what is going on in such complex environments. They have lost none of their ability to construct accurate accounts on the basis of their experience. However this knowledge turns out to be of no real use, for their practical expertise never improves. And their 'learning' is not accompanied by any intuitive promptings, as normal people's is. It is as if our hunches and feelings, far from being primitive or irrational, are a vital part of our learning and knowing. Anthony Damasio, who conducted these studies of brain damaged patients, concludes that 'intuition' is actually the glue that holds intelligent action and conscious understanding together. Without it they become disconnected, and the level of 'articulate incompetence' becomes dangerous (Bechara et al. 1997).

The ability to listen to, and the willingness to trust, the inarticulate voice of intuition is one of the hallmarks of the most creative people. A recent survey of 83 Nobel science laureates revealed that around 90 per cent of them relied upon intuition in one way or another (Marton et al. 1994). One said: 'We felt at times almost as if there was a hand guiding us, because we would go from one step to the next and somehow we would know which way to go. And I really can't tell you how we knew that.' Another talked about an intuitive sense of knowing which results to trust. He said: 'I am not always right, but I do have feelings about what is an important observation and what is probably trivial.' A third referred to the almost magical appearance of insight. 'You've been thinking about something without willing to for a long time, and then the problem is opened to you in a flash and you suddenly see the answer.' Igor Sikorsky, renowned aircraft designer and manufacturer, echoed the scientists when he said that sometimes:

> in a moment, a solution of a difficult and complicated problem comes in with remarkable clarity, and so convincingly that no doubts are left as to its correctness. Quite often it is possible to select one out of a dozen sketches of proposed solutions and state positively that it is the best, when it is still not possible to say why. (Sikorsky 1997)

Incubation

Hare Brain tends to be relentless in its search for solutions. It sees no value in less focused mental activity or in 'time off task'. Yet this is another of the ways in which it stifles creativity. For there is plenty of evidence that the innovative mind needs to move between open-minded playfulness and concentrated purposefulness, and to do so with a range of different rhythms and tempos. We have already seen the value of allowing pauses and gaps in the train of thought. A few seconds of 'down time' can allow a fuller and more integrated mental picture of a situation to emerge, enabling a response to be less impulsive and more 'thoughtful'.

Taking a few minutes away from a problem that is proving recalcitrant can also be very productive. Studies have shown that problems on which people have got stuck are more likely to be solved after a break of a few minutes than if problem solving is persistent (Smith 1995). In hare brain mode, it is easy to get locked in, as we have seen, to a view of the problem that may contain some unnecessary or misleading assumptions. By taking a break and thinking about something else, you increase the likelihood that these assumptions will lose their strength and dissolve away, so that when you return to the problem, you may be able to take a fresh approach. Collectively, it can be very helpful to suggest such a 'hunch break' in a meeting that has become blocked, or where positions have become entrenched. Even a ten-minute recess can allow minds to soften and emotions to cool, so that greater creativity can emerge.

On a slightly longer time-scale, it has been shown that creative individuals tend to structure their daily routines so that they contain significant periods of playtime or rest. A recent survey of outstandingly creative people in the USA found that: 'Many of the individuals we interviewed structured their day to include a period of solitary time that follows a period of hard work... Without this solitary quiet time, they would never have their most important ideas. Several respondents kept their minds idle by engaging in repetitive physical activity.' For example one said: 'Generally the really high ideas come to me when I'm gardening, or when I'm doing something steadying with my hands' (Csikszentmihalyi and Sawyer 1996). Longer-term still, there are too many accounts to ignore of people who discovered solutions to complex problems whilst they were on holiday. The 30 page document that outlined the structure of the first consumer banking enterprise in the US has become widely known in financial circles as the 'memo from the beach'.

Desensitization

Finally, too much hard thinking undermines innovation by closing people off to their own existing resources of knowledge and experience, and renders their perception of current events coarser and more conventional. When people are searching earnestly, anxiously or impatiently for a solution, they tend to see what they expect or want to see, and the incongruous detail or the small but vital clue gets overlooked. The good tracker, or the insightful detective, possesses a large body of knowledge, skill and experience – much of which is not systematically formulated in consciousness – but the way they make use of this rich memory is more through resonance than rationality. They take time to absorb the fine details of the situation, and to allow this subtle image to resonate gently with their accumulated wisdom in a way that could not be described as intellectual or explicit. Sherlock Holmes, you may recall, when faced with a particularly difficult case, would not spend hours checking the Interpol database on his computer, but having inspected the scene of the crime would retire to his room with a full tobacco pouch, saying 'Do not disturb me, Watson. This is, I think, a three pipe problem.'

It is as if there is a variable threshold between the conscious and the unconscious minds, and an analytical, critical attitude, or too much pressure for results, causes this threshold to be raised, so that information that is subtle or equivocal becomes unavailable. This happens even at the level of bare perception. People who are looking at a screen in order to detect faint flashes of light are better at doing so when they are not trying too hard. Perception is more sensitive when you are relaxed, just allowing what is faintly there to 'pop up' by itself. Interestingly, however, this effect is reduced when people do not feel comfortable adopting such a receptive attitude. For people who found it difficult to allow themselves to respond spontaneously, or who rated themselves as more highly motivated to do well, the advantage of the 'pop up' condition was removed (Snodgrass et al. 1993). Learning to ease up, and let the mind 'do its own thing' clearly has its advantages.

Implications for innovation

Taken together, this research shows that the relentless application of the Hare Brain mind-set is antithetical to innovation in organizations. The innovative mind needs to be able to move fluidly between its different modes.

There are many indications in the foregoing review of how the innovative mind can be supported and cultivated. Let me conclude by highlighting just a few of these. First, there needs to be a widespread intellectual reappraisal of the nature of human thinking. The idea that systematic, rational, clear purposeful conscious thinking is the best tool for all jobs has to be replaced by the realization that the mind has a variety of different modes, all of which have their place, and which need to be in dynamic balance with each other.

Second, we need a broader conception of what counts as 'data'. There is more to information than spreadsheets, bullet points and glossy reports. Brief informal conversations and direct experience may be of greater use to a manager than a detailed report. Anita Roddick, founder of The Body Shop, is famous for the 'board walk', in which senior executives make time to stroll around and chat to people on the shop floor. Andy Grove, CEO of Intel, says: 'The type of information most useful to me comes from quick, often casual conversational exchanges, many of them on the telephone.' Formal reports, he says, may be worth writing, in that they force the author to clarify their thinking – but they are often not worth reading. Much valuable information is, at least to start with, unsystematic, experiential and intuitive, and is none the worse for that. The mind is at least as much like a rich compost heap as it is like the Library of Congress.

Third, managers need to learn to listen to and respect their hunches and inklings. Note, 'respect', not 'trust', because intuition can be as wrong as logic can. Logic based on a crude or rigid perception of the situation can produce stupid 'solutions'. So can intuitions based on a plausible but inappropriate analogy. Somewhere between uncritical acceptance and dismissing it out of hand there is an attitude which notices the uneasy feeling, the odd detail, the nagging question, the flash of an idea, and takes it seriously.

Fourth, people need to learn the rhythms of thinking as much as the skills of any one particular type. Often the creation of a 'problem space' starts with some kind of niggling dissatisfaction or disappointment – the underperformance of a highly qualified team; poor returns on a marketing campaign – which needs to be sharpened using some hard-nosed thinking and research. But then there may need to be a phase – time-limited if necessary – of pondering and playing with possibilities. Finally there may need to be careful analysis of proposals and monitoring of implementation. And within this broad cycle, there will be many smaller loops and rhythms as well. A natural sense of these rhythms, and the patience to wait while ideas may come to the surface, are essential attributes of the innovative mind.

Fifth, managers need to create for themselves, and for the people they manage, physical and social conditions that are conducive to innovative thinking. Some people can enter a state of reverie in the midst of a busy open-plan office, but not all can. More commonly people need a little peace and quiet, and some informal and playful interaction. In an innovative culture, activity is not confused with productivity, and breaks are seen as being an essential counterpoint to focused busy-ness. Gordon Gekko may famously have said in *Wall Street* that 'lunch is for wimps', but it is also for the creative. An atmosphere of incessant rush and panic militates against innovation. So does an ethos in which 'thinking out loud' or 'wondering' are seen as risky activities.

Creating an innovative culture is not so much a matter of instituting new practices as it is of remembering to import and value in the workplace modes and states of mind which we all know and make use of in our leisure hours. The hare brained manager might immediately ask for a list of 'how to' points and the address of a good tortoise mind 'trainer', but to do so is to miss the point. Slow and soft thinking are not new mental technologies like 'brain gym' or 'synectics'. They are modes of mind to which everyone has access, and in which we are all more or less well versed. In fact, if you look below the surface of managers' practice – how they actually think, rather than how they say they do – you find that slow tortoise mind and the use of intuition are alive and well. Senior managers in particular will admit that they get most of their ideas in the bath or on the beach – but they feel obliged to pretend that they developed them through purely rational means (Isenberg 1984). All that is required is to replace the lop-sided view of the mind as ideally articulate, with a slightly more subtle model that embraces a variety of mental modes – and then to create cultures in which these modes can all flourish.

Note

I would like to thank John Cleese, Sean Hardie, Natasha Owen and Michael West for many stimulating conversations which helped to clarify the relevance of the ideas in *Hare Brain, Tortoise Mind* to the business world.

References

Bahrick, H.P., Fitts, P.M. and Rankin, R.E. (1952) 'Effect of incentives upon reactions to peripheral stimuli', *Journal of Experimental Psychology* 44: 400–6.

Baker-Sennett, J. and Ceci, S.J. (1996) 'Cue-efficiency and insight: unveiling the mystery of inductive leaps', *Journal of Creative Behaviour* 30: 153–72.

Bechara, A., Damasio, H., Tranel, D. and Damasio, A.R. (1997) 'Deciding advantageously before knowing the advantageous strategy', *Science* 275: 1293–5.

Berry, D.C. and Dienes, Z.P. (1993) *Implicit Learning: Theoretical and Empirical Issues*. Hove: Lawrence Erlbaum.

Boersma, F.J. and O'Bryan, K. (1968) 'An investigation of the relationship between creativity and intelligence under two conditions of testing', *Journal of Personality* 36: 341–8.

Bowers, K.S., Regehr, G., Balthazard, C. and Parker, K. (1990) 'Intuition in the context of discovery', *Cognitive Psychology* 22: 72–110.

Claxton, G.L. (1997/9) *Hare Brain, Tortoise Mind: Why Intelligence Increases when You Think Less*. London: Fourth Estate (1997), Hopewell, NJ: Ecco Press (1999).

Csikszentmihalyi, M. and Sawyer, K. (1996) 'Creative insight: the social dimension of a solitary moment', in R.J. Sternberg and J.E. Davidson (Eds) *The Nature of Insight*. Cambridge, MA: Bradford/MIT Press.

Dunbar, K. (1996) 'How scientists really reason: scientific reasoning in real-world laboratories', in R.J. Sternberg and J.E. Davidson (Eds) *The Nature of Insight*. Cambridge, MA: Bradford/MIT Press.

GMAT Bulletin (1996) 'About the GMAT'. Princeton, NJ: Educational Testing Service.

Isen, A.M., Daubman, K.A. and Nowicki, G.P. (1987) 'Positive affect facilitates creative problem solving', *Journal of Personality and Social Psychology* 52: 1122–31.

Isenberg, D.J. (1984) 'How senior managers think', *Harvard Business Review*, November/December. Reprinted in Agor, W.H. (Ed.) *Intuition in Organizations: Leading and Managing Productively*. London: Sage.

Krass, P. (1997) *The Book of Business Wwisdom*. New York: Wiley.

Lynn, S.J. and Rhue, J.W. (1986) 'The fantasy prone person: hypnosis, imagination and creativity', *Journal of Personality and Social Psychology* 51: 404–8.

Marton, F., Fensham, P. and Chaiklin, S. (1994) 'A Nobel's eye view of scientific intuition: discussions with Nobel prize-winners in physics, chemistry and medicine (1970–1986)', *International Journal of Science Education* 16: 457–73.

Postman, N. (1992) *Technopoly*. New York: Knopf.

Prince, G. (1975) 'Creativity, self and power', in I..A. Taylor and J.W. Getzels (Eds) *Perspectives in Creativity*. Chicago: Aldine.

Rokeach, M. (1950) 'The effect of perception time upon the rigidity and concreteness of thinking', *Journal of Experimental Psychology* 40: 206–16.

Rowan, R. (1986) *The Intuitive Manager*. Boston: Little, Brown.

Schon, D.A. (1983) *The Reflective Practitioner: How Professionals Think in Action.* New York: Basic Books.

Schooler, J.W., Ohlsson, S. and Brooks, K. (1993) 'Thought beyond words: when language overshadows insight', *Journal of Experimental Psychology: General* 122: 166–83.

Sikorsky, I.I. (1997) 'A mysterious faculty', in P. Krass (ed.) *The Book of Business Wisdom.* New York: Wiley.

Smith, S.M. (1995) 'Fixation, incubation and insight in memory and creative thinking', in S.M. Smith, T.B. Ward and R.A. Finke (Eds) *The Creative Cognition Approach.* Cambridge, MA: Bradford/MIT Press.

Snodgrass, M., Shevrin, H. and Kopka, M. (1993) 'The mediation of intentional judgments by unconscious perceptions: the influence of task strategy, task preference, word meaning and motivation', *Consciousness and Cognition* 2: 169–93.

West, M.A. (1999) 'Creativity and innovation implementation in work groups', *Applied Psychology: An International Review* in press.

Wilson, T. and Schooler, J. (1991) 'Thinking too much: introspection can reduce the quality of preferences and decisions', *Journal of Personality and Social Psychology* 60: 181–92.

4 Creativity and Problem Solving

Geir Kaufmann

Problems are frequently described as varying on a continuum from 'well-structured' to 'ill-structured' (ISP) (Simon 1973, p. 181). Mintzberg et al. defines an ill-structured problem as a task calling for 'decision processes that have not been encountered in quite the same form and for which no predetermined and explicit set of ordered responses exists' (1976, p. 246). It is important to distinguish between different determinants of ill-structuredness which may be quite distinct. These are *novelty, complexity* and *ambiguity*. It is easy to see that these dimensions can be varied systematically and *independently* of each other. The important point is that novelty, complexity and ambiguity may call for the use of quite different capacities and strategies on the part of the problem solver. In operating with an undifferentiated concept of an ill-structured problem, important differentiations in the problem-solving domain may be lost. It is reasonable to argue that the novelty component of difficulty is of primary importance and should be a specific focus in creativity research.

Another source of difficulty in the creativity domain may materialize in what we will term 'deceptive problems'. In many tasks the problem may lie in 'apparent familiarity', when the presentation (or representation) of the task is such that a conventional, well-programmed line of attack is suggested which is, however, not adequately tailored to the solution, and a new twist is necessary to meet the goal specifications.

There is an important distinction to be made between handling a situation that is novel, and recognized as such, and a situation which looks familiar, but deceptively directs the problem solving to look for conventional solutions where a novel one is really required. In the former case, search for new information and creative use of past experience is required. In the latter case, successful problem solving requires the individual to shake off a misleading representation and to realize that solutions along conventional lines do not adequately meet the goal specifications.

The anatomy of creativity

Creativity is most intimately linked to problem solving that results in high-novelty solutions. However, novelty in thought product does not constitute a sufficient condition for defining creativity. The weird ideas of a psychotic person may rank high in originality and novelty, but we would hardly regard them as creative. To justify the use of the term 'creative thinking' a thought product also has to satisfy the criterion of having some *use* or *value*. Newell et al. (1979) suggest some additional criteria:

• Creative thinking normally feeds on high motivation and persistence and takes place either over a relatively long period of time – continuously or intermittently – or at high-level intensity.
• Newell et al. (1979) argue that a problem that requires creative thinking is normally vague and ill-defined, and that part of the task is to formulate the problem itself. This point suggests that creative thinking is seen most clearly in the category of 'constructed problems', where the main share of creativity may lie in the formulation of the problem itself. The criterion of creativity also applies, of course, to the process of identifying a productive problem definition in a presented problem.

The prevailing general theory of human problem solving as presently worked out is not adequately developed to deal with the creativity aspects of problem solving.

Theory of problem solving

The theory that dominates and directs research in the problem-solving field is worked out from an explicit information-processing perspective, where the computer-metaphor is the cornerstone of the edifice (e.g. Simon 1978).

Of particular relevance for the creativity aspect is the distinction made with regard to the nature of problem spaces. There is a striking tendency in contemporary problem-solving literature to hold forth the case of the *too large* problem space as the only interesting one. This aspect is, of course, prominent when the difficulty of the task lies in its complexity. However, it is not as obvious when the problem is one of novelty or ambiguity, or in the case of the 'deceptive problem'. Quite the contrary, the difficulties observed in these tasks may often be aptly described as related to a *too narrow* problem space, where the problem solver has to enlarge the space and see new possibilities in order to succeed in solving the problem. There is a clear tendency for human problem solvers to stick too closely to established lines or procedures when the problem requires new lines of attack. With ambiguity, the problem is rather one of choosing between different *kinds* of problem spaces that are conflicting alternatives. In the case of the 'deceptive problem', an adequate description of the difficulties facing the problem solver is that the task directs the individual into the wrong problem space, where a solution cannot possibly be located.

Phases of problem solving

There is a striking agreement in the literature describing the phases of a problem-solving event. Normally, three major phases are identified. Johnson (1955) distinguishes between 'preparation' – understanding and identifying the problem; 'production' – development of different solution alternatives; and 'judgment' – which involves choice of the best solution. Johnson and his collaborators have provided evidence that suggests that these three phases are empirically distinguishable and independent of each other in important ways. An interesting implication is that there are important individual differences in profiles of problem-solving ability. High ability in one phase does not seem to imply success in other phases of problem solving. Simon has suggested a trichotomy that is essentially commensurate with the Johnson formulation. 'Intelligence' describes the phase of identifying the nature of the problem, 'design' involves 'inventing, developing and analyzing possible courses of action' (1977, p. 41). The third phase deals with the 'selection' of a particular course of action from those available. (When dealing with problems in a practical management context, Simon argues that we may distinguish a fourth phase termed 'review', which involves evaluating past choices.) The finest and most extensive research on phases has probably been done by Mintzberg et al. (1976). On the basis of comprehensive studies of real-life problem solving, Mintzberg et al. were able to confirm the trichotomy theory of phases in problem solving. Mintzberg et al. distinguish the three major phases under the headings of 'identification', 'development' and 'selection', and go on to give a detailed picture of the microstructure of the problem-solving process by identifying seven recurring central 'routines' within the tripartite structure.

The evidence presented by Mintzberg et al. seems to demonstrate very clearly that a simple, straightforward sequence is the rare case. Normally, the cycle of phases is a lot more complex, and a high degree of overlapping occurs with lots of commuting between the different phases.

According to Hayes, what sets an ill-defined problem apart from a well-defined one is that 'ill-defined problems require problem solvers to contribute to the *problem definition*' (1978, p. 212). Newell et al. (1979) make the very same point when they claim that problems that require creative thinking are typically vague and ill-defined when initially posed and that an important part of the task is to formulate the problem itself. Perkins (1981) argues that the danger of 'premature closure' is a major obstacle to creativity. Premature closure means that the problem is encapsulated in too narrow a perspective which in turn prevents the consideration of alternative solution routes that may lead to high-quality, creative solutions to a problem. What these views have in common is the singling out of the problem identification and definition as a particularly delicate phase in problem solving.

The view that choice of representation can make an important difference in our problem-solving performance has attracted quite a bit of research interest in contemporary experimental studies of thinking. To exemplify the point, we may consider the problem of the Mutilated Checkerboard, as illustrated in Figure 4.1.

The task consists of an ordinary checkerboard with 64 squares and a set of 32 rectangular dominoes. Each domino covers 2 checkerboard squares. Thus, the 32 dominoes can be arranged to cover the complete board. The problem is the following one: suppose that two black squares are cut from opposite corners of the board, as shown in Figure 4.1, is it possible to cover the remaining 62 squares of the checkerboard by using exactly 31 dominoes?

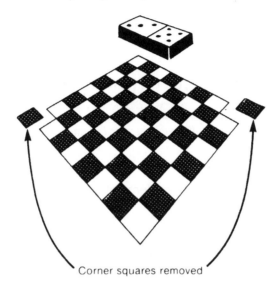

Corner squares removed

Figure 4.1 The Mutilated Checkerboard problem

Put this way, the problem is exceedingly difficult and very few can solve it (Hayes 1978). The correct answer is 'No', for the following reason: since each domino covers 1 white square and 1 black square, 31 dominoes will cover 31 white squares and 31 black squares. But the two corners that have been removed are both black. The mutilated checkerboard therefore has 32 white squares and 30 black ones. Thus it cannot be covered by 31 dominoes. It is easily seen that a correct identification of the problem gives the correct solution immediately. Hayes contrasts the Mutilated Checkerboard problem with a so-called problem-isomorph, i.e. the same problem described in a different context: 'In a small but very proper Russian village, there were 32 bachelors and 32 unmarried women. Through timeless efforts, the village matchmaker succeeded in arranging 32 highly satisfactory marriages. The village was proud and happy. Then one Saturday night of drinking, two bachelors, in a test of strength, stuffed each other with pirogies and died. Can the matchmaker, through some quick arrangements, come up with 31 satisfactory marriages among the 62 survivors?'

This Matchmaker problem is an exact parallel to the Mutilated Checkerboard problem and is trivially easy to solve. This example rather dramatically illustrates that the same problem can differ vastly in difficulty when presented in different ways, thus underscoring the importance of problem definition for success in subsequent problem solving.

Hayes and Simon (1977) have demonstrated that changes in problem representation may cause a large difference in performance (by a factor of 2). As Hayes (1978) points out, the effect is particularly prone to occur in 'discovery tasks', where search activity is often of minimal importance after the 'correct' (or productive) representation of the problem has been achieved.

It is reasonable to claim that the identification phase of problem solving is a particularly sensitive area and a potentially important bottleneck in the process of finding creative solutions to problems.

Main areas of research on human problem solving

We will now consider five areas of research: [*capacity* limitations, problem-solving *strategies, symbolic tools, expertise* and *antecedent and situational conditions*].

Capacity limitations and problem solving

A major direction for research on human problem solving is given in the theory of *bounded rationality* developed by Simon (1983). Rather than maximizing, the individual will follow a strategy of *satisficing*, directed by a realistic aspiration level of what is 'good enough'. More precisely, the thinker is assumed to select the first alternative he encounters which meets some minimum standard of satisfaction. Substituting satisficing for maximizing greatly reduces the demands upon the computational capabilities of the thinker.

Research on capacity limitations in the human information-processing system has clearly corroborated the basic thesis in Simon's theory. There are important bottlenecks in the cognitive system that easily impose cognitive strain on the individual confronted with a non-trivial task. Available evidence seems to show that only a small number of such limits exist, but these seem to be constant across a wide variety of tasks, and are of crucial importance for the processing capabilities involved in solving problems. Thus, insight into cognitive capacity limitations may have great implications for our understanding of basic features of problem-solving behaviour.

Schiffrin (1978) has argued that many of the computational limitations observed in cognitive tasks may be traced back to basic limitations in short-term memory (including working memory): 7 ± 2 units of information has been given as a 'magical number' (Miller 1956) of the storage capacity of short-term memory. Research by Simon (1979) suggests that this is an over-estimation, and that the true number is in the order of 5 units. Roughly, we may define a unit of information as the information contained in a unitary concept. The size of the unit may vary (letter, word, sentence) and it is interesting to note that the parameter seems to be constant across size of unit. To increase memory capacity the individual has to organize information in higher-order, unitary 'packages' called 'chunks of information'. The letters U, C, B represent three units of information. Drawn together they may mean University of California, Berkeley, which is one unit. Such capacity-increasing 'chunking' may be of great importance in tasks of memory and problem solving (e.g. Anderson 1985). Another bottleneck in the human cognitive system is given in the time it takes to transfer information from short- to long-term memory. Research reported by Simon (1979) indicates that it takes 8–10 seconds to transfer a new unit of information from short- to long-term memory. Again it is interesting to note that this parameter seems to be invariant across different types of information.

Strategies in problem solving

Heuristics of simplification

Heuristics of simplification are particularly relevant when the task is one of *complexity*. Hayes (1978) distinguishes between three varieties of search aimed at short-cutting the problem: proximity methods, pattern matching and planning.

Proximity methods

The hot and cold strategy – Problem solvers often look for 'hot' signals to move closer to, and 'cold' signals to move away from, [such as] the loudness of another person's voice.

Hill climbing – This is from the analogy of climbing a hill under foggy conditions one step at a time and evaluating its consequences.

Means–end analysis – Means–end analysis offers a choice among different *means* of approaching the goal. Search is guided by attempts to *reduce the difference* between the initial state and the goal state. The main purpose is to solve an ill-structured problem by reducing it to a series of smaller well-structured problems. This also illustrates the important heuristic of the *sub-goal strategy*.

Planning methods

Another class of heuristics that may be used to confine search in complex task environments is the planning methods, (Hayes 1978).

Planning by modelling – To guide complex activities in a rational way, it is useful to construct a simplified model of the situation to avoid going in wrong directions and making errors. Before making a suit the tailor needs to draw a model of it.

Planning by analogy – Plans may be formed by analogy where the solution of one problem is used as a platform for solving another problem. An example would be exploiting the energy in waves by way of the principle of a lens.

Planning by abstraction – Plans are formed by abstraction when the original problem is simplified to a related but easier one. The solution of the simpler problem can then be used as a plan for solving the original more complex problem. Writing a book for the first time may be approached by building on the successful solution of writing a paper on a related topic.

Working backwards

The ordinary directional strategy in problem solving is to work forwards from initial state to goal state. However, it may be more useful to work backwards from the goal to the givens. The reason is that fewer paths lead to the solution from the goal than from the givens.

Heuristics of variation

In creative thinking tasks, where *novelty* is the dominating determinant of difficulty, the problem is often that of operating within a too restricted problem space, or – as in 'deceptive problems' – in the wrong space. Heuristics of stimulus variation contain exactly the kind of strategies that would be expected to be useful in typical creative thinking tasks.

Adding stimuli

New stimuli may be needed to expand a too narrow problem perspective, and to set up new patterns of activity in the representational system. One way of achieving this aim is to present the problem in *different terms*. It is interesting to note that creative thinkers often shift between concrete and abstract ways of representing the problem (Kaufmann 1980).

Thinking in analogies is another way of adding stimuli. Gordon (1961) has reported numerous examples of using this strategy. In one case the problem was to construct a roof that would absorb heat under cold conditions and reflect heat under hot conditions. The analogy of a flounder that can change colour according to variations in light conditions was used. The problem was solved on the basis of this analogy by constructing a roof impregnated with white plastic balls that would contract under low temperatures, rendering the roof black, and expand under high temperatures, thus reflecting heat.

Removing stimuli

Particularly relevant to the case of the 'deceptive problem' is the presence of irrelevant or misleading stimuli that may lure the problem solver into the wrong space. Adamson and Taylor (1954) have shown that fixations in problem solving may decay over a period of some days. Weaker items are forgotten more rapidly than stronger ones. It is reasonable to believe that in most cases incorrect items are weaker than stronger ones.

Rearranging stimuli

A final way of achieving the aim of restructuring a problem space by deliberate, strategical means is to rearrange stimuli. Temporal orderings may here play a significant role. Given the task of crossing out the word that does not fit into the sequence *skyscraper, female, cathedral, prayer,* a subject will normally choose *prayer*. When the list is presented in the reverse order, the word *skyscraper* is most likely to be crossed out (Anderson 1975, p. 285). Spatial arrangements are also important.

Symbolic activity in problem solving

The spotlight of research has been cast on the use of imagery as a symbolic medium. Reports pertaining to major inventions and scientific discoveries suggest that the inventors were visualizing complex situations when their revealing 'flash of insight' took place (Kaufmann 1980; Shepard 1978). Such informal evidence suggests that somehow imagery is of particular service to creative thought. Reviews of the experimental literature suggest quite strongly that imagery gains increasing importance in direct proportion to the degree of ill-structuredness of the task. With high novelty, complexity or ambiguity the subject seems to switch from a linguistic–propositional code to an imagery-based representation (Kaufmann 1984). We have suggested that imagery is a back-up system that gives access to a set of simpler cognitive processes of a perceptual kind.

Expert performance

We have considered the use of very general strategies and capacities that may facilitate performance in ill-structured task environments. This picture needs to be supplemented with research evidence that relates to the significance of domain-specific knowledge for effective and creative problem solving.

In his seminal work on human intelligence, Spearman (1927) arrived at the conclusion that successful problem solving is determined by two factors: general intelligence and knowledge specifically bearing on the task in question. The factor of general intelligence has been unpacked by Sternberg (1985). He claims that the realities behind the term 'general intelligence' consist of the efficient use of highly general problem-solving strategies.

In addition it seems that expertise in problem solving is highly dependent on the availability of extensive, well-organized domain-specific knowledge. Chase and Simon (1973a,b) conclude that the chess master's superior ability is due to the possession of a vast number of stored patters in long-term memory which allow them to match perceived board positions with stored memory representations. Thus, the master can organize his information in a more efficient way. Chase and Simon estimated that a chess master has stored in memory 50,000–100,000 such 'chunks' of information. It is the advantage of possessing this extensive and well-organized knowledge that makes for superior problem-solving ability. McKeithen et al. (1981) have corroborated these findings in a study with computer programmers. Where novices and experts in other domains like physics and architecture have been studied, the same results are found (Kahney 1986).

Differences in the strategies employed by experts and novices have also been studied. The results of the research on expertise seem to show that the possession of extensive, well-organized domain-specific knowledge is a crucial factor in expert performance. The important point is that a higher level of organized, domain-specific knowledge gives the expert access to more powerful problem-solving methods. Thus, high-level cognitive abilities should not be seen as existing apart from knowledge. Rather, powerful cognitive operations seem only to materialize in a system of well-organized, extensive knowledge. This is an important insight in cognitive psychology.

Creative problem solving may be seen as expert performance that produces new insights. We may now expect that high-level creativity is crucially dependent on a large amount of well-organized domain-specific knowledge. Before the fruits of real creativity can be reaped, then, we may expect that a long history of building up domain-specific knowledge and skills must precede.

Hayes (reported in Simon 1983) has examined this question by way of biographical evidence on famous chess masters, composers, painters, and mathematicians. Hayes concludes that, for top performance, ten years of work in the field seems to be a magic number. Almost none of the individuals studied had produced world-class performance without first having invested at least ten years of intensive learning and practice. It is interesting to note that the folklore surrounding child prodigies seems to be distorted. For instance, by the standard Hayes used (five appearances in the Swann catalogue), he found no world-class work of Mozart before the age of seventeen. On the basis of Hayes' extensive and systematic observations, Simon concludes: 'a *sine qua non* for outstanding work is diligent attention to the field over a decade or more' (1983, p. 28).

In general, expertise and high-level creativity seem to require an extensive base of well-organized domain-specific knowledge that takes a long time to acquire. The point is, of course, not that having extensive knowledge in itself guarantees creativity of high rank. Rather, it seems to be a *necessary condition* for high-level performance. Wallach (1988) seems to be entirely justified when he argues that there has been a narrow perspective in the field of creativity research that has focused mainly on very general capacities underlying creativity at the expense of the extensive domain-specific knowledge and skills that have to be present for high-level creativity to unfold.

Antecedent and situational determinants of problem solving

This section identifies antecedent and situational conditions that affect problem-solving performance: conditions that *facilitate* and those that *inhibit* productive problem solving.

Facilitating conditions

Exploring the problem situation
We presented evidence to the effect that the initial *problem identification* is a most sensitive part of the problem-solving process. Differences in *problem representation* may strongly affect the success of solving a problem. It is to be expected that this relationship holds true especially in the area of creative

thinking. Here we are often dealing with 'discovery tasks', where formulation of the problem is of critical importance for success, as is seen in the problem of the Mutilated Checkerboard.

Raaheim's (1964) subjects were given a typical 'insight problem' to solve. The experimental group was carefully instructed to find out exactly what was missing, and then to replace it with the object available before starting on solving the problem. The control group was given no such instructions. The results showed an impressive 50 per cent increase in correct solutions in the experimental group compared with the control group. Again it seems that spending time working out a suitable problem representation may greatly facilitate insightful problem-solving performance.

Turning a choice situation into a problem situation

Maier and Hoffman have argued that 'there is a tendency to seek solutions before the problem is understood' (1970, p. 139). When the aim is for creative solutions to a problem, it is therefore important that an attitude of 'problem-mindedness' replaces the attitude of 'solution-mindedness'. Maier and Hoffman submitted this hypothesis to experimental test by having the subjects obtain a second solution after a first one had been produced. The problem given was the so-called Change of Work Procedure, where the task is to find a productive solution to an assembly-line problem. The assembly operation was divided into three positions and workers adopted a system of hourly rotation among the three jobs. Each worker has a best position, and the issue is to find a new method that would increase productivity. The interesting feature of this problem is that there are several possible solutions that may be graded on a scale of creativity. The creative solutions are called integrative. Maier and Hoffman confirmed their hypothesis by showing that, whereas only 16 per cent of the subjects produced integrative solutions on the first try, 52 per cent of the second solutions were of this type.

Such findings underscore the importance of sufficient problem exploration for creative problem solving and point to the critical importance of a problem representation for finding high-quality solutions to a problem.

Separated idea generation and idea evaluation

Osborn (1963) has argued that a major block in creative thinking is the tendency to premature evaluation of ideas. Consequently, Osborn argues for a strategy of 'brainstorming' in problem solving where creativity is a major requirement. The basic idea of brainstorming is to separate idea generation from idea evaluation.

Much experimental research has gone into testing the soundness of this principle. The general design has been to determine the effects of brainstorming instructions on originality and productivity when used as a group problem-solving method. The results have been rather depressing for the brainstorming thesis. Brainstorming instructions often turn out to have a *detrimental* effect on the quality and productivity of problem solving, as compared to the effect of neutral instructions. However, Parnes (1963) has reminded us that the brainstorming technique is not inherently a group technique. Anxiety over negative evaluations from others when suggesting 'wild ideas' may, indeed, block the productivity of the individual performing in a group setting. Research on the deferment-of-judgement principle used in individual problem solving tends to show a positive effect on performance. Furthermore, encouraging the subjects to 'free-wheel' and not resist wild ideas is not a necessary feature of the principle. Maier (1973), on the basis of several experiments, reports that the principle of separating idea generation and idea evaluation in itself seems to be sound policy for promoting productive problem solving.

Rickards and Freedman (1978) presented interesting evidence to the effect that a greater *variance* in quality of ideas is obtained under the deferment-of-judgement principle. This means that a greater number of poor solutions *and* high-quality solutions are obtained. These findings suggest that there is a special place for the deferment-of-judgement principle in idea-deficient situations, where the requirements for creativity are particularly strong.

Conflictual thinking

In the literature on problem solving and creativity, the conditions of a *conflict* between opposing ideas are seen as a potentially powerful spur for productive thinking (e.g. Duncker 1945). The general idea is that such a conflict puts pressure on the problem solver which may be resolved by finding a new idea containing elements from the two opposing base ideas.

Rothenberg (1976) has defined a process termed 'Janusian thinking' that is held to be characteristic of creative thought. Janusian or 'oppositional thinking' is 'the capacity to conceive and utilise two or more opposite or contrary ideas, concepts, or images simultaneously' (Rothenberg 1976, p. 313). This feature is also found in great scientific discoveries (the 'double helix' springs out of the notion of identical chains running in opposite directions). Rothenberg has pursued the issue by gathering clinical and experimental evidence on the importance of thinking in conflictual opposites in creativity. In his studies, highly acclaimed writers (winners of Pulitzer prizes, etc.) and novice writers of high creative potential (rated by literary critics and teachers) have been compared with 'non-creative' persons who try to write a work of fiction or poetry for financial reward. Janusian thinking figures frequently in the works of the creative writers, but never in non-creative persons. Special association tasks were given to prominent and novice creative writers. The results show a high tendency to rapid oppositional associations in these groups as well. The evidence tends to support the general idea that thinking in a context of cognitive conflict will promote creativity in solving problems.

High motivation and persistence

An attitude of persistence is mentioned as a defining criterion of creativity in problem solving. Simon (1966) has pointed out that high-level creativity is a rare event in scientific discovery, and a theory of creativity also needs to account for this rarity of occurrence. The idea that high-level creativity requires extraordinarily high persistence fits nicely into this observation. Creativity often involves 'going against the tides' and a lot of resistance to change has to be overcome. Anderson (1980) also points to the possibility that high persistence may have to do with the openness that high-level creativity requires. He posits that highly creative individuals may be willing to continue working because they are less willing than others to accept the many conflicting facts that are present on the route to creativity. Several findings suggest that high motivation and persistence are indeed vital ingredients in the creative process. Roe (1953) examined characteristics of a group of 64 American physicists, biologists, and social scientists selected for the importance of their contributions to their fields. The only trait that Roe found to be common to her subjects was willingness to work extremely hard. MacKinnon (1962), in his studies of creative architects, reports that his highly creative subjects had developed a 'healthy obsession' with their problems.

Hyman (1964) made the interesting observation that when people were asked to continue working on a problem beyond the point where they thought they had come up with their best effort, they frequently were able to produce the ideas that were even more creative than their previous ones.

Inhibiting conditions

According to the theory of bounded rationality, a strategy of satisficing is chosen to reduce the strain on the computational capabilities of the thinker. This is a rational strategy that makes for good adjustment given the cognitive limitations of the human information processor. It may be argued, however, that preserving cognitive economy means keeping variation and changes to a minimum. Thus, we may expect dysfunctional consequences of this orientation where restructuring and creative change are required. To relinquish established perspectives and standard operating procedures that are associated with safety and predictability may conflict with the individual's striving for cognitive economy and meet with resistance to change. Thus, a rational orientation to solving problems, guided by the motive of preserving cognitive economy, may entail a danger of rigidity and stereotype when faced with a situation where a restructuring of established conceptions and lines of procedure is required.

The psychological literature on human problem solving confirms this expectation through many examples of rigidity, stereotype and dysfunctional resistance to change. A major orientation in the experimental psychology of creative thinking has, indeed, been to investigate the conditions that inhibit creativity in problem solving. We will describe some fixations and resistance to change in problem solving.

The Einstellung effect

The so-called 'Einstellung' effect shows itself under conditions where the individual has discovered a strategy that initially functions well in solving certain tasks, but later on blocks the realization of new and simpler solutions to similar problems. Luchins (1942) has investigated this phenomenon in a series of experiments and shown it to be a reliable and robust one. The general conclusion from the Luchins water jar experiments is that the fixation in problem solving is dramatically strong. While just about all of the subjects in the control group solve the test problems by way of the simplest formulas, as many as 80 per cent in the experimental group use the complicated standard procedure on later problems. About 60 per cent are not at all able to solve the problem where the formula breaks down.

The Einstellung phenomenon also shows up in other types of task, like anagrams (letter combinations), concept formation tasks, and geometry tasks. Thus, it seems to reflect a dysfunctional consequence of the normal, rational way of approaching problems that may block the establishment of a new perspective and more appropriate lines of procedure in task environments that resemble those encountered before. It is interesting to note that Cyert and March (1963) have observed similar behaviour among managers in real-life contexts. Typical managerial search is seen as 'simple minded', and as over-emphasizing previous experience, by selectively searching in regions close to where previous solutions have been found.

Functional fixedness

Duncker (1945) has also investigated how past experience may block productive problem solving. Duncker coined the term 'functional fixedness' to refer to a block against using an object in a new way that is required to solve a problem. In the so-called Box Problem the task was to mount a candle vertically on a screen nearby to serve as a lamp. The experimental group was given a box containing matches, a second box holding candles, and a third one that contained tacks. The same supplies were given to the control group, but with the matches, tacks and candles outside the boxes. The solution to the problem is to mount a candle on top of a box. This may be achieved by melting wax onto the box, sticking the candle to it, and then tacking the box to the screen. This was much harder for the experimental group. Similar effects were found in other tasks. Duncker takes the results of his experiments as a demonstration of how previous experience may have dysfunctional consequences in problem solving by blocking new insights and necessary restructuring in the face of the requirements of the task.

Some interesting examples of how the factor of functional fixedness may operate in real-life contexts and seriously hamper the process of technical invention are given by Weizenbaum (1984). According to Weizenbaum the steam engine had been in use for a hundred years to pump water out of mines before Trevithick had the idea of using it as a source of locomotive power. Another example is the computer, which for a long time was seen just as a calculator before its potential as general symbol manipulator was conceived.

Hidden assumptions

A similar dysfunctional effect of a mental set is due to the 'hidden assumption'. Fixation in problem solving may be caused by certain assumptions of how a problem has to be solved which delimit the search for productive solutions. An illustrative demonstration is provided by Scheerer (1963) through the case of the so-called Nine Dot Problem.

Confirmation bias

A number of experiments seem to show that people have a natural propensity to seek confirming evidence and to avoid disconfirmation or discard disconfirming evidence when it is present. Wason (1968) observed a marked confirmation bias. The majority of subjects did not actively seek disconfirming evidence and tended to ignore it when it occurred. Einhorn and Hogarth (1978) observed that confidence in a hypothesis generally increases more following positive feedback than it decreases following negative feedback. Doherty et al. (1979) found that many people do not consult observations relevant to an alternative hypothesis, even when such observations are readily available.

Conservatism in hypothesis testing

Closely related to the experiments described above are a series of experiments purporting to demonstrate a marked bias in hypothesis-testing behaviour. People have been observed to manifest a *conservative bias* in hypothesis testing consisting of a reluctance to reduce their confidence in a decision following disconfirmation. Phillips and Edwards (1966) investigated the effects on posterior probability estimates of (1) prior probabilities, amount of data, and diagnostic impact of data; (2) payoffs; and (3) response modes. In all the experiments the subjects typically behaved conservatively. Pitz (1969) has argued that commitment is an important cause of this 'inertia effect'. (See Pitz, 1975, for a review of experiments on conservatism in hypothesis testing.)

Taken together, the experiments on hypothesis-testing behaviour seem to suggest that there is a basic, natural tendency to resist change and restructuring in problem solving. Together with the experiments on Einstellung and fixations they point to dysfunctional cognitive tendencies that we may expect to block creativity in problem solving.

Are there 'creativity specials'?

The domain of creative thinking harbours special features of cognition that are not easily described or explained within the framework of a rational information-processing model. The processes that are the dominant driving forces behind creative thinking are held to be largely unconscious, and stand in need of being described and explained within the framework of a totally different conceptual scheme. The processes referred to here are mainly those of 'intuition' and 'incubation' – both held to depend on the workings of the unconscious mind and to be driven by illogical, irrational processes. These phenomena are often described as being intimately related to the process of high-level creativity in prominent scientists and artists (e.g. Patrick 1938), and present a challenge to the information-processing approach.

Intuition – ESP or IPS?

In the popular writings, intuition is often described in rather occult terms as a kind of indefinable gift that only the highly creative person possesses to a full degree. In this view, intuition is not an ordinary, natural part of an information-processing system (IPS). Rather, it is a kind of extra-rational, ESP-like ability that allows the individual who possesses it to point out the correct directions in problem solving without knowing why. It is like having a friendly homunculus in the back of the head that whispers sweet answers to the searching mind. Often such views are coupled with naïve and oversimplified ideas about the human brain. According to the popular theory (e.g. Blakesley 1980), the left brain is the site of logic and language and is dry and editorial, while the right brain harbours all the goodies of intuition, imagination and imagery, and is the engine of creativity.

   With the case of intuition, Simon (1983) has thrown some cold water into the veins of the most ardent proponents of the extra-rational model. According to Simon, intuition is something that we all have, and it is not dependent on a mysterious, indescribable process. Intuition has to do with making a correct judgement without conscious awareness of the process behind it. Such a capacity is not the exclusive property of the chosen few. Rather it is a common ingredient in everyday, cognitive functioning. The skilled chess player will be able to make a move in a mid-game situation in just a few seconds without exactly knowing why, and often it turns out to be correct move. The explanation of such good intuition is well known to cognitive psychologists. It depends on the availability of a large, well-organized knowledge base and a corresponding elaborate discrimination net that makes for quick and accurate judgements. According to Simon, it is no more mysterious than the ordinary ability to recognize immediately one of your friends in the street. The recognition ability here is likewise dependent on considerable experience with a large number of 'friends'. Thus, we have an elaborate, well-organized sorting net that allows us to perform the correct judgement very quickly.

   We can now see that the phenomenon of intuition may depend on elaborate sorting nets derived from extensive experience. Since the knowledge is well organized in 'chunks', processing will occur at very high speed, largely outside the conscious awareness of the individual. Thus, it is not necessary to postulate fancy and elusive processes behind the power of human intuition. The phenomenon is real and available to every human information processor that possesses elaborate and well-organized discrimination nets derived from extensive experience.

Incubation – fact or fiction?

Incubation is said to occur when the individual sets the problem aside for a while and does something else that is unrelated to the problem. At a later occasion – often very suddenly – the correct solution springs to mind. Many dramatic examples of the phenomenon have been described in the literature (e.g. Ghiselin 1952; Patrick 1938). According to popular theory, incubation runs on active unconscious processes that go on in the interval. This is, however, not the only possible explanation. It may be due to the breaking of an unproductive set, stress reduction, reduction of fatigue, selective forgetting, and the facilitating effects of incidental stimuli (Olton and Johnson 1976). According to Hayes (1978), selective forgetting is the most likely explanation for incubation effects. Simon (1966) has given the following detailed explanation of the possible mechanisms behind incubation:

> When the problem is approached again after a delay, the old plan is forgotten, and a new one has to be formed. The new plan is based on better information about the nature of the problem than the old one and is likely to be a better plan. The break therefore should have the effects of increasing the probability of solution, and this is exactly what is supposed to happen during incubation.

It seems that we do not have to borrow ingredients from extra-rational theories to account for the creativity domain of human problem solving.

From problem solving to problem finding

There is an unduly myopic view of the world of problems that seems to reflect the traditional view of humans as basically reactive and responding to 'stimuli' or 'inputs'. To cover the full territory of problem solving, we may need a broader view.

There are three broad kinds of problems that a theory of human problem solving has to deal with in a satisfactory way. First, there are *presented problems*. The individual is faced with a difficulty that has to be handled. Such a situation may be well-structured (initial conditions, goal conditions, and operators are clearly definable). At the other pole is the unstructured problem situation, where the number of unknowns is at a maximum. But these are not the only problems people deal with. There is also a class of problems that may be called *foreseen problems*: that is, the individual anticipates that a problem (serious pollution, a massive traffic jam, etc.) will result if present developmental trends continue. Evasive action may then be taken. Even more interesting in the context of the present discussion is the class of problems that may be called *constructed problems*. The initial condition may here be a consistently reinforcing, satisfactory state of affairs. Nevertheless, a problem may arise when an individual compares the existing situation to a future, hypothetical state of affairs that could represent an improvement over the present situation. An example would be the present TV technology which may be said to be quite satisfactory. Yet, an individual might see a problem here in that there is no TV set with an adjustable-sized monitor unit.

Getzels and Csikszentmyhalyi (1976) present evidence to the effect that *problem finding* is more intimately related to creativity than is problem solving in the traditional sense. In the case of 'discovered problems' success is dependent on problem sensitivity, whereas with 'constructed problems' the driving force seems to be 'innovation-orientation' or 'opportunity seeking'.

It is interesting to note that this important aspect of problem solving has been clearly seen by researchers observing managerial problem solving in real-life contexts. Mintzberg et al. identify an important class of problems as 'opportunity decisions' which are 'initiated on a purely voluntary basis, to improve an already secure situation, such as the introduction of a new product to enlarge an already secure market share' (1976, p. 251). These are to be contrasted with 'crisis decisions', where individuals and organizations 'respond to intense pressures' (p. 251).

Working in 'discovered' and 'constructed' problem environments, thus, seems to be intimately related to the creativity aspect of problem solving. It is possible that the computer metaphor has put blinkers on students of problem solving. [It does] not capture the human processes involved in the identification of problems on weak signals, and definitely not the creation of 'tensions' and discrepancies between existing and imagined situations. It is important to point out discrepancies between human and computer capabilities that may block perspectives and narrow our views or problem solving to those aspects that are assimilable to a computer-metaphor.

References

Adamson, R.W. and Taylor, D.W. (1954) 'Functional fixedness as related to elapsed time and to set', *Journal of Experimental Psychology* 47:122–6.

Anderson, B.F. (1975) *Cognitive Psychology.* New York: Academic Press.

Anderson, B.F. (1980) *The Complete Thinker.* Englewood Cliffs, N.J: Prentice Hall.

Anderson, F.R. (1985) *Cognitive Psychology and its Implications.* San Francisco: Freeman.

Blakesley, T.R. (1980) *The Right Brain.* New York: Doubleday & Company.

Chase, W.G. and Simon, H.A. (1973a) 'Perception in chess', *Cognitive Pschology* 4: 55–81.

Chase, W.G. and Simon, H.A. (1973b) 'The mind's eye in chess', in W.G. Chase (Ed.) *Visual Information Processing.* New York: Academic Press.

Cyert, R.M. and March, J.G. (1963) *A Behavioural Theory of the Firm.* Englewood Cliffs, NJ: Prentice Hall.

Duncker, K. (1945) 'On problem solving', *Psychological Monographs* 58(5) (whole No. 270).

Einhorn, H.J. and Hogarth, R.M. (1978) 'Confidence in judgement: persistence of the illustion of validity', *Psychological Review* 85: 395–416.

Getzels, F. and Csikszentmyhalyi, M. (1976) *The Creative Vision: A Longitudinal Study of Problem Solving in Art.* New York: Wiley.

Ghiselin, B. (1952) *The Creative Process.* Berkeley, CA: University of California Press.

Gordon, W.J. (1961) *Synectics.* New York: Harper & Row.

Hayes, J.R. (1978) *Cognitive Psychology. Thinking and Creating.* Homewood, IL: Dorsey Press.

Hayes, J.R. and Simon, H.A. (1977) 'Psychological differences among problem isomorphs', in N.J. Castellan, D.B. Pisoni and G.R. Potts (Eds), *Cognitive Theory* Vol. 2. Hillsdale, NJ: Erlbaum.

Hoffmann, L.R. (1961) 'Conditions for creative problem solving', *Journal of Psychology* 52: 429–44.

Hyman, R. (1964) 'Creativity and the prepared mind: the role of information and induced attitudes', in C.W. Taylor (ed.) *Widening Horizons in Creativity.* New York: Wiley.

Johnson, D.M. (1955) *The Psychology of Thought.* New York: Harper & Row.

Kahney, H. (1986) *Problem Solving: A Cognitive Approach.* Milton Keynes: Open University Press.

Kaufmann, G. (1980) *Imagery, Language and Cognition.* Oslo/Bergen/Tromsø: Norwegian University Press.

Kaufmann, G. (1984) 'Mental imagery in problem solving', *International Review of Mental Imagery* 23–55.

Kaufmann, G. (1986) 'The conceptual basis of cognitive imagery models: a critique and a theory', in D. Marks (ed.) *Theories of Image Formation.* New York: Brandon House.

Kaufmann, G. (1987) 'Mental imagery and problem solving', in M. Denis (ed.) *Imagery and Cognitive Processes.* Amsterdam: Martinus Nijhoff.

Luchins, A.A. (1942) 'Mechanization in problem solving: the effect of Einstellung', *Psychological Monographs* 54 (whole No. 248).

MacKinnon, D.W. (1962) 'The nature and nurture of creative talent', *American Psychologist* 17: 484–95.

Maier, N.R.F. (1963) *Problem Solving Discussions and Conferences.* New York: McGraw-Hill.

Maier, N.R.F. and Hoffman, L.R. (1970) 'Quality of first and second solutions in group problem solving', in N.R.F. Maier (ed.) *Problem Solving and Creativity.* Belmont, CA: Brooks/Cole.

McKeithen, K.B., Raitman, J.S., Ruchter, H.H. and Hirtle, S.C. (1981) 'Knowledge organization and skill differences in computer-programmers', *Cognitive Psychology* 13: 307–25.

Miller, G.A. (1956) 'The magical number seven, plus or minus two: some limits on our capacity for processing information', *Psychological Review* 63: 81–97.

Mintzberg, H., Duru, R. and Theortet, A. (1976) The structure of unstructured decision processes', *Administrative Science Quarterly* 21:246–75.

Newell, A. and Simon, H.A. (1972) *Human Problem Solving.* Englewood Cliffs, NJ: Prentice-Hall.

Newell, A., Shaw, J.C. and Simon, H.A. (1958) 'Elements of a theory of human problem solving', *Psychological Review* 65: 151–66.

Newell, A., Shaw, J.C. and Simon, H.A. (1979) 'The processes of creative thinking', in H.A. Simon (ed.) *Models of Thought.* New Haven: Yale University Press.

Olton, R.M. (1980) 'Experimental studies of incubation: searching for the elusive', *Journal of Creative Behavior* 13: 9–22.

Olton, R.M. and Johnon, D.M. (1976) 'Mechanisms of incubation in problem solving', *American Journal of Psychology* 89: 617–30.

Osborn, A.F. (1963) *Applied Imagination.* New York: Scribners.

Paivio, A. (1971) *Imagery and Verbal Processes.* New York: Holt, Rinehart & Winston.

Paivio, A. (1986) *Mental Representations.* Oxford: Oxford University Press.

Parnes, S.J. (1963) 'The deferment of judgment principle: a clarification of the literature', *Journal of Experimental Psychology* 72:346–54.

Patrick, C. (1938) 'Scientific thought', *Journal of Psychology* 5: 55–83.

Perkins, D.N. (1981) *The Mind's Best Work.* Cambridge, MA: Harvard University Press.

Phillips, L. and Edwards, W. (1966) 'Conservatism in a simple probability inference task', *Journal of Psychology* 72: 346–54.

Pitz, G.F. (1969) 'An inertia effect (resistance to change) in the revision of opinion', *Canadian Journal of Psychology* 23: 24–33.

Pitz, G.F. (1975) 'Bayes' Theorem: Can a theory of judgment and inference do without it?' in F.R. Restle, R.M. Schiffrin, N.J. Castellan, H.R. Lindman and D.B.Pisoni (Eds), *Cognitive Theory* Vol. 1. Hillsdale, NJ: Erlbaum.

Raaheim, K. (1964) 'Analysis of the missing part in problem solving', *Scandinavian Journal of Psychology* 5: 149–52.

Raaheim, K. (1974) *Problems solving and intelligence.* Oslo/Bergen/Tromsø: Norwegian Universities Press.

Reitman, W.R. (1965) *Cognition and Thought.*, New York: Wiley.

Rickards, T. and Freedman, B.L. (1978) 'Procedures for management in idea-deficient situations: and examination of brainstorming approaches', *The Journal of Management Studies* 15: 149–52.

Roe, A. (1953) 'A psychological study of eminent psychologists and a comparison with biological and physical scientists', *Psychological Monographs* 67(2) (whole No. 352).

Rothenberg, A. (1976) 'The process of Janusian thinking', in A. Rothenberg (ed.) *The Creativity Question.* Durham, NC: Duke University Press.

Scheerer, M. (1963) 'Problem solving', *Scientific American* 208: 118–28.

Schiffrin, R.M. (1978) 'Capacity limitations in information processing, attention and memory', in W.K.Estes (ed.) *Handbook of Learning and Cognitive Processes.* New York: Wiley.

Shepard, R.N. (1978) 'The mental image', *American Psychologist*, pp. 125–37.

Simon, H.A. (1966) 'Scientific discovery and the psychology of problem solving', in R.G. Colodny (ed.) *Mind and Cosmos: Essays in Contemporary Science and Philosophy.* Pittsburgh: University of Pittsburgh Press.

Simon, H.A. (1969) *The Sciences of the Artificial.* Cambridge, MA: MIT Press.

Simon, H.A. (1973) 'The structure of ill-structured problems', *Artificial Intelligence* 4: 181–201.

Simon, H.A. (1977) *The New Science of Management Decision.* Englewood Cliffs, NJ: Prentice-Hall.

Simon, H.A. (1978) 'Information processing theory of human problem solving', in W.K. Estes (ed.) *Handbook of Learning and Cognitive Processes.* New York: Wiley.

Simon, H.A. (1979) *Models of Thought.* New Haven: Yale University Press.

Simon, H.A. (1981) 'Cognitive science: the newest science of the artificial', in D. Norman (ed.) *Perspectives on Cognitive Science.* Hillsdale, NJ: Erlbaum.

Simon. H.A. (1983) *Reason in Human Affairs.* Oxford: Basil Blackwell.

Simon, H.A. and Sumner, R.K. (1968) 'Pattern in music', in B. Kleinmuntz (ed.) *Formal Representation of Human Judgement.* New York: Wiley.

Simon, H.A. et al. (1986) 'Report of research briefing panel on decision making and problem solving', *Research Briefings 1986.* Washington, DC: National Academy Press.

Spearman, C. (1927) *The Abilities of Man.* New York: Macmillan.

Sternberg, R.J. (1979) 'The nature of mental abilities', *American Psychologis* 34, pp. 214–30.

Sternberg, R.J. (1985) *Beyond IQ.* Cambridge: Cambridge University Press.

Wallach, M.A. (1988) 'Creativity and talent: a master symposium on the applications of psychology to the teaching and learning of music', Music Educators National Conference.

Wason, P.C. (1968) '"On the failure to eliminate hypotheses" – a second look', in P.C. Wason and P. Johnson-Laird (eds) *Thinking and Reasoning.* Baltimore: Penguin.

Weizenbaum, J. (1984) *Computer Power and Human Reason.* Harmondsworth: Penguin.

Source: Edited version of Chapter in K. Gronberg and G. Kaufmann, *Innovation: A Cross-disciplinary Perspective,* 1988, Oslo: Norwegian University Press, pp. 87–139.

5 Organizational Knowledge Creation

Ikujiro Nonaka and Hirotaka Takeuchi

The distinctive approach of Western philosophy to knowledge has profoundly shaped the way organizational theorists treat knowledge. The Cartesian split between subject and object, the knower and the known, has given birth to a view of the organization as a mechanism for 'information processing'. According to this view, an organization processes information from the external environment in order to adapt to new circumstances. Although this view has proven to be effective in explaining how organizations function, it has a fundamental limitation. When organizations innovate, they do not simply process information, from the outside in, in order to solve existing problems and adapt to a changing environment. They actually create new knowledge and information, from the inside out, in order to redefine both problems and solutions and, in the process, to re-create their environment.

To explain innovation, we need a new theory of organizational knowledge creation. Like any approach to knowledge, it will have its own 'epistemology' (the theory of knowledge), although one substantially different from the traditional Western approach. The cornerstone of our epistemology is the distinction between tacit and explicit knowledge. The key to knowledge creation lies in the mobilization and conversion of tacit knowledge. And because we are concerned with organizational knowledge creation, as opposed to individual knowledge creation, our theory will also have its own distinctive 'ontology', which is concerned with the levels of knowledge-creating entities (individual, group, organizational and inter-organizational). Figure 5.1 presents the epistemological and ontological dimensions in which a knowledge-creation 'spiral' takes place.

We present the four modes of knowledge conversion that are created when tacit and explicit knowledge interact with each other. These four modes – which we refer to as socialization, externalization, combination and internalization – constitute the 'engine' of the entire knowledge-creation process. These modes are what the individual experiences. They are also the mechanisms by which individual knowledge gets articulated and 'amplified' into and throughout the organization.

Knowledge and information

Knowledge is similar to and different from information. First, knowledge, unlike information, is about *beliefs* and *commitment*. Knowledge is a function of a particular stance, perspective, or intention. Second, knowledge, unlike information, is about *action*. It is always knowledge 'to some end'. And third, knowledge, like information, is about *meaning*. It is context-specific and relational.

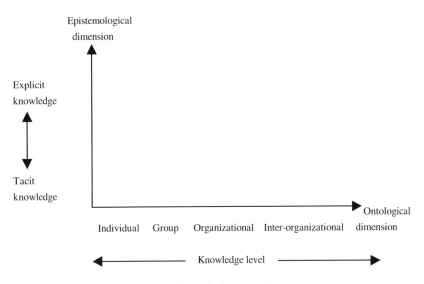

Figure 5.1 Two dimensions of knowledge creation

While traditional epistemology emphasizes the absolute, static and nonhuman nature of knowledge, typically expressed in propositions and formal logic, we consider knowledge as *a dynamic human process of justifying personal belief toward the 'truth'*.

Information is a flow of messages, while knowledge is created by that very flow of information, anchored in the beliefs and commitment of its holder. This understanding emphasizes that *knowledge is essentially related to human action*. We focus attention on the active, subjective nature of knowledge represented by such terms as 'commitment' and 'belief' that are deeply rooted in individuals' value systems.

Both information and knowledge are context-specific and relational in that they depend on the situation and are created dynamically in social interaction among people. Berger and Luckmann (1966) argue that people interacting in a certain historical and social context share information from which they construct social knowledge as a reality, which in turn influences their judgment, behaviour and attitude. Similarly, a corporate vision presented as an equivocal strategy by a leader is organizationally constructed into knowledge through interaction with the environment by the corporation's members, which in turn affects its business behaviour.

Two dimensions of knowledge creation

Although much has been written about the importance of knowledge in management, little attention has been paid to how knowledge is created and how the knowledge-creation process is managed. In a strict sense, knowledge is created only by individuals. An organization cannot create knowledge without individuals. The organization supports creative individuals or provides contexts for them to create knowledge. Organizational knowledge creation, therefore, should be understood as a process that 'organizationally' amplifies the knowledge created by individuals and crystallizes it as a part of the knowledge network of the organization. This process takes place within an expanding 'community of interaction', which crosses intra- and inter-organizational levels and boundaries.[1]

As for the epistemological dimension, we draw on Michael Polanyi's (1966) distinction between *tacit knowledge* and *explicit knowledge*. Tacit knowledge is personal, context-specific, and therefore hard to formalize and communicate. Explicit or 'codified' knowledge, on the other hand, refers to knowledge that is transmittable in formal, systematic language. Polanyi contends that human beings acquire knowledge by actively creating and organizing their own experiences. Thus, knowledge that can be expressed in words and numbers represents only the tip of the iceberg of the entire body of knowledge. As Polanyi (1966) puts it, 'We can know more than we can tell' (p. 4).[2]

In traditional epistemology, knowledge derives from the separation of the subject and the object of perception; human beings as the subject of perception acquire knowledge by analysing external objects. In contrast, Polanyi contends that human beings create knowledge by involving themselves with objects, that is, through self-involvement and commitment, or what Polanyi called 'indwelling'. To know something is to create its image or pattern by tacitly integrating particulars. In order to understand the pattern as a meaningful whole, it is necessary to integrate one's body with the particulars. Thus indwelling breaks the traditional dichotomies between mind and body, reason and emotion, subject and object, and knower and known. Therefore, scientific objectivity is not a sole source of knowledge. Much of our knowledge is the fruit of our own purposeful endeavours in dealing with the world.[3]

Tacit knowledge includes cognitive and technical elements. The cognitive elements centre on what Johnson-Laird (1983) calls 'mental models', in which human beings create working models of the world by making and manipulating analogies in their minds. Mental models, such as schemata, paradigms, perspectives, beliefs, and viewpoints, help individuals to perceive and define their world. On the other hand, the technical element of tacit knowledge includes concrete know-how, crafts, and skills. It is important to note here that the cognitive elements of tacit knowledge refer to an individual's images of reality and visions for the future, that is, 'what is' and 'what ought to be'. The articulation of tacit mental models, in a kind of 'mobilization' process, is a key factor in creating new knowledge.

Some distinctions between tacit and explicit knowledge are shown in Table 5.1. Features generally associated with the more tacit aspects of knowledge are listed on the left, while the corresponding qualities related to explicit knowledge are shown on the right. For example, knowledge of experience tends to be tacit, physical, and subjective, while knowledge of rationality tends to be explicit, metaphysical, and objective. Tacit knowledge is created 'here and now' in a specific, practical context and entails what Bateson (1973) referred to as 'analog' quality. Sharing tacit knowledge between individuals through communication is an analogue process that requires a kind of 'simultaneous processing' of the complexities of issues shared by the individuals. On the other hand, explicit knowledge is about past events or objects 'there and then' and is oriented toward a context-free theory.[4]

Table 5.1 Two types of knowledge

Tacit Knowledge (subjective)	*Explicit Knowledge (objective)*
Knowledge of experience (body)	Knowledge of rationality (mind)
Simultaneous knowledge (here & now)	Sequential knowledge (there & then)
Analogue knowledge (practice)	Digital knowledge (theory)

Knowledge conversion: interaction between tacit and explicit knowledge

The history of Western epistemology can be seen as a continuous controversy about which type of knowledge is more truthful. While Westerners tend to emphasize explicit knowledge, the Japanese tend to stress tacit knowledge. However, tacit knowledge and explicit knowledge are not totally separate but mutually complementary entities. They interact with and interchange into each other in the creative activities of human beings. Our dynamic model of knowledge creation is anchored to a critical assumption that human knowledge is created and expanded through social interaction between tacit knowledge and explicit knowledge. We call this interaction 'knowledge conversion'. It should be noted that this conversion is a 'social' process *between* individuals and not confined *within* an individual.[5] According to the rationalist view, human cognition is a deductive process of individuals, but an individual is never isolated from social interaction when he or she perceives things. Thus, through this 'social conversion' process, tacit and explicit knowledge expand in terms of both quality and quantity (Nonaka 1990).

The idea of 'knowledge conversion' may be partially consonant with [certain models] in cognitive psychology. The hypothesis is that for cognitive skills to develop, all declarative knowledge, which corresponds to explicit knowledge in our theory, has to be transformed into procedural knowledge, which corresponds to tacit knowledge, used in such activities as riding a bicycle or playing the piano.[6] Proponents of this model consider knowledge transformation as mainly unidirectional from declarative (explicit) to procedural (tacit), whereas we argue that the transformation is interactive and spiral.

Four modes of knowledge conversion

The assumption that knowledge is created through the interaction between tacit and explicit knowledge allows us to postulate four different modes of knowledge conversion. They are as follows: (1) from tacit knowledge to tacit knowledge, which we call socialization; (2) from tacit knowledge to explicit knowledge, or externalization; (3) from explicit knowledge to explicit knowledge, or combination; and (4) from explicit knowledge to tacit knowledge, or internalization.[7] Three of the four types of knowledge conversion – socialization, combination, and internalization – have been discussed from various perspectives in organizational theory. For example, socialization is connected with the theories of group processes and organizational culture; combination has its roots in information processing; and internalization is closely related to organizational learning. However, externalization has been somewhat neglected.[8] Figure 5.2 shows the four modes of knowledge conversion. Each of these four modes of knowledge conversion will be discussed in detail below, along with actual examples.

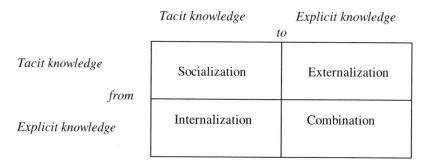

Figure 5.2 Four modes of knowledge conversion

Socialization: from tacit to tacit

Socialization is a process of sharing experiences and thereby creating tacit knowledge such as shared mental models and technical skills.[9] An individual can acquire tacit knowledge directly from others without using language. Apprentices work with their masters and learn craftsmanship not through language but through observation, imitation and practice. In the business setting, on-the-job training uses basically the same principle. The key to acquiring tacit knowledge is experience. Without some form of shared experience, it is extremely difficult for one person to project her- or himself into another individual's thinking process. The mere transfer of information will often make little sense, if it is abstracted from associated emotions and specific contexts in which shared experiences are embedded. The following three examples illustrate how socialization is employed by Japanese companies within the product development context.

The first example of socialization comes from Honda, which set up 'brainstorming camps' (*tama dashi kai*) – informal meetings for detailed discussions to solve difficult problems in development projects. This kind of brainstorming camp is not unique to Honda but has been used by many other Japanese firms. It is also not unique to developing new products and services but is also used to develop managerial systems or corporate strategies. Such a camp is not only a forum for creative dialogue but also a medium for sharing experience and enhancing mutual trust among participants.[10] It is particularly effective in sharing tacit knowledge and creating a new perspective. It reorients the mental models of all individuals in the same direction, but not in a forceful way. Instead, brainstorming camps represent a mechanism through which individuals search for harmony.

The second example, which shows how a tacit technical skill was socialized, comes from the Matsushita Electric Industrial Company. A major problem at the Osaka-based company in developing an automatic home bread-making machine in the late 1980s centred on how to mechanize the dough-kneading process, which is essentially tacit knowledge possessed by master bakers. Dough kneaded by a master baker and by a machine were x-rayed and compared, but no meaningful insights were obtained. Ikuko Tanaka, head of software development, knew that the area's best bread came from the Osaka International Hotel. To capture the tacit knowledge of kneading skill, she and several engineers volunteered to apprentice themselves to the hotel's head baker. Making the same delicious bread as the head baker's was not easy. No one could explain why. One day, however, she noticed that the baker was not only stretching but also 'twisting' the dough, which turned out to be the secret for making tasty bread. Thus she socialized the head baker's tacit knowledge through observation, imitation, and practice.

Socialization also occurs between product developers and customers. Interactions with customers before product development and after market introduction are, in fact, a never-ending process of sharing tacit knowledge and creating ideas for improvement. The way NEC developed its first personal computer is a case in point. The new-product development process began when a group from the Semiconductor and IC Sales Division conceived of an idea to sell Japan's first microcomputer kit, the TK-80, to promote the sales of semiconductor devices. Selling the TK-80 to the public at large was a radical departure from NEC's history of responding to routine orders from Nippon Telegraph and Telephone (NTT). Unexpectedly, a wide variety of customers, ranging from high school students to professional computer enthusiasts, came to NEC's BIT-INN, a display service center in Akihabara district of Tokyo, which is famous for its high concentration of electronic goods retailers. Sharing experiences and continuing dialogues with these customers at the BIT-INN resulted in the development of NEC's best-selling personal computer, the PC-8000, a few years later.

Externalization: from tacit to explicit

Externalization is a process of articulating tacit knowledge into explicit concepts. It is a quintessential knowledge-creation process in that tacit knowledge becomes explicit, taking the shapes of metaphors, analogies, concepts, hypotheses, or models. When we attempt to conceptualize an image, we express its essence mostly in language – writing is an act of converting tacit knowledge into articulable knowledge (Emig 1983). Yet expressions are often inadequate, inconsistent, and insufficient. Such discrepancies and gaps between images and expressions, however, help promote 'reflection' and interaction between individuals.

The externalization mode of knowledge conversion is typically seen in the process of concept creation and is triggered by dialogue or collective reflection.[11] A frequently used method to create a concept is to combine deduction and induction. Mazda, for example, combined these two reasoning methods when it developed the new RX-7 concept, which is described as 'an authentic sports car that provides an exciting and comfortable drive'. The concept was *deduced* from the car maker's corporate slogan: 'create new values and present joyful driving pleasures' as well as the positioning of the new car as 'a strategic car for the US market and an image of innovation'. At the same time, the new concept was *induced* from 'concept' trips, which were driving experiences by development team members in the United States as well as from 'concept clinics', which gathered opinions from customers and car experts. When we cannot find an adequate expression for an image through analytical methods of deduction or induction, we have to use a nonanalytical method. Externalization is, therefore, often driven by metaphor and/or analogy. Using an attractive metaphor and/or analogy is highly effective in fostering direct commitment to the creative process. Recall the Honda City example. In developing the car, Hiroo Watanabe and his team used a metaphor of 'Automobile Evolution'. His team viewed the automobile as an organism and sought its ultimate form. In essence, Watanabe was asking, 'What will the automobile eventually evolve into?'

I insisted on allocating the minimum space for mechanics and the maximum space for passengers. This seemed to be the ideal car, into which the automobile should evolve. The first step toward this goal was to challenge the 'reasoning of Detroit', which had sacrificed comfort for appearance. Our choice was a short but tall car ... spherical, therefore lighter, less expensive, more comfortable, and solid.[12]

The concept of a tall and short car – 'Tall Boy' – emerged through an analogy between the concept of 'man-maximum, machine-minimum' and an image of a sphere that contains the maximum volume within the minimum area of surface, which ultimately resulted in the Honda City.

The case of Canon's Mini-Copier is a good example of how an analogy was used effectively for product development. One of the most difficult problems faced by the development team was producing at low cost a disposable cartridge, which would eliminate the necessity for maintenance required in conventional machines. Without a disposable cartridge, maintenance staff would have to be stationed all over the country, since the copier was intended for family or personal use. If the usage frequency were high, maintenance costs could be negligible. But that was not the case with a personal copier. The fact that a large number of customers would be using the machine only occasionally meant that the new product had to have high reliability and no or minimum maintenance. A maintenance study showed that more than 90 per cent of the problems came from the drum or its surrounding parts. Aimed at cutting maintenance costs while maintaining the highest reliability, the team developed the concept of a disposable cartridge system in which the drum or the heart of the copier is replaced after a certain amount of usage.

The next problem was whether the drum could be produced at a cost low enough to be consistent with the targeted low selling price of the copier. A task force assigned to solve this cost problem had many heated discussions about the production of conventional photosensitive drum cylinders with a base material of aluminum-drawn tube at a low cost. One day Hiroshi Tanaka, leader of the task force, sent out for some cans of beer. Once the beer was consumed, he asked, 'How much does it cost to manufacture this can?' The team then explored the possibility of applying the process of manufacturing the beer can to manufacturing the drum cylinder, using the same material. By clarifying similarities and differences, they discovered a process technology to manufacture the aluminum drum at a low cost, thus giving rise to the disposable drum.

These examples within Japanese firms clearly show the effectiveness of the use of metaphor and analogy in creating and elaborating a concept (see Table 5.2). As Honda's Watanabe commented, 'We are more than halfway there, once a product concept has been created.' In this sense, the leaders' wealth of figurative language and imagination is an essential factor in eliciting tacit knowledge from project members.

Among the four modes of knowledge conversion, externalization holds the key to knowledge creation, because it creates new, explicit concepts from tacit knowledge. How can we convert tacit knowledge into explicit knowledge effectively and efficiently? The answer lies in a sequential use of metaphor, analogy and mode. As Nisbet noted, 'much of what Michael Polanyi has called "tacit knowledge" is expressible – in so far as it is expressible at all – in metaphor' (1969, p. 5). Metaphor is a way of perceiving or intuitively understanding one thing by imaging another thing symbolically. It is most often used in abductive reasoning or nonanalytical methods for creating radical concepts (Bateson 1973). It is neither analysis nor synthesis of common attributes of associated things. Donnellon, Gray and Bougon argue that 'metaphors create novel interpretation of experience by asking the listener to see one thing in terms of something else' and 'create new ways of experiencing reality' (1986, pp. 48, 52). Thus, 'metaphors are one communication mechanism that can function to reconcile discrepancies in meaning' (p. 48).[13]

Table 5.2 Metaphor and/or analogy for concept creation in product development

Product (Company)	Metaphor/Analogy	Influence on Concept Creation
City (Honda)	'Automobile Evolution' (metaphor)	Hint of maximizing passenger space as ultimate auto development 'Man-maximum, machine minimum' concept created
	The sphere (analogy)	Hint of achieving maximum passenger space through minimizing surface area 'Tall and short car (Tall Boy)' concept created
Mini-Copier (Canon)	Aluminum beer can (analogy)	Hint of similarities between inexpensive aluminum beer can and photosensitive drum manufacture 'Low-cost manufacturing process' concept created
Home Bakery (Matsushita)	Hotel bread (metaphor)	Hint of more delicious bread
	Osaka International Hotel head baker (analogy)	'Twist dough' concept created

Moreover, metaphor is an important tool for creating a *network* of new concepts. Because a metaphor is 'two thoughts of different things ... supported by a single word, or phrase, whose meaning is a resultant of their interaction' (Richards 1936, p. 93), we can continuously relate concepts that are far apart in our mind, even relate abstract concepts to concrete ones. This creative, cognitive process continues as we think of the similarities among concepts and feel an imbalance, inconsistency, or contradiction in their associations, thus often leading to the discovery of new meaning or even to the formation of a new paradigm.

Contradictions inherent in a metaphor are then harmonized by analogy, which reduces the unknown by highlighting the 'commonness' of two different things. Metaphor and analogy are often confused. Association of two things through metaphor is driven mostly by intuition and holistic imagery and does not aim to find differences between them. On the other hand, association through analogy is carried out by rational thinking and focuses on structural/functional similarities between two things, and hence their differences. Thus analogy helps us understand the unknown through the known and bridges the gap between an image and a logical model.[14]

Once explicit concepts are created, they can then be modeled. In a logical model, no contradictions should exist and all concepts and propositions must be expressed in systematic language and coherent logic. But in business terms, models are often only rough descriptions or drawings, far from being fully specific. Models are usually generated from metaphors when new concepts are created in the business context.[15]

Combination: from explicit to explicit

Combination is a process of systemizing concepts into a knowledge system. This mode of knowledge conversion involves combining different bodies of explicit knowledge. Individuals exchange and combine knowledge through such media as documents, meetings, telephone conversations, or computerized communication networks. Reconfiguration of existing information through sorting, adding, combining and categorizing of explicit knowledge (as conducted in computer databases) can lead to new knowledge. Knowledge creation carried out in formal education and training at schools usually takes this form. An MBA education is one of the best examples of this kind.

In the business context, the combination mode of knowledge conversion is most often seen when middle managers break down and operationalize corporate visions, business concepts, or product concepts. Middle management plays a critical role in creating new concepts through networking of codified information and knowledge. Creative uses of computerized communication networks and large-scale databases facilitate this mode of knowledge conversion.[16]

At Kraft General Foods, a manufacturer of dairy and processed foods, data from the POS (point-of-sales) system of retailers is utilized not only to find out what does and does not sell well but also to create new 'ways to sell', that is, new sales systems and methods. Kraft successfully manages its product sales through supermarkets by controlling four elements of the 'category management' methodology – consumer and category dynamics, space management, merchandizing management, and pricing management.[17]

At the top management level of an organization, the combination mode is realized when mid-range concepts (such as product concepts) are combined with and integrated into grand concepts (such as a corporate vision) to generate a new meaning of the latter. Introducing a new corporate image in 1986, for example, Asahi Breweries adopted a grand concept dubbed 'live Asahi for live people'. The concept stood for the message that 'Asahi will provide natural and authentic products and services for those who seek active minds and active lives.' Along with this grand concept, Asahi inquired into the essence of what makes beer appealing, and developed Asahi Super Dry beer based on the new-product concept of 'richness and sharpness'. The new-product concept is a mid-range concept that made the grand concept of Asahi more explicitly recognizable, which in turn altered the company's product development system. The taste of beer was hitherto decided by engineers in the production department without any participation by the sales department. The 'richness and sharpness' concept was realized through co-operative product development by both departments.

Other examples of interaction between grand concepts and mid-range concepts abound. For example, NEC's 'C&C' (computers and communication) concept induced the development of the epoch-making PC-8000 personal computer, which was based on the mid-range concept of 'distributed processing'. Canon's corporate policy, 'Creation of an excellent company by transcending the camera business' led to the development of the Mini-Copier, which was developed with the mid-range product concept of 'easy maintenance'. Mazda's grand vision, 'Create new values and present joyful driving', was realized in the new RX-7, 'an authentic sports car that provides an exciting and comfortable drive'.

Internalization: from explicit to tacit

Internalization is a process of embodying explicit knowledge into tacit knowledge. It is closely related to 'learning by doing'. When experiences through socialization, externalization, and combination are internalized into individuals' tacit knowledge bases in the form of shared mental models or technical know-how, they become valuable assets. All the members of the Honda City project team, for example, internalized their experiences of the late 1970s and are now making use of that know-how and leading R&D projects in the company. For organizational knowledge creation to take place, however, the tacit knowledge accumulated at the individual level needs to be socialized with other organizational members, thereby starting a new spiral of knowledge creation.

For explicit knowledge to become tacit, it helps if the knowledge is verbalized or diagrammed into documents, manuals, or oral stories. Documentation helps individuals internalize what they experienced, thus enriching their tacit knowledge. In addition, documents or manuals facilitate the transfer of explicit knowledge to other people, thereby helping them experience the experiences of others indirectly (i.e. 're-experiencing' them). GE, for example, documents all customer complaints and inquiries in a database at its Answer Center in Louisville, Kentucky, which can be used, for example, by members of a new-product development team to 're-experience' what the telephone operators experienced. GE established the Answer Center in 1982 to process questions, requests for help and complaints from customers on any product 24 hours a day, 365 days a year. Over 200 telephone operators respond to as many as 14,000 calls a day. GE has programmed 1.5 million potential problems and their solutions into its computerized database system. The system is equipped with an on-line diagnosis function utilizing the latest artificial intelligence technology for quick answers to inquiries; any problem-solution response can be retrieved by the telephone operator in two seconds. In case a solution is not available, 12 specialists with at least four years of repair experience think out solutions on site. Four full-time programmers put the solutions into the database, so that the new information is usually installed into the system by the following day. This information is sent to the respective product divisions every month. Yet, the product divisions also frequently send their new-product development people to the Answer Center to chat with the telephone operators or the 12 specialists, thereby 're-experiencing' their experiences.

Internalization can also occur even without having actually to 're-experience' other people's experiences. For example, if reading or listening to a success story makes some members of the organization feel the realism and essence of the story, the experience that took place in the past may change into a tacit mental model. When such a mental model is shared by most members of the organization, tacit knowledge becomes part of the organizational culture. This practice is prevalent in Japan, where books and articles on companies or their leaders abound. Freelance writers or former employees publish them, sometimes at the request of the companies. One can find about two dozen books on Honda or Soichiro Honda in major bookstores today, all of which help instil a strong corporate culture for Honda.

An example of internalization through 'learning by doing' can be seen at Matsushita when it launched a company-wide policy in 1993 to reduce yearly working time to 1,800 hours. Called MIT'93 for 'Mind and Management Innovation Toward 1993', the policy's objective was not to reduce costs but to innovate the mind-set and management by reducing working hours and increasing individual creativity. Many departments were puzzled about how to implement the policy, which was clearly communicated as explicit knowledge. The MIT'93 promotion office advised each department to experiment with the policy for one month by working 150 hours. Through such a bodily experience, employees got to know what working 1,800 hours a year would be like. An explicit concept reducing working time to 1,800 hours, was internalized through the one-month experience.

Contents of knowledge and the knowledge spiral

Organizational knowledge creation is a continuous and dynamic interaction between tacit and explicit knowledge. This interaction is shaped by shifts between different modes of knowledge conversion, which are in turn induced by several triggers (see Figure 5.3).

First, the socialization mode usually starts with building a 'field' of interaction. This field facilitates the sharing of members' experiences and mental models. Second, the externalization mode is triggered by meaningful 'dialogue or collective reflection', in which using an appropriate metaphor or analogy helps team members to articulate hidden tacit knowledge that is otherwise hard to communicate. Third, the combination mode is triggered by

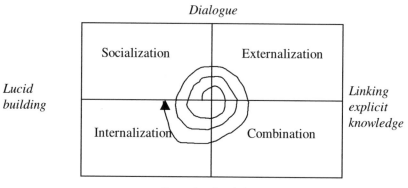

Dialogue

Socialization	Externalization
Internalization	Combination

Lucid building

Linking explicit knowledge

Learning by doing

Figure 5.3 The knowledge spiral

'networking' newly created knowledge and existing knowledge from other sections of the organization, thereby crystallizing them into a new product, service, or managerial system. Finally, 'learning by doing' triggers internalization.

The content of the knowledge created by each mode of knowledge conversion is naturally different (see Figure 5.4). Socialization yields what can be called 'sympathized knowledge', such as shared mental models and technical skills. The tacit skill of kneading dough in the Matsushita example is a sympathized knowledge. Externalization outputs 'conceptual knowledge'. The concept of 'Tall Boy' in the Honda example is a conceptual knowledge created through the metaphor of 'Automobile Evolution' and the analogy between a sphere and the concept of 'man-maximum, machine-minimum'. Combination gives rise to 'systemic knowledge', such as a prototype and new component technologies. The micro-merchandizing programme in the Kraft General Foods example is a systemic knowledge, which includes retail management methods as its components. internalization produces 'operational knowledge' about project management, production process, new-product usage, and policy implementation. The bodily experience of working 150 hours a month in the Matsushita case is an operational knowledge of policy implementation.

These contents of knowledge interact with each other in the spiral of knowledge creation. For example, sympathized knowledge about consumers; wants may become explicit conceptual knowledge about a new-product concept through socialization and externalization. Such conceptual knowledge becomes a guideline for creating systemic knowledge through combination. For example, a new-product concept steers the combination phase, in which newly developed and existing component technologies are combined to build a prototype. Systemic knowledge (e.g. a simulated production process for the new product) turns into operational knowledge for mass production of the product through internalization. In addition, experience-based operational knowledge often triggers a new cycle of knowledge creation. For example, the users' tacit operational knowledge about a product is often socialized, thereby initiating improvement of an existing product or development of an innovation.

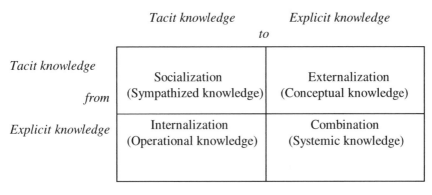

	Tacit knowledge	*Explicit knowledge*
Tacit knowledge	Socialization (Sympathized knowledge)	Externalization (Conceptual knowledge)
Explicit knowledge	Internalization (Operational knowledge)	Combination (Systemic knowledge)

Figure 5.4 Contents of knowledge created by the four modes

Thus far, we have focused our discussion on the epistemological dimension of organizational knowledge creation. As noted before, however, an organization cannot create knowledge by itself. Tacit knowledge of individuals is the basis of organizational knowledge creation. The organization has to mobilize tacit knowledge created and accumulated at the individual level. The mobilized tacit knowledge is 'organizationally' amplified through four modes of knowledge conversion and crystallized at higher ontological levels. We call this the 'knowledge spiral', in which the interaction between tacit knowledge and explicit knowledge will become larger in scale as it moves up the ontological levels. Thus, organizational knowledge creation is a spiral process, starting at the individual level and moving up through expanding communities of interaction, that crosses sectional, department, divisional and organizational boundaries.

This process is exemplified by product development. Creating a product concept involves a community of interacting individuals with different backgrounds and mental models. While the members from the R&D department focus on technological potential, those from the production and marketing departments are interested in other issues. Only some of those different experiences, mental models, motivations and intentions can be expressed in explicit language. Thus, the socialization process of sharing tacit knowledge is required. Moreover, both socialization and externalization are necessary for linking individuals' tacit and explicit knowledge. Many Japanese companies have adopted brainstorming camps as a tool for that purpose.

The product created by this collective and co-operative process will then be reviewed for its coherence with mid-range and grand concepts. Even if the newly created product has superior quality, it may conflict with the divisional or organizational goals expressed by the mid-range and grand concepts. What is required is another process at a higher level to maintain the integrity of the whole, which will lead to another cycle of knowledge creation in a larger context.

Enabling conditions for organizational knowledge creation

The role of the organizational knowledge-creation process is to provide the proper context for facilitating group activities as well as the creation and accumulation of knowledge at the individual level. In this section we will discuss five conditions required at the organizational level to promote the knowledge spiral.

Intention

The knowledge spiral is driven by organizational intention, which is defined as an organization's aspiration to its goals. Efforts to achieve the intention usually take the form of strategy within a business setting. From the viewpoint of organizational knowledge creation, the essence of strategy lies in developing the organizational capability to acquire, create, accumulate, and exploit knowledge. The most critical element of corporate strategy it to conceptualize a vision about what kind of knowledge should be developed and to operationalize it into a management system for implementation.

Autonomy

The second condition for promoting the knowledge spiral is autonomy. At the individual level, all members of an organization should be allowed to act autonomously as far as circumstances permit. By allowing them to act autonomously, the organization may increase the chance of introducing unexpected opportunities. Autonomy also increases the possibility that individuals will motivate themselves to create new knowledge. Moreover, autonomous individuals function as part of the holographic structure, in which the whole and each part share the same information. Original ideas emanate from autonomous individuals, diffuse within the team, and then become organizational ideas. In this respect, the self-organizing individual assumes a position that may be seen as analogous to the core of a series of nested Russian dolls. From the viewpoint of knowledge creation, such an organization is more likely to maintain greater flexibility in acquiring, interpreting, and relating information. It is a system in which the 'minimum critical specification' principle (Morgan 1986) is met as a prerequisite for self-organization, and therefore autonomy is assured as much as possible.

Fluctuation and creative chaos

The third organizational condition for promoting the knowledge spiral is fluctuation and creative chaos, which stimulate the interaction between the organization and the external environment. Fluctuation is different from complete disorder and characterized by 'order without recursiveness.' It is an order whose pattern is hard to predict at the beginning (Gleick 1987). If organizations adopt an open attitude toward environmental signals, they can exploit those signals' ambiguity, redundancy, or noise in order to improve their own knowledge system.

Redundancy

Redundancy is the fourth condition that enables the knowledge spiral to take place organizationally. To Western managers who are preoccupied with the idea of efficient information processing or uncertainty reduction (Galbraith 1973), the term 'redundancy', may sound pernicious because of its connotations of unnecessary duplication, waste, or information overload. What we mean here by redundancy is the existence of information that goes beyond the immediate operational requirements of organizational members. In business organizations, redundancy refers to intentional overlapping of information about business activities, management responsibilities, and the company as a whole.

Requisite variety

The fifth condition that helps to advance the knowledge spiral is requisite variety. According to Ashby (1956), an organization's internal diversity must match the variety and complexity of the environment in order to deal with challenges posed by the environment. Organizational members can cope with many contingencies if they possess requisite variety, which can be enhanced by combining information differently, flexibly, and quickly, and by providing equal access to information throughout the organization. To maximize variety, everyone in the organization should be assured of the fastest access to the broadest variety of necessary information, going through the fewest steps (Numagami et al. 1989).

[See original article for examples of each of these enabling conditions.]

Summary

Knowledge conversion takes place between tacit knowledge and explicit knowledge. Four modes of this conversion – socialization, externalization, combination and internalization – were discussed. These modes are not independent of each other, but their interactions produce a spiral when time is introduced as the third dimension. We introduced five organizational conditions – intention, fluctuation/chaos, autonomy, redundancy and requisite variety – that enable the four modes to be transformed into a knowledge spiral.

Knowledge created by individuals is transformed into knowledge at the group and organizational levels. These levels are not independent of each other, but interact with each other iteratively and continuously. The five-phase process of organizational knowledge creation [involves] sharing tacit knowledge, creating concepts, justifying concepts, building archetypes and cross-levelling knowledge.

Notes

1. Brown and Duguid's (1991) work on 'evolving communities of practice' shows how individuals' actual ways of working and learning might be very different from relatively rigid, official practices specified by the organization. In reality, informal groups evolve among individuals seeking to solve a particular problem or pursuing other commonly-held objectives. Membership in these groups is decided by individuals' abilities to trade practically valuable information. Orr (1990) argues that members exchange ideas and share narratives or 'war stories', thereby building a shared understanding out of conflicting and confusing information. This knowledge creation includes not only innovation but also learning that can shape and develop approaches to daily work.

2. For example, we recognize our neighbour's face without being able to explain how to do so in words. Moreover, we sense others' feelings from their facial expressions, but explaining them in words is more difficult. Put another way, while it is virtually impossible to articulate the feelings we get from our neighbour's face, we are still aware of the overall impression. For further discussion on tacit knowledge, see Polanyi (1958) and Gelwick (1977).

3. Michael Polanyi was a renowned chemist and rumoured to be very close to the Nobel Prize until he turned to philosophy at the age of fifty.

4. Brown argues that 'The organizations of the future will be "knowledge refineries" in which employees will synthesize understanding and interpretations from the sea of information that threatens to flood them from all sides' (1992, p. 3). In a knowledge refinery, he continues, workers need to collaborate with both the past and the present. While collaboration with the present is about sharing tacit knowledge, collaboration with the past draws on experiences gained from previous ways of doing things.

5. According to Maturana and Varela, 'The linguistic domain as a domain of orienting behavior requires at least two interacting organisms, so that a cooperative system of consensual interactions may be developed. The central feature of human existence is its occurrence in a linguistic cognitive domain. This domain is constitutively social' (1980, pp. xxiv, 41).

6. This model is consonant with Ryle's (1949) categorization of knowledge into knowing that something 'exists' and knowing 'how' it operates. Squire (1987) listed contending taxonomies with more than a dozen labels, such as 'implicit' vs. 'explicit' and 'skill memory' vs. 'fact memory'.

7. A survey of 105 Japanese middle managers was conducted to test the hypothesis that the knowledge-creation construct is comprised of four knowledge-conversion processes – socialization, externalization, combination and internalization. Factor loading from first-order and second-order factor analyses empirically validated the existence of these four conversion processes. For details see Nonaka et al. (1994).

8. For a limited analysis of externalization from a viewpoint of information creation, see Nonaka (1987).

9. Cannon-Bowers et al. define 'shared mental models' as 'knowledge structures held by members of a team that enable them to form accurate explanations and expectations for the task, and in turn, to coordinate their actions and adapt their behavior to demands of the task and other team members' (1993, p. 228), based upon their extensive review of the literature on the shared mental model and their research on team decision making.

10. Condon (1976) argues that communication is a simultaneous and contextual phenomenon in which people feel a change occurring, share the same sense of change, and are moved to take action. In other words, he says, communication is like a wave that passes through people's bodies and culminates when everyone synchronizes with the wave.

11. Graumann (1990) views dialogue as multiperspective cognition. As noted before, language is inherently related to action. Dialogue, therefore, may be seen as a collective action. Moreover, according to Kant, creating concepts is creating the world.

12. Interviewed on 25 January 1984.

13. These authors emphasize the importance of creating shared meaning for organized action. According to Rosch (1973), we understand things not through theory attributes bur through better examples of them, or what she called 'prototypes'.

14. The following famous episode illustrates the process. F.A. Kekule, a German chemist, discovered the chemical structure of benzene – a hexagonal ring of carbon atoms – through a dream of a snake gripping its own tail. In this case, the snake pattern was a metaphor, and possible combinations of the pattern became analogies of other chemical compounds. Thus, Kekule developed the structural model of organic chemistry.

15. According to Lakoff and Johnson, 'metaphor is pervasive in everyday life, not just in language but in thought and action' (1980, p. 3).

16. Information and communications technologies used for this purpose include VAN (Value-Added Network), LAN (Local Area Network), E-Mail (Electronic mail), POS (Point-Of-Sale) system, 'Groupware' for CSCW (Computer Supported Cooperative Work), and CAD/CAM (Computer-Aided Design/Manufacturing).

17. In the triad database system, data from the Market Metrics' Supermarket Solutions system, which integrates POS data from supermarkets nationwide, is hooked to customized data on shopping behaviours provided by Information Resources, and lifestyle data from Equifax Marketing Decisions System's Microvision database. For more information see 'Micro-merchandizing with KGF', *Food and Beverage Marketing* 10(6) 1991, 'Dawn of brand analysis', *Food and Beverage Marketing* 10(10) 1991, and 'Partnering', *Supermarket Business* 46(5) 1991.

References

Ashby. W.R. (1956) *An Introduction to Cybernetics.* London: Chapman and Hall.

Bateson, G. (1973) *Steps to an Ecology of Mind.* London: Paladin.

Berger, P.L. and Luckmann, T. (1966) *The Social Construction of Reality.* Garden City, NY: Doubleday.

Brown, J.S. (1992) *Reflections on the Document.* Mimeograph: Xerox Palo Alto (CA) Research Center.

Brown, J.S. and Duguid, P. (1991) 'Organizational learning and communities-of-practice: towards a unified view of working, learning and innovation', *Organization Science* 2(1): 40–57.

Cannon-Bowers, J.A., Salas, E. and Converse, S. (1993) 'Shared mental models in expert team decision making', in N.J. Castellan (Ed.) *Individual and Group Decision Making.* Hillsdale, NJ: Lawrence Erlbaum, pp 221–46.

Condon, W.S. (1976) 'An analysis of behavioural organization', *Sign Language Studies* 13.

Donnellon, A., Gray, B., and Bougon, G. (1986) 'Communication, meaning and organized action', *Administrative Science Quarterly* 31: 43–55.

Emig, J. (1983) *The Web of Meaning.* Upper Montclair, NJ: Boynton/Cook.

Galbraith, J. (1973) *Designing Complex Organizations.* Reading, MA: Addison-Wesley.

Gelwick, R. (1977) *The Way of Discovery.* Oxford: Oxford University Press.

Gleick, J. (1987) *Chaos: Making a New Science.* New York: Viking.

Graumann, C.F. (1990) 'Perspectival structure and dynamics in dialogues', in I. Markova and K. Foppa (Eds) *The Dynamics of Dialogue.* Hemel Hempstead: Harvester Wheatsheaf.

Johnson-Laird, P.N. (1983) *Mental Models.* Cambridge: Cambridge University Press.

Lakoff, G. and Johnson, M. (1980) *Metaphors We Live By.* Chicago, IL: University of Chicago Press.

Maturana, H.R. and Varela, F.J. (1980) *Autopoesis and Cognition.* Dordrecht, Holland: Reidel.

Morgan, G. (1986) *Images of Organization.* Beverly Hills, CA: Sage.

Nisbet, R. A. (1969) *Social Change and History.* Oxford: Oxford University Press.

Nonaka, I. (1987) 'Managing the firm as information creation process'. Working Paper, Institute of Business Research, Hitotsubashi University.

Nonaka, I. (1990) *A Theory of Organizational Knowledge Creation.* Tokyo: Nihon-Keizeai-Shimbunsha (In Japanese).

Nonaka, I. Byosiere, P., Boruki, C. and Komo, N. (1994) Organizational Knowledge Creation Theory Test, *International Business Review*, Special Issue

Numagami, T., Ohta, I. and Nonaka, T. (1989) *Case Study SMIP 91 16 CN* (Japanese text) Tokyo: Nomura School of Advanced Management.

Orr, J.E. (1990) 'Sharing knowledge, celebrating identity', in D. Middleton and D. Edwards (Eds) *Collective Remembering.* Newbury Park, CA: Sage, pp. 169–189.

Polanyi, M. (1966) *The Tacit Dimension.* London: Routledge.

Richards, I.A. (1936) *The Philosophy of Rhetoric.* Oxford: Oxford University Press.

Rosch, E.H. (1973) 'Natural categories', *Cognitive Psychology* 4: 328–350.

Ryle, G. (1949) *The Concept of Mind.* London: Hutchinson.

Squire, L.R. (1987) *Memory and Brain*, New York: Oxford University Press.

Source: Edited extract from Chapter 3, *The Knowledge-Creating Company: how companies create the dynamics of innovation*, 1995, Oxford: Oxford University press.

Section C   Perception

Perceptions of management are changing. Here Mintzberg outlines what he sees as wrong with current rhetoric, Morgan argues for the use of metaphor and analogical thinking as a means of opening up perceptions, and Broekstra charts the changing management paradigm and accompanying metaphors.

Henry Mintzberg is a Canadian Professor who has been a thorn in the back of orthodox management theorists for the last thirty years. In detailed studies, he has shown that what the manager actually does is at odds with the rhetoric management science tends to use to describe management (Mintzberg 1973). He has also pointed out the shortcomings of planning as a guiding metaphor for management processes (Mintzberg 1994). Here, in a light piece, he summarizes some of his objections to management as propagated by American business schools.

Morgan shows how perceptions are necessarily subjective and partial. He advocates consciously adopting different metaphors as a means of accessing the different perspectives they reveal. He suggests the conscious use of these different frames will reveal new ways of seeing and acting.

Broekstra is one of many writers who have drawn attention to the changing management paradigm. He charts the move from organization as machine through organization as organism to organization as brain, arguing that the brain provides a more appropriate metaphor for today's networked organization with its capacity to reinvent itself and that the science of complexity also offers new insights for today's organization.

References

Mintzberg, H. (1973) *The Nature of Managerial Work.* New York: Harper and Row.
Mintzberg, H. (1994) *The Rise and Fall of Strategic Planning: reconceiving roles for planning, plans, planners.* Englewood Cliffs, NJ: Prentice Hall.

6 Ten Ideas Designed to Rile Everyone Who Cares about Management

Henry Mintzberg

The object of this exercise is to shake us all out of the complacency that surrounds too much of the practice of management today, a practice that I believe is undermining many of our organizations and hence our society. We had better take a good look at what is wrong with this hype called management.

1 Organizations don't have tops and bottoms

These are just misguided metaphors. What organizations really have are the *outer* people, connected to the world, and the *inner* ones, disconnected from it, as well as many so-called *middle* managers, who are desperately trying to connect the inner and outer people to each other.

The sooner we stop talking about top management (nobody dares to say *bottom* management), the better off we shall be. The metaphor distorts reality. After all, organizations are spread out geographically, so that even if the chief executive sits 100 stories up in New York, he is not nearly as high as a lowly clerk on the ground floor in Denver.

The only thing a chief executive sits atop is an organization chart. And all that silly document does is demonstrate how mesmerized we are with the abstraction called management. The next time you look at one of these charts, cover the name of the organization and try to figure out what it actually does for a living. This most prominent of all corporate artefacts never gets down to real products and real services, let alone the people who deal with them every day. It's as if the organization exists for the management.

Try this metaphor. Picture the organization as a circle. In the middle is the *central* management. And around the outer edges are those people who develop, produce, and deliver the products and services – the people with the knowledge of the daily operations. The latter see with complete clarity because they are closest to the action. But they do so only narrowly, for all they can see are their own little segments. The managers at the centre see widely – all around the circle – but they don't see clearly because they are distant from the operations. The trick, therefore, is to connect the two groups. And for that, most organizations need informed managers in between, people who can see the outer edge and then swing around and talk about it to those at the centre. You know – the people we used to call middle managers, the ones who are mostly gone.

2 It is time to delayer the delayerers

As organizations remove layers from their operations, they add them to the so-called top of their hierarchies – new levels that do nothing but exercise financial control and so drive everyone else crazy.

I used to write books for an independent publishing company called Prentice-Hall. It was big – very big – but well organized and absolutely dedicated to its craft. Then it was bought by Simon & Schuster, which was bought by Paramount. Good old Prentice-Hall became a 'Paramount Communications Company'. It was at about this time that one of my editors quoted her new boss as saying, 'We're in the business of filling the OI (operating income) bucket.' Strange, because my editor and I both had thought the company was in the business of publishing books and enlightening readers. Next, publisher Robert Maxwell got involved, and not long ago the whole thing was bought yet again, so that now Prentice-Hall has become a 'Viacom Company'. After all this, will publishing books remain as important as satisfying bosses?

Take the metaphor of the circular organization and plunk a financial boss on top of the chief in the centre, then pile on another and perhaps another. The weight can become crushing. To use a favourite management expression, the new layers don't 'add value' at all. By focusing on the numbers, they depreciate true value and reduce the richness of a business to the poverty of its financial performance. Listen to what *Fortune* wrote a few years ago: 'What's truly amazing about P&G's historic restructuring is that it is a response to the consumer market, not the stock market' (6 November 1989). What's truly amazing about this statement is the use of the phrase 'truly amazing'.

With controllers looking over their shoulders, division chiefs get impatient for numerical results.

Nowhere does the harshness of such attitudes appear more starkly than in the delayering of all those middle managers. Delayering can be defined as the process by which people who barely know what's going on get rid of those who do. Delayering is done in the name of the 'empowerment' of those who remain. But too many of them, at the outer edges, become disconnected instead, while the real database of the organization, the key to what was its future, lines up at the unemployment office. Isn't it time that we began to delayer the delayerers?

3   Lean *is* mean and doesn't even improve long-term profits

There is nothing wonderful about firing people. True, stock market analysts seem to love companies that fire frontline workers and middle managers (while increasing the salaries of senior executives). Implicitly, employees are blamed for having been hired in the first place and are sentenced to suffer the consequences while the corporations cash in. Listen to this sample of contemporary management wisdom: 'In the face of the dismaying results that began in 1985, just after John Akers became CEO, and that persisted, IBM failed to accept the reality that its so-called full-employment practice, in which it forswore layoffs, was no longer workable. A retired IBM manager who worked closely for years with IBM's top executives recalls the mystique that grew up around this practice: "It was a religion. Every personnel director who came in lived and died on defending that practice. I tell you, this was like virginity." Just recently, a day late and a dollar short, IBM at last gave it up' (*Fortune*, 3 May 1993).

You can almost feel the writer gloating and thinking, isn't this wonderful – finally IBM has joined the club. The magazine article, about big companies in decline, was entitled 'Dinosaurs?' But everyone knows that dinosaurs lasted a couple of hundred million years and, even then, probably succumbed to natural forces. With mass firings and other callous behaviours toward one another, we could well be getting rid of ourselves after barely a few hundred thousand years.

I did some work recently for a large US insurance company, with no market analysts to worry about because it is a mutual. I was told a story about a woman there who was working energetically to convert a paper database to an electronic one. Someone said to her, 'Don't you know you are working yourself out of a job?' 'Sure,' she retorted. 'But I know they'll find something else for me. If I didn't, I'd sabotage the process.' Imagine how much her feeling of security is worth to that company. Or imagine the case of no job security. A few years ago, some middle managers at one of the major Canadian banks formed what they called their 50/50 club. They were more than 50 years old and earning more than \$50,000 per year, and it was clear to them that many members of the group were systematically being fired just before they qualified for their pensions. How much sabotage was going on at that bank?

Lean *is* mean. So why do we keep treating people in these ways? Presumably because we are not competitive. And just why aren't we competitive? To a large extent because we have been unable to meet Japanese competition. So how do we respond? By managing in exactly the opposite way from the Japanese. Will we never learn?

4 The trouble with most strategies are chief executives who believe themselves to be strategists

Great strategists are either creative or generous. We have too few of either type. We call the creative ones visionaries – they see a world that others have been blind to. They are often difficult people, but they break new ground in their own ways. The generous ones, in contrast, bring strategy out in other people. They build organizations that foster thoughtful inquiry and creative action. (You can recognize these people by the huge salaries they don't pay themselves. Their salaries signal their people, We're all in this together. Salaries are not used to impress fellow CEOs.) The creative strategists reach out from the centre of that circular organization to touch the edges, while the generous ones strengthen the whole circle by turning strategic thinking into a collective learning process.

Most so-called strategists, however, just sit on top and pretend to strategize. They formulate ever so clever strategies for everyone else to implement. They issue glossy strategic plans that look wonderful and take their organizations nowhere with great fanfare. Strategy becomes a game of chess in which the pieces – great blocks of businesses and companies – get moved around with a ferocity that dazzles the market analysts. All the pieces look like they fit neatly together – at least on the board. It's all very impressive, except that the pieces themselves, ignored as every eye focuses on the great moves, disintegrate. Imagine if we took all this energy spent on shuffling and used it instead to improve *real* businesses. I don't mean 'financial services' or 'communications', I mean banking or book publishing.

Consider how we train strategists in the MBA classrooms. We take young people with little business experience – hardly selected for their creativity, let alone their generosity – and drill them in case after case in which they play the great strategists sitting atop institutions they know nothing about. An hour or two the night before to read 20 pithy pages on Gargantuan Industries and its nuclear reactors and then off to 80 supercharged minutes in the classroom to decide what Gargantuan must do with itself into the next millennium. Is it any wonder that we end up with case studies in the executive suites – disguised as strategic thinking?

5 Decentralization centralizes, empowerment disempowers, and measurement doesn't measure up

The buzzwords are the problem, not the solution. The hot techniques dazzle us. Then they fizzle. *Total quality management* (TQM) takes over and no one even remembers *quality of work life* – same word, similar idea, no less the craze, not very long ago. How come quality of work life died? Will TQM die a similar death? Will we learn anything? Will anyone even care?

**How much
sabotage will result
if employees are
fired right before
qualifying for
pensions?**

The TQM concept has now magically metamorphosed into empowerment. What empowerment really means is stopping the disempowering of people. But that just brings us back to hierarchy, because hierarchy is precisely what empowerment reinforces. People don't get power because it is logically and intrinsically built into their jobs; they get it as a gift from the gods who sit atop those charts. *Noblesse oblige*. If you doubt this, then contrast empowerment with a situation in which the workers really do have control. Imagine a hospital director empowering the doctors. They are perfectly well empowered already, with no thanks to any hospital managers. Their power is built into their work. (Indeed, if anything, doctors could stand a little disempowering – but by nurses, not by managers.)

Better still, consider a truly advanced social system: the beehive. Queen bees don't empower worker bees. The worker bees are adults, so to speak, who know exactly what they have to do. Indeed, the queen bee has no role in the genuinely strategic decisions of the hive, such as the one to move to a new location. The bees decide collectively, responding to the informative dances of the scouts and then swarming off to the place they like best. The queen simply follows. How many of our organizations have attained that level of sophistication? What the queen bee does is exude a chemical substance that holds the system together. She is responsible for what has been called the 'spirit of the hive'. What a wonderful metaphor for good managers – not the managers on top but those in the centre.

If empowering is about disempowerment, then is decentralization about centralizing? We have confounded our use of these words, too, ever since Alfred P. Sloan, Jr., centralized General Motors in the 1920s in the name of what came to be called decentralization. Recall that Sloan had to rein in a set of businesses that were out of control. There was no decentralization in that.

Part and parcel of this so-called decentralization effort has been the imposition of financial measures – control by the numbers. If division managers met their targets, they were ostensibly free to manage their businesses as they pleased. But the real effect of this decentralization *to* the division head has often been centralization *of* the division: the concentration of power at the level of the division chief, who is held personally responsible for the impersonal performance. No wonder that now, in reaction, we have all this fuss about the need for empowerment and innovation.

Buzzwords are the problem, not the solution. Hot techniques dazzle us, then fizzle.

Division chiefs – and headquarters controllers looking over their shoulders – get very fidgety about surprises and impatient for numerical results. And the best way to ensure quick, expected results is never to do anything interesting: always cut, never create. That is how the rationalization of costs has become to today's manager what bloodletting was to the medieval physician: the cure for every illness.

As a consequence of all this (de)centralizing and (de)layering, measurement has emerged as the religion of management. But how much sensible business behaviour has been distorted as people have been pushed to meet the numbers instead of the customers?

'After all you've done for your customers, why are they still not happy?' asked the title of a recent article (*Fortune*, 11 December 1995). The answer: because business 'has not yet figured out how to define customer satisfaction in a way that links it to financial results'. Be quite clear what this means: customers will be satisfied and happy only when companies can put a dollar sign on them.

To explain its point, *Fortune* included a box labelled 'What's a Loyal Customer Worth?' It offered several steps to answering that question: first, 'decide on a meaningful period of time over which to do the calculations'; next 'calculate the profit ... customers generate each year'; after that, 'it's simple to calculate net present value. ... The sum of years one through *n* is how much your customer is worth.'

Just a few easy steps to a happier customer. Because no article on management today can be without its list of easy steps, here come my 'Five Easy Steps to Destroying Real Value' (any step will do):

- *Step 1*. Manage the bottom line (as if companies make money by managing money).
- *Step 2*. Make a plan for every action. (No spontaneity please, definitely no learning.)
- *Step 3*. Move managers around to be certain they never get to know anything but management well, and let the boss kick himself upstairs so that he can manage a portfolio instead of a real business. (For *herself*, see Musing 9, below).
- *Step 4*. When in trouble, rationalize, fire and divest; when out of trouble, expand, acquire and still fire (it keeps employees on their toes); above all, never create or invent anything (it takes too long).
- *Step 5*. Be sure to do everything in five easy steps.

If this sort of thing sounds familiar, it's because the analytical mentality has taken over the field of management. We march to the tune of the technocrat. Everything has to be calculated, explicated, and categorized. The trouble is that technocrats never get much beyond the present. They lack the wisdom to appreciate the past and the imagination to see the future. Everything is centred on what's 'in', what's 'hot'. To plan, supposedly to take care of the future, they forecast, which really means they extrapolate current quantifiable trends. (The optimists extrapolate positive trends, the pessimists negative ones.) And then, when an unexpected 'discontinuity' occurs (meaning, most likely, that a creative competitor has invented something new), the technocrats run around like so many Chicken Littles, crying, 'The environment's turbulent! The environment's turbulent!'

Measurement is fine for figuring out when to flip a hamburger or how to fill the O.I. bucket at that 'communications' company. But when used to estimate the market for a brand new product or to assess the worth of a complicated professional service, measurement often goes awry. Measurement mesmerizes no less than management. We had better start asking ourselves about the real costs of counting.

6 Great organizations, once created, don't need great leaders

Organizations that need to be turned around by such leaders will soon turn back again. Go to the popular business press and read just about any article on any company. The whole organization almost always gets reduced to a single individual, the chief at the 'top': ABB exists in the persona of Percy Barnevik. And General Motors is not an incredibly complex web of three quarters of a million people. It's just one single hero: 'CEO Jack Smith didn't just stop the bleeding. With a boost from rising auto sales, he made GM healthy again' (*Fortune*, 17 October 1994). All by himself!

Switzerland is an organization that really works. Yet hardly anybody even knows who's in charge, because seven people rotate in and out of the job of head of state on an annual basis. We may need great visionaries to create great organizations. But after the organizations are created, we don't need heroes, just competent, devoted, and generous leaders who know what's going on and exude that spirit of the hive. Heroes – or, more to the point, our hero worship – reflect nothing more than our own inadequacies. Such worship stops us from thinking for ourselves as adult human beings. Leadership becomes the great solution. Whatever is wrong, the great one will make it right.

Bill Agee was the great hero at Bendix. Out he went. Jim Robinson played the same role at American Express. Suddenly that flipped over, too. And on it goes. Who's next? The popular business press is amazing for its ability to turn on a dime. Every magazine issue is a whole new ball game – no responsibility for what was written just a few weeks earlier. Too bad the press has developed the technocrat's blindness to the past.

Part of this cult of leadership involves an emphasis on the 'turning around' of old, sick companies. Just look what we invest in that! Think of all those consulting firms specializing in geriatrics, ready to help – hardly a pediatric, let alone an obstetric, practice to be found. Why don't we recognize when it's time for an old, sick organization to die? Would we say that it was one of the great wrongs of this century to have let a talent like Winston Churchill die? Of course not; it was a natural event, part of the life cycle. But when it comes to the great old companies, we feel compelled to keep them alive – even if it means we must resort to interventionist life-support systems.

What we really need, therefore, is a kind of Dr Kevorkian for the world of business – someone to help with pulling the plug. Then young, vibrant companies would get the chance to replace the old, spent ones. Letting more big companies die – celebrating their contributions at grand funerals – would make our societies a lot healthier.

7 Great organizations have souls; any word with a *de* or a *re* in front of it is likely to destroy those souls

Well, there are still some healthy big organizations out there. You can tell them by their individuality. They stay off the bandwagon, away from the empty fads. Did you ever wonder why so many really interesting ones headquarter themselves far from the chic centres of New York and London, preferring places like Bentonville, Arkansas (Wal-Mart Stores), and Littlehampton, West Sussex (The Body Shop)?

If you really want to adopt a new technique, don't use its usual name, especially with a *de* or *re*. Call it something completely different. Then you will have to explain it, which means you will have to think about it. You see, techniques are not the problem; just the mindless application of them. Wouldn't it be wonderful if the editors of HBR printed a skull and crossbones next to the title of every article, like those on medicine bottles: an example might be 'Warning! For high-technology companies only; not to be taken by mass-production manufacturers or government agencies.'

**We should let old,
sick companies die –
and have grand
funerals for them.**

Consider the mindless application of re-engineering. I opened the popular book on the topic and at first thought, this is not a bad idea. But when I saw the claim on page 2 that the technique 'is to the next revolution of business what specialization of labor was to the last', namely, the Industrial Revolution, I should have closed the book right there. Hype is the problem in management; the medium destroys the message. But I read on. Wasn't this what the Ford Motor Company did to automobile production at the turn of the century, what McDonald's did to fast food 30 years ago? Every once in a while, a smart operator comes along and improves a process. Companies like Ford and McDonald's did not need the book; quite the contrary. They needed imagination applied to an intimate knowledge of a business.

In other words, there is no re-engineering in the idea of re-engineering. Just reification, just the same old notion that the new system will do the job. But because of the hype that goes with any new management fad, everyone has to run around re-engineering everything. We are supposed to get superinnovation on demand just because it is deemed necessary by a manager in some distant office who has read a book. Why don't we just stop re-engineering and delayering and restructuring and decentralizing and instead start thinking?

8 It is time to close down conventional MBA programs

We should be developing real managers, not pretending to create them in the classroom.

I have been doing a survey. I ask people who know a lot about US business to name a few of the really good US chief executives, the leaders who really made or are making, a major *sustained* difference. I am not talking about the turnaround doctors but the real builders. (Stop here and make your own list.)

You know what? Almost never has anyone been named who has an MBA. No one ever seems to mention Bill Agee or measurement maven Robert McNamara, two of Harvard's best-known graduates. Many do name Jack Welch, Andy Grove, Bob Galvin and Bill Gates. This is rather interesting because all these people have been either seriously educated (Welch and Grove both have doctorates in chemical engineering) or hardly formally educated at all (Galvin and Gates never finished bachelor's degrees).

Years ago, when things were going better in US business, I used to think that the brilliance of the country's management lay in its action orientation. Managers didn't think a lot; they just got things done. But now I find that the best managers are very thoughtful people (whether or not they have PhDs) who are also highly action-oriented. Unfortunately, too many others have stopped thinking. They want quick, easy answers. There is an overwhelming need to be in the middle of whatever is popular. Getting an MBA may be just another example of that need.

It is plain silly to take people who have never been managers – many of whom have not even worked full-time for more than a few years – and pretend to be turning them into managers in a classroom. The whole exercise is too detached from context. We need to stop dumping management theories and cases on people who have no basis even to judge the relevance.

Let's begin by recognizing today's MBA for what it is: technical training for specialized jobs, such as marketing research and financial analysis. (And these are *not* management.) Then maybe we can recognize good management for what *it* is: not some technical profession, certainly not a science or even an applied science (although sometimes the application of science) but a practice, a craft. We have some good things to teach in management schools; let's teach them to people who know what's going on.

It used to be that the MBA was a licence to parachute into the middle of an organization, there to climb the proverbial ladder without ever having developed an intimate understanding of what lies below – in order to boss around the people who have.

That was bad enough. But now we have a new and more insidious track to the executive suite. After the MBA, you work as a consultant with some prestigious firm for a time, skipping from one client organization to another. And then you leap straight into the chief executive chair of some company, making judicious moves to others in the hope that you may one day end up running a company like IBM. That system might work on occasion. But it is no way to build a strong corporate sector in society.

I think of that approach as a cookie model of management cause it was born in what might be called generic consumer-products companies – the ones that sell consumer goods that come out identically, like cookies, one after another. Certain critical skills in these businesses reside in marketing and can be carried from one company to another, but only within this narrow consumer-goods sphere. Cookie management just doesn't work for running nuclear reactors or conducting liver transplants. So there has to be a better way to select and develop managers. Maybe the Groves, Galvins, Gateses and Welches of this world – who, incidentally, have devoted their careers to single companies – know of one.

Managers keep operating on their systems, hoping to fix them – usually by cutting things out.

9 Organizations need continuous care, not interventionist cures

That is why nursing is a better model for management than medicine and why women may ultimately make better managers than men. The French term for a medical operation is 'intervention'. Intervening is what all surgeons and too many managers do. Managers keep operating on their systems, radically altering them in the hope of fixing them, usually by cutting things out. Then they leave the consequences of their messy business to the nurses of the corporate world.

Maybe we should try nursing as a model for management. Organizations need to be nurtured – looked after and cared for, steadily and consistently. They don't need to be violated by some dramatic new strategic plan or some gross new re-organization every time a new chief executive happens to parachute in.

In a sense, caring is a more feminine approach to managing, although I have seen it practised by some excellent male chief executive officers. Still, women do have an advantage, in which case the corporate world is wasting a great deal of talent. Let us, therefore, welcome more women into the executive suites as perhaps our greatest hope for coming to our senses.

A few years ago, I spent a day following around the head nurse of a surgical ward in a hospital. I say 'following around' because she spent almost no time in her office; she was continually on the floor. (Bear in mind that, long ago, the partners of Morgan Stanley operated on the floor, too: their desks were right on the trading floor.)

But being on the floor has not been favoured style of management, in nursing or elsewhere. Two other styles have been preferred. One can be called the *boss* style, in which the manager knows and controls everything personally, like Nurse Ratched in *One Flew Over the Cuckoo's Nest*. This style has gradually been replaced by the currently popular *professional* style, in which whoever knows management can manage anything, regardless of experience. Here credentials are what matter, and these, together with the absence of firsthand experience, help to keep managers in their offices reading performance reports and supposedly empowering their subordinates. Professional management is management by remote control.

At the first sign of trouble, empowerment becomes encroachment by senior managers who, because they don't know what is going on, have no choice but to intervene. And so the organization gets turned into a patient to be cured, even if it was not really sick in the first place. It finds itself alternating between short bouts of radical surgery and long doses of studied inattention.

There is a third style, not nearly common enough but practised by that head nurse I followed around and by other effective managers. Let's call it the *craft* style of managing. It is about inspiring, not empowering, about leadership based on mutual respect rooted in common experience and deep understanding. Craft managers get involved deeply enough to know when not to get involved. In contrast to professional managers who claim 'hands off, brain on', the craft manager believes that if there is no laying on of hands (to extend our metaphor), the brain remains shut off.

Women complain about glass ceilings. They can see what goes on up there, at the so-called top; they just cannot easily get through. Well, glass ceilings apply to all sorts of people in all sorts of situations, and that includes the people above, who cannot touch what is below, who cannot even be heard when they shout. But worse still may be the concrete floors. Too many managers can't even see what is going on at the ground level of their organizations, where the products are made and the customers served (presumably). This suggests that we need more than *transparency* in management. We need to smash up the ceilings and bust down the floors as well as break through the walls so that people can work together in that one big circle.

In her book, *Female Advantage: Women's Ways of Leadership* (Doubleday, 1990), Sally Helgesen found that women managers 'usually referred to themselves as being in the middle of things. Not at the top, but in the center; not reaching down, but reaching out.' Does that sound like our metaphor of the circle? I guess we have now come full circle, so it is time to conclude with our last musing – about which I will add nothing.

10 The trouble with today's management is the trouble with this article: everything has to come in short, superficial doses

Source: Extract from 'Musings on management', *Harvard Business Review*, 1996, July, pp. 32–8.

7 The Theory Behind the Practice

Gareth Morgan

Some philosophical background

As the twentieth century has progressed, increasing attention has been devoted to understanding how language, images, and ideas shape social reality and our understanding of the world at large.

The focus on language as a means of revealing how humans construct and *make* reality has proved very insightful. Take, for example, the process through which we use languages to construct meaning. Meanings and actions are always mediated by external contexts and points of reference. *Black* only acquires significance in relation to the concept and meaning of *white*, just as *day* takes form in relation to *night*. To grasp and understand even the simplest meanings, it seems that we have to draw on all kinds of implicit knowledge and engage in complex acts of social construction and interpretation that are tentative, paradoxical, and always in danger of breaking down. The worlds in which we live, it seems, are truly extensions of ourselves and the forms of life through which we experience and engage them.

These ideas have been enormously influential, laying the basis for a general social constructionist view that, whatever the characteristics of the 'objective' world, they are *always* known and experienced subjectively. Humans play an active role in *constructing*, *making*, and *enacting* their realities (Berger and Luckman 1966; Gadamer 1975, 1976; Gergen 1982, 1985; Weick 1979). But this view itself raises fascinating paradoxes, for, while humans can in principle be seen as active agents in perceiving, constructing, and acting on their worlds, they do so in circumstances that are not of their own choosing. For example, as philosophers like Michel Foucault (1973, 1980) have shown, there are all kinds of power relations embedded in the language, routines, and discourses that shape everyday life. People's views of reality are influenced by conscious and unconscious social constructions associated with language, history, class, culture, and gender experience. Often, these exert a decisive impact, locking people into a feeling that they are hemmed in by deterministic forces over which they have no control. As a result, despite our ability to enact or make our world, existing social constructions of reality often become difficult to break, with people becoming no more than passive 'voices', reflecting and 'speaking' their social contexts.

These paradoxes have brought the social constructionist movement to an interesting point in its development, which can fork in at least two ways. One path leads to the view that, whether they know it or not, humans have the potential to make and transform themselves and their world through individual and collective enactments that can 'real-ize' new images, ideas, and worldviews. The other leads to the conclusion that, while this may be true in principle, the deep structure of power relations lends the world a resilient logic of its own. While the former encourages people to see and grasp the liberating potential of new individual and collective enactments, the latter tends to dwell on the idea that, to change the social constructions that shape our world, one has to begin by addressing underlying power relations.

Along with educators like Paolo Freire (1970), who emphasize the liberating potential of human consciousness, I believe that people *do* make and shape their world and have the ability to do so anew. As the 'power theorists' suggest, people often get trapped by the cultural beliefs and social practices through which they make their reality 'real'. They frequently lose sight of the ideas, attitudes, assumptions, and other social constructions that are ultimately shaping the structure and experience of their daily realities. But, despite this, they always have the potential to break into new modes of consciousness and understanding. This, I believe, can be a fundamental source of individual and social change and is the premise on which my approach to imaginization builds.

Knowledge as objective or literal truth places too much emphasis on the *object* of knowledge and not enough on the paradigm, perspective, assumptions, language games, and frames of reference of the observer. The challenge before us now is to achieve a better balance, by recognizing that all knowledge is the product of an interpretive process. To achieve this, we need fresh metaphors for thinking about the process through which knowledge is generated. Instead of placing emphasis on the need for 'solid', 'literal', 'foundational', 'objective truth', we need more dynamic modes of understanding that show how knowledge results from some kind of implicit or explicit 'conversation', 'dialogue', 'engagement', or interaction between the interests of people and the world in which they live (Bernstein 1983; Checkland 1981; Checkland and Scholes 1990; Gergen 1982; Morgan 1983; Rorty 1979, 1985). Instead of seeing knowledge as an objective, known 'thing', we need to see it as a capacity and potential that can be developed in the 'knower' – hence my interest in imaginization as a process through which, metaphorically, we 'read' and 'write' the world of organization and management.

The majority of books on organization and management offer a specific theory for understanding and managing organizations or try to develop an integrated framework that highlights certain dimensions over others. They reduce our understanding of organization to a particular way of seeing. My approach, on the other hand, was to suggest that, because any *particular* way of seeing is limited (including the one being advocated!), the challenge is to become skilled in the 'art of seeing', in the art of 'understanding', in the art of 'interpreting' and 'reading' the situations we face.

In many respects, the approach fits what is known as a postmodern approach to understanding organizational life. The postmodernist movement has grown in strength and significance over the last few decades, suggesting that the search for universal, authoritative, 'true' explanations of social reality are always problematic and incomplete because they end up elevating the priority of a particular perspective while downplaying others. As it is sometimes put, 'the presence' of the ideas and insights highlighted by a particular theory or perspective always creates 'an absence': the insights, ideas, and perspectives that are pushed from view. This creates a problem for anyone who wishes to interpret and explain something.

For the most part, postmodernism has only resulted in critiques of modes of writing and social processes that elevate one view over another: to disrupt what is typically viewed as 'normal' and self-evident so that the problematic nature of 'normality' becomes clear. This critical stance has done much to help us understand how biases and blind spots can accompany and sometimes dominate ways of seeing and how all 'explanations' are only forms of rhetoric that seek to persuade people to join or accept a particular point of view (see, for example, Berman 1988; Calas and Smircich 1988; Cooper 1989; Cooper and Burrell 1988; Harvey 1989; Linstead and Grafton-Small 1992; Martin 1990; Reed and Hughes 1992).

But there is another way in which the postmodern perspective can be developed: by recognizing that, because partiality, incompleteness, and distortion are ever present in explanations of how we see and understand the world, perhaps we need to develop ways of theorizing and explaining the world that explicitly recognize and deal with the distorting nature of knowledge. Imaginization, as a mode of theorizing is an approach to social change that seeks to help people mobilize highly relativistic, open-ended, evolving interpretive frameworks for guiding understanding and action. The postmodern worldview, which, of interest, is paralleled in aspects of the new science emphasizing the chaotic, paradoxical, and transient nature of order and disorder (see, for example, the work of writers like Gleick 1987; Hampden-Turner 1990; Jantsch 1980; Nonaka 1988; Prigogine and Stengers 1984; Quinn 1990; Smith and Berg 1987), requires an approach that allows the theory and practice of organization and management to acquire a more fluid form, a relativistic, self-organizing approach to management

The hermeneutic school of social theory specializes in the art of interpretation (see, for example, Boland 1989; Gadamer 1975, 1976; Hollinger 1985; Rorty 1979, 1985; Shotter 1990; Turner 1983). It recognizes that, as readers and authors of our everyday realities, we all have limited horizons, shaped by the values, assumptions, worldviews, interests and perspectives that we possess as individuals and as members of social groups. Hence our readings and subsequent authorings tend to be partial and one sided, committing us to live realities reflecting all kinds of conscious and unconscious social constructions associated with class, gender, culture, and the daily context in which we live. The hermeneutic perspective focuses on understanding the never-ending circle of relations underlying this social construction of reality.

The essential relativity of imaginization links to 'foundational' versus 'conversational' approaches to knowledge. A foundational view leads one to look for authoritative, 'this is the way it is!' interpretations of a situation. Imaginization, on the other hand, builds around the paradox that any given situation may have multiple dimensions and multiple meanings, which acquire significance in the context of interpretation. None of these is necessarily absolute or 'true'. The challenge is to recognize that as interpreters and constructors of reality we face many options and that, just like scientists studying light as waves or particles, we can't study all dimensions at the same time. Our challenge is to dialogue and converse with the situations with which we are involved, to 'real-ize' meaningful knowledge, knowledge that will allow us to be edified or to act in a personally significant way. That doesn't necessarily satisfy those who are looking for an absolute meaning or 'truth' in a situation. But it does capture what seems to be the nature of the human condition: that, as humans, we can only ever acquire limited, partial, *personally significant* ways of knowing the world.

Viewed in this way, we are encouraged to see the 'reading' and knowledge generation process in terms of what Donald Schön (1983) has described as 'reflective practice', as the product of a craft shaped by assumptions and perspectives of all kinds. Imaginization is a form of 'reflective practice' encouraging us to become skilled interpreters of the situations with which we have to deal. It encourages us to develop our skills of framing and reframing, so that we can learn to see the same situation in different ways, so that we can remain open and flexible to multiple meanings, so that we can generate new insights and become comfortable with the paradox that the same situation can mean many things at the same time. It encourages us to become reflective, creative, and expansive in understanding the situations with which we have to deal. A reflective practitioner is someone who is aware of how implicit images, ideas, theories, frames, metaphors, and ideas guide and shape his or her practice and how they can be used to create new possibilities.

In this context, and in terms of my own reflective practice, it is appropriate to recognize that the concept of imaginization is itself a metaphor and, as such, has inherent strengths and limitations. In fusing the concepts of imagination and organization, it seeks to open the process of organizing to an expansive, creative mode of thinking, as opposed to the reductive mode that has dominated the development of mechanistic thought. It highlights and stresses creative possibility. But, at the same time, as critics may rush to point out, it can gloss and downplay the importance of existing power relations, and may underestimate some of the deep structural rigidities in patterns of both thought and action. It thus suffers the fate of all metaphors, and indeed of all paradigms, concepts, and modes of understanding, in that it elevates the importance of certain aspects of reality over others.

People writing on the theory of change (e.g., Argyris and Schön 1974; Watzlawick et al. 1974) have made important distinctions between superficial change where the context remains invariant (called single-loop learning or first- order change) and change where the context is also transformed (called double-loop learning or second order change). This has important implications for the practice of imaginization, because it highlights how one may be able to generate hundreds of new insights without substantial impact. The challenge of imaginization is to create insights that allow one to reframe contexts substantially rather than superficially. It's the old problem of rearranging the deck chairs on the Titanic! Superficially, one can create the impression of making a lot of changes; but, at base level, nothing of significance may have really changed.

Imaginization as personal empowerment

We have all probably experienced situations where individuals or groups have tried to imaginize and act on a new reality only to find the process reversed by those exercising power over their lives. We have all probably experienced situations where the gulfs and divides between rival stakeholders are so deep that those involved would rather continue occupying entrenched battle lines than find a shared way forward. We have all read stories of *successful* individuals, communities, and organizations that suffer dramatic reversals in fortune, perhaps being more or less eliminated overnight as the result of uncontrollable changes in the world economy. These are some of the harsh, all-too-real aspects of the socioeconomic context with which we have to deal.

Yet, if we dwell on the enormity of the problems, our powerlessness soon becomes a self-fulfilling prophesy. For everyone, at every level, can see themselves as being hemmed in by processes and situations over which they feel they have no control. Employees often feel constrained by the perspectives, biases, and interests of their managers. The managers, in turn, feel constrained by 'the culture' of the organization and the expectations that they feel *their* managers are imposing. These more senior managers, in turn, feel hemmed in by the dictates of HQ, stock analysts reports, and general corporate policy. Even the chief executive or chairman of the board can point to her powerlessness as she sees forces of global change buffeting and reshaping the economic context with which she has to deal. If we pursue the logic of this kind of thinking, we quickly find that no one seems to have any real power to do anything of any real significance.

But we do! And that's why I bring the core challenge of imaginization right down to the issue of personal empowerment. There are, no doubt, deep structures of power shaping the structure and logic of the global company. We are, no doubt, caught up in all kinds of sedimented patterns of culture, ideology, and social practice that inhibit capacities for change. The power of macro global forces does encourage a sense of inevitability and powerlessness when it comes to having a significant impact on our world. Indeed, even the leaders of major countries sometimes feel that they have no power to shape things and have no option but to swim with the prevailing tide.

That's why we have to bring it all back down to the level of the individual and individual capacities for change – for change is an individual affair! Individuals can form groups, and groups can become social movements. But the process begins and ends with the commitments and actions of individuals. Certainly, it makes a big difference if one is the head of a large corporation as opposed to the average man or woman in the street. But it is the individual involved who has to move.

That's why I present imaginization as an attitude of mind that encourages people to become their own personal theorists, playing an active role in 'writing' the realities that they would like to realize. I believe that our innate imaginizing capacities can serve us well in tackling some of the major social and organizational problems of the current time. We are reaching the end of a line of development associated with the mechanistic thinking of the industrial age and are in need of an alternative. We need new metaphors that can help us *remake* ourselves, our society, and our relations with planet Earth.

References

Argyris, C. and Schön, D. (1974) *Theory in Practice*. Reading, MA: Addison-Wesley.

Berger, P. and Luckmann, T. (1966) *The Social Construction of Reality.* Garden City, NY: Doubleday.

Berman, A. (1988) *From the New Criticism to Deconstruction.* Urbana, IL: University of Illinois Press.

Bernstein, R.J. (1983) *Beyond Objectivism and Relativism: Science, Hermeneutics and Praxis.* Philadelphia: University of Pennsylvania Press.

Boland, R.J. (1989) 'Beyond the objectivist and the subjectivist: learning to read accounting as text', *Accounting, Organizations and Society* 14: 591–604.

Calas, M. and Smircich, L. (1988) 'Reading leadership as a form of cultural analysis', in J.G. Hunt, R.D. Belliga, H.P. Dachler, and C.A. Schriesheim (Eds) *Emerging Leadership Vistas.* Lexington, MA: Lexington, pp. 201–26.

Checkland, P. (1981) *Systems Thinking, Systems Practice.* Chichester: John Wiley.

Checkland, P. and Scholes, J. (1990) *Soft Systems Methodology in Action.* Chichester: John Wiley.

Cooper, R. (1989) 'Modernism, postmodernism and organizational analysis 3: the contribution of Jacques Derrida', *Organization Studies* 10(4): 479–502.

Cooper, R. and Burrell, G. (1988) 'Modernism, postmodernism and organizational analysis: an inroduction', *Organization Studies* 9: 91–112.

Foucault, M. (1973) *The Order of Things: The Archeology of the Human Sciences.* new York: Vintage.

Foucault, M. (1980) *Power/Knowledge,* C. Gordon (ed.) Brighton: Harvester Wheatsheaf.

Freire, P. (1970) *Pedagogy of the Oppressed.* New York: Seabury.

Gadamer, H.G. (1975) *Truth and Method.* New York: Seabury.

Gadamer, H.G. (1976) *Philosophical Hermeneutics.* Berkeley: University of California Press.

Gergen, K.G. (1982) *Toward Transformation in Social Knowledge.* New York: Springer-Verlag.

Gergen, K.G. (1985) 'The social constructionist movement in modern psychology', *American Psychologist* 40(3): 266–75.

Gleick, J. (1987) *Chaos: Making a New Science.* New York: Viking.

Hampden-Turner, C. (1990) *Charting the Corporate Mind.* New York: Free Press.

Harvey, D. (1989) *The Condition of Postmodernity.* Oxford: Basil Blackwell.

Hollinger, R. (Ed.) (1985) *Hermeneutics and Practice.* Notre Dame: University of Notre Dame Press.

Jantsch, E. (1980) *The Self Organizing Universe.* Oxford: Pergamon.

Linstead, S. and Grafton-Small, R. (1992) 'On reading organizational culture', *Organization Studies* 13: 331–56.

Martin, J. (1990) 'Deconstructing organizational taboos: the suppression of gender conflict in organizations', *Organization Studies* 1: 339–59.

Morgan, G. (Ed.) (1983) *Beyond Method: Strategies for Social Research.* Beverly Hills, CA: Sage.

Nonaka, I. (1988) 'Creating organizational order out of chaos: self-renewal in Japanese firms', *California Management Review* Spring: 57–73.

Prigogine, I. and Stengers, I. (1984) *Order Out of Chaos.* New York: Bantam.

Quinn, R.E. (1990) *Beyond Rational Management: Mastering the Paradoxes and Competing Demands of High Performance.* San Francisco: Jossey-Bass.

Reed, M. and Hughes, M. (Eds) (1992) *Rethinking Organization.* London: Sage.

Rorty, R. (1979) *Philosophy and the Mirror of Nature.* Princeton, NJ: Princeton University Press.

Rorty, R. (1985) *Consequences of Pragmatism.* Minneapolis: University of Minneapolis Press.

Schön, D.A. (1983) *The Reflective Practitioner.* New York: Basic Books.

Shotter, J. (1990) 'The manager as author', paper presented to the Conference on Social-Organizational Theory, St. Gallen, August.

Smith, K.K. and Berg, D.N. (1987) *Paradoxes of Group Life.* San Francisco: Jossey-Bass.

Turner, S. (1983) 'Studying organization through Levi-Strauss's structuralism', in G. Morgan (Ed.) *Beyond Method: Strategies for Social Research.* Beverly Hills, CA: Sage.

Watzlawick, P, Weakland, J. and Fisch, R. (1974) *Change: Principles of Problem Formation and Problem Resolution.* New York: Norton.

Weick, K.E. (1979) *The Social Psychology of Organizing.* Reading, MA: Addison-Wesley.

Source: Edited extract from Appendix A in *Imaginization: the art of creative management*, 1993, Newbury Park, CA: Sage, pp. 271–94.

8 Metaphor and the Evolution of the Living Organization

Gerrit Broekstra

The flurry of new techniques and ideas about organizing and managing signals a transition towards a fundamentally new paradigm: the evolutionary paradigm. This paradigm is associated with the intriguing metaphor of the brain. As such it provides an articulation of the emerging more intelligent network forms of the living organization. The argument presented here is that, at a time when continual organizational self-renewal is a necessary condition for survival, organizations once thought of as machines controlled by managers are now better thought of as brains. It is argued that the brain metaphor is particularly appropriate to the modem organization, which is in effect a complex dynamic system poised at the edge of order and chaos, and largely, as Kelly (1994) maintains, out of control.

In the 1980s a plethora of highly trumpeted change philosophies, methods and techniques, ranging from quality circles to core competencies, and from culture change to empowerment, were eagerly adopted by thousands of managers and corporations. However, in many cases, they were hastily dropped again with little or no positive effect, usually in an atmosphere of blaming everything and everyone, and particularly blaming that never resting phantom in the organization called 'resistance to change'. As a result of these failed attempts to change the entrenched assumptions and ingrained ways of doing things, frustration and even cynicism prevail in many firms. They suffer from the failed-change syndrome.

Despite the obvious failures the merry-go-round continues. Pascale et al. (1993) caustically remind us that the definition of insanity is quite appropriate here: doing the same thing over and over again, like banging your head against the wall, but expecting different results each time. There appears, then, to be a certain mindlessness in all this. Most organizations still seem to be relatively unintelligent things when it comes to changing their ways of providing value to society. As cybernetician Stafford Beer (1979) would have it, organizations are inclined to be pathologically autopoietic, that is, they tend towards the closing of the organizational mind indulging primarily in self-serving and self-maintaining behaviour.

The fallacy of modern Taylorism

Peddling buzzwords, the new gurus of the 1980s were propelled into the highly profitable status of emperors of the business world — without any serious questions being raised about their clothes. In 1986 *Business Week* pointed out 'how faddishness has come to dominate management thinking', and warned of the general tendency among companies to 'evade the basic challenges they face'. In the first half of the 1990s, this early counter-voice started to gain in strength. For example, in 1990, Michael Beer et al., on the basis of their pioneering research on the revitalization attempts of a diverse range of companies, warned against the 'fallacy of programmatic change', and emphasized the widespread lack of understanding of what it takes to really bring about fundamental change. In 1992, Eccles and Nohria took a swing at the 'obsession with newness', and in advocating a deeper understanding of the essence of management they suggested there was indeed life beyond the hype.

In 1993, Pascale et al. referred to the managerial propensity to indiscriminately adopt business fads as the 'doing trap'. Being confronted with transformational change rather than incremental change, they suggested that managers meditate on the deeper levels or the 'hidden dimension' of a company's being. In the same vein, Drucker (1994) challenged corporate change efforts by claiming that all these allegedly new business techniques were basically 'how to do' tools, whereas the central corporate focus should be on 'what to do'. Drucker argued that the 'theory of the business' of most companies today no longer fits reality.

It may be self-evident that most new business techniques are solutions in search of a problem, but it is worse when the change attempts are directing precious energy towards 'doing things right', rather than 'doing the right thing'. And here we come to the heart of the matter: the prevailing managerial ideology. Managers are primarily efficiency – rather than effectiveness-oriented. The result is, as Janov (1994) contends, a means – end confusion. Related to this perennial efficiency-effectiveness dilemma, is the part – whole distinction as observed in systems thinking. Without exception, business fads constitute partial approaches to improving the business. Some are directed at changing attitudes of people (e.g. empowerment), others at changing the task (e.g. Business Process Re-engineering), and so on, to the virtual exclusion of all other aspects.

Change initiatives which go beyond incremental improvements arising from a predominantly efficiency orientation require an entirely different change logic that we have barely begun to explore. Transforming or remaking a company requires a systemic logic which is much more far-reaching than anything that is offered by the present hype.

The complexity perspective

A more benevolent way of looking at the phenomenon of the rise and fall of business fads is obtained in expanding our view in a more encompassing frame of organizational evolution. We clearly live in a time of transition in which the global social-economic system is undergoing large-scale transformations. The buzzwords are widely recognized as symbols of deep shifts on a worldwide scale announcing the demise of the Industrial Era and its associated institutions. Globalization of competition, newly emerging economies, information technology, mass customization, knowledge society, postmodernism and fundamentalism come to mind.

Viewed from an evolutionary perspective, business organizations as well as public institutions are interacting players in this worldwide transforming organizational ecosystem. They are experiencing the resultant pressures and struggle to respond individually by experimenting with new forms and functions. Such a period of transition may indeed be characterized by frantic evolutionary experimentation with novel ways of coping with the new complexities. Moreover, it can be regarded as a sign of deep self-organizing forces at work.

The new sciences of chaos and complexity, which have also recently gained such enormous popularity, may shed some light on this phenomenon (Waldrop 1992). The Santa Fe Institute's interpretation of the science of complexity suggests that new structure and order may spontaneously arise as a consequence of newly emergent behaviour in non-linear, complex, dynamic systems. This has been described as a transitional phase where 'unrestrained evolutionary experimentation' may lead to an initial proliferation of new types of social organization (Lewin 1992). An anthology of all the newly promoted organizational forms proves the point: the hollow, virtual, horizontal, intelligent, network, knowledge-creating, inventive, spider-web, cluster, learning organization, and so on.

A complex non-linear system may essentially exhibit three classes of behaviour: (1) relatively frozen and (2) entirely chaotic separated by (3) a small 'edge of chaos' (Lewin 1992: 53). The latter narrow transition region between order and chaos is the more interesting as it constitutes the 'no-man's land, where chaos and stability pull in opposite directions' (Lewin 1992: 51). This edge of chaos appears to be analogous to a phase transition and also appears to be the locus of maximum creativity for the system. Even more striking, if unrestrained, systems appear to have a tendency to self-adapt to this edge of chaos where the maximum capacity for innovation is exhibited (Kauffman 1993).

Most business fads have a short and somewhat uninfluential lifetime, such as Theory Z and the One-Minute Manager. Relatively few have a far greater impact. Total Quality Management perhaps belongs to this category. The explosive burst of fads has the signature of a system that has got itself into a critical state.

The science of complexity teaches us that complex dynamic systems, whether physical, biological or societal, have the same underlying internal dynamics and exhibit common emerging patterns. Poised at the edge of chaos, a long period of stability may be punctuated by a relatively rapid period of tremendous instability and a transition between different levels of organization, perhaps, though unpredictable, towards increasing levels of complexity. The flurry of collective activity that accompanies such transitions may also be a sign of impending collapse, or at least some form of mini-collapse (Lewin, 1992).

We are currently experiencing a major paradigm shift which runs deeper than any of the surface turbulence which organizations are experiencing may indicate. The new science of complexity has revolutionary insights to offer here that may help to articulate the new paradigm.

Paradigms of change

Oversimplifying somewhat for clarity, it is possible to distinguish between three different paradigms in the short history of conceptualizations of organizing and the management of change (Broekstra, 1992). The distinction presented has been inspired particularly by the work on self-organizing systems by the systems thinkers, Jantsch (1973, 1980) and Nicolis and Prigogine (1989). Jantsch (1973) foresaw the tremendous implications of the new second-order cybernetics and related developments in physical chemistry and biology, which he subsumed under the banner of the paradigm of self-organization. He briefly indicated a description of three types of systems:

1 mechanistic systems do not change their internal organization;
2 adaptive (or organismic) systems adapt to changes in the environment through changes in their internal organization by using pre-programmed information;
3 inventive (or human action) systems change their internal organization in accordance with their intentions to change the environment by inventing (internally generating) information.

These three descriptions show a remarkable insight in the evolution of the paradigms that also govern our present state of thinking about organizations. Table 8.1 shows the three paradigms of organizing and organizational change: mechanistic, organismic and evolutionary. They will be discussed further, together with the associated main organizational forms: the functional, divisional and network organization.

The corresponding metaphors are the machine, the organism and the brain. These three main metaphors were popularized in Morgan's (1986) seminal book *Images of Organization*. Inspiration for the paradigms presented in Table 8.1 has also been derived from the work of Miles and Snow (1984, 1994), who published extensively on the evolution of organizational forms or configurations. Nonaka and Takeuchi's (1995) pioneering work on the knowledge-creating company and processes of self-renewal in Japanese companies has also helped to sharpen the formulation of the third paradigm.

Table 8.1 The force, fit and fluctuation paradigms of change

Paradigm	System thinking	Metaphor	Order through	Organization form
Mechanistic	Closed	Machine	Force	Functional
Organismic (Equilibrium)	Open	Organism (Information processing)	Fit	Divisional & Business Unit
Evolutionary Non-equilibrium self-organizing	Complex (Knowledge-creating)	Brain	Fluctuation	Network

It is worth noting that the three organizational forms (Table 8.1) are not seen as mutually exclusive, but rather as progressively encompassing, representing increasingly higher levels of complexity. Each higher level encompasses, though in a considerably modified form, the previous lower levels. This will become much clearer during the subsequent discussion contained in this chapter.

The mechanistic paradigm

The oldest paradigm is the mechanistic one, where the organization is basically viewed as a special-purpose clockwork machine. Rooted in the nineteenth-century materialist/reductionist worldview, this was the dominant paradigm which started with the inception and rapid rise of large hierarchical business organizations after the Great Depression of the 1870s. The environment, including customers, was a non-issue, hence closed system thinking focused managerial attention inward on the efficient running of the internal organization. The 'business fads' of those days were the management techniques developed under the banner of Scientific Management, of which the American engineer Frederick Taylor was the most well-known proponent.

According to the nineteenth-century mechanistic outlook and fuelled by the division-of-labour specialization philosophy, humans were supposed to behave like the efficient parts of a machine. The alienating effects of these scientific management practices and the classical bureaucracy principles of organizing were later seemingly softened up by the Human Relations movement.

The principles of impersonalized bureaucracy led to an emphasis on centralized hierarchy, position, power distance, uniformity of rules and practices, conformity, routinization and an obsession with vertical control. Still quite visible in the machine-like way many of today's organizations operate, these mechanical principles ensure that 'organizational life is often routinized with the precision demanded of clockwork', thus on the flip side, as the German sociologist Max Weber already argued, 'eroding the human imperative, which by virtue of its basically coercive character, may well be referred to as 'order through force'.

The emergence of the functional organization

The rise during the nineteenth century of the big modern industrial enterprise commences in the decades preceding the economic depression of the 1870s. The civil engineers of the railroad companies in the US pioneered a new organizational form, naturally acting from the same mechanistic philosophy underlying the construction of their company's physical machinery and infrastructure. From an evolutionary viewpoint, this story is quite relevant.

Briefly, in the post-depression period of the 1840s, when the railroad (and telegraph communication) infrastructures expanded rapidly, the centralized administrative hierarchy gradually emerged as the dominant form among the railroad companies. However, this did not happen without having been contested by the remarkably more effective decentralized divisional form of the Pennsylvania Railroad Company (Chandler 1977). This is another salient instance of the systemic phenomenon of 'lock-in', the evolutionary caprice proposed by scientists at the Santa Fe Institute. Lock-in occurs when one system, often an inferior one, succeeds, while a superior one fails. An overt illustration being the way in which the market locked into the technologically inferior VHS videotape format in preference to Betamax (Waldrop 1992). It comes therefore as no surprise that some people who take a keen interest in the history and future of organizational forms tend to view the dominance of the bureaucratic hierarchy in the last century as a historical aberration (Hock 1995).

At the start of the Great Depression of the 1870s, the large vertically integrated, multifunctional industrial organization was virtually non-existent. However, as the American business historian Alfred Chandler (1977) has pointed out, this had changed by the turn of the century. To assure the high-volume flow of goods, major American industries adopted a multifunctional bureaucratic form by integrating mass production and mass distribution processes. These efficient 'special-purpose machines' were designed to produce and distribute a limited line of goods and services in large volume and at low cost, governed by the principle of centrally co-ordinated specialization (Miles and Snow 1994).

The sudden emergence of a new form of social organization, and the tremendous evolutionary experimentation associated with it, appears to constitute an authentic example of a big change phase transition in a spontaneously self-organizing ecology of organizations driven to the edge of chaos. The interesting pattern we may discern during this transition runs somewhat as follows. First, we saw the development of new technologies and infrastructures (railroads and telegraph) during a period of relative economic expansion. Then, those enterprises involved in these developments pioneered a new organizational form to deal with the arising complexities of their own creation. Next, after a severe economic recession, the new form acted as a precursor. Not until it was adopted on a large scale by other organizations, thus enabling them to harness the new technologies, did the economies start to greatly expand again. A similar pattern occurred around the emergence of the divisional form, and appears to be occurring now around the evolving network form of organization (Broekstra 1993).

The emergence of the divisional organization

The story of the development of the multidivisional organization is extensively dealt with in Chandler's (1962) study of the expansion and subsequent decentralization of some of the largest US enterprises. It began with a sharp economic downturn in the early 1920s that almost toppled General Motors (GM). Related diversification of products and market segmentation had become the name of the organizational logic governing the new competitive game. Toffler (1985: 41) called it 'destandardization of output in response to rising consumer demands for variety', which in turn was fuelled by a 'push toward individualization'. The functional form was a good fit for the mass markets and standardized products required prior to the First World War, but gradually became a misfit in a world of increasing variety and diversity.

In the early 1920s, Alfred Sloan at GM pioneered the multidivisional organization headed by a general office. At first it was merely a new way to administer more effectively its sprawling aggregate of companies and to boost corporate financial synergy (Sloan 1963). Soon the advantages of this more decentralized structure became apparent, in as much as each product division focused on a distinct market to meet the demands of product diversification – a car for every pocket. What Miles and Snow (1984) called an 'early fit' of strategy and structure helped GM grasp the largest share of the automobile market in the US and, for decades, maintain its position as the leading car manufacturer in the world.

Not until after the Great Depression of the 1930s and subsequently the Second World War, when the economies started to boom again, was the divisional form copied by most large corporations. With occasional 'ups-and-downs', the decentralization tendency has endured, although it is now frequently seen under the banner of the autonomous business unit. It should be noted, however, that a business unit itself is usually organized according to the functional form. A business unit is largely a self-sufficient entrepreneurial form comprised of all those functions needed to effectively add value to a particular product – market – technology combination or geographical area. It operates of course within the context of an overall strategic direction and, hence, is subject to centrally controlled performance evaluation. In short, the divisional organization has a great capacity for adaptation (Miles and Snow 1994: 39).

The organismic paradigm

Shortly after the Second World War, when the organizational logic of divisionalization gained wide popularity, a new paradigm was born which, while encompassing the mechanistic one as a special ease, transcended way beyond it. This new way of thinking about organizations constituted a perfect conceptual underpinning of the divisionalization philosophy according to which each unit of organization has to adapt to its own environmental circumstances, and therefore needs to be largely self-sufficient and autonomous. The organismic image is that of a biological organism which by adapting to its external environment has a better chance of survival. Some organizational units faced with a more stable and predictable environment would therefore flourish with a more mechanistic form and operating logic, others in a more turbulent and unpredictable environment would be better off with a more organic form. Strategic choice became an option, thus allowing for different 'species' of organization (Morgan 1986).

In 1950, one of the founding fathers of the systems movement, the Austrian biologist and philosopher Ludwig von Bertalanffy, published a seminal article on open systems in physics and biology in *Science*. His organismic approach exerted a major influence on the development of the sociotechnical systems approach to organizations pioneered by the famous Tavistock Institute in London. Based on Bertalanffy's systems ideas, they conceived an organization as a system that is embedded in, and open to, a changing environment to which it needs to adapt in order to survive. This system, then, consists of a collection of aspects, technical, social, and so on, which interact in a balanced way to form an integral whole, thus imposing the need for external and internal fit on the system. The Tavistock notion of a sociotechnical system has been elaborated by a number of scientists to become the standard view in organizational analysis and understanding in the second half of this century.

Lawrence and Lorsch (1967) and Miles and Snow (1978) were among the most influential scholars in establishing this organismic paradigm characterized by open-systems thinking. Using a closely related line of argument Galbraith (1973) advocated the concept of an organization as an information-processing system. His insights into the intricacies of organization design are intimately matched by the traditional first-order cybernetics notions of control, such as those represented by Ashby's Law of Requisite Variety. Despite all the hype, even today's trendy ideas around the learning organization still fall largely into this realm of traditional cognitive, information-processing, open-systems thinking (Nonaka and Takeuchi 1995).

Many conceptual working frameworks were developed to express the order-through-fit principle. Clearly, the organismic paradigm was less efficiency-oriented and more effectiveness-oriented than the mechanistic paradigm. However, the environment was regarded as more or less a given concrete entity to which the organization had to adapt, and not as a complex system of processes that co-evolved with those of the organization.

Furthermore, the rationality of the consistency and configuration approach was basically dominated by a belief in an equilibrium perspective.

Thus the organismic paradigm became the epitome of near-Darwinian gradualism emphasizing linear, incremental change in groping towards an ever better fit of the organizational unit with its environmental niche, interpreted as an equilibrium state. The term 'equilibrium' is, however, somewhat of a misnomer, equilibrium would mean death, 'temporary stability' would be a more accurate expression. From Prigogine's work we know that complex systems, like business organizations, which belong to the class of dissipative structures, exhibit order as a kind of temporary stability only in far-from-equilibrium conditions.

Temporary stability may hold true during a period of convergence towards a particular consistency configuration (Tushman and Romanelli 1985). Yet, at a time when wholesale organizational renewal is at stake, fluctuations such as inconsistencies, paradoxes, conflicts and misfits become more important. As Miles and Snow (1994) noted, fit is a dynamic process, and yesterday's fit may become today's failure. This is precisely the situation that many organizations are facing today. Thus, a more encompassing perspective is needed, and is indeed gradually taking shape.

The emergence of the network organization

Sensing an 'organizational revolution' in the making, Miles and Snow (1984, 1986) were among the first to forecast the emergence of more flexible network forms of organizations, which started to pop up in more significant numbers mainly after the recession of the early 1980s. They made a distinction between various forms, such as stable, internal and dynamic external networks (Miles and Snow 1992, 1994), and contrasted them with the older functional and divisional forms. The latter were perceived as less well suited to the demands of the new environments of global competition and rapid technological changes.

Although the network form has not yet reached a definitive mature form, and its complete system of underlying organizing principles is not yet well crystallized, some features stand out more clearly than others. For example, the complexity of, and, in particular, the innovation rate demanded by the new environments forced companies to focus their units on their respective distinctive competencies, and out-source non-distinctive activities. Thus networks of loosely coupled and collaborating dependencies are gradually created among basically autonomous units, both internally and externally.

Badaracco (1991) has argued that this focusing, and vertical disaggregation combined with loose coupling, cause a 'blurring of boundaries' between and within companies. Limerick and Cunnington noted that another distinguishing feature of these networks is the renewed search for synergies, but that 'synergies are sought and achieved by the parts themselves, and not superimposed on them by various structures or staff' (1993: 60). Miles and Snow (1992) added that networks rely more on contractual market mechanisms than administrative processes to co-operatively manage resource flows.

Limerick and Cunnington (1993) contended that the central idea of the new paradigm underlying the network of relationships is the twin concepts of autonomy and collaboration. They invented the paradoxical term 'collaborative individualism' for this phenomenon. Bartlett and Ghoshal (1989) perceived a similar trend among large multinational corporations in search of a 'transnational solution': the integrated network. They noticed the tendency among large corporations to disperse, yet specialize their assets and capabilities through the use of strong interdependencies. This pattern of interdependency was achieved by self-enforced co-operation among otherwise autonomous units.

The most conspicuous feature of the network organization is its capacity for self-renewal. In viewing an organization as multiple relationships in action, Janov (1994) contrasted the newly emerging vision-driven inventive organizations with the older goal-driven fixed and mission-driven adaptive organizations. Emphasizing innovation and renewal, she urged managers to go beyond adaptation, and 'provide the unexpected'.

Likewise, recognizing innovation as the key competitive issue today, the Japanese management scholar Nonaka (1988) urges us to think about innovation and renewal in a whole new way. He has written extensively about organizational self-renewal, most recently with Takeuchi (1995). Central to their insights is that knowledge creation is the driving force behind innovation and self-renewal. Japanese companies tend to distinguish between the explicit, which typically characterizes the Western orientation, and tacit aspects of knowledge creation, which is more typical for the oriental approach. Badaracco (1991) used the terms 'migratory' versus 'embedded' knowledge to describe these differing approaches. This distinction allows for a more holistic, dynamic and multilevel approach to innovation. Tacit knowledge includes subjective insights, intuition, experience, emotions and the use of metaphors. This type of knowledge can be thought of as that which is embedded in the deep structure of an organization (Broekstra, 1995).

In this context, Nonaka and Takeuchi's 1995 seminal book also proposed a new type of organizational form, which includes a middle – up – down management process and the hypertext structure. The latter structure is particularly interesting because the underlying idea makes sense from an evolutionary point of view, and builds on previous insights about parallel or collateral structures (Broekstra 1986; Kanter 1980; Zand 1981). Briefly, Nonaka and Takeuchi proposed that bureaucracy and task force structures are complementary, so that their type of inventive organization has a non-hierarchical, self-organizing structure that co-exists with its formalized hierarchical structure. The hierarchical structure handles the routine work. The parallel structure constitutes a network of horizontal, across-units and project teams pursuing creativity and innovation. This is not to be confused with the matrix structure, because at any one point in time, in the hypertext organization organizational members belong and report to only one structure.

It would be a mistake to assume that the network organization has minimal, if any, formal authority or order-giving hierarchies. Hierarchy-bashing may be fashionable, but is pure nonsense. Certainly, the evolution of organizations has shown a punctuated process of dehierarchization since the swift emergence of the steep hierarchical pyramid over a century ago. The progressive 'complexification' of the world at large and the associated increasing rate of innovation appear to be the main driving forces behind the process of dehierarchization of organizations. As the pyramid flattens, self-steering emerges through increasingly smaller self-sufficient units. Thus, there also appears to be a concomitant process of miniaturization: from bureaucracy, through divisions, to business units, and finally to self-organizing teams.

The network organization of the future may contain elements, though considerably modified, of all previous organizational forms. As a result of this evolutionary development, the network organization of the future may consist of three overlapping layers: the hierarchy, autonomous units and the 'cerebral cortex' of an intelligent network of relationships, greatly facilitated by the emerging electronic infrastructures. A good example of such a development has been proposed by Hock (1995), founder and retired chief executive of the VISA organization, a non-stock, for-profit, membership corporation. Contemplating its original radical organizational principles – equitable ownership, maximally distributed power and governance, etc. – and to express his idea that this organization was profitably balancing on the edge between chaos and order, he dubbed the innovative term the 'chaordic organization' for this type of network. Another radical example is the 'Internet organization', where 'no part knows the whole, the whole does not know all the parts and none has any need to' (Hock 1995: 14). This may almost sound like blasphemy to today's modern managers. But, beware, the chaords of the future are already among us, quietly preparing to totally alter the competitive landscape.

The evolutionary paradigm

The new science of complexity may become an important pillar for the new evolutionary paradigm. Complex dynamic systems, while getting 'better' at their games of interaction as time passes, tend to generate order of increasing complexity which emerges spontaneously. Of particular importance for organization theory and change are previous developments in complexity science such as Prigogine's dissipative structures (Nicolis and Prigogine 1989) and Maturana and Varela's notion of autopoiesis (Varela 1979). Recognizing an organization as a living system (the third paradigm), Nonaka and Takeuchi (1995) also concede that a knowledge-creating organization is basically an autopoietic system.

Limerick and Cunnington (1993) contend that the primary motivation behind the design and use of network organizations is to provide the stimulation necessary for innovation. Of particular importance is their insight that loose coupling is the central notion of the network concept. They refer to Orton and Weick, who point out that loose coupling implies 'a situation in which elements are responsive, but retain separateness and identity' (1990: 203). Loose coupling is to be distinguished from tight coupling and decoupling.

The science of complexity would suggest that decoupling refers to the frozen regime, whereas tight coupling entails that any disturbance would rapidly diffuse throughout the entire system, causing chaos. For example, too little communication could stifle an organization into a frozen status quo, whereas an overload of communication could cause confusion and chaos. The small edge between frozen order and chaos is the region of loose coupling. This makes a lot of sense because, as noted, the edge of chaos is also the region of the highest creativity and innovation.

The brain, as the most highly developed form of a living organization, becomes a natural candidate for a metaphor which may help explicate the most salient features of the new organizational network form.

The brain metaphor

Through the science of complexity, and the related alternative orientation in cognitive science called connectionism, 'the brain has once more become the main source of metaphors and ideas' (Varela et al. 1991: 87). Self-organization and the emergence of global coherence, from local rules in neural-like nets, have received considerable attention in the last few years. Particularly, the debate about the origin of mind and consciousness as emerging distributed phenomena of the intrinsic operation of the brain itself has gained best-selling status.

There are a number of intriguing similarities between the evolution of the brain and the evolution of the three organizational forms discussed above. With the emergence of the network organization, interest in the 'intelligent organization' has been increasing (Broekstra 1992).

Encompassing the two older brain systems [the reptilian brain at the base of the forbrain and the limbic system] (Beer 1972), sits the more recently developed neocortex: seat of verbal communication, intelligent learning, problem solving, creativity, and so on. Its orientation is primarily towards the external world and is more long-termist than the limbic system.

Like the brain, the architecture of the internal network organization comprises three layers in one: the functional layer, the layer of units, and the parallel circuitry of teams, task forces and other 'horizontal' institutionalized relationships, overlaying the evolutionary older systems. They constitute three different modes of organizational intelligence, functional, unit and network intelligence, which need to be clearly distinguished both conceptually and structurally.

An example of this is provided by a successful Dutch co-operative bank, consisting of hundreds of local co-operative banks and a central organization, once, a century ago, itself an innovative concept to provide credit to farmers. Now, in this bank functional intelligence relates to providing standard products, such as checking and saving. Unit intelligence refers not so much to the autonomy of the local banks, though important, as to the bank's institutionalized product/market segmentation, providing more advanced mass-customized products and services. Both are heavily supported by information technology and are basically more or less centralized. The essence and strength of the co-operative system, however, are revealed in its hard-to-copy network intelligence. Through decentralized, and intimate, local interactions with their members, the local co-operative banks have a unique opportunity to greatly enhance innovation with long-term effects (this is comparable to Hock's chaordic membership organization).

A remark should be made about the position of top management. Although senior managers and executives should be largely involved in corporate renewal, the organizational 'neocortex' is not thought to be located at the apex of the traditional pyramid. On the contrary, the creative intelligence is thought to be distributed like a neural network across the entire organization. However, top management, guided by a vision of appropriate organizing principles, has an important role as the architect of this network and as a catalyst to promote self-organizing processes in it, keeping the organization poised on the edge between the Scylla and Charybdis of frozen order and complete chaos.

Does an organization have a mind?

Most organizations, public and private, come across as pretty mindless. But there is some hope. If the brain is the seat of the mind, and organizations are developing the kind of network connectedness that is apparently needed to attain some minimal complexity for mind-like phenomena to emerge, the above question becomes quite pertinent, if not gripping. Inevitably, the next question would then be about consciousness. Gustavsson (1992), in his treatise on consciousness in organizations, noted that culture may be better viewed as a manifestation of an underlying collective (un)consciousness. Allen and Kraft (1982) played on that idea in calling culture the 'organizational unconscious', a term reminiscent of Jung's collective unconscious.

Arguably, it is time that we start to take the concept of corporate consciousness seriously. This does not just mean 'conscious-of-ness'. Organizations already employ terms like cost consciousness, quality consciousness, and so on, meaning to be aware of costs and quality. The consideration of corporate consciousness should not preclude the analysis of characteristics such as its holographic nature (Cardamone 1986; see also Morgan 1986), its architecture and its transcendental nature, as a collective, subjective experience with a sense of self. This is not as far-fetched as it may sound and brings us back to Pascale et al.'s (1993) reference to the hidden dimension of a company's *being*. The need for a sense of shared selfhood is frequently expressed by, for example, the need to identify a corporate identity through shared values.

Under the two previous paradigms organizations were basically subject to forces of fragmentation. Fragmented consciousness can only be the source of limited, local intelligence, and hence the cause of undesirable side effects upon 'the whole'. With the advent of the more holistic network organization, the development of coherence in corporate consciousness holds the promise of increased creative intelligence and synergy in its inventive parts, such as self-managing task forces geared towards product and process innovation.

Gregory Bateson (1979) has formulated a set of criteria that, if satisfied by any system, will lead us to recognize that the system is a mind. He added that if one wants to understand such a system, one will 'need sorts of explanation different from those which would suffice to explain the characteristics of its smaller parts' (1979: 67). Among these criteria of mind he listed the following:

1 A mind is an aggregate of interacting parts (equivalent to the notion of the loosely coupled network).
2 Interaction between the parts of mind is triggered by difference (corresponding to the present emphasis on order-through-fluctuation, contention and paradox).
3 The mind requires collateral energy (which reminds us of the Gestalt approach's emphasis on raising awareness to mobilize energy in change processes (Nevis 1987), but also Prigogine's (1989) conception of the brain as a dissipative structure).
4 The mind requires circular chains of determination (compare the concepts of organizational closure (Broekstra 1991) and catalytic closure (Kauffman 1993), both necessary, according to the artificial life movement, for the emergence of coherent order in living systems).

The implications of the new evolutionary paradigm and the brain metaphor run far deeper, particularly for business organizations, than the above cursory excursion into corporate consciousness may have revealed. Pondering on the quantum revolution in technology and economics, Gilder (1989: 17) opened his influential book with the assertion that: 'The central event of the twentieth century is the overthrow of matter', that is, by information. In an equally profound book on the bio-logic of the new machines, Kelly (1994: 126) asserted that: 'The central event of the twenty-first century will be the overthrow of information.' There he referred to the emergence of self and self-consciousness from the 'out-of-control' circularities in network systems, the same strangely attracting self-referential things the science of complexity, including second-order cybernetics, and the artificial life movement have been coming up with.

We now see that the evolutionary drift appears to manifest a beautiful sequence of, first, matter being replaced by information as the dominant paradigm and, next, while we are virtually drowning in information overload, information being replaced by consciousness. In our scheme, matter, information and consciousness also figure as the fundamental consecutive notions behind the organization as a machine, an organism and a brain, respectively.

As Einstein rightly said: 'Scientists are tamed metaphysicists.' It may sound like a pipe dream to think that managers, one day, will talk in terms of 'anchoring our organization in a coherent corporate consciousness'. But the world is moving much faster today, and if we agree that 'knowledge is the new competitive resource' (Nonaka and Takeuchi 1995: 7), and we follow the ancient Vedic wisdom that 'knowledge is structured in consciousness', logic would require that consciousness is the new competitive resource. After all, the world is as we see it.

References

Allen, R.F. and Kraft, C. (1982) *The Organizational Unconscious.* Englewood Cliffs, NJ: Prentice-Hall.

Badaracco, J.L. (1991) *The Knowledge Link: How Firms Compete through Strategic Alliances.* Boston: Harvard Business School Press.

Bak, P. and Chen, K. (1991) 'Self-organized criticality', *Scientific American* 264(1): 46–53.

Bartlett, C.A. and Ghoshal, S. (1989) *Managing across Borders: The Transnational Solution.* London: Century Business.

Bateson, G. (1979) *Mind and Nature: A Necessary Universe.* London: Wildwood House.

Beer, M., Eisenstatt, R.A. and Spector, B. (1990) *The Critical Path to Corporate Renewal.* Boston: Harvard Business School Press.

Beer, S. (1972) *Brain of the Firm.* London: Allen Lane.

Beer, S. (1979) *The Heart of Enterprise.* Chichester: John Wiley and Sons.

Bertalanffy, L. von (1950) The theory of open systems in physics and biology', *Science* 111: 23–9.

Broekstra, G. (1986) 'Organizational humanity and architecture: duality and complementarity of papa-logic and mama-logic in managerial conceptualizations of change', *Cybernetics and Systems: An International Journal* 17: 13–41.

Broekstra, G. (1991) 'Consistency, configuration, closure and change', in R.J. in't Veld (Ed.) *Autopoiesis and Configuration Theory: New Approaches to Societal Steering.* Dordrecht: Kluwer, pp. 113–26.

Broekstra, G. (1992) 'Toward a theory of organizational change: The chaos hypothesis', in R. Trappl (Ed.) *Cybernetics and Systems Research 92.* Singapore: World Scientific, pp. 1023–30.

Broekstra, G. (1993) 'Chaos, the fifth environment and the revolution of inter-organizational cooperation', in R. Glanville and O. de Zeeuw (Eds) Problems of Support, Survival and Culture, Special Issue, *Systemica* 9 (1–6), Amsterdam: Thesis Publishers, pp. 21–31.

Broekstra, G. (1995) 'Organizations are closed systems', in R. Glanville and O. de Zeeuw (Eds) Problems of Excavating the Foundations of Cybernetics, Special Issue, *Svstemica.* 10 (1–6), Amsterdam: Thesis Publishers, pp. 1–6.

Business Week Reporters (1986) 'What's in – what's out', *Business Week,* 27 January, 30–9.

Cardamone, MA. (1986) 'The likeness of mind', in R.K.Ragade (Ed.) *General Systems: Yearbook of the Society for General Systems Research,* Louisville, KY: SGSR, p. 49.

Chandler, A.D. (1962) *Strategy and Structure: Chapters in the History of the Industrial Enterprise.* Cambridge, MA: MIT Press.

Chandler, A.D. (1977) *The Visible Hand: The Managerial Revolution in American Business.* Cambridge, MA: Belknap Press.

Drucker, P.F. (1994) 'The theory of the business', *Harvard Business Review,* Sept.–Oct: 95–104.

Eccles, R.G. and Nohria, N. (1992) *Beyond the Hype: Rediscovering the Essence of Management*. Boston: Harvard Business School Press.

Galbraith, J.R. (1973) *Designing Complex Organizations*. Reading, MA: Addison-Wesley.

Gilder, G. (1989) *Microcosm: the quantum revolution in economics and technology*. New York: Simon and Schuster.

Gustavsson, B. (1992) *The Transcendent Organization*. Stockholm: University of Stockholm.

Harrnan, W. (1988) *Global Mind Change: The Promise of the Last Years of the 20th Century*. Indianapolis: Knowledge Systems.

Hock, D.W. (1995) 'The chaordic organization: Out of control and into order', *World Business Academy Perspectives* 9(1): 5-18.

Janov, J. (1994) *The Inventive Organization: Hope and Daring at Work*. San Francisco: Jossey- Bass.

Jantsch, E. (1973) 'Forecasting and systems approach: a frame of reference', *Management Science* 19(12): 1355–68.

Jantsch, E. (1980) *The Self-Organizing Universe: Scientific and Human Implications of the Emerging Paradigm of Evolution*. Oxford: Pergamon.

Jones, R.S. (1982) *Physics as Metaphor*. New York: Meridian.

Kanter, R.M. (1980) 'Building the parallel organization: creating mechanisms for permanent QWL', *Journal of Applied Behavioral Science* 16(4): 371–88.

Kauffman, S.A. (1993) *The Origins of Order: Self-Organization and Selection in Evolution*. Oxford: Oxford University Press.

Kelly, K. (1994) *Out of Control: The New Biology of Machines, Social Systems and the Economic World*. Reading, MA: Addison-Wesley.

Lawrence, P.R. and Lorsch, J.W. (1967) *Organization and Environment: Managing Differentiation and Integration*. Boston: Harvard University Press.

Lewin, R. (1992) *Complexity: Life at the Edge of Chaos*. New York: Macmillan.

Limerick, D. and Cunnington, B. (1993) *Managing the New Organization: A Blueprint for Networks and Strategic Alliances*. San Francisco: Jossey-Bass.

MacLean, P.D. (1990) *The Triune Brain in Evolution*. New York: Plenum Press.

Miles, R.E. and Snow, CC. (1978) *Organizational Strategy, Structure, and Process*. New York: McGraw-Hill.

Miles, RE. and Snow, CC. (1984) 'Fit, failure and the Hall of Fame', *California Management Review* XXVI(3): 10–28.

Miles, R.E. and Snow, C.C. (1986) 'Organizations: New concepts for new forms', *California Management Review* XXVII(3): 62–73.

Miles, RE. and Snow, C.C. (1992) 'Causes of failure in network organizations', *California Management Review* Summer: 53–72.

Miles, R.E. and Snow, CC. (1994) *Fit, Failure, and the Hall of Fame: How Companies Succeed or Fail*. New York: Free Press.

Morgan, G. (1986) *Images of Organization*. Beverly Hills, CA: Sage.

Nevis, E.C. (1987) *Organizational Consulting: A Gestalt Approach*. New York: Gardner Press.

Nicolis, O. and Prigogine, I. (1989) *Exploring Complexity: An Introduction*. New York: Freeman.

Nonaka, I. (1988) 'Creating organizational order out of chaos: self-renewal in Japanese firms', *California Management Review* Spring: 57–73.

Nonaka, I. and Takeuchi, H. (1995) *The Knowledge-Creating Company: How Japanese Companies Create the Dynamics of Innovation.* New York: Oxford University Press.

Orton, J.D. and Weick, K.E. (1990) 'Loosely coupled systems: a reconceptualization', *Academy of Management Review* 15(2): 203–23.

Pascale, R.T., Goss, T. and Athos, A. (1993) 'The reinvention roller coaster: risking the present for a powerful future', *Harvard Business Review* Nov.–Dec.: 97–108.

Ray, M. and Rinzler, A. (Eds) (1993) *The New Paradigm in Business.* New York: Putnam.

Sloan, A.P. (1963) *My Years with General Motors.* New York: Doubleday.

Toffler, A. (1985) *The Adaptive Corporation.* London: Pan Books.

Trist, E.L., Higgin, G.W., Murray, H. and Pollock, A.B. (1963) *Organizational Choice.* London: Tavistock Publications.

Tushman, M.L. and Romanelli, E. (1985) 'Organizational evolution: a metamorphosis model of convergence and reorientation', in L.L.Cummings and B.M. Staw (Eds) *Research in Organizational Behavior,* Vol. 7. Greenwich, CT: JAI Press, pp. 171–222.

Varela, F.J. (1979) *Principles of Biological Autonomy.* New York: North Holland.

Varela, F.J., Thompson, E. and Rosch, E. (1991) *The Embodied Mind: Cognitive Science and Human Experience.* Cambridge, MA: MIT Press.

Waldrop, M.M. (1992) *Complexity: The Emerging Science at the Edge of Order and Chaos.* Harmondsworth: Penguin.

Zand, D.E. (1981) *Information, Organization, and Power: Effective Management in the Knowledge Society.* New York: McGraw-Hill.

Source: Adapted from Chapter 3 in D. Grant and C. Oswick, *Metaphor and Organizations*, 1996, London: Sage.

Part 2

Style

Section D   Emotion

Emotion is a sadly neglected topic in psychology and management, witness the purely cognitive intelligence tests commonly used in education from the 11+ through to the GMAT. However management through people is now recognized as a, if not the, key management skill, though it is generally approached from a largely cognitive angle, i.e. deficient skills are analysed and training is seen as the magic bullet that will insert the missing competency into people's brains. Here Goleman and Gabriel give prominence to the role of emotional competencies and psychodynamics in organizations.

Daniel Goleman has come to prominence through his work on emotional intelligence (EQ), a catchy phrase under which he has drawn together certain key personal and interpersonal skills, namely self-awareness, self-regulation, motivation, empathy and social skill. Leaders are often thought to need particular skills, often characterized in popular literature as the capacity to inspire loyalty through an appealing vision, but studies of leaders of companies who achieve long-term success, show that neither charismatic leadership nor a particular vision are necessary for an organization's continuation (Collins and Porras 1995). Here Goleman argues that it is emotional intelligence that makes the difference between the performance of good and bad leaders. He recognizes that EQ has a genetic component and that it improves with age. He argues that emotional skills can be learnt, but only through a lengthy process of individualized coaching not short-term training.

Yiannis Gabriel addresses the deeper reaches of emotion through psychodynamics, arguing that this operates at the organizational as much as individual and team levels. Psychodynamics describes the various processes of sublimation, repression, rationalization etc. that people use, both individually and collectively, to defend against unwanted and unpleasant irrational thoughts such as the pain of overwhelming anxiety. He uses the Challenger disaster to explain how senior management at NASA continued to believe their 'all is well' rhetoric, despite clear signs to the contrary. It has been suggested that organizations are particularly prone to repression, and that bureaucracy itself, acts as a defence against the anxieties inherent in the work. Also that the endemic impersonalization in bureaucratic organizations prevents trust being established and leaves empty psychological space that is ripe for psychological fantasy and that such fantasies can explain the overreaction and irrational actions that are often a feature of organizational life.

This is of course only the tip of the iceberg as regards the pervasive role of emotion in organization and business life. Various writers have suggested ways in which management colonizes the subjectivity of their employees, creating dependence by becoming surrogate authoritative parents (Hirshorn 1988) or manipulating the type of self-regulation the employee practices, through their internalization of the values in the company's culture. Stacy (1996) suggests that a feature of the creative and innovative organization is their capacity to live with the ambiguity and anxiety their more bureaucratic counterpart feels obliged to control and/or deny.

References

Collins, J. and Porras, J. (1995) 'Building a visionary company', *California Management Review* 37(2): 80–100.

Hirschorn, L. (1988) *The Workplace Within*. Cambridge, MA: MIT Press.

Stacy, R.D. (1996) *Complexity and Creativity in Organizations*. San Francisco: Berrett-Koehler.

9 What Makes a Leader?

Daniel Goleman

Every business person knows a story about a highly intelligent, highly-skilled executive who was promoted into a leadership position only to fail at the job. And they also know a story about someone with solid – but not extraordinary – intellectual abilities and technical skills who was promoted into a similar position and then soared.

Such anecdotes support the widespread belief that identifying individuals with the 'right stuff' to be leaders is more art than science. After all, the personal styles of superb leaders vary: some leaders are subdued and analytical; others shout their manifestos from the mountain tops. And just as important, different situations call for different types of leadership. Most mergers need a sensitive negotiator at the helm, whereas many turnarounds require a more forceful authority.

I have found, however, that the most effective leaders are alike in one crucial way: they all have a high degree of what has come to be known as *emotional intelligence*. It's not that IQ and technical skills are irrelevant. They do matter, but mainly as 'threshold capabilities'; that is, they are the entry-level requirements for executive positions. But my research, along with other recent studies, clearly shows that emotional intelligence is the *sine qua non* of leadership. Without it, a person can have the best training in the world, an incisive, analytical mind, and an endless supply of smart ideas, but he still won't make a great leader. In the course of the past year, my colleagues and I have focused on how emotional intelligence operates at work. We have examined the relationship between emotional intelligence and effective performance, especially in leaders. And we have observed how emotional intelligence shows itself on the job. How can you tell if someone has high emotional intelligence, for example, and how can you recognize it in yourself? In the following pages, we'll explore these questions, taking each of the components of emotional intelligence – self-awareness, self-regulation, motivation, empathy, and social skill – in turn.

Evaluating emotional intelligence

Most large companies today have employed trained psychologists to develop what are known as 'competency models' to aid them in identifying, training, and promoting likely stars in the leadership firmament. The psychologists have also developed such models for lower-level positions. And in recent years, I have analysed competency models from 188 companies, most of which were large and global and included the likes of Lucent Technologies, British Airways, and Credit Suisse.

In carrying out this work, my objective was to determine which personal capabilities drove outstanding performance within these organizations, and to what degree they did so. I grouped capabilities into three categories: purely technical skills like accounting and business planning; cognitive abilities like analytical reasoning; and competencies demonstrating emotional intelligence such as the ability to work with others and effectiveness in leading change.

Table 9.1 The Five components of emotional intelligence at work

	Definition	*Hallmarks*
Self-awareness	The ability to recognize and understand your moods, emotions and drives, as well as their effect on others	Self-confidence, realistic self-assessment, self-deprecating sense of humour
Self-regulation	The ability to control or redirect impulses and moods, a propensity to suspend judgement – to think before acting	Trustworthiness and integrity, comfort with ambiguity, openness to change
Motivation	A passion to work for reasons that go beyond money or status, a propensity to pursue goals with energy and enthusiasm	Strong drive to achieve optimism, even in the face of failure, organizational commitment
Empathy	Ability in managing meaningful relationships and building networks, skill in treating people according to their emotional reactions	Expertise in building and retaining talent, cross-cultural sensitivity, service to clients and customers
Social skill	Proficiency in managing relationships and building networks, an ability to find common ground and support	Effectiveness in leading change, persuasiveness, expertise in building and leading teams

To create some of the competency models, psychologists asked senior managers at the companies to identify the capabilities that typified the organization's most outstanding leaders. To create other models, the psychologists used objective criteria such as a division's profitability to differentiate the star performers at senior levels within their organizations from the average ones. Those individuals were then extensively interviewed and tested, and their capabilities were compared. This process resulted in the creation of lists of ingredients for highly effective leaders. The lists ranged in length from 7 to 15 items and included such ingredients as initiative and strategic vision.

When I analysed all this data, I found dramatic results. To be sure, intellect was a driver of outstanding performance. Cognitive skills such as big-picture thinking and long-term vision were particularly important. But when I calculated the ratio of technical skills, IQ, and emotional intelligence as ingredients of excellent performance, emotional intelligence proved to be twice as important as the others for jobs at all levels.

Moreover, my analysis showed that emotional intelligence played an increasingly important role at the highest levels of the company, where differences in technical skills are of negligible importance. In other words, the higher the rank of a person considered to be a star performer, the more emotional intelligence capabilities showed up as the reason for his or her effectiveness. When I compared star performers with average ones in senior leadership positions, nearly 90% of the difference in their profiles was attributable to emotional intelligence factors rather than cognitive abilities.

Other researchers have confirmed that emotional intelligence not only distinguishes outstanding leaders but can also be linked to strong performance. The findings of the late David McClelland, the renowned researcher in human and organizational behaviour, are a good example. In a 1996 study of a global food and beverage company, McClelland found that when senior managers had a critical mass of emotional intelligence capabilities, their divisions outperformed yearly earnings goals by 20%. Meanwhile, division leaders without that critical mass underperformed by almost the same amount. McClelland's findings, interestingly, held as true in the company's US divisions as in its divisions in Asia and Europe.

In short, the numbers are beginning to tell us a persuasive story about the link between a company's success and the emotional intelligence of its leaders. And just as important, research is also demonstrating that people can, if they take the right approach, develop their emotional intelligence (see Box 9.1).

Self-awareness

Self-awareness is the first component of emotional intelligence (see Table 9.1) – which makes sense when one considers that the Delphic oracle gave the advice to 'know thyself' thousands of years ago. Self-awareness means having a deep understanding of one's emotions, strengths, weaknesses, needs, and drives.

Box 9.1 Can emotional intelligence be learned?

For ages, people have debated if leaders are born or made. So too goes the debate about emotional intelligence. Are people born with certain levels of empathy, for example, or do they acquire empathy as a result of life's experiences? The answer is both. Scientific inquiry strongly suggests that there is a genetic component to emotional intelligence. Psychological and developmental research indicates that nurture plays a role as well. How much each perhaps will never be known, but research and practice clearly demonstrate that emotional intelligence can be learned.

One thing is certain: emotional intelligence increases with age. There is an old-fashioned word for the phenomenon: maturity. Yet even with maturity, some people still need training to enhance their emotional intelligence. Unfortunately, far too many training programmes that intend to build leadership skills – including emotional intelligence – are a waste of time and money. The problem is simple: they focus on the wrong part of the brain.

Emotional intelligence is born largely in the neuro-transmitters of the brain's limbic system, which governs feelings, impulses, and drives. Research indicates that the limbic system learns best through motivation, extended practice, and feedback. Compare this with the kind of learning that goes on in the neocortex, which governs analytical and technical ability. The neo-cortex grasps concepts and logic. It is the part of the brain that figures out how to use a computer or make a sales call by reading a book. Not surprisingly – but mistakenly – it is also the part of the brain targeted by most training programs aimed at enhancing emotional intelligence. When such programmes take, in effect, a neo-cortical approach, my research with the Consortium for Research on Emotional Intelligence in Organizations has shown they can even have a negative impact on people's job performance.

To enhance emotional intelligence, organizations must refocus their training to include the limbic system. They must help people break old behavioural habits and establish new ones. That not only takes much more time than conventional training programs, it also requires an individualized approach.

Imagine an executive who is thought to be low on empathy by her colleagues. Part of that deficit shows itself as an inability to listen; she interrupts people and doesn't pay close attention to what they're saying. To fix the problem, the executive needs to be motivated to change, and then she needs practice and feedback from others in the company.

A colleague or coach could be tapped to let the executive know when she has been observed failing to listen. She would then have to replay the incident and give a better response; that is, demonstrate her ability to absorb what others are saying. And the executive could be directed to observe certain executives who listen well and to mimic their behaviour.

With persistence and practice, such a process can lead to lasting results. I know one Wall Street executive who sought to improve his empathy – specifically his ability to read people's reactions and see their perspectives. Before beginning his quest, the executive's subordinates were terrified of working with him. People even went so far as to hide bad news from him. Naturally, he was shocked when finally confronted with these facts. He went home and told his family – but they only confirmed what he had heard at work. When their opinions on any given subject did not mesh with his, they, too, were frightened of him.

Enlisting the help of a coach, the executive went to work to heighten his empathy through practice and feedback. His first step was to take a vacation to a foreign country where he did not speak the language. While there, he monitored his reactions to the unfamiliar and his openness to people who were different from him. When he returned home, humbled by his week abroad, the executive asked his coach to shadow him for parts of the day, several times a week, in order to critique how he treated people with new or different perspectives. At the same time, he consciously used on-the-job interactions as opportunities to practice 'hearing' ideas that differed from his. Finally, the executive has himself videotaped in meetings and asked those who worked for and with him to critique his ability to acknowledge and understand the feelings of others. It took several months, but the executive's emotional intelligence was reflected in his overall performance on the job.

It's important to emphasize that building one's emotional intelligence cannot – will not – happen without sincere desire and concerted effort. A brief seminar won't help; nor can one buy a how-to manual. It is much harder to learn to empathize – to internalize empathy as a natural response to people – than it is to become adept at regression analysis. But it can be done. 'Nothing great was ever achieved without enthusiasm,' wrote Ralph Waldo Emerson. If your goal is to become a real leader, these words can serve as a guidepost in your efforts to develop high emotional intelligence.

People with strong self-awareness are neither overly critical nor unrealistically hopeful. Rather, they are honest – with themselves and with others.

People who have a high degree of self-awareness recognize how their feelings affect them, other people, and their job performance. Thus a self-aware person who knows that tight deadlines bring out the worst in him plans his time carefully and gets his work done well in advance. Another person with high self-awareness will be able to work with a demanding client. She will understand the client's impact on her moods and the deeper reasons for her frustration. 'Their trivial demands take us away from the real work that needs to be done,' she might explain. And she will go one step further and turn her anger into something constructive.

Self-awareness extends to a person's understanding of his or her values and goals. Someone who is highly self-aware knows where he is headed and why, so, for example, he will be able to be firm in turning down a job offer that is tempting financially but does not fit with his principles or long-term goals. A person who lacks self-awareness is apt to make decisions that bring on inner turmoil by treading on buried values. 'The money looked good so I signed on,' someone might say two years into a job, 'but the work means so little to me that I'm constantly bored.' The decisions of self-aware people mesh with their values; consequently, they often find work to be energizing.

How can one recognize self-awareness? First and foremost, it shows itself as candour and an ability to assess oneself realistically. People with high self-awareness are able to speak accurately and openly – although not necessarily effusively or confessionally – about their emotions and the impact they have on their work. For instance, one manager I know of was skeptical about a new personal-shopper service that her company, a major department-store chain, was about to introduce. Without prompting from her team or her boss, she offered them an explanation: 'It's hard for me to get behind the rollout of this service,' she admitted, 'because I really wanted to run the project, but I wasn't selected. Bear with me while I deal with that.' The manager did indeed examine her feelings; a week later, she was supporting the project fully.

Such self-knowledge often shows itself in the hiring process. Ask a candidate to describe a time he got carried away by his feelings and did something he later regretted. Self-aware candidates will be frank in admitting to failure – and will often tell their tales with a smile. One of the hallmarks of self-awareness is a self-deprecating sense of humour.

Self-awareness can also be identified during performance reviews. Self-aware people know – and are comfortable talking about – their limitations and strengths, and they often demonstrate a thirst for constructive criticism. By contrast, people with low self-awareness interpret the message that they need to improve as a threat or a sign of failure.

Self-aware people can also be recognized by their self-confidence. They have a firm grasp of their capabilities and are less likely to set themselves up to fail by, for example, overstretching on assignments. They know, too, when to ask for help. And the risks they take on the job are calculated. They won't ask for a challenge that they know they can't handle alone. They'll play to their strengths.

Consider the actions of a mid-level employee who was invited to sit in on a strategy meeting with her company's top executives. Although she was the most junior person in the room, she did not sit there quietly, listening in fearful silence. She knew she had a head for clear logic and the skill to present ideas persuasively, and she offered cogent suggestions about the company's strategy. At the same time, her self-awareness stopped her from wandering into territory where she knew she was weak.

Despite the value of having self-aware people in the workplace, my research indicates that senior executives don't often give self-awareness the credit it deserves when they look for potential leaders. Many executives mistake candour about feelings for 'wimpiness' and fail to give due respect to employees who openly acknowledge their shortcomings. Such people are too readily dismissed as 'not tough enough' to lead others.

In fact, the opposite is true. In the first place, people generally admire and respect candour. Further, leaders are constantly required to make judgment calls that require a candid assessment of capabilities – their own and those of others. Do we have the management expertise to acquire a competitor? Can we launch a new product within six months? People who assess themselves honestly – that is, self-aware people – are well suited to do the same for the organizations they run.

Self-regulation

Biological impulses drive our emotions. We cannot do away with them – but we can do much to manage them. Self-regulation, which is like an ongoing inner conversation, is the component of emotional intelligence that frees us from being prisoners of our feelings. People engaged in such a conversation feel bad moods and emotional impulses just as everyone else does, but they find ways to control them and even to channel them in useful ways.

Imagine an executive who has just watched a team of his employees present a botched analysis to the company's board of directors. In the gloom that follows, the executive might find himself tempted to pound on the table in anger or kick over a chair. He could leap up and scream at the group. Or he might maintain a grim silence, glaring at everyone before stalking off.

But if he had a gift for self-regulation, he would choose a different approach. He would pick his words carefully, acknowledging the team's poor performance without rushing to any hasty judgment. He would then step back to consider the reasons for the failure. Are they personal – a lack of effort? Are there any mitigating factors? What was his role in the debacle? After considering these questions, he would call the team together, lay out the incident's consequences, and offer his feelings about it. He would then present his analysis of the problem and a well-considered solution.

Why does self-regulation matter so much for leaders? First of all, people who are in control of their feelings and impulses – that is, people who are reasonable – are able to create an environment of trust and fairness. In such an environment, politics and infighting are sharply reduced and productivity is high. Talented people flock to the organization and aren't tempted to leave. And self-regulation has a trickle-down effect. No one wants to be known as a hothead when the boss is known for her calm approach. Fewer bad moods at the top mean fewer throughout the organization.

Second, self-regulation is important for competitive reasons. Everyone knows that business today is rife with ambiguity and change. Companies merge and break apart regularly. Technology transforms work at a dizzying pace. People who have mastered their emotions are able to roll with the change. When a new change programme is announced, they don't panic; instead, they are able to suspend judgement, seek out information, and listen to executives explain the new programme. As the initiative moves forward, they are able to move with it.

Sometimes they even lead the way. Consider the case of a manager at a large manufacturing company. Like her colleagues, she had used a certain software programme for five years. The programme drove how she collected and reported data and how she thought about the company strategy. One day, senior executives announced that a new programme was to be installed that would radically change how information was gathered and assessed within the organization. While many people in the company complained bitterly about how disruptive the change would be, the manager mulled over the reasons for the new programme and was convinced of its potential to improve performance. She eagerly attended training sessions – some of her colleagues refused to so – and was eventually promoted to run several divisions, in part because she used the new technology so effectively.

I want to push the importance of self-regulation to leadership even further and make the case that it enhances integrity, which is not only a personal virtue but also an organizational strength. Many of the bad things that happen in companies are a function of impulsive behaviour. People rarely plan to exaggerate profits, pad expense accounts, dip into the till, or abuse power for selfish ends. Instead, an opportunity presents itself, and people with low impulse control just say yes.

By contrast, consider the behaviour of the senior executive at a large food company. The executive was scrupulously honest in his negotiations with local distributors. He would routinely lay out his cost structure in detail, thereby giving the distributors a realistic understanding of the company's pricing. This approach meant the executive couldn't always drive a hard bargain. Now, on occasion, he felt the urge to increase profits by withholding information about the company's costs. But he challenged that impulse – he saw that it made more sense in the long run to counteract it. His emotional self-regulation paid off in strong, lasting relationships with distributors that benefited the company more than any short-term financial gains would have.

The signs of emotional self-regulation, therefore, are not hard to miss: a propensity for reflection and thoughtfulness; comfort with ambiguity and change; and integrity – an ability to say no to impulsive urges.

Like self-awareness, self-regulation often does not get its due. People who can master their emotions are sometimes seen as cold fish – their considered responses are taken as a lack of passion. People with fiery temperaments are frequently thought of as 'classic' leaders – their outbursts are considered hallmarks of charisma and power. But when such people make it to the top, their impulsiveness often works against them. In my research, extreme displays of negative emotion have never emerged as a driver of good leadership.

Motivation

If there is one trait that virtually all effective leaders have, it is motivation. They are driven to achieve beyond expectations – their own and everyone else's. The key word here is *achieve*. Plenty of people are motivated by external factors such as a big salary or the status that comes from having an impressive title or being part of a prestigious company. By contrast, those with leadership potential are motivated by a deeply embedded desire to achieve for the sake of achievement.

If you are looking for leaders, how can you identify people who are motivated by the drive to achieve rather than by external rewards? The first sign is a passion for the work itself – such people seek out creative challenges, love to learn, and take great pride in a job well done. They also display an unflagging energy to do things better. People with such energy often seem restless with the status quo. They are persistent with their questions about why things are done one way rather than another; they are eager to explore new approaches to their work.

A cosmetics company manager, for example, was frustrated that he had to wait two weeks to get sales results from people in the field. He finally tracked down an automated phone system that would beep each of his salespeople at 5pm every day. An automated message then prompted them to punch in their numbers – how many calls and sales they had made that day. The system shortened the feedback time on sales results from weeks to hours.

That story illustrates two other common traits of people who are driven to achieve. They are forever raising the performance bar, and they like to keep score. Take the performance bar first. During performance reviews, people with high levels of motivation might ask to be 'stretched' by their superiors. Of course, an employee who combines self-awareness with internal motivation will recognize her limits – but she won't settle for objectives that seem too easy to fulfill.

And it follows naturally that people who are driven to do better also want a way of tracking progress – their own, their team's, and their company's. Whereas people with low achievement motivation are often fuzzy about results, those with high achievement motivation often keep score by tracking such hard measures as profitability or market share. I know of a money manager who starts and ends his day on the Internet, gauging the performance of his stock fund against four industry-set benchmarks.

Interestingly, people with high motivation remain optimistic even when the score is against them. In such cases, self-regulation combines with achievement motivation to overcome the frustration and depression that come after a setback or failure. Take the case of an another portfolio manager at a large investment company. After several successful years, her fund tumbled for three consecutive quarters, leading three large institutional clients to shift their business elsewhere.

Some executives would have blamed the nosedive on circumstances outside their control; others might have seen the setback as evidence of personal failure. This portfolio manager, however, saw an opportunity to prove she could lead a turnaround. Two years later, when she was promoted to a very senior level in the company, she described the experience as 'the best thing that ever happened to me; I learned so much from it.'

Executives trying to recognize high levels of achievement motivation in their people can look for one last piece of evidence: commitment to the organization. When people love their job for the work itself, they often feel committed to the organizations that make that work possible. Committed employees are likely to stay with an organization even when they are pursued by headhunters waving money.

It's not difficult to understand how and why a motivation to achieve translates into strong leadership. If you set the performance bar high for yourself, you will do the same for the organization when you are in a position to do so. Likewise, a drive to surpass goals and an interest in keeping score can be contagious. Leaders with these traits can often build a team of managers around them with the same traits. And of course, optimism and organizational commitment are fundamental to leadership – just try to imagine running a company with out them.

Empathy

Of all the dimensions of emotional intelligence empathy is the most easily recognized. We have all felt the empathy of a sensitive teacher or friend; we have all been struck by its absence in an unfeeling coach or boss. But when it comes to business, we rarely hear people praised, let alone rewarded, for their empathy. The very word seems unbusinesslike, out of place amid the tough realities of the marketplace.

But empathy doesn't mean an 'I'm okay you're okay' mushiness. For a leader, that is, it doesn't mean adopting other people's emotions as one's own and trying to please everybody. That would be a nightmare – it would make action impossible. Rather, empathy means thoughtfully considering employees' feelings – along with other factors – in the process of making intelligent decisions.

For an example of empathy in action, consider what happened when two giant brokerage companies merged, creating redundant jobs in all their divisions. One division manager called his people together and gave a gloom speech that emphasized the number of people who would soon be fired. The manager of another division gave his people a different kind of speech. He was upfront about his own worry and confusion and he promised to keep people informed and treat everyone fairly.

The difference between these two managers was empathy. The first manager was too worried about his own fate to consider the feelings of his anxiety-stricken colleagues. The second knew intuitively what his people were feeling, and he acknowledged their fears with his words. Is it any surprise that the first manager saw his division sink as many demoralized people, especially the most talented, departed. By contrast, the second manager continued to be a strong leader, his best people stayed, and his division remained as productive as ever.

Empathy is particularly important today as a component of leadership for at least three reasons – the increasing use of teams; the rapid pace of globalization; and the growing need to retain talent.

Consider the challenge of leading a team. As anyone who has ever been a part of one can attest, teams are cauldrons of bubbling emotions. They are often charged with reaching a consensus – hard enough with two people and much more difficult as the numbers increase. Even in groups with as few as four or five members, alliances form and clashing agendas get set. A team's leader must be able to sense and understand the viewpoints of everyone around the table.

That's exactly what a marketing manager at a large information technology company was able to-do when she was appointed to lead a troubled team. The group was in turmoil, overloaded by work and missing deadlines. Tensions were high among the members. Tinkering with procedures was not enough to bring the group together and make it an effective part of the company.

So the manager took several steps. In a series of one-on-one sessions, she took the time to listen to everyone in the group – what was frustrating them, how they rated their colleagues, whether they felt they had been ignored. And then she directed the team in a way that brought it together: she encouraged people to speak more openly about their frustrations, and she helped people raise constructive complaints during meetings. In short, her empathy allowed her to understand her team's emotional makeup. The result was not just heightened collaboration among members but also added business, as the team was called on for help by a wider range of internal clients.

Globalization is another reason for the rising importance of empathy for business leaders. Cross-cultural dialogue can easily lead to miscues and misunderstandings. Empathy is an antidote. People who have it are attuned to subtleties in body language; they can hear the message beneath the words being spoken. Beyond that, they have a deep understanding of the existence and importance of cultural and ethnic differences.

Consider the case of an American consultant whose team had just pitched a project to a potential Japanese client. In its dealings with Americans, the team was accustomed to being bombarded with questions after such a proposal, but this time it was greeted with a long silence. Other members of the team, taking the silence as disapproval, were ready to pack and leave. The lead consultant gestured them to stop. Although he was not particularly familiar with Japanese culture, he read the client's face and posture and sensed not rejection but interest – even deep consideration. He was right: when the client finally spoke, it was to give the consulting firm the job.

Finally, empathy plays a key role in the retention of talent, particularly in today's information economy. Leaders have always needed empathy to develop and keep good people, but today the stakes are higher. When good people leave, they take the company's knowledge with them.

That's where coaching and mentoring come in. It has repeatedly been shown that coaching and mentoring pay off not just in better performance but also in increased job satisfaction and decreased turnover. But what makes coaching and mentoring work best is the nature of the relationship. Outstanding coaches and mentors get inside the heads of the people they are helping. They sense how to give effective feedback. They know when to push for better performance and when to hold back. In the way they motivate their protégés, they demonstrate empathy in action.

In what is probably sounding like a refrain, let me repeat that empathy doesn't get much respect in business. People wonder how leaders can make hard decisions if they are 'feeling' for all the people who will be affected. But leaders with empathy do more than sympathize with people around them: they use their knowledge to improve their companies in subtle but important ways.

Social skill

The first three components of emotional intelligence are all self-management skills. The last two, empathy and social skill, concern a person's ability to manage relationships with others. As a component of emotional intelligence, social skill is not as simple as it sounds. It's not just a matter of friendliness, although people with high levels of social skill are rarely mean-spirited. Social skill, rather, is friendliness with a purpose: moving people in the direction you desire, whether that's agreement on a new marketing strategy or enthusiasm about a new product.

Socially skilled people tend to have a wide circle of acquaintances, and they have a knack for finding common ground with people of all kinds – a knack for building rapport. That doesn't mean they socialize continually; it means they work according to the assumption that nothing important gets done alone. Such people have a network in place when the time for action comes. Social skill is the culmination of the other dimensions of emotional intelligence. People tend to be very effective at managing relationships when they can understand and control their own emotions and can empathize with the feelings of others. Even motivation contributes to social skill. Remember that people who are driven to achieve tend to be optimistic, even in the face of setbacks or failure. When people are upbeat, their 'glow' is cast upon conversations and other social encounters. They are popular, and for good reason.

Because it is the outcome of the other dimensions of emotional intelligence, social skill is recognizable on the job in many ways that will by now sound familiar. Socially skilled people, for instance, are adept at managing teams – that's their empathy at work. Likewise, they are expert persuaders – a manifestation of self-awareness, self-regulation, and empathy combined. Given those skills, good persuaders know when to make an emotional plea, for instance, and when an appeal to reason will work better. And motivation, when publicly visible, makes such people excellent collaborators; their passion for the work spreads to others, and they are driven to find solutions.

But sometimes social skill shows itself in ways the other emotional intelligence components do not. For instance, socially skilled people may at times appear not to be working while at work. They seem to be idly schmoozing – chatting in the hallways with colleagues or joking around with people who are not even connected to their 'real' jobs. Socially skilled people, however, don't think it makes sense to arbitrarily limit the scope of their relationships. They build bonds widely because they know that in these fluid times, they may need help someday from people they are just getting to know today.

For example, consider the case of an executive in the strategy department of a global computer manufacturer. By 1993, he was convinced that the company's future lay with the Internet. Over the course of the next year, he found kindred spirits and used his social skill to stitch together a virtual community that cut across levels, divisions, and nations. He then used this de facto team to put up a corporate Web site, among the first by a major company. And, on his own initiative, with no budget or formal status, he signed up the company to participate in an annual Internet industry convention. Calling on his allies and persuading various divisions to donate funds, he recruited more than 10 people from a dozen different units to represent the company at the convention.

Management took notice: within a year of the conference, the executive's team formed the basis for the company's first Internet division, and he was formally put in charge of it. To get there, the executive had ignored conventional boundaries, forging and maintaining connections with people in every corner of the organization.

Is social skill considered a key leadership capability in most companies? The answer is yes, especially when compared with the other components of emotional intelligence. People seem to know intuitively that leaders need to manage relationships effectively; no leader is an island. After all, the leader's task is to get work done through other people, and social skill makes that possible. A leader who cannot express her empathy may as well not have it at all. And a leader's motivation will be useless if he cannot communicate his passion to the organization. Social skill allows leaders to put their emotional intelligence to work.

It would be foolish to assert that good old-fashioned IQ and technical ability are not important ingredients in strong leadership. But the recipe would not be complete without emotional intelligence. It was once thought that the components of emotional intelligence were 'nice to have' in business leaders. But now we know that, for the sake of performance, these are ingredients that leaders 'need to have'.

It is fortunate, then, that emotional intelligence can be learned. The process is not easy. It takes time and, most of all, commitment. But the benefits that come from having a well-developed emotional intelligence, both for the individual and for the organization, make it worth the effort.

Source: *Harvard Business Review*, 1998, November, pp. 93–102.

10 Psychodynamics, Psychoanalysis, and Organizations

Yiannis Gabriel[1]

At first glance, psychoanalysis and organizations do not go well together. We think of psychoanalysis in terms of individuals, their worries, irrationalities and mental disorders. But organizations are different. We think of them as orderly places where people behave in a rational, business-like way. What can psychoanalysis tell us about organizations? Can it tell us only about the unusual, pathological individuals or events within organizations? Or only about the occasional organization characterized by so much irrationality that it may be said to have gone crazy? In this chapter, I shall argue that the psychoanalytic conception of organizations goes far beyond the examination of the pathological and the unusual. Psychoanalysis can provide a deep understanding of many organizational features, even those that appear perfectly straightforward and ordinary. It does so not by addressing the behaviour of individuals in organizations, but rather the *meaning* of their behaviour and the deeper *motives* for their actions.

When we look into meanings of events and motives of actions, distinctions between rational and irrational become blurred. Actions which appear on the surface to make perfectly good sense can turn out to serve ends which have little to do with organizational efficiency and rationality. Such actions may in the end turn out to be better understood by reference to motives which some organizational members may not openly acknowledge or may prefer not to understand. Distinctions between order and disorder become equally blurred as tension, conflict, and flux often threaten to disrupt even the best laid plans. This chapter introduces a psychoanalytic perspective to the study of organizations. It argues that psychoanalysis enables us to make sense of those irrational phenomena that from time to time afflict organizations, but also to study systematically the demands which they make on their members and the costs at which these demands are met.

A psychoanalytic interpretation of the Challenger disaster

It is telling to start with a well-known example of a widely debated organizational disaster.[2] Disasters are instructive not because they are common-place or typical, but because they lay bare some of the organizational stresses and tensions that normally go unnoticed. Following the Challenger disaster, the

United States government created a commission, headed by former Secretary of State William P. Rogers, to investigate the causes. At first, the commission was in the dark concerning the causes of the disaster, viewing it as a freak accident at odds with the technological sophistication, competence and responsibility epitomized by NASA at the time. So, when Richard C. Cook, a budget analyst, presented a story at variance with this image of NASA, they tended to be dismissive.

Cook's job had been to keep track of the development of the space shuttle's solid rocket boosters (SRB), the element whose failure was ultimately found to have caused the explosion. In a memorandum written in July 1985, six months before the disaster, Cook warned that flight safety was being compromised by erosion of the boosters' O-ring seals and that failure of these parts could be catastrophic. Following the explosion, he wrote another memo referring to the earlier one, which someone leaked to the Rogers Commission. He was then called to testify on 12 February 1986. In his testimony, Cook claimed that his information was solely based on what engineers on the SRB project had told him, something that turned out to be accurate. Yet, when NASA officials were invited to comment on his charges, they categorically refuted them (*The New York Times*, 13 February, Section B, Page 11). *The Times* reported further that a 'parade' of NASA officials testified that Mr Cook's concerns were out of proportion and that the issue of seal erosion had been dealt with carefully by NASA engineering experts and managers. They said, quite erroneously as it turned out,[3] that seal problems had diminished in 1985. While they did not deny Cook's claim that the seals had eroded, they did claim that more competent professionals than he had concluded they were safe.[4]

The next day, *The Times* invited Cook to respond. Cook's version was at odds with that of the officials; more importantly his general image of NASA was substantially different.

> In his first major interview, ... Richard C. Cook, said that propulsion engineers at the National Aeronautics and Space Administration 'whispered' in his ear since he arrived last July that the seals were unsafe and even 'held their breath' when earlier shuttles were launched...
>
> Mr Cook said he based his warning memorandum last July on conversations with engineers in the agency's propulsion division who were concerned about erosion of the rocket's safety seals. 'They began to tell me that some of these were being eaten away,' he said, 'and rather innocently I asked what does that mean?'
>
> 'They said to me, almost in a whisper in my ear, that the thing could blow up,' he continued. 'I was shocked.' In his July memorandum, Mr Cook explained, 'I was simply paraphrasing what this engineering group was telling me. I was not making it up that flight safety was being compromised and the results could be catastrophic. I didn't put it in my memorandum, but one of them said to me, "When this thing goes up, we hold our breath."'(14 February 1986: B4)

Compare this image of NASA with that held by one of its senior officials:

Today, L. Michael Weeks, deputy associate Administrator for space flight, the space agency's second-ranking shuttle official, said that the climate at the agency actually encouraged individuals two or three levels below him to speak their minds on safety concerns. He said that working-level engineers 'don't hesitate to tell Mike Weeks anything' and 'quite often will argue right on the spot at a significant meeting with me or Jesse,' a reference to Jesse W. Moore, the top shuttle official. (14 February 1986: B4)

Now the picture of NASA presented by Cook and that presented by NASA officials were at loggerheads. Cook's NASA was a place where engineers agonized over flaws in their product and feared for the lives of astronauts; it was a place where they felt that they could not voice their concerns. NASA management's NASA, on the other hand, was a place in which communication between ranks was open and free, in which concerns about safety were addressed directly and competently; safety was simply not a matter they needed to be worried about. It does not appear that NASA officials were lying or being disingenuous. Rather, they appeared to maintain their views with perfect conviction. Nor was it simply that certain elements of organizational functioning were not within their purview, for in fact they had a very elaborate idea of how those elements functioned; it is just that their perception was contrary to the reality as experienced by Mr Cook and the engineers who had talked to him. From the perspective of the senior officials, the Challenger disaster was a one-off, unpredictable aberration. From the perspective of Mr Cook and his informants, it is surprising that the accident did not happen earlier – in fact, the accident was the natural culmination of an organization in which people are afraid to speak their mind.

Each of these two images of NASA leads to very different conclusions about the causes of the disaster, as well as its *meaning*. One, held by management, is an image of an organization that is open to communication, in which everyone can say openly what they think. This image is positive, desirable and consistent with NASA's earlier successes. The other image, emerging from Cook's account and supported by the testimonies of many engineers, is one of an organization ridden with enforced silence and conformity, which muffles its employees and is impervious to criticism. In the former image, the employees emerge as independent professionals, doing a job which contributes to the organization's formidable technical achievements. In the latter, the employees are individuals merely earning a living, frightened to do anything that may jeopardize their livelihoods. How can two images at such variance co-exist within the same organization? How can different people working together maintain such different perceptions? Furthermore, is it possible that the same individual may hold both images at the same time?

The Challenger disaster has been the topic of numerous books and articles which enable us to address some of these questions (McConnell 1987; Trento 1987; McCurdy 1993; Vaughan 1996; Adams and Balfour 1998). While their authors differ in many points of interpretation and explanation, they generally agree that the agency's senior officials failed to recognize numerous warning signals, both in terms of technical failures and in terms of the ways in which technical failures were identified and discussed. They seemed to be blind to the failures themselves, and they were blind to the fact the agency was preventing its staff from expressing legitimate concerns. Their blindness was not the result of ignorance, stupidity or innocence. Rather, it is as if *they kept themselves from knowing*, as if it was too painful to acknowledge that an organization they loved was fallible or that it was experienced by some of its members as tyrannical and oppressive.

This is where psychoanalysis can make a contribution. Non-psychoanalytic approaches may content themselves in arguing that, to defend their interests, individuals lie, distort and disregard inconvenient facts. A psychoanalytic approach, on the other hand, envisages a possibility where individuals deceive themselves, without actually lying or being disingenuous. Our perceptions and ideas about social reality are not neutral. They are shaped by feelings, such as pride, anxiety and pain, as well as by earlier experiences in our lives which, unknown to us, have left deep marks on our mental personality. If we sometimes deceive ourselves, it is because reality is too painful or too complex and our desires too precious to forsake. Seen from this perspective, the blindness of the NASA officials to technical flaws with catastrophic potential as well as to their organization's unwillingness to tolerate 'bad news' was not accidental – it was the product of *repression*, a process whereby dangerous or unpleasant ideas are prevented from reaching consciousness and restricted to an *unconscious* part of the mind. Managers worried about potential disasters *may* disregard signs of danger and discard warnings as defeatist talk of nay-sayers; in this way, troubling parts of reality are avoided by being replaced by desirable but unrealistic fictions. This process may be reinforced if managers are surrounded by others who are likewise inclined to re-shape their view of reality according to their desires, or if current worries trigger off memories of earlier painful events in their personal histories which threaten to overwhelm them.

Psychoanalysis and the unconscious

Unconscious ideas and desires do not behave like conscious ones. They cannot be accessed through introspection (i.e. by asking questions of oneself and looking inward); they cannot be corrected or changed by appeal to logic or material evidence; they do not lead to action geared at achieving desired results. Above all, unconscious ideas and desires cannot be discussed freely, for the reason that powerful psychic forces keep them repressed. We all spend much mental energy defending ourselves against disturbing or embarrassing ideas and desires, by keeping them unconscious. In this way, much as the NASA officials did, we censor our thoughts, our desires and even our feelings. If political censors seek to eliminate ideas and images which threaten the regime, mental censors seek to suppress those ideas and desires which they envisage as threatening our psychological well-being or even survival. *The idea that repression is a form of mental defense against threatening psychic phenomena lies at the heart of Freudian psychology.*[5]

If the unconscious is by definition inaccessible to consciousness how can we be sure of its existence, how can we ever hope to know its contents? To answer these questions, Freud relied on his view that unconscious material (ideas, desires, thoughts and feelings) is the result of a process of repression in the service of psychological defence. But he also used a key corollary of this idea, which he initially formulated through his study of neurotic symptoms (such as a compulsive cough or an irrational fear of horses) and dreams. *Repressed ideas do not disappear without trace from a person's life, but they seek expression in various subterfuges.* During sleep, for instance, when the censors are less vigilant, repressed ideas may be expressed through dreams. In waking life, a repressed feeling may be manifested by changing into its opposite or by being *displaced* onto a different object. Interpretation is a process whereby we can access unconscious material through its conscious manifestations. It is a powerful but also a dangerous process, capable of yielding extraordinary insights into human motivation; but it is also a dangerous process which, when abused, can lead to false and potentially destructive conclusions. It is a process that cannot be reduced to a number of simple steps, but requires practice and experience. It is a process whose outcomes are virtually always provisional, open to refinement, correction and re-evaluation.

Interpretation is a kind of detective work, such as that practised by Sherlock Holmes and his less famous imitators relying on small clues to construct a general picture (Ricoeur 1970; Ginzburg 1980; Shepherd 1985). But Freud was even keener in the parallel between psychoanalysis and archaeology, a discipline which held an acute fascination for him. Like an archaeologist, Freud imagined himself as someone who extrapolates latent structures from manifest ones, by undoing the work of time. Yet, what Freud also realized, like some archaeologists also do, was that the material he was starting with, the dream, the neurotic symptom, the returning memory, had not just deteriorated with the passage of time, but had been deliberately tampered with, in order to frustrate and mislead the attempts at interpretation.

The intimate, personal details of dreams and the vast panorama of thousands of people working to put spaceships into space seem to belong to different worlds. Dreams appear to spring from the irrational recesses of each individual's unconscious whereas an organization like NASA appears to be the epitome of technical rationality, science and order. And yet. Is it not the case that behind the massive resources mobilized by NASA lie the dreams of millions of people? How many children have not dreamt of becoming astronauts, of going to the moon or beyond? And how many adults did not share Kennedy's dream of putting a man on the moon and bringing him back safely by the end of the decade? How many did not shed tears as they lined the roads to give the early astronauts the welcome reserved for conquering emperors in antiquity? It would seem that, however rational and ordered organizations appear to be they are often carriers of strong emotional forces, unconscious desires and hopes, similar to those expressed in dreams.

The two worlds, the public arena of technical and cultural achievements and the private world of emotions and dreams, are not as far apart as they seem at first. In both, we encounter human desires finding different expressions. The unconscious link between the fantasy life of individuals and groups and an organization's mission, symbols and practices allows us to broaden the scope of psychoanalytic interpretations. Thus repressed desires and censored fantasies, shared by many organizational participants, find expression and partial fulfilment in the organization, the way it is symbolically experienced, the emotions it generates, the stories it spawns. By interpreting organizational stories, mission statements, artefacts and symbols it is possible to access the deeper psychological experiences of individuals as members of organizations.[6]

Psychodynamics

The contribution of psychoanalysis to organizational phenomena is not exhausted with the recognition that individual desires, fantasies and emotional aberrations find their way into organizational life. Organizations themselves, the psychological demands which they make on individuals, call for a special type of analysis which seeks to uncover how our emotional functioning and our behaviour is affected by group participation. How often is it that a group of highly talented and sensitive individuals find it impossible to work together, without being overwhelmed by powerful emotions, such as envy, suspicion, anger and fear? The field of psychodynamics has developed psychoanalytic insights into the unconscious life of groups and organizations seeking to identify what forces influence group functioning, what distinguishes effective and ineffective groups and how individuals interact with each other. Three contributions of psychodynamics stand out:

- Groups and organizations are characterized by their own unconscious processes, which radically mould the experiences of their members and influence their effectiveness.
- Many of these processes have as their aim the control of anxiety, an emotion which can have an incapacitating influence on individuals or may galvanize them to action.
- The ways in which individuals respond to groups and organizations are influenced by their earlier experiences as members of a family.

As members of groups (such as committees, crowds, work-teams and organizations) our mental processes operate in distinct ways. Since the pioneering work of 19th century French psychologist Gustave Le Bon, it has been known that crowds exacerbate unconscious, irrational forces through which individuals surrender part of their self-control to the crowd, their mind being, at least in part, taken over by the group mind. Emotions, such as dedication, enthusiasm, anger and panic, tend to be amplified and easily communicated from person to person as though they were contagious. Rational judgement and intelligence are often hampered, as individuals find themselves under pressure to conform to group norms and values. Thus groups are capable of great violence and horror, just as they are capable of miracles of team work, dedication and performance.

Current group dynamics theory is indebted to psychoanalyst Wilfred Bion (1961), whose theories were based on observations he made during group therapy sessions with military personnel mentally traumatized during World War II. Bion noted that the groups he treated seemed to focus on the task at hand only some of the time. At other times, they were overwhelmed by their emotions and became unable to focus on work. He referred to these diversions as 'basic assumption' activity, the group was acting *as if* they held shared certain assumptions about each other, about the therapist/leader, or about the subject of discussion. When a group was in "work group' mode, members were intent on furthering the task; they maintained close contact with reality and used rational means to address the demands of the task. In basic assumption mode, on the other hand, members seemed focused primarily on easing anxiety and avoiding the painful interactions. They quickly lost touch with reality and embraced collective delusions.

Bion argued that basic assumption sets in when the group is gripped by anxiety which it is unable to contain. He identified three types of basic assumption – dependency, fight-flight, and pairing – each with a characteristic set of behaviors and emotions.

In basic assumption *dependency* (baD) mode, group members act as if a leader (who may be formal or informal) is possessed of almost supernatural powers to protect the group and make its decisions. The members regress to a state of child-like powerlessness and paralysis, experiencing towards the leader feelings akin to those directed at the parents in early childhood. In this state, the group quickly becomes stymied, as subsequent events prove the leader all too human and fallible. Disappointment then often leads the group to 'depose' the former leader and 'elect' another.

In *fight-flight* (baF) mode, the group acts as if there is a great danger that must be attacked or fled from. This imagined danger can be internal or external, identifiable in the group's apparent panic. The baF group is typically led by a member who 'specializes' in fight or flight. He/she may be regularly mobilized to fight with the group's official leader. Scapegoating, recrimination and mobbing are common features of this type of group, which is marked by a different type of regression from the dependency group – a regression to animal-like fight-or-flight response to threat.

Basic assumption *pairing* (baP) is characterized by feelings of hopefulness and optimism. In this mode, the group acts as if two members of the group will get together to generate an idea ('give birth to a messiah') which will solve all the group's problems. This hope can have a religious (Messianic), sexual (pregnancy), or reparative (world peace) theme but in all cases, the focus of the group turns away from immediate, difficult issues to a fantasized future in which all such difficulties are overcome. Again, certain group members may be chosen for their propensity to pair, but the group may use any combination of members, depending on the issue at hand.

Organizations, anxiety and defence

Bion's basic assumption theory has proven one of the most robust and useful ideas in psychodynamics. Much effort has been devoted at diagnosing the imminence of basic assumption and the factors which restore a group's focus on the task, keeping emotional forces under control. The containment of anxiety is vital in preventing a group from lapsing into basic assumption, and an important function of leadership. At the same time, however, anxiety is directly linked to various bureaucratic features of organizations, such as hierarchies, rules and impersonality. The theories developed by Elliott Jaques, Isabel Menzies Lyth, Eric Trist, Harold Bridger, Eric Miller and other scholars of the Tavistock Institute in London have sought to demonstrate that many bureaucratic features of organizations (features such as formal rules, hierarchies, etc.) function not directly to enhance performance but to contain anxiety.

In her influential study of hospital staff, Menzies (1960) found that nurses constantly confront strong emotions from patients and their relatives, ranging from gratitude to admiration, from envy to resentment. Their own feelings towards the patients, especially feelings of closeness and personal caring, are tempered by the knowledge that the patient may die. Faced with such emotions, many nurses experience acute anxieties from which they seek to defend themselves. The hospital's own bureaucratic features, its rules and procedures, rotas, task-lists, checks and counterchecks, paperwork, hierarchies and so on, act as supports for defensive techniques. By allowing for 'ritual task performance', by depersonalizing relations with the patients, by relying on organizational hierarchies, nurses contained their anxiety. Yet, such organizational defences against anxiety were ultimately unsuccessful:

> The system made little provision for confronting anxiety and working it through, the only way in which a real increase in the capacity to cope with it and personal maturation would take place. As a social defense system, it was ineffectual in containing anxiety. (Menzies Lyth 1991, p. 363)

The system's inadequacy is evidenced by its failure to train and retain nurses, a chronically low morale, high levels of stress and burn-out and absence of work satisfaction. Menzies Lyth views the role of the consultant as one who can help restore an organization to health, by implementing a number of principles. These include acknowledging and working through anxiety, receiving support in confronting and dealing problems, accepting the suffering and pain which is part of their work and instituting more visible relations between efforts and rewards symbolic and material. Menzies Lyth's prescriptions have been taken up with greater or lesser success by numerous psychoanalytically-orientated consultants. Countless instances of backfiring social defences against anxiety have been documented by writers working within this psychodynamic perspective (Diamond 1985; Hirschhorn 1988; Hirschhorn 1989; Hirschhorn and Gilmore 1989; Krantz 1989; Lapierre 1989; Diamond 1993; Gould 1993).

In *The Workplace Within*, Hirschhorn (1988) uses his experiences as an organizational consultant to show how anxiety in organizations triggers off child-like fears of annihilation, which in turn call for social defences. To Bion's basic assumption, Hirschhorn adds two further modes of social defence, organizational rituals and covert coalitions. Following Menzies Lyth, Hirschhorn views organizational rituals as depersonalized routines, which create a distance between the individuals and their roles, screening out threatening emotional involvements and replacing them with a set of mechanical actions. Covert coalitions, on the other hand, constitute a kind of unconscious psychological deal, whereby members of an organization call a truce to conflict or disagreement, by assuming roles drawn from family life, which provides them with a model for anxiety containment. The price of such a truce, observes Hirschhorn, is the creation of taboo subjects which may not be referred to and the perpetuation of dysfunctional arrangements within the organization. Hirschhorn documents several instances where management training and socialization reproduces and perpetuates defensive techniques. Hirschhorn argues that successful organizations in future will need members whose anxieties are confronted and worked through, rather than members who look for suitable scapegoats to victimize or suitable regulations behind which to take cover. In this manner, Hirschhorn envisages the possibility of the emergence of an organizational culture that accepts complexity and supports learning and growth processes, both at the individual and the organizational levels.

The view that organizations function as social defences against anxiety has gained considerable currency. Even rationality itself, the use of quasi-scientific procedures like forecasting, planning, monitoring, testing and so on can be seen as emotional rituals whose main function is in allaying anxieties in times of unpredictability and even chaos. The distinct contribution of psychoanalysis to the discussion of control over external forces lies in the view that the fear of outer chaos and the threats issuing from it are themselves related to anxiety over inner chaos, chaos which arises from our own disorderly desires, impulses and inhibitions. Of considerable interest is Stacey's (1992, 1995) combination of the psychoanalytic theory of social defences with complexity theory to argue that successful organizations are those which function in a state of bounded instability, a near-chaos state which is neither one of catastrophic disequilibrium nor one of static ossification and death. Functioning in this mode, organizations are unpredictable beyond a very small time span. Outdated procedures of control are virtually useless in such circumstances; by contrast, creativity and innovation are the result of learning to operate at the edge of the abyss and being able to live with the attendant anxiety.

Organizational causes of anxiety

If organizations offer some more or less successful mechanisms for the containment of anxiety, they are also sources of anxiety. Like Hirschhorn, Howell S. Baum in *The Invisible Bureaucracy* (1987) explores the matching of psychological and organizational processes, only his emphasis is in the opposite direction. Bureaucracy, argues Baum, contains certain features which function as systematic generators of anxiety. Foremost among these is hierarchy which disperses responsibility while concentrating power. The responsibilities of individuals become ambiguous; trust is undermined by endemic impersonality and distance between individuals across organizational ranks. Individuals adopt a defensive attitude seeking to cover their back at all times.

Bureaucratic impersonality creates an empty psychological space between subordinates and superiors, which is filled with fantasies (Levinson 1968/1981, Levinson 1972). Baum notes two especially common fantasies among subordinates, the 'moral paragon' and the 'superiority in competence and strength'. Each of these sets off its own type of anxiety, the former guilt anxiety, the latter shame anxiety. When wrongly accused, individuals frequently feel threats of annihilation out of proportion to the actual blame placed on them. The strong feelings of rage, anxiety and fear generated by such events are evidence of regression to an earlier, more vulnerable age. Blame and credit become the vital currency in which organizational participants continuously trade:

> Organizational hierarchies become highways along which blame travels: superiors blame subordinates for filling-in the wrong forms or pulling the wrong levers; subordinates blame superiors for designing forms and levers wrongly or giving the wrong instructions. Apportioning blame can become a highly unpredictable business. Under these circumstances, people may learn the simple, but demoralizing lesson, that the best thing to do is simply to protect themselves. (Fineman and Gabriel 1996, p. 119)

If organizations harbour unseen dangers, potential victimization, unexpected responsibilities and dormant or unknown regulations, anxiety warns the individual of such threats and offers a partial inoculation against injury when misfortune strikes. In many organizations, especially oppressive authoritarian ones, a continuous level of anxiety is maintained through alarmist gossip and horror stories of sadism and humiliation which alert individuals to potential threats but also enable them to claim the moral superiority accorded to victims of oppression and injustice (Gabriel 1991, 1998, 2000).

Conclusion

The distinct contribution of psychoanalysis to the study of organizations lies in its ability to penetrate the non-conscious dimension of human life – the dimension which includes those psychic realities which individually or in groups that we keep concealed from ourselves as well as what is taken for granted and becomes invisible. Psychoanalysis stresses that our actions can be driven by motives which are unknown to us, that we frequently deceive ourselves and that we sacrifice accuracy and truth in the interest of desire and emotion. In addition, psychoanalysis teaches us that in defending ourselves against anxiety, pain and suffering, we often regress to primitive or infantile modes of behaviour. From time to time, we are possessed by strange desires and driven to the most unpredictable or irrational acts. Above all, psychoanalysis teaches us that our psyche:

> ... is not a coherent, integrated entity, but an area of conflict and turmoil; our soul is not a simple thing; on the contrary, it is a hierarchy of superordinated and subordinated agents, a labyrinth of impulses striving independently of one another towards action, corresponding with the multiplicity of instincts and of relations with the outer world, many of which are antagonistic to one another and incompatible. (Freud 1917, 187)

Organizations are not immune from the consequences of such an emotional cauldron. They easily become terrains where irrational fears and fantasies are acted out, where relations between subordinates and superiors regress to infantile relations between children and parents, where perceptions are systematically coloured by feeling, and where order and stability are constantly battered by inner as well as outer forces of disorder and chaos. It is by recognising the precarious and endlessly shifting foundation on which organizations are built that we can properly appreciate the amazing effort that goes into keeping them going, as well as the mental costs and sacrifices that this calls for.

Notes

1. Some of the arguments in this article come from Gabriel (2000), which was written in collaboration with Howard S. Schwartz, Larry Hirschhorn and Marion McCollom Hampton. My thanks to all three.
2. The example is drawn from Gabriel (2000) and owes much the analysis offered by Schwartz (1988, 1989, 1990).
3. In fact, of nine flights in 1985, O-ring erosion occurred in seven, with blow-by occurring in six. This compared with four instances of erosion and three of blow-by for the six flights of 1984, when the problem began developing on a regular basis (Rogers 1986, pp. 130–1).
4. It is also important to note that, as investigation revealed, NASA's problems were by no means limited to the Solid Rocket Boosters, but affected every aspect of their activity. They had hardware problems in other areas, and had lost technical, financial, and operational control over what they were doing. There can be no doubt that NASA's problems were systemic (Schwartz 1990).
5. Freud's notion of the unconscious is, in the first place, the state of ideas and desires which have undergone repression.
6. For practical examples of this approach see Gabriel (1991a, b, 1995).

References

Adams, G. B. and Balfour, D.L. (1998) 'An historical analysis of destructive organizational culture: the von Brown team, the Marshall space flight center and the space shuttle Challenger disaster', *Administrative Theory and Praxis* 20(3): 300–13.

Baum, H. S. (1987) *The Invisible Bureaucracy*. Oxford: Oxford University Press.

Bion, W. R. (1961) *Experiences in Groups*. London: Tavistock.

Diamond, M.A. (1985) 'The social character of bureaucracy: anxiety and ritualistic defense', *Political Psychology* 6(4): 6633–79.

Diamond, M.A. (1993) *The Unconscious Life of Organizations: Interpreting Organizational Identity*. London: Quorum Books.

Fineman, S. and Gabriel, Y. (1996) *Experiencing Organizations*. London: Sage.

Freud, S. (1917) *A Difficulty in the Path of Psycho-Analysis*. London: Hogarth Press.

Freud, S. (1923/1984) 'The ego and the id', in *On Metapsychology: the theory of psychoanalysis*. Great Britain, Pelican Freud Library. 11: 341–406.

Gabriel, Y. (1991a) 'Organizations and their discontents: a psychoanalytic contribution to the study of corporate culture', *Journal of Applied Behavioural Science* 27: 318–36.

Gabriel, Y. (1991b) 'Turning facts into stories and stories into facts: a hermeneutic exploration of organizational folklore', *Human Relations* 44(8): 857–75.

Gabriel, Y. (1995) 'The unmanaged organization: stories, fantasies, subjectivity', *Organization Studies* 16(3): 477–501.

Gabriel, Y. (1998) 'An introduction to the sociology of insults in organizations', *Human Relations* 51(11): 1329–54.

Gabriel, Y. (2000) *Organizations in Depth*. London: Sage.

Ginzburg, C. (1980) '"Morelli, Freud and Sherlock Holmes: clues and scientific method', *History Workshop* 9: 5–36.

Gould, L. (1993) 'Contemporary perspectives on personal and organizational authority: the Self in a system of work relations', in L. Hirschhorn and C. K. Barnett (Eds) *The Psychodynamics of Organizations*. Philadelphia: Temple University Press, pp. 49–66.

Hirschhorn, L. (1988) *The Workplace Within*. Cambridge, MA: MIT Press.

Hirschhorn, L. (1989) 'Professionals, authority and group life: a case study of a law firm', *Human Resource Management* 28(2): 235–52.

Hirschhorn, L. and Gilmore, T.N. (1989) 'The psychodynamics of a cultural change: learning from a factory', *Human Resource Management* 28 (2): 211–33.

Krantz, J. (1989) 'The managerial couple: superior–subordinate relationships as a unit of analysis', *Human Resource Management* 28(2): 161–76.

Lapierre, L. (1989) 'Mourning, potency and power in management', *Human Resource Management* 28(2): 177–89.

Levinson, H. (1968/1981) *Executive*. Cambridge, MA: Harvard University Press.

Levinson, H. (1972) *Organizational Diagnosis*. Cambridge, MA: Harvard University Press.

McConnell, M. (1987) *Challenger: a major malfunction*. New York: Doubleday.

McCurdy, H. E. (1993) *Inside NASA: high technology and organizational change in the US space program*. Baltimore, MD: Johns Hopkins University Press.

Menzies, I. (1960) 'A case study in functioning of social systems as a defence against anxiety', *Human Relations* 13: 95–121.

Menzies Lyth, I. (1991) 'Changing organizations and individuals: psychoanalytic insights for improving organizational health', in M.F.R.K. de Vries (Ed.) *Organizations on the Couch.* San Francisco: Jossey-Bass.

Ricoeur, P. (1970) *Freud and Philosophy: an essay on interpretation.* New Haven, CT: Yale University Press.

Rogers, W.P. (1986) *Report of the Presidential Commission on the space shuttle Challenger accident.* Washington, DC: US Government Printing Office.

Schwartz, H.S. (1988) 'The symbol of the space shuttle and the degeneration of the American Dream', *Journal of Organizational Change Management* 1/2: 5–20.

Schwartz, H.S. (1989) 'Organizational disaster and organizational decay: the case of the National Aeronautics and Space Administration', *Industrial Crisis Quarterly* 3: 319–34.

Schwartz, H.S. (1990) *Narcissistic Process and Corporate Decay.* New York: New York University Press.

Shepherd, M. (1985) *Sherlock Holmes and the Case of Dr Freud.* London: Tavistock.

Stacey, R.D. (1992) *Managing Chaos: dynamic business strategies in an unpredictable world.* London: Kogan Page.

Stacey, R.D. (1995) 'The science of complexity: an alternative perspective for strategic change processes', *Strategic Management Journal* 16: 477–95.

Trento, J.J. (1987) *Prescription for Disaster: From the glory of Apollo to the betrayal of the shuttle.* New York: Crown.

Vaughan, D. (1996) *The Challenger Launch Decision: risky technology, culture, and deviance at NASA.* Chicago, IL: Chicago University Press.

Section E Style

Personality research is undergoing something of a resurgence at present with the increasing consensus that there are five main personality traits known as the Big Five – extraversion, agreeableness, conscientiousness, emotional stability and openness. Many personality tests can be related to these five factors, notably the most commonly used personality inventory, the MBTI.

In a short article, Hampson reviews the state of personality testing, the prominence of the Big Five and implications for whether or not we can change. A number of commentators feel that at least 40% of the variance in the Big Five factors is accounted for by genetic inheritance. Test–retest scores over 3 to 30 years are about .65 for the Big Five measures, suggesting relatively little change in adult personality, though of course we may get much better at self-presentation.

Bayne explains the relationship between the Big Five traits and MBTI types. He points out the merits of the positive interpretation of both poles of the MBTI dimensions compared to the largely negative characteristics often used to describe one pole on Big Five measures.

Historically creativity in the West has been associated with the big breakthrough – the radical innovation, but towards the end of the 20th century the West has begun to appreciate the importance of the hitherto somewhat neglected incremental creativity, the sort that builds on what has gone before and that people in the East seem to excel at. Through his Adaption Innovation inventory Kirton has drawn attention to the idea of creative style, emphasizing that there are different ways of being creative – people who like to do things differently or innovatively and those that prefer to do things better or adaptively, and that both approaches are valuable. This is a very different idea from the old notion of testing for creative ability to try and differentiate between those who are creative and those who are not. Here Kirton describes the theory underlying his Adaption Innovation theory and the implications for the way people behave. Adaption Innovation is related the Big Five openness factor and the intuition and sensing dimension on the MBTI.

11 State of the Art: Personality

Sarah Hampson

Back in the 1960s, normal personality was largely studied with some version of trait theory. Personality traits (e.g. extraversion) are relatively stable dispositions that give rise to characteristic patterns of behaviour (e.g. a preference for activities involving other people to being alone), and logically depend on evidence of behavioural consistency. Mischel (1968) compiled a seemingly devastating critique of traits in which he demolished the idea that people behave consistently regardless of situation. 30 years later personality is alive and well. Indeed, these days, personality research is popular and personality testing is profitable.

Units of analysis

In the 1980s, a new generation of personality psychologists responded to the critique of traits by advocating different units of analysis (Buss and Cantor 1989) A hierarchy of units of analysis of personality emerged, with the whole person at the apex branching down through middle-level units such as 'life tasks' to traits and behaviours at the base.

Middle-level units dealing with smaller chunks of life history, such as 'personal strivings' (e.g. 'be myself and not do things to please others') (Emmons 1986), and 'life tasks' (e.g. 'maturing beyond my high school mentality') (Cantor and Kihlstrom 1987) These middle-level units are personal goals that reflect elements of motivation and personality. That is, a first-year undergraduate with a strong need for affiliation (motivation) and who scores highly on extraversion (personality) might have a personal goal of 'having a thriving social life by the end of the first term'. This goal might be achieved via life tasks such as 'make at least one friend every week' and personal strivings such as 'become a more witty and entertaining person'. By focusing on middle-level units, personality psychologists have become interested in the processes involved in translating personality into goals, and goals into behaviour.

Norem (1989) described another kind of middle-level unit, the cognitive strategy of defensive pessimism, by which people protect themselves from the disappointment of failing to achieve a desired goal by playing through the 'worst-case' scenario. For example, a defensive pessimist who very much desires to get a first-class degree, and who has a track record of first-class marks, will nevertheless dwell on the possibility of failing the degree. Personality types are another form of middle-level approach.

Towards the base of the pyramid we have units on a scale at a similar level to traits, such as motives (wishes and desires) and values (aspects of life we deem especially important) At this level, the debates are about whether there is a real difference between traits and motives, or motives and values. For example, in an almost convincing study, Winter et al. (1998) argued that motives describe unique aspects of personality not captured by traits, and that both units of analysis are necessary for a complete understanding of personality. These alternative units do not rely on the same evidence for their validity as do traits, so the arguments and data marshalled against traits do not apply. Instead, they bring their own challenges, such as how they differ from traits and how they all fit together. There is no 'right' unit, but there is a large range to choose from depending on the scale of the research question.

The Big Five

Despite the alternatives to traits, a significant chunk of personality psychology is still built around the trait concept. The big debate of the 1990s has been about the structure of trait terms: in particular, how many broad traits are needed to provide a comprehensive description of personality.

Eysenck remained a strong advocate of three: extraversion, neuroticism and psychoticism (e.g. Eysenck 1991), whereas Cattell believed in about 15 plus intelligence (Cattell et al. 1970) However, the winning number in this lottery is undoubtedly five, Digman (1990), Goldberg (1993), John (1990) and McCrae and Costa (1997) are all compelling advocates for a five-factor structure, composed of broad domains of personality known as the Big Five. The Big Five and their trait descriptors are summarized in Table 11.1.

Table 11.1 The Big Five personality domains and representative traits

Domain	Desirable traits	Undesirable traits
extraversion (I)	outgoing, sociable, assertive	introverted, reserved, passive
agreeableness (II)	kind, trusting, warm	hostile, selfish, cold
conscientiousness (III)	organized, thorough, tidy	careless, unreliable, sloppy
emotional stability (IV)	calm, even-tempered, imperturbable	moody, temperamental, nervous
intellect or openness (V)	imaginative, intelligent, creative	shallow, unsophisticated, imperceptive

One major advantage of the Big Five framework is that it can assimilate other structures. For example, Goldberg and Rosolack (1994) demonstrated empirically that Eysenck's three-factor system of extraversion, neuroticism and psychoticism can be integrated into the Big Five. Psychoticism is a combination of undesirable Big Five III (low conscientiousness) and undesirable Big Five II (low agreeableness), while Eysenck's extraversion is equivalent to Big Five I (also called extraversion) and Eysenck's neuroticism to Big Five IV (emotional stability, which is simply the desirable pole of neuroticism)

The Big Five makes a useful structure for organizing the large and confusing number of traits and their measures in vogue today. However, it remains, for the most part, a description of normal personality and therefore is not as useful in clinical applications as it is in other areas such as occupational psychology.

Personality consistency

Mischel developed an alternative to traits, called social cognitive units. These units incorporate a person's cognitions, affect and action assessed in relation to the situations in which they occur (Mischel 1973) The focus on what the person does cognitively, affectively and behaviourally, rather than on what the person has in terms of traits. They include cognitive activities, encoding strategies, expectancies, values, preferences and goals.

More recently, Mischel and his colleagues have developed these ideas into a cognitive-affective personality system that accounts for intra-individual consistency and predictable patterns of variability across situations (Mischel and Shoda 1995, 1998) For example, a person may be shy in small groups but be an excellent public speaker. This pattern of behaviour would be cross-situationally inconsistent if viewed in purely trait terms. But if the difference in the psychological situation is taken into account, it becomes a meaningful and predictable pattern of responding: speaking to a large group does not require engaging personally with any one individual, whereas making conversation in a small group does.

An important feature of these developments is that they incorporate situational factors as a moderating influence on individual differences. This is a more sophisticated response to the critique of traits than pure situationism (in which behaviour is solely a function of situations) or mechanistic interactionism (in which behaviour is viewed as a function of independent situational factors and trait factors in an analysis of variance framework)

A moderator approach to personality allows for social cognitive units to operate in combination with traits. Moderator approaches attempt to explain why traits alone do not always predict behaviour reliably. The general principle behind such approaches is that consistency will not be found for all of the people for all of the time, and must instead be sought for certain types of behaviour of certain types of people in certain types of situation.

Several different ways of moderating traits (i.e. of determining under what conditions behavioural consistency will be found) have been proposed. For example, Biesanz et al. (1998) demonstrated that individuals with higher test–retest stability of their trait ratings had more self–other agreement on these ratings than those with less temporal stability. That is, people who regard themselves as more stable over time on a particular trait (e.g. punctuality) will also be rated more accurately by others on this trait.

Another approach to the consistency problem, which connects to the units of analysis issue, is to use personality measures at different levels of abstraction. Depending on the level of precision required for the given prediction task. The idea is that broad traits such as the Big Five serve to predict broad classes of behaviour, but will not be as good as narrower traits at predicting specific behaviours (Lay 1997) For example, a measure of Big Five conscientious will predict whether or not a person will arrive for meeting on time with less precision than a measure of the highly specific trait of punctuality.

When working with large units of analysis, such as entire life histories, inconsistencies become increasingly apparent. As novelists and laypeople have been telling us for hundreds of years, people are not consistent and descriptions of ourselves and others contain inconsistencies. We know we can be both hardworking and lazy, friendly and reserved. Studies of trait ratings indicate that we use more inconsistencies in trait descriptions of ourselves than of other people: I am more likely to describe myself as both hardworking and lazy than to describe a colleague in this way.

When we describe ourselves or another with two inconsistent traits, they are most likely to be from the Big Five domain of emotional stability (e.g. 'I am both relaxed and nervous'), whereas we are least likely to use two inconsistent traits from the domain of intellect (e.g. 'I am both deep and shallow') (Hampson 1997) Inconsistencies can be a subtle way of signalling a negative evaluation of a disliked person by attributing both a desirable and an undesirable trait describing the same aspect of personality (e.g. 'my boss is both friendly and cold' is inconsistent on Big Five agreeableness) (Hampson 1998)

Given that behaviour is not always stable across time and across situations, but can to some extent be understood and predicted, contemporary personality psychology is not so much concerned with consistency as with coherence. We recognize that people show cross-situational variability in their behaviour but that this can be understood when other factors are taken into account, such as the influence of moderator variables described earlier.

When trying to understand our own inconsistent behaviours, we often appeal to some form of situational account: 'I am usually a helpful person but this year I did not volunteer to organize the office party because I was too busy with other things.' Coherence recognizes that a person's behaviour can be understood, and perhaps even predicted, despite not necessarily being strictly consistent.

Personality testing

While academic psychologists agonized about whether there was such a thing as personality, the personality testing business started to take off and is now enjoying huge success. Although personality tests can contribute to the prediction of job performance (e.g. Barrick and Mount 1991), their predictive power is relatively low compared with other types of assessment, such as of cognitive abilities (Hunter and Hunter 1984) and decisions to hire or fire based on personality test scores are being challenged in the courts.

The testing business depends on surrounding its tests with a degree of mystique. Consequently, published personality tests protected by copyright become fossilized. They do not undergo constant revision and improvement as a result of research by the scientific community at large. Producing new versions of tests and new methods of scoring them is expensive and annoying for customers, and does not happen very often. Meanwhile, research may have revealed serious limitations.

In response to the inherently unscientific nature of copyrighted tests, Goldberg has produced a website in which he places in the public domain over 1200 personality items which can be grouped into scales to create measures equivalent to those found in many of the well-known copyrighted tests (ipip.ori.org/) Goldberg provides the necessary statistics to demonstrate which personality constructs these alternative scales assess, and not infrequently the new scales outperform those on which they are modelled (Goldberg in press)

This new development should improve the quality of personality tests, and may lead to a more equal and informed relationship between the tester and those tested as a result of test-takers having easy access via the internet to information about the purpose of a test and how it is scored.

Nature versus nurture

Over the last 20 years, the pendulum has swung towards the nature side of the nature–nurture debate in personality development and, as with the behavioural consistency problem, the nature–nurture debate has become much more complicated. Behaviour is the result of the complex interplay of traits and situations. Similarly, behaviour is the result of the complex interplay of nature and nurture, with genes implicated in both (Plomin 1994)

An accumulation of evidence from family, twin and adoption studies has led to the conclusion that approximately 40 per cent of the variation in personality is genetic (Plomin et al. 1990) Contrary to the wisdom encapsulated in newspaper headlines, personality traits are unlikely to each be determined by a single gene. It is much more likely that there are polygenic influences on personality. With advances in molecular genetics permitting the study of individuals' actual DNA, the variance attributed to genetic factors inferred from family, twin and adoption studies can now be studied at the physiological level.

Changing personalities

The genetic foundation to personality suggests immutability, and, according to McCrae and Costa (1990), adult personality is stable and does not change after

30 years of age. However, others have evidence for the malleability of personality in adulthood (e.g. Helson and Wink 1992)

Which is right? Is personality stable or does it change? The answer is: it depends what you mean by personality. Personality as defined by trait scores (e.g. the Big Five) appears to remain relatively stable in adulthood. The median correlation for measures of the Big Five assessed across time points of three to 30 years apart is $r = 0.65$ (Costa and McCrae 1994)

Those who advocate different personality units, such as life tasks, personal strivings, or even the study of entire biographies, are more likely to assert that personality changes (McAdams 1994) Genetics and life circumstances may place limits on personality, but within these limits there is room for growth and adaptation. Life events such as parenthood provide an opportunity for new facets of personality to emerge, such as playfulness or a sense of responsibility. On the negative side, an emotionally stable person may become more neurotic as a consequence of worrying about a problem child. Moreover, for those aspects of personality that are linked to self-presentation and are therefore socially constructed, such as friendliness or conformity, we have the power to influence how we appear to others by modifying this self-presentation (Hampson, 1988) For a deeper examination of these issues, an excellent airing of the various arguments concerning personality stability versus change is to be found in Heatherton and Weinberger (1994)

References

Ajzen, I. (1988) *Attitudes, Personality and Behaviour.* Milton Keynes: Open University Press.

Barrick, M.R. and Mount, M.K. (1991) 'The Big Five personality dimensions and job performance: a meta-analysis' *Personnel Psychology* 44: 1–26.

Biesanz, J.C., West, S.G. and Graziano, W.G. (1998) 'Moderators of self-other agreement: reconsidering temporal stability in personality', *Journal of Personality and Social Psychology* 75: 467–77.

Block, J. (1995) 'A contrarian view of the Five-Factor approach to personality description', *Psychological Bulletin* 117: 187–215.

Buss, D.M. and Cantor, N. (1989) *Personality Psychology: recent trends and emerging directions.* New York: Springer-Verlag.

Cantor, N and Kihlstrom, J.K. (1987) *Personality and Social Intelligence.* New York: Prentice-Hall.

Cattell, R.B., Eber, H. and Tatsuoka, M.M. (1970) *Handbook for the Sixteen Personality Factor Questionnaire (16PF).* Champaign, IL: Institute for Personality and Ability Testing.

Costa, P.T. and McCrae, R.R. (1994) 'Set like plaster! Evidence for the stability of adult personality', in T.F. Heatherton and J.L. Weinbeiger (Eds) *Can Personality Change?* Washington, DC: American Psychological Association.

Digman, J.M. (1990) 'Personality structure: emergence of the five-factor model', *Annual Review of Psychology* 41: 417–446.

Emmons, R.A. (1986) 'Personal strivings: an approach to personality and subjective well-being', *Journal of Personality and Social Psychology* 51: 1058–68.

Eysenck, H.J. (1991) 'Dimensions of personality: 16, 5, or 3? Criteria for a taxonomic paradigm', *Personality and Individual Differences* 12 773–90.

Goldberg, L.R. (1993) 'The structure of phenotypic personality traits', *American Psychologist* 48: 26–34.

Goldberg, L.R. (in press) 'A broad-bandwidth, public domain, personality inventory measuring the lower-level facets of several five-factor models', in I. Mervielde, I. Deary, F. De Fruyt and F. Ostendorf (Eds) *Personality Psychology in Europe*, vol. 7. Tilburg: Tilburg University Press.

Goldberg, L.R. and Rosolack, T.K. (1994) 'The Big Five factor structure as an integrative framework: an empirical comparison with Eysenck's P-E-N model', In C.F. Halverson Jr., G.A. Kohnstamm and R.P. Martin (Eds) *The Developing Structure of Temperament and Personality from Infancy to Adulthood*. New York: Lawrence Eribaum.

Hampson, S.E. (1997) 'Determinants of inconsistent personality description: trait and target effects', *Journal of Personality* 65: 250–90.

Hampson, S.E. (1998) 'When is an inconsistency not an inconsistency? Trait reconciliation in personality description and impression formation', *Journal of Personality and Social Psychology* 74: 102–17.

Heatherton, T.F. and Weinberger, J.L. (Eds) (1994) *Can Personality Change?* Washington, DC: American Psychological Association.

Helson, R and Wink, P. (1992) 'Personality change in women from the early 40s to the early 50s', *Psychology and Ageing* 7: 46–55.

Hogan, R., Johnson, J. and Briggs, S. (Eds) (1997) *Handbook of Personality Psychology*. San Diego, CA: Academic Press.

Hunter, J.E. and Hunter, R.F. (1984) 'Validity and utility of alternative predictors of job performance', *Psychological Bulletin* 96: 72–98.

John, O.P. (1990) 'The "Big Five" taxonomy: dimensions of personality in the natural language and in questionnaires', in L.A. Pervin (Ed.) *Handbook of Personality: Theory and Research*. New York: Guildford Press.

Lay, C.H. (1997) 'Explaining lower-order traits through higher-order factors: the case of trait procrastination, conscientiousness, and the specificity dimensions', *European Journal of Personality* 11: 267–78.

McAdams, D.P. (1994) 'Can personality change? Levels of stability and growth in personality across the life span', in T.F. Heatherton and J. K. Weinberger (Eds) *Can Personality Change?* Washington, DC: American Psychological Association.

McAdams, D.P. (1996) 'Personality, modernity, and the storied self: a contemporary framework for studying persons', *Psychological Inquiry* 7: 295–321.

McCrae, R.R. and Costa, P.T. (1990) *Personality in Adulthood*. New York: Guildford Press.

McCrae, R.R. and Costa, P.T. (1997) 'Personality trait structure as a human universal', *American Psychologist* 52: 509–16.

Mischel, W. (1968) *Personality and Assessment*. New York: Wiley.

Mischel, W. (1973) 'Toward a cognitive social-learning reconceptualisation of personality', *Psychological Review* 80: 252–83.

Mischel, W. and Shoda, Y. (1995) 'A cognitive-affective system theory of personality: reconceptualising situations, dispositions, dynamics and invariance in personality structure', *Psychological Review* 102: 246–68.

Mischel, W and Shoda, Y. (1998) 'Reconciling processing dynamics and personality dispositions', *Annual Review of Psychology* 49: 229–58.

Nasby, W. and Read, N.W. (1997) 'The inner and outer voyages of a solo circumnavigator: an integrative case study', Special Issue, *Journal of Personality* 65: 757–1116.

Norem, J.K. (1989) 'Cognitive strategies as personality: effectiveness, specificity, flexibility, and change', in D.M. Buss and N. Cantor (Eds) *Personality Psychology: Recent Trends and Emerging Directions.* New York: Springer-Verlag.

Pervin, L.A. and John, O.P. (Eds) (in press) *Handbook of Personality Theory and Research.* Second edition. New York: Guildford Press.

Plomin, R. (1994) *Genetics and Experience: The Interplay between Nature and Nurture.* Thousand Oaks, CA: Sage.

Plomin, R., Chipur, H.M. and Loehlin, J.C. (1990) 'Behavioural genetics and personality', in L.A. Pervin (Eds) *Handbook of Personality Theory and Research.* New York: Guildford Press.

Winter, D.G., John, O.P., Stewart, A.J., Klohnen, E.C. and Duncan, L.E. (1998) 'Traits and motives: toward an integration of two traditions in personality research', *Psychological Review* 105: 230–50.

York, K.L. and John, O.P. (1992) 'The four faces of Eve: a typological analysis of women's personality at midlife', *Journal of Personality and Social Psychology* 63: 494–508.

Source: Edited extract from *Psychologist* 1999, 12(6): 284–8.

12 The Big Five versus the Myers-Briggs

Rowan Bayne

The 'Big Five' factor theory of personality dominates current research on personality traits while the Myers-Briggs Type Indicator is probably the most widely-used personality measure in occupational and counselling psychology. Both theories are highly relevant to job choice, job performance, training and development.

Five factor theory

There is considerable agreement about the current pre-eminence of the 'Big Five'. McAdams (1992) remarks that 'After decades of doubt and defensiveness, traits are back on top' (p. 329). However, the agreement is not completely unanimous (Waller and Ben-Porath 1987; Eysenck 1992) and there are problems in interpreting and naming the factors. Perhaps the most accepted terms are: Extraversion (factor one), Agreeableness (two), Conscientiousness (three), Neuroticism (four), and Openness or Intellect (five). The fifth factor is the most problematic. The corresponding MBTI term, Intuition (versus Sensing), may capture its meaning better; it is close to 'Imagination', mentioned in passing by Goldberg (1993, p. 30), and more neutral than Openness or Intellect.

The MBTI

Psychological type theory suggests that the four most important individual differences, arranged in pairs of opposites, are: Extraversion (E) versus Introversion (I), Sensing (S) versus Intuition (N), Thinking (T) versus Feeling (F), and Judging (J) versus Perceiving (P). The sixteen combinations of these four pairs – called preferences – give 16 types, e.g. ESFJ, ENFP. The MBTI results are given in letters and numbers, the latter indicating how clearly the respondent has chosen each preference.

Type theory assumes that one of the central four preferences (S, N, T or F) is the main characteristic in each personality. This preference is called the 'dominant function' and the other three the auxiliary, third and fourth functions. Usually the dominant is the most developed and comfortable to use, the auxiliary next most, and so on. The theory thus recognizes that people are fairly versatile in their behaviour, but claims that while most of us generally behave in accord with our own types (using our dominant and auxiliary preferences most of the time), we sometimes behave like some of the other types as well. However – and this is a key point – we do not generally do so with equal facility or fulfilment, either because those aspects of ourselves are not as developed or because they are not our 'true type' (Myers 1980; Myers and McCaulley, 1985).

The terms Extraversion etc. used in the MBTI and the underlying theory are taken from Jung (e.g. 1921/1971) and there is some controversy about how consistent the MBTI is with Jung's ideas (e.g. Garden 1991), and how much it matters. I see Jung's work as historically important and still a source of ideas, but the MBTI and Myers' approach as a considerable clarification and development. A major difference between the two lies in Jung's view of normal behaviour as heavily influenced by unconscious motives, and Garden (1991) criticizes the MBTI for not being Jungian enough in this respect. I think this quality of the MBTI and Myers' theory is a strength not a problem, and one supported well by research, e.g. Thorne and Gough (1991) and the study discussed in the next section.

McCrae and Costa's study

McCrae and Costa (1989a) gave their self-report and rating measures of the five factors and the standard form of the MBTI (Form G) to a large sample of the general population. The correlations (Table 12.1) between the Extraversion and Openness factors of their self-report measure and two of the four MBTI preferences (EI and SN) were as high as is likely in this kind of research, and there were substantial correlations between Agreeableness and Conscientiousness and the other two MBTI preferences. Correlations between ratings and the MBTI were lower but the same pattern (cf. Funder and Sneed 1993). The Neuroticism factor in five-factor theory does not have a counterpart in the standard MBTI. These results are very striking: two questionnaires developed in very different traditions (factor analysis and psychotherapy respectively) agree closely on four of the five most general personality variables (Dachowski 1987).

Table 12.1 Relationships between four of the Five Factors (self-report) and MBTI continuous scores

	Extraversion	*Openness*	*Agreeableness*	*Conscientious-ness*
EI	-0.69 (-0.74)			
SN		0.69 (0.72)		
TF			0.46 (0.44)	
JP				-0.46 (-0.49)

Note: $N = 468$ (201 men and 267 women).

Source: Part of Table 3, McCrae and Costa (1989a, p. 30).

McCrae and Costa (1989a) also attempted to test the validity of an aspect of MBTI types. They argued that 'The dominant function is the most highly developed, so the individual should show the clearest preference for it' (p. 27) i.e. the dominant function should have a higher number than the auxiliary in each person's MBTI results. They found that this was so only about half the time. Myers and McCaulley in the MBTI Manual (1985, p60) had earlier reported the same finding.

McCrae and Costa concluded: 'there is no evidence that MBTI types represent unique configurations; they merely summarise four additive main effects' (1989a, p.34). However, they were confusing two very different interpretations of the number results: clarity of choice and development. The number results are designed to measure the first of these, not the second: a result of T43 is a much clearer vote for Thinking than one of T7 but says nothing about which person is more skilful in Thinking or in Feeling. Further, taking one person's MBTI results e.g. E23 S11 T43 P21, it is tempting to say this person is more developed in T than S, but on the clearness of vote interpretation this is not so.

McCrae and Costa's error is understandable because the MBTI Manual (Myers and McCaulley 1985) is unclear on the number results, stating for example that the developmental interpretation is 'not necessarily correct' (p. 3), and 'The most frequent error that occurs when interpreting the numerical portion of MBTI scores is assuming that strength of preference implies excellence' (p. 58), but also that, 'According to theory the dominant will show a clearer preference than will the auxiliary' (p. 58). Moreover, the MBTI (as McCrae and Costa's main results confirm) functions well as a trait measure in the sense that it correlates strongly with other instruments which measure relevant traits.

A further distinction may help resolve this problem, between (1) behaving more in the ways indicated by the particular preference and type, and (2) behaving in more developed, more skilful ways. The number in MBTI results may measure the former more than the latter or high number results may be more informative than low ones. Alternatively, it may be more consistent with the MBTI's rationale and purpose – as a categorizing indicator which provides non-evaluative feedback – to ignore the numbers for most purposes.

Meaning and value of 'type'

'Type' is often used merely as a language of convenience, to describe groups on a dimension, while a more rigorous use implies some form of discontinuity, a difference in kind. Myers uses type in the latter, distinctive form sense – the MBTI is explicitly a categorizing measure. However, the MBTI types are also ideal types, i.e. intended to fit actual people to varying degrees and to help in understanding them, rather than to fit anyone perfectly. The question of whether type or dimensions is the most useful concept for describing personality is not usually asked (Gangestad and Snyder 1985), and most MBTI research so far has treated the MBTI as a measure of dimensions and ignored it as a type measure.

There are several approaches to testing the validity of the MBTI typology (e.g. Hicks 1984, 1985; Thorne and Gough 1991), e.g. the relationship predicted between the fourth function and reactions to high levels of stress (Barger 1992). The fourth function is the least developed, and appears (anecdotally) to take over at such times, in characteristic ways. These are summarized in Table 12.2. In each case, the person is seen as 'in the grip of' the behaviour and as if it is 'not really them'.

Table 12.2 Type and reactions to a high level of stress

Type	Fourth Function	Reaction
ISTJ/ISFJ ESFP/ESTP	N	See very gloomy possibilities, or feel doomed and trapped.
INTJ/INFJ ENFP/ENTP	S	Overdo something, e.g. make lots of long lists, overeat, or behave obsessively in some other way.
INTP/ISTP ESTJ/ENTJ	F	Emotional outbursts, or feel isolated and unloved.
ISFP/INFP ESFJ/ENFJ	T	Lots of analysing or very critical, or feel useless and incompetent.

Source: Adapted from Barger (1992) and Hirsh and Kummerow (1990 p. 10).

Personality description

McCrae and Costa (1989a) suggest that although the MBTI descriptions of personality are 'reasonably good', it may be better to reinterpret them in terms of the five-factor model, to include for example 'the antagonistic side of Thinking types and the lazy and disorganised side of Perceiving types' (1989a, p. 36). Type and five factor theory differ markedly in tone, as these examples imply. All five factors, except perhaps extraversion, have a positive and a negative end. In contrast, the MBTI descriptions are much more positive, indeed almost glowing, because each preference and type is described mainly in terms of its distinctive strengths.

Thus, someone with a preference for Perceiving (low Conscientiousness in Big Five terms) is described as 'flexible' and 'adaptable'. Of course, flexibility taken to an extreme becomes disorganization but, equally, extreme Conscientiousness becomes rigidity and obsessiveness rather than organization and self-discipline. The MBTI language, which describes aspects of personality in positive terms first, while adding in effect that strengths have weaknesses, and that strengths can be under and over-developed, is a much less threatening approach to understanding self and others than the Big Five's – even though it is describing much the same behaviours. Moreover, it also includes the idea, useful in giving and receiving feedback, that strengths tend to have corresponding weaknesses (e.g. Bayne 1993).

Conversely, five-factor terms may clarify and add to type descriptions. 'Agreeableness' for example seems to capture part of the meaning of 'Feeling'. Components of the primary constructs in each approach have also been distinguished: 30 facets for five-factor theory (Costa et al. 1991), 20 subscales for the Expanded Analysis Report (EAR) of the MBTI (Kummerow and Quenk 1992). Comparison at this finer level should also be useful. For example, the six facets for Extraversion in five-factor theory do not include equivalents of the subscales Expressive/Contained and Auditory/Visual in the EAR. 'Auditory' can be briefly described as more participative, preferring to speak and listen, 'visual' as more reflective, preferring to read and write.

Three further differences between the two approaches are related to the content of the descriptions. The first is the Big Five factor of Neuroticism, defined by McCrae and Costa as including 'the predisposition to experience negative affects ... and other cognitive and behavioral manifestations of emotional instability' (1989a, p. 23). It would detract too much from the MBTI's positive tone to include Neuroticism in standard-type descriptions. Second, type theory includes a model of personality development while five-factor theory – though it does provide an interesting perspective on personality change and counselling (Costa and McCrae 1986) – is mainly descriptive. Third, much more attention has been paid so far to interactions between the MBTI preferences than those between the five factors, both additive (numerous combinations are possible e.g. Myers and McCaulley 1985, pp. 31–8) and dynamic (e.g. Quenk 1993).

Conclusions

1. The MBTI's validity as a measure of four major personality factors or traits is considerably strengthened by its relationship with the Big Five.
2. The MBTI's validity as a measure of type is a separate issue, not addressed successfully by McCrae and Costa (1989a) because they, like others, misused the number part of the MBTI results as measures of development. What the number scores do mean may be worth clarifying and testing further.
3. The MBTI personality descriptions are much more positive in 'tone' than those of five-factor theory. The benefits and costs of this in various settings are worth investigating.
4. Both the MBTI and five-factor theory can gain from close study of each other's descriptions. When McCrae and Costa (1989b, p 452) write that the MBTI descriptions 'would be even more valuable' if reinterpreted in terms of five-factor theory, they ignore the opposite possibility.

References

Barger, N. (1992) *Type and Stress*. Annual Conference of the British Association for Psychological Type, Manchester.

Bayne, R. (1993) 'Psychological type, conversations and counselling', in R. Bayne and P. Nicholson (Eds) *Counselling and Psychology for Health Professionals*, London: Chapman and Hall.

Costa, P.T. and McCrae, R.R. (1986) 'Personality stability and its implications for clinical psychology', *Clinical Psychology Review* 6(5): 407–23.

Costa, P.T., McCrae, R.R. and Dye, D.A. (1991) 'Facet scales for Agreeableness and Conscientiousness: a revision of the NEO Personality Inventory', *Personality and Individual Differences* 12: 887–98.

Dachowski, M. MCC. (1987) 'A convergence of the tender-minded and the tough-minded?', *American Psychologist* 42: 886–7.

Eysenck, H.J. (1992) 'Four ways five factors are not basic', *Personality and Individual Differences* 13(6): 667–73.

Funder, D.C. and Sneed, C.D. (19930 'Behavioral manifestations of personality: an ecological approach to judgmental accuracy', *Journal of Personality and Social Psychology* 64(3): 479–90.

Gangestad, S. and Snyder, M. (1985) 'To carve Nature at its joint: on the existence of discrete classes in personality', *Psychological Review* 92(3): 317–49.

Garden, A-M. (1991) 'Unresolved issues with the Myers-Briggs Type Indicator', *Journal of Psychological Type* 22: 3–14.

Goldberg, L.R. (1992) 'The development of markers for the big-five factor structure', *Psychological Assessment* 4(1): 26–42.

Goldberg, L.R. (1993) 'The structure of phenotypic personality traits', *American Psychologist* 48(1): 26–34.

Hicks, L.E. (1984) 'Conceptual and empirical analysis of some assumptions of an explicitly typological theory', *Journal of Personality and Social Psychology* 46(5): 1118–31.

Hicks, L.E. (1985) 'Dichotomies and typologies: summary and implications', *Journal of Psychological Type* 10: 11–13.

Hirsh, S.K. and Kummerow, J.M. (1990) *Introduction to Type in Organizations*, 2nd edn. Palo Alto, CA: Consulting Psychologists Press.

Jung, C.G. (1927/1971) *Psychological Types*. London: Routledge.

Kummerow, J.M. and Quenk, N.L. (1992) *Interpretive Guide for the MBTI Expanded Analysis Report*. Palo Alto, CA: Consulting Psychologists Press.

McAdams, D.P. (1992) 'The five-factor model in personality: a critical appraisal', *Journal of Personality* 60(2): 329–61.

McCrae, R.R. and Costa, P.T. (1989a) 'Reinterpreting the Myers-Briggs Type Indicator from the perspective of the five factor model of personality', *Journal of Personality* 57(1): 17–37.

McCrae, R.R. and Costa, P.T. (1989b) 'More reasons to adopt the five-factor model', *American Psychologist* 44(2): 451–2.

Myers, I.B. (1980) *Gifts Differing*. Palo Alto, CA: Consulting Psychologists Press.

Myers, I.B. and McCaulley, M.H. (1985) *Manual: A Guide to the Development and Use of the Myers-Briggs Type Indicator*. Palo Alto, CA: Consulting Psychologists Press.

Quenk, N.L. (1993) *Beside Myself: The Inferior Function in Everyday Life*. Palo Alto, CA: Consulting Psychologists Press.

Rawling, K. (1992) *Introverting and Extraverting the Functions: The Cambridge Type Inventory.* Annual Conference of the British Association for Psychological Type, Manchester.

Thorne, A. and Gough, H. (1991) *Portraits of Type.* Palo Alto, CA: Consulting Psychologists Press.

Waller, N.G. and Ben-Porath, Y.S. (1987) 'Is it time for clinical psychology to embrace the five-factor model of personality?', *American Psychologist* 42: 887–9.

York, K.L. and John, O.P. (1992) 'The four faces of Eve: a typological analysis of women's personality at mid-life', *Journal of Personality and Social Psychology* 63(3): 494–508.

Source: *Psychologist*, 1994, 7(1): 14–16.

13 Adaptors and Innovators: why new initiatives get blocked

Michael J. Kirton

Background

The Adaption–Innovation theory defines and measures two styles of decision making (Kirton 1976, 1977, 1980) clarifying earlier literature on problem solving and creativity which concentrates more on defining and assessing *level* rather than *style*. This shift of emphasis has advantages in the practical world of business, commerce and administration.

According to the Adaption–Innovation theory, everyone can be located on a continuum ranging from highly adaptive according to their score on the Kirton Adaption–Innovation Inventory. The range of responses is relatively fixed and stable (Kirton 1977),[1] and in the general population approaches the normal curve distribution. For the purpose of clarity the following descriptions characterize those individuals at the extreme ends of the continuum.

Adaptors characteristically produce a sufficiency of ideas,[2] based closely on, but stretching, existing agreed definitions of the problem and likely solutions. They look at these in detail and proceed within the established mores (theories, policies, practices) of their organizations. Much of their effort to change is in improving and 'doing better' (which tends to dominate management , e.g. Drucker 1969).

Innovators, by contrast, are more likely in the pursuit of change to reconstruct the problem, separating it from its enveloping accepted thought, paradigms and customary viewpoints, and emerge with much less expected and probably less acceptable solutions (see Figure 13.1). They are less concerned with 'doing things better' than with 'doing things differently'.

The development of the A–I theory began with observations made and the conclusions reached as a result of a study of management initiative (Kirton 1961). The aim of this study was to investigate the ways in which ideas had led to radical changes in the companies studied were developed and implemented.

In each of the examples of initiative studied the resulting changes had required the co-operation of many managers and others in more than one department.

Numerous examples of successful 'corporate' initiative, such as the introduction of a new product or new accounting procedures, were examined, and this analysis highlighted the stages through which such initiative passed on the way to becoming part of the accepted routine of the company, i.e. perception of the problem, analysis of the problem, analysis of the solution,

Adaptor	Innovator
Characterized by precision, reliability, efficiency, methodicalness, prudence, discipline, conformity	Seen as undisciplined, thinking tangentially, approaching tasks from unsuspected angles
Concerned with resolving problems rather than finding them	Could be said to discover problems and discover avenues of solution
Seeks solutions to problems in tried and understood ways	Queries problems' concomitant assumptions; manipulates problems
Reduces problems by improvement and greater efficiency, with maximum of continuity and stability	Is catalyst to settled groups, irreverent of their consensual views; seen as abrasive, creating dissonance
Seen as sound, conforming, safe, dependable	Seen as unsound, impractical; often shocks his opposite
Liable to make goals of means	In pursuit of goals treats accepted means with little regard
Seems impervious to boredom, seems able to maintain high accuracy in long spells of detailed work	Capable of detailed routine (system maintenance) work for only short bursts; quick to delegate routine tasks
Is in authority within given structures	Tends to take control in unstructured situations
Challenges rules rarely, cautiously, when assured of strong support	Often challenges rules, has little respect for past custom
Tends to high self-doubt. Reacts to criticism by closer outward conformity. Vulnerable to social pressures and authority; compliant	Appears to have low self-doubt when generating ideas, not needing consensus to maintain certitude in face of opposition
Is essential to the functioning of the institution all the time, but occasionally needs to be 'dug out' of his or her systems	In the institution is ideal in unscheduled crises, or better still to help to avoid them, if he or she can be controlled
When collaborating with innovators: Supplies stability, order and continuity to the partnership	*When collaborating with adaptors:* Supplies the task orientations, the break with the past and accepted theory
Sensitive to people, maintains group cohesion and co-operation	Appears insensitive to people, often threatens group cohesion and co-operation
Provides a safe base for the innovator's riskier operations	Provides the dynamics to bring about periodic radical change, without which institutions tend to ossify

Source: Originally published in Kirton (1976)

Figure 13.1 Behaviour descriptions of adaptors and innovators

agreement to change, acceptance of change, delegation and finally implementation.

The study also looked at what went wrong at these various stages, and how the development of a particular initiative was thus affected. From this, a number of anomalies were thrown up that at the time remained unexplained.

1) Delays in introducing change

Despite the assertion of managers that they were collectively both sensitive to the need for changes and willing to embark on them, the time lag between the first public airing of most of the ideas studied, and the date on which an idea was clearly accepted as a possible course of action, was a matter of years – usually two or three. Conversely, a few were accepted almost immediately, with the bare minimum of in-depth analysis. (The size of proposed changes did not much affect this timescale, although all the changes studied were large.)

2) Objections to new ideas

All too often, the new idea had been formally blocked by a series of well-argued and reasoned objections which were upheld until some critical event – a 'precipitating event' – occurred, so that none of these quondam, cogent contrary arguments (lack of need, lack of resource, etc.) was ever heard again. Indeed, it appeared at times as if management had been hit by almost total collective amnesia concerning past objections.

3) Rejection of individuals

There was a marked tendency for the majority of ideas which encountered opposition and delays to have been put forward by managers who were themselves unacceptable to an 'establishment' group, not just before, but also after the ideas they advocated had not only become accepted, but even been rated highly successful. At the same time, other managers putting forward the more palatable ideas not only were themselves initially acceptable, but remained so, even if these ideas were later rejected or failed.

The A–I theory offers a rational, measured explanation of these findings.

Adaptors and innovators – two different styles of thinking

Adaptive solutions are those that depend directly and obviously on generally agreed paradigms, are more easily grasped intellectually, and therefore more readily accepted by most – by adaptors as well as the many innovators not so directly involved in the resolution of the problem under scrutiny. The familiar assumptions on which the solution depends are not under attack, and help 'butter' the solution advanced, making it more palatable. Such derived ideas, being more readily acceptable, favourably affect the status of their authors, often even when they fail – and the authors of such ideas are much more likely to be themselves adaptors, characterized as being personally more acceptable to the 'establishment' with whom they share those underlying familiar assumptions (Kirton 1976). Indeed, almost irrespective of their rank, they are likely to be part of that establishment, which in the past has led innovators to claim somewhat crudely that adaptors owe their success to agreeing with their bosses. However, Kirton (1977a) conducted a study in which KAI scores were compared with superior/subordinate identification in a sample of 93 middle managers. No connection was found between KAI scores and tendency to agree with one's bosses. Instead a more subtle relationship is suggested, i.e. that those in the upper hierarchy are more likely to accept the same paradigms as their adaptor juniors, and that there is, therefore, a greater chance of agreement between them on broad issues and on approved courses of action. Where they disagree on detail within the accepted paradigm, innovators may be inclined to attach less significance to this and view the broad agreements reached as simple conformity.

It can thus be seen how failure of ideas is less damaging to the adaptor than to the innovator, since any erroneous assumptions upon which ideas were based were also shared with colleagues and other influential people. The consequence is that such failure is more likely to be written off as 'bad luck' or due to 'unforeseeable events', thereby directing the blame away from the individuals concerned.

In stark contrast to this, innovative ideas, not being as closely related to the group's prevailing, relevant paradigms, and even opposing such consensus views, are more strongly resisted, and their originators are liable to be treated with suspicion and even derision. This rejection of individuals tends to persist even after their ideas are adopted and acknowledged as successful. (It should be noted that both these and the further descriptions to come are put in a rather extreme form (as heuristic device) and usually therefore occur in a somewhat less dramatic form.)

Differences in behaviour

Evidence is now accumulating from a number of studies that *personality* is implicated in these characteristic differences between adaptors and innovators (Kirton 1976, 1977; Carne and Kirton 1982). Indeed it must be so, since the way in which one thinks affects the way in which one behaves, and is seen to behave, in much the same way as there are differences in personality characteristics between those who are left brain dominated and those who are right brain dominated – the former being described as tending towards methodical, planned thinking and the latter towards more intuitive thinking (there is a significant correlation between left–right brain preference scores and adaption–innovation (Torrance 1982)). The personality characteristics of adaptors and innovators that are part of their cognitive style are here described.

Innovators are generally seen by adaptors as being abrasive and insensitive, despite the former's denial of these traits. This misunderstanding usually occurs because the innovator attacks the adaptor's theories and assumptions, both explicitly when he feels that the adaptor needs a push to hurry him in the right direction or to get him out of his rut, and implicitly by showing a disregard for the rules, conventions, standards of behaviour, etc. What is even more upsetting for the adaptor is the fact that the innovator does not even seem to be aware of the havoc he is causing. Innovators may also appear abrasive to each other, since neither will show much respect for the other's theories, unless of course their two points of view happen temporarily to coincide. Adaptors can also be viewed pejoratively by innovators, suggesting that the more extreme types are far more likely to disagree than collaborate. Innovators tend to see adaptors as stuffy and unenterprising, wedded to systems, rules and norms which, however useful, are too restricting for their (the innovators) liking. Innovators seem to overlook how much of the smooth running of all around them depends on good adaptiveness but are acutely aware of the less acceptable face of efficient bureaucracy (Weber 1970; Merton 1957). Disregard of convention when in pursuit of their own ideas has the effect of isolating innovators in a similar way to Rogers' (1957) creative loner.

While innovators find it difficult to combine with others, adaptors find it easier. The latter will more rapidly establish common agreed ground, assumptions, guidelines and accepted practices on which to ground their collaboration. Innovators also have to do these things in order to fit at all into a company but they are less good at doing so, less concerned with finding out the anomalies within a system, and less likely to stick to the patterns they help form. This is at once the innovators' weakness and a source of potential advantage.

Where are the innovators and the adaptors?

Much of Kirton's earlier research was devoted to the description and classification of these two cognitive styles. More recently, attention has been focused on the issue of how they are distributed and whether any distinctive patterns emerge. It has been found from a large number of studies that KAI scores are by no means haphazardly distributed. Individuals' scores are derived from a 32-item inventory, giving a theoretical range of 32–160, and a mean of 96. The observed range is slightly more restricted, 46–146, based on over 1000 subjects; the observed mean is near to 95 and the distribution conforms almost exactly to a normal curve. The studies have also shown that variations by identifiable subsets are predictable, their means shifting from the population mean in accordance with the theory. However, the group's range of scores is rarely restricted – even smallish groups showing ranges of approximately 70–120 – a finding with important implications for change, against the background of differences found at cultural level, at organizational level, between jobs, between departments and between individuals within departments. This is a somewhat arbitrary grouping since norms of cognitive style can be detected wherever a group of people define themselves as differing or distinct from others, by whatever criteria they choose, be it type of work, religion, philosophy, etc. However, while allowing for a certain amount of overlap, the majority of research studies can be classified according to these groupings.

Innovators and adaptors in different cultures

A considerable amount of research information has been accumulating regarding the extent to which mean scores of different samples shift from culture to culture. For example, published normative samples collected from Britain (Kirton 1976, 1977, 1980; Kirton and Pender 1982), USA (Keller and Holland 1978), Canada (Kirton 1980), and New Zealand (Kirton 1978) have all produced remarkably similar means. When the KAI was validated on a sample of Eastern managers from Singapore and Malaysia (Thomson 1980) their mean scores of 95 were compatible with those of their Western counterparts (e.g. UK managerial sample had a mean of 97; compared to general UK samples which together yielded a mean of 95.3).

However, samples of Indian and Iranian managers yielded lower means (91) than similar samples in the UK, USA, Canada and Singapore (Dewan 1982, Hossiani 1981, Khaneja 1982)). More adaptive norms were also found in work still in progress in a sample of black South African business students (Pottas). These differences may not simply be a split between Western and Chinese Western groups versus others, since tentative results from a sample of Flemish-speaking job applicants for professional posts in a leading Belgian pharmaceutical company (Peeters) have yielded an even more adaptive mean (85.6) than that of the South African sample.[3] Clearly there may be cultural differences of adaptor–innovator norms.

There is also a further speculation put forward by Kirton (1978a) that people who are most willing to cross boundaries of any sort are likely to be more innovative, and the more boundaries there are and the more rigidly they are held, the higher the innovative score should be of those who cross. In the Thomson study managers in Western-owned companies in Singapore scored higher in innovativeness then either those working for a private local company or those in the Civil Service, and those in this last category had the most adaptive scores of the triad. Further evidence for cultural differences emerges in work on Indian and Iranian managers (Dewan 1982; Hossaini 1981; Khaneja 1982). Here, it was found that, as expected, entrepreneurs scored higher on the KAI than non-entrepreneurs (97.9 and 90.5 as opposed to 77.2 for Government Officers), but Indian women entrepreneurial managers were found to be even more innovative than their male counterparts. They had to cross two boundaries: they broke with tradition by becoming a manager in the first place, and they had succeeded in becoming a manager in a risky entrepreneurial business.

Innovators and adaptors in different organizations

Organizations in general (Weber, Gerth and Mills 1970; Bakke 1965; Mulkay 1972) and especially organizations which are large in size and budget (Swatez 1970; Veblen 1928) have a tendency to encourage bureaucracy and adaptation in order to minimize risk. It has been said by Weber (1970), Merton (1957) and Parsons (1951) that the aims of a bureaucratic structure are precision, reliability and efficiency, and that the bureaucratic structure exerts constant pressure on officials to be methodical, prudent and disciplined, and to attain an unusual degree of conformity. These are the qualities that the adaptor–innovator theory attributes to the 'adaptor' personality. For the marked adaptor, the longer an institutional practice has existed, the more he feels it can be taken for granted. So when confronted by a problem, he does not see it as a stimulus to question or change the structure in which the problem is embedded, but seeks a solution within that structure, in ways already tried and understood – ways which are safe, sure, predictable. He can be relied upon to carry out a thorough, disciplined search for ways to eliminate problems by 'doing things better' with a minimum of risk and a maximum of continuity and stability. This behaviour contrasts strongly with that of the marked innovator. The latter's solution, because it is less understood, and its assumption untested, appears more risky, less sound, involves more 'ripple-effect' changes in areas less obviously needing to be affected; in short, it brings about changes with outcomes that cannot be envisaged so precisely. This diminution of predictive certainty is unsettling and not to be undertaken lightly, if at all, by most people – but particularly by adaptors, who feel not only more loyal to consensus policy but less willing to jeopardize the integrity of the system (or even the institution). The innovator, in contrast to the adaptor, is liable to be less respectful of the views of others, more abrasive in the presentation of his solution, ore at home in a turbulent environment, seen initially as less relevant in his thinking towards company needs (since his perceptions may differ as to what is needed), less concerned with people in the pursuit of his goals than adaptors readily tolerate. Tolerance of the innovator is thinnest when adaptors feel under pressure from the need for imminent radical change. Yet the innovators' very disadvantages to institutions make them as necessary as the adaptors' virtues in turn make them.

Every organization has its own particular 'climate', and at any given time most of its key individuals reflect the general outlook. They gradually communicate this to others in the organization, and in time due to recruitment, turnover and such processes the cognitive style will reflect the general organizational ethos. However, the range seems to remain unaffected, and this is critical when one wishes to consider who might be the potential agents for a change in the mode of the whole group.

Sufficient evidence has been collected to enable predictions to be made about not only the direction of, but the extent to which these shifts in KAI mean will occur from organization to organization. For example, Kirton (1977, 1980) hypothesized that the mean scores of managers who work in a particularly stable environment will incline more towards adaption, while the mean scores of those whose environment could be described as turbulent will tend towards innovation. This hypothesis was supported by Thomson (1980), whose study showed that a Singapore sample of middle-ranking Civil Servants were markedly adaptor-inclined (mean = 89) whereas the means of a sample of managers in multi-national companies were just as markedly innovator-inclined (mean = 107).

A dissertation by Holland (1982) suggests that bank employees are inclined to be adaptors; so are local government employees (Hayward and Everett 1983). Two of these studies support and refine the hypothesis that, given time, the mean KAI score of a group will reflect its ethos. Both Holland and Hayward and Everett found the groups of new recruits had means away from those of the established groups they were joining. However, within 3 (Holland) or at most 5 (Hayward and Everett) years, as a result of staff changes, the gaps between the means of the new groups and the established groups narrowed sharply.

If there are predictable variations between companies wherever selection has been allowed to operate for a sufficient length of time, then variations may be expected within a company as adaptors and innovators are placed in the parts of the organization which suit them best. It is unlikely (as well as undesirable), that any organization is so monolithic in its structure and in the 'demands' on its personnel that it produces a total conformity of personality profiles. This hypothesis was tested and supported by Kirton (1980) when adaptors were found to be more at home in departments of a company that must concentrate on solving problems which mainly emanate from within their departmental system (e.g. production) and innovators tend to be more numerous in departments that acts as interfaces (e.g. sales, progress chasing). Studies by Keller and Holland (1978, 1978a, 1979) in American R & D departments found that adaptors and innovators had different roles in internal company communications: adaptors being more valued for communications on the workings of the company and innovators being more valued for communications on advanced technological information (Keller and Holland 1979). Kirton (1980, 1980a) also found that managers who tend to select themselves to go on courses (i.e. selected) will have significantly different mean KAI scores from the managers on courses who were just sent as part of the general scheme (i.e. personally unselected), the former being innovator-inclined. Members of three groups of courses were tested: one British 'unselected', one British 'selected' and one Canadian 'selected'. The results (Kirton 1980a) showed that the unselected managers scored significantly more adaptively than the selected groups. Among the Canadian sample of managers, there was sufficient information on their job titles to be able to divide them into two groups of occupations: those liable to be found in adaptor-oriented departments (e.g. line manager) and those liable to be found in innovator-oriented departments (e.g. personnel consultant). The latter group were found to be significantly more innovative than the former, having a mean of 116.4 for non-line managers as opposed to a mean of 100.14 for line managers.[4] These findings later led to a full-scale study (Kirton and Pender 1982) in which data on 2375 subjects collected in 15 independent studies were cross-tabulated with reference to different occupational types and varying degrees of self-selection to courses. Engineering instructors and apprentices were studied as examples of occupations involving a narrow range of paradigms, thorough rigid training and closely structured environment, while research and development personnel were examined as examples of occupations involving a number of flexible paradigms and a relatively unstructured environment. The differences were large, significant and in the expected direction.

These variations which exist between companies and between occupational groups are also found within the relatively narrow boundaries of the job itself. For example, work in progress suggests that within a job there may be clear subsets whose tasks differ and whose cognitive styles differ, e.g. an examination of the job of quality control workers for a local government body revealed that the job contained two major aspects. One was the vital task of monitoring, and one was the task of solving anomalies which were thrown up in the system from time to time. The first of these tasks was carried out by an adaptive inclined group, and the second by an innovative one.

Such knowledge about jobs and who is inclined to do them could eventually lead to better integration of adaptors and innovators within a company.

Who are the change agents?

It has already been noted that the mean adaptor–innovator score of a group may shift quite considerably depending on the population in question, whilst the range remains relatively stable. This suggests that many a person is part of a group whose mean adaptor–innovator score is markedly different from his own. There are three possible reasons why these individuals should be caught up in this potentially stressful situation:

(a) they are in transit, for example, under training schemes;
(b) they are trapped and unhappy and may soon leave (Holland 1982, Hayward and Everett 1983);
(c) they have found a niche which suits them and have developed a particular role identity.

(These three categories should be regarded as fluid, since given a change in the individual's peer group, boss, department or even organizational outlook, he may well find himself shifting from one category to another.)

It is the identification of the third category which will most repay further investigation since it contains refinements of the A–I theory which have considerable practical implications, though these are as yet speculations and work is currently being undertaken to explore their ramifications more fully.

The individual who can successfully accept and be accepted into an environment alien to his own cognitive style must have particular survival characteristics, and it is those characteristics which make him a potential agent for change within that particular group. In order to effect a change an individual must first have job 'know-how' which is also an important quality keeping him functioning as a valuable group member when major changes are not needed. He must also be able to gain the respect of his colleagues and superiors, and with this comes commensurate status, which is essential if he wants his ideas to be recognized. Lastly, if a person is embarked on a course of action for change, he will of course require the general capacity, e.g. leadership, management qualities, to carry out such a task. His different cognitive style gives him a powerful advantage over his colleagues in being able to anticipate events which others may not see (since due to their cognitive styles, they may not think to look in that direction).

Therefore, the agent for change can be seen as a competent individual who has enough skill to be successful in a particular environment (which he may in fact have made easier by selecting or being selected for tasks within the unit less alien to his or her cognitive style). At this point he plays a supportive role to the main thrust of the group with its contrasting cognitive style. Given a 'precipitating event' however (particularly if he has anticipated and prepared for it), the individual becomes at once a potential leader in a new situation. In order to be able to take advantage of this position, he must have personal qualities to bring to bear, management must have the insight to recognize the position, and management development must have also played its part. However, this may need to be reinforced by individual and group counselling which makes use of an understanding of Adaption–Innovation theory (Lindsay, Davies).

It should be emphasized here that the change agent can be either an adaptor or an innovator, and this is solely determined by the group composition, so that if it is an innovator group, the change agent will be an adaptor, and vice versa. This discovery challenges traditional assumptions that heralding and initiating change is the innovator's prerogative because a precipitating event could demand either an adaptive or innovative solution, depending on the original orientation of the group and the work. An example in which an adaptor is the change agent in a team of innovators might be where the precipitating event takes the form of a bank's refusal to give further financial support to a new business enterprise. At this stage the change agent (who may have been anticipating this event for months) is at hand with the facts, figures and a cost- cutting contingency plan all neatly worked out. It is now that the personal qualities of know-how, respect, status and ability will be crucial for success. All this assumes that many groups will have means away from the centre. It seems likely that the more the mean is displaced in either direction, the harder it will be, the bigger the precipitating event needed, to pull the group back to the middle, which may be unfortunate both for the group and change agent. However, an 'unbalanced' team is what may be required at any particular time. To hold such a position and yet to be capable of flexibility is a key task of management to which this theory may make a contribution.

In a wider context, it is hoped that the Adaption–Innovation theory will offer an insight into the interactions between the individual, the organization and change. By using the theory as an additional informational resource when forward planning, it may also be possible to anticipate, and retain control in the face of changes brought about by extraneous factors. This hopefully will enable such changes to take place amid less imbalance and confusion, thereby rendering them more effective.

Notes

1. Test–retest coefficients of 0.82 for 6th formers ($N = 412$) on one New Zealand study after 8 months (Kirton 1978); South African study after 5 months on $N = 143$, means: 91.19, S.D. 9.31; and 91.10, S.D. 8.52 (Pottas unpublished).
2. Factor analyses show that total adaptor–innovator scores are composed of three traits: sufficiency versus proliferation of originality; degree of (personal) efficiency and degree of group-rule conformity. They are closely related respectively to Rogers' creative loner, and Weber's and Merton's typical bureaucratic behaviour.
3. Caution: based on a Dutch version of KAI which is still being tested.
4. Because of the nature of this course and selection system, both groups' means were displaced towards innovativeness; however, they retain their distance *vis-à-vis* each other.

References

Bakke, E.W. (1965) 'Concept of the social organisation', in M. Haire (Ed.) *Modern Organisation Theory*. New York: Wiley.

Carne, J.C. and Kirton, M.J. (1982) 'Styles of creativity: test score correlations between the Kirton Adaption–Innovation Inventory and the Myers-Briggs Type Indicator', *Psychological Reports* 50: 31–6.

Davies, G.B. Unpublished data (in preparation), Cambridge Management Centre.

Dewan, S. (1982) 'Personality characteristics of entrepreneurs', PhD Thesis, Institute of Technology: Delhi.

Hayward, G. and Everett, C. (1983) 'Adaptors and innovators: data from the Kirton Adaption–Innovation Inventory in a local authority setting', *Journal of Occupational Psychology* 56: 339–42.

Holland, P.A. (1982) 'Creative thinking: an asset of liability in employment', MEd Dissertation, University of Manchester.

Hossaini, H.R. (1981) 'Leadership effectiveness and cognitive style among Iranian and Indian middle managers', PhD Thesis, Institute of Technology: Delhi.

Keller, R.T. and Holland, W.E. (1978) 'A cross-validation study of the Kirton Adaption-Innovation Inventory in three research and development organizations', *Applied Psychological Measurement* 2: 563–70.

Keller, R.T. and Holland, W.E. (1978a) 'Individual characteristics of innovativeness and communication in research and development organisations', *Journal of Applied Psychology* 63: 759–62.

Keller, R.T. and Holland, W.E. (1979) 'Towards a selection battery for research and development professional employees', *IEEE Transactions on Engineering Management* EM-26(4) November.

Khaneja, D.K. (1982) 'Relationship of the adaption–innovation continuum to achievement orientation in entrepreneurs and non-entrepreneurs', PhD Thesis, Institute of Technology: Delhi.

Kirton, M.J. (1961) *Management Initiative.* London: Acton Society Trust.

Kirton, M.J. (1976) 'Adaptors and innovators: a description and measure', *Journal of Applied Psychology* 61: 622–29.

Kirton, M.J. (1977) *Manual of the Kirton Adaption-Innovation Inventory.* London: National Foundation for Educational Research.

Kirton, M.J. (1977a) 'Adaptors and innovators and superior-subordinate identification', *Psychological Reports* 41: 289–90.

Kirton, M.J. (1978) 'Have adaptors and innovators equal levels of creativity?', *Psychological Reports* 42: 695–98.

Kirton, M.J. (1978a) 'Adaptors and innovators in culture clash', *Current Anthropology* 19: 611–12.

Kirton, M.J. (1980) 'Adaptors and innovators: the way people approach problems', *Planned Innovation* 3: 51–4.

Kirton, M.J. (1980a) 'Adaptors and innovators in organizations', *Human Relations* 3: 213–24.

Kirton, M.J. and Pender, S.R. (1982) 'The adaption–innovation continuum: occupational type and course selection', *Psychological Reports* 51: 883–6.

Lindsay, P. Unpublished data (in press), Cambridge Management Centre.

Merton, R.K. (Ed.) (1957) 'Bureaucratic structure and personality', in *Social Theory and Social Structure.* New York: Free Press of Glencoe.

Mulkay, M.S. (1972) *The Social Process of Innovation.* London: Macmillan.

Parsons, T. (1951) *The Social System.* New York: Free Press of Glencoe.

Peeters, L. Unpublished data, Janssen Pharmaceutical, Belgium.

Pottas, C.D. Unpublished data, University of Pretoria, South Africa.

Rogers, C.R. (1957) 'Towards a theory of creativity', in H.H. Anderson (Ed.), *Creativity And Its Cultivation.* New York: Harper.

Swatez, G.M. (1980) 'The social organisation of a university laboratory', *Minerva, A Review of Science Learning & Policy* VIII: 36–58.

Thomson, D. (1970) 'Adaptors and innovators: a replication study on managers in Singapore and Malaysia', *Psychological Reports* 47: 383–87.

Torrance, E.P. (1982) 'Hemisphericity and creative functioning', *Journal of Research and Development in Education* 15 29–37.

Veblen, T. (1928) *The Theory of the Leisure Class.* New York: Vanguard Press.

Weber, M. (1970) In H.H. Gerth and C.W. Mills (Eds and trans.) *From Max Weber: Essays in Sociology.* London: Routledge & Kegan Paul.

Source: *Long Range Planning* 1984 17(2): 137–43.

Section F Learning

The three articles in this section set learning in a slightly wider context than convention dictates. Reason advocates a participative and reflective approach to action learning that aims to improve behaviour in problem situations through collective inquiry. Argyris shows how psychological defences can inhibit a manager's personal learning and defeat their organizational change efforts. Both advocate more open communication in organizations. Krackhardt and Hanson illustrate the use of network maps as an aid to decision making.

Peter Reason co-created co-operative enquiry with John Heron. This is one form of a series of related approaches to action learning that entail a collaborative and emergent approach to learning by cycling through repeated phases of reflection and action. Here Reason introduces some of the historical antecedents of action research, including experiential learning, participatory action research and Revan's action learning. He explains the practical, participative and situated approach action learning takes, and describes how this usually entails personal reflection and co-operative inquiry with others over time, and sometimes participation in a wider community.

Chris Argyris (1991, 1994) is well-known for his articulation of the practical effects of the shadow side of organizations. He differentiates between theories in action and theories in use and explains how defensive routines prevent learning. Here, he explains some of the inherent contradictions typically found in organizational change programmes designed to bring about empowerment. Recognizing that empowerment necessarily entails a commitment that comes about through participation, Argyris explains how organizational change efforts are often sabotaged through a design that pre-specifies top managers' preferred strategy and process. This pre-specification comforts top management with the control it appears to afford them, but leaves little scope for staff to identify with or feel ownership of the programme.

Krackhardt and Hanson show how managers can map informal advice and trust networks and how this information can be used to determine the most appropriate manager for the job.

References

Argyris, C. (1991) 'Teaching smart people how to learn', *Harvard Business Review* May–Jun, 99–110.

Argyris, C. (1994) 'Good communication that blocks learning', *Harvard Business Review*, July–Aug, 77–85.

14 Learning and Change through Action Research

Peter Reason

Historical roots

Action research has a long history, going back to social scientists' attempts to help solve practical problems in wartime situations in both Europe and America. Greenwood and Levin (1998, p. 1445) trace its origins to the work of Kurt Lewin in the 1940s to design social experiments that could take place in natural settings. Lewin is credited with the phrase 'Nothing is as practical as a good theory" and the suggestion that if you want to understand an organization the best thing to do is try to change it. According to Greenwood and Levin, these early action research experiments, together with the pioneering work of the Tavistock Institute in London after the war, showing how production technology and work organization are inextricably linked, strongly influenced the links between *action research* and social democracy in Scandinavia. Pioneering work with Volvo, Saab-Scania and Alfa Laval helped change our understanding of industrial organization away from rigid Taylorist approaches to work design, and toward the more flexible forms of semi-autonomous work organization with which we are more familiar today.

But the origins of action research do not rest only in Western social science. Another important influence has been *liberationist* movements particularly among underprivileged people of the South, where approaches to research, evaluation and education have been used as tools for social change. The argument here is that the creation of knowledge is in the hands of the rich and powerful elements of an increasingly global society, and works to enhance their interests against those of the disenfranchised majority world.

Selener (1997) traces the theoretical roots of what has come to be called *participatory action research* to liberationist writers such as Marx, Engels and Gramsci. Freire (1970) in particular has emphasized the importance of helping disadvantaged people develop critical thinking so that they could understand the ways in which they were disadvantaged by the political and economic conditions of their lives and could develop their own organized action in order to address these issues.

So participatory research has a double objective. One aim is to produce knowledge and action directly useful to a group of people – through research, through adult education, and through sociopolitical action. The second aim is to empower people at a second and deeper level through the process of constructing and using their own knowledge: they 'see through' the ways in which the establishment monopolizes the production and use of knowledge for the benefit of its members. This is the meaning of consciousness raising or *conscientization*, a term popularized by Freire for a 'process of self-awareness through collective self-inquiry and reflection' (Fals-Borda and Rahman 1991, p. 16). The tradition of participatory rural appraisal similarly is concerned with 'putting the first last' and creating practical knowledge of use to the underpriviledged members of our world (Chambers 1997).

Other important influences on action research have been the *experiential learning* movement (Kolb 1984), *action learning* (Revans 1980), *humanistic psychology* (Heron 1992), popular education (Gaventa 1991), organization development (Shani 1985) and feminist thinking (Mies 1993, p. 61). A recent special issue of the journal *Management Learning* (Raelin 1999, p. 1560) contains articles exploring Action Research (Dickens and Watkins 1999), Participatory Research (Park 1999), Action Learning (Marsick and O'Neil 1999), Action Science (Putman 1999), Action Inquiry (Torbert 1999) and Cooperative Inquiry (Reason 1999). These are all contemporary forms of action-oriented research which place emphasis on a full integration of action and reflection, so that the knowledge developed in the inquiry process is directly relevant to the issues being studied – as Torbert (1981) puts it, creating a form of knowledge useful to the actor and the point of action. They also place great importance on the democratic nature of the research process: as Greenwood and Levin emphasize, action research 'is fundamentally about the transformation of power relations in the direction of greater democracy' (Greenwood and Levin 1998, p. 88, see also Toulmin and Gustavsen 1996). This is first because democracy is of over-arching value in its own right, and second because inappropriate, authoritarian use of power in all societies, means that only a tiny fraction of knowledge and capacities are used to confront important problems. Thus contemporary forms of action research place great importance on collaboration between all those involved in the inquiry project, aiming to help the individual practitioner develop skills of reflective practice and organization and community members develop a culture of open inquiry as part of their work life, to develop learning organizations or communities of inquiry.

There are thus many ways of approaching action research and action learning, and in the rest of this chapter I offer one way of thinking about different approaches to action research which are based in our own work at the Centre for Action Research in Professional Practice at the University of Bath, and my collaboration with colleagues worldwide. More extended discussions of both theory and practice can be found by consulting the references cited (e.g Reason and Bradbury 2000).

Characteristics of action research practice

I want to emphasize four important characteristics of action research which, I believe, distinguish it from more traditional forms of management research.

First, while the primary purpose of academic research is to contribute to an abstract 'body of knowledge' available to third-persons, it has long been argued that 'the findings in our scholarly management journals are only remotely related to the real world of practicing managers' (Susman 1978, p. 582). In contrast, the primary purpose of action research is to develop *practical knowing* embodied moment-to-moment action by the research practitioner, and the development of learning organizations – communities of inquiry rooted in communities of practice (Argyris and Schön 1974, 1996; Argyris et al. 1985; Senge 1990).

Second, as we have seen above, action research has a *collaborative intent*: a primary value of action research strategies is to increase people's involvement in the creation and application of knowledge about them and about their worlds. Fundamentally, if one accepts that human persons are agents who act in the world on the basis of their own sensemaking; and that human community involves mutual sensemaking and collective action, it is no longer possible to do research *on* persons. It is only possible to do research *with* persons, including them both in the questioning and sensemaking that inform the research, *and* in the action which is the focus of the research. Of course, this collaboration between persons is not something which can be produced by fiat, as it were: collaborative relationships emerge over time, and may require careful facilitation for them to emerge at all. In many ways we can say that the development of organizations and communities able to inquire into and learn from their experience is the primary purpose of all action research strategies, and as we have seen above, this is important as a fundamental expression of human rights (Payne 1791).

Third, while most forms of academic research separate the knower from what it is to be known, and conduct their research from a distance (through surveys and questionnaires, for example) action research is rooted in each participant's in-depth, critical and practical experience of the *situation* to be understood and acted in.

This leads to the fourth characteristic of action research, that truth is not solely a property of formal propositions, but is a human activity that must be managed for human purposes (Mitroff 1998) which leads action research practitioners to take into account many *different forms of knowing* – knowledge of our purposes as well of our ideas, knowledge that is based in intuition as well as the senses, knowledge expressed in aesthetic form such as story, poetry and visual arts as well as propositional language, and practical knowledge expressed in skill and competence. Table 14.1 shows a version of the extended epistemology based on the work of Heron and Reason (e.g. Heron 1971, 1992, 1996; Reason 1988, 1994, 1999; Reason and Heron 1995). Others, notably Park (1999) and Torbert (1991) use different descriptions with similar intentions.

Knowing will be more valid– richer, deeper, more true to life and more useful – if these four ways of knowing are congruent with each other: if our knowing is grounded in our experience, expressed through our stories and images, understood through theories which make sense to us, and expressed in worthwhile action in our lives.

Table 14.1 Types of knowing in co-operative action learning

- *Experiential knowing* is through direct face-to-face encounter with person, place or thing; it is knowing through empathy and resonance, and is almost impossible to put into words.
- *Presentational knowing* emerges from experiential knowing, and provides its first expression through forms of imagery such as poetry and story, drawing, sculpture, movement, dance and so on.
- *Propositional knowing* 'about' something, is knowing through ideas and theories, and is expressed in abstract language or mathematics.
- *Practical knowing* is knowing 'how to' do something and is expressed in a skill, knack or competence.

Source: After Heron (1971) and Reason (1988).

Finally, action research aims to develop theory which is not simply abstract and descriptive but is a guide to inquiry and action in present time. A good theory arises out of practical experience, articulates qualities of practice to which we aspire, and challenges us, moment to moment in our professional and personal lives, to discover ways to realize these qualities in action.

Thus we can highlight the radical shift between the basic aims of most managerial research and participatory action inquiry: the former aims at *universalizable, valid certainty in reflection about particular pre-designated questions,* participatory action inquiry aims at *timely, voluntary, mutual, validity-testing, transformative action at all moments of living.*

Strategies for action research and practice

We can identify three broad strategies of action research practice (Reason and Torbert in preparation, Torbert 1998):

- First-person action research/practice skills and methods address the ability of the researcher to foster an inquiring approach to his or her own life, to act awarely and choicefully, and to assess effects in the outside world while acting.
- Second-person action research/practice addresses our ability to inquire face-to-face with others into issues of mutual concern – for example in the service of improving our personal and professional practice both individually and separately. Second-person inquiry is also concerned with how to create communities of inquiry or learning organizations.
- Third-person research/practice aims to create a wider community of inquiry involving persons who, because they cannot be known to each other face-to-face (say, in a large, geographically dispersed corporation), have an impersonal quality.

Naturally, the fullest kind of action research will engage all three strategies: first-person research practice is best conducted in the company of friends and colleagues who can provide support and challenge; such a company is most likely to evolve into a second-person co-operative inquiry process. On the other hand, attempts at third-person research which are not based in rigorous first-person inquiry into one's purposes and practices is open to distortion through unregulated bias.

The following account from Bob Hudson shows how one manager's first-person research evolved to include immediate colleagues (second-person) and on into the wider organization (third-person). As CEO of an NHS Trust in Wales, Bob led his organization's response to the reorganization of the health service in Wales which challenges the independent existence of the Trust and with it his job as CEO.

> The reaction from the Board down was to defend our position and to seek to build a power base that would enable us to survive as an independent organization. While this was my own initial position, I could also see that that competitive relationships between organizations were hindering the delivery of service.
>
> My initial attempts to engage the Board in a constructive debate on these issues didn't go down too well – the concern was about winning in the merger process. Speaking widely with my colleagues over the following weeks I discovered a mixed range of concerns, from personal survival and a desire to defend the patch to anxieties about the implications for clinical services.
>
> My response was to concentrate on the process of debate rather than the solution. I reasoned that we needed to surface within the Board the complexities of the issues and the range of views held if we were to collectively find a way forward. Our first attempt suggested that what we needed was an organization that looked like the one we had but was bigger! We had simply distorted our process to support the views we had brought to the meeting and there was a moment of collective recognition that this was what we had done. At a later session, using a process that forced us to articulate the assumptions we were using, we began to discuss openly the benefits of a range of merger models.
>
> From this we engaged with the other organizations plus a wide range of other stakeholders. We did not propose a solution and seek to sell it to them, we sold a process on the basis that we might all learn something more ourselves. The final outcome was an agreement to the creation of a single Trust to replace the existing three – a solution that no one thought politically achievable at the outset. Support was not universal, the board of one trust continued to oppose the idea throughout but general stakeholder support was forthcoming and the idea survived.
>
> There are a number of key points in this story for me:
>
> • My own reflective practice was making me more open to different perspectives and more sensitive to reactions from organizational members to new thinking.

• I was beginning to develop corporate processes within the Trust that allowed a more open and reflective consideration of complex issues.

• I learnt to separate my personal future from these discussions: I openly acknowledged that I did not see myself competing for the post of CEO in the new organization. This was a very liberating thing to do if risky.

• As a manager I have shifted from being a provider of solutions to someone who seeks to introduce new ideas and create spaces in which they can be discussed. I have taken this learning into my new job developing new strategy for NHS Wales as a whole.

First-person action research/practice

First-person inquiry is in many ways the experiential and practical foundation of all other forms of inquiry. It invites the individual – in their personal and professional, public and private lives – to attend to questions such as:

- Who am I? What is important to me? What is worthwhile engaging with?
- What frameworks of thinking/feeling do I bring to my life and work? What creative and distorting perspectives do I bring? Am I stuck in one frame or able to appreciate and delight in alternative frames?
- What is the quality of my behaviour? Do I have a range of behaviours appropriate to the situation? In particular, can I act in such a way as to increase the quality of the conversation? Am I flexible, diplomatic *and* outrageous, cunning *and* simple, wise *and* foolish? Is my behaviour congruent with my purposes?
- Am I awake to what is happening within me and in the world around me?
- How do I act *now* to increase the quality of dialogue and inquiry?

First-person research/practice brings scholarship to life, brings inquiry into more and more of our moments of action – not as outside researchers but as organizational and family members, and in our spiritual, artistic, craft, exercise, conversational, sexual, and other activities. It is open to anyone willing to commit to integrating inquiry and practice in everyday personal and professional settings. In fact, we all inevitably integrate inquiry and practice *implicitly* in our everyday conduct – although to integrate inquiry and practice both explicitly and implicitly in our everyday conduct is of course hugely demanding.

Some of the origins of first-person inquiry lie in the work of Argyris and Schön and their descriptions of action science to explore the fit and misfit between theories-in-use and espoused theories (Argyris et al. 1985) and the 'reflective practitioner' (Schön 1983) developing skills of both reflection *on* practice and reflection *in* practice. Torbert has described action inquiry as exploring the fit and misfit between four territories of human experience – between one's *purposes* and intuitive sense of what needs to be attended to; how one *understands and frames* the situation to hand, one's espoused theory; the qualities of one's *actual behaviour*; and what is going on in the *world outside*.

Torbert argues that all good inquiring conversations will explicitly incorporate these four territories of experience. In conversation this means explicit *framing* – making clear the perspective you are taking and the purposes you are pursuing; *advocating* – being clear about the course of action you are proposing; *illustrating* – grounding this advocacy in a particular concrete example; and *inquiring* – inviting others to comment and respond. One can then find ways to monitor one's conversations, seeking to balance the four types of speech in one's own performance, listening to and seeking to help others in the conversation similarly. This kind of inquiry practice can over time transform conversations from habitual, unaware and repetitive rituals toward inquiring dialogue (Fisher et al. 2000).

Bob Hudson's first-person research enabled him to re-evaluate his own assumptions about his organization, to separate his own interests from wider purposes, and to change his behaviour away from being solutions-oriented toward creating processes for open debate.

Second-person action research/practice

Second-person research/practice starts when we engage with others face-to-face to enhance our respective first-person inquiries. Maybe the most fundamental form of second-person research/practice is friendship, and most forms of professional practice are at their best forms of mutual inquiry. The relationship between manager and managed, between doctor and patient, between consultant and client are often seen as based primarily on authority and expertise, but can all be reframed as processes of mutual inquiry to which all involved bring their own different perspectives, knowledge, skills, and arenas of action. Thus a significant form of second-person research/practice may be to make explicit and systematic these everyday, tacit forms.

One of the most clearly articulated approaches to second-person research/practice is co-operative inquiry (Heron 1996, p. 24; Reason and Heron 1996, p. 7). In a co-operative inquiry, all those involved in the research endeavour are both co-researchers, whose thinking and decision-making contributes to generating ideas, designing and managing the project, and drawing conclusions from the experience; and *also* co-subjects, participating in the activity which is being researched. A typical inquiry group will consist of between six and twenty people. As co-researchers they participate in the thinking that goes into the research – framing the questions to be explored, agreeing on the methods to be employed, and together making sense of their experiences. As co-subjects they participate in the action being studied. The co-researchers engage in cycles of action and reflection: in the action phases they experiment with new forms of personal or professional practice; in the reflection phase they reflect on their experience critically, learn from their successes and failures, and develop theoretical perspectives which inform their work in the next action phase.

Mark Baldwin worked with groups of social workers to explore the tensions between professional discretion and bureaucratic procedures in the front-line implementation of social welfare policy. The groups were established following a day-long workshop at which these questions were identified, explored, and a shared commitment made to developing more effective practice. The groups met for a half-day session eight times over a six-month period. One group provides a good example of the approach: group members agreed to explore how they used one particular bureaucratic document – a consent form which was legally required but often not completed since, in the professional judgement of the social workers, it was inappropriate to do so because it would be threatening or oppressive to their clients. They agreed to reflect carefully about each instance when they did or did not complete this form, to keep notes on what they did, and to bring all this to each inquiry group meeting for collective reflection. In this way their own first-person inquiries were systematized and integrated with second-person inquiry within the group. As a result of these reflections over time they were able to understand much better the intuitive processes by which they reached decisions in their practice, and to develop practices of mutual reflection and support which provided much improved professional practice and managerial control over what was before an entirely uncontrolled activity. Not only did they learn about how to manage professional discretion within the team, they also began to incorporate the processes of co-operative inquiry into their team practices in a sustained fashion. (Baldwin 1998)

Bob Hudson extends his first-person inquiries into the second-person arena first by initiating reflective one-to-one conversations and then by creating workshop events at which his Board can reflect together about the challenges that face them.

Third-person action research/practice

The practices of first- and second-person action research, while certainly challenging, are relatively well established: the inquiry processes an individual manager can undertake to develop his or her practice have been widely described and have been explored by probably thousands of managers and professionals worldwide; similarly well described and practised are the second-person processes a group of people may undertake, whether through co-operative inquiry, democratic dialogue, learning history and so on. One of the significant challenges for the field is how to develop third-person approaches to action research that engage large systems in democratic inquiry. Third-person research/practice attempts to create conditions which awaken and support the inquiring qualities of first- and second-person research/practice in a wider community, thus empowering participants to create their own knowing-in-action in collaboration with others.

For example, Toulmin and Gustavsen point to the major challenge of extending the relatively small-scale action research projects so that 'rather than being defined exclusively as "scientific happenings" they (are) also defined as

"political events" with links to a broader debate on industrial democracy'
(1996, p. 11). They have begun to experiment with 'dialogue conferences'
which engage thousands of people in democratic dialogue on developmental
tasks. Chisholm (1998) describes a large-scale action research to build network
organizations in the New Baldwin Corridor, and a depressed region of
Pennsylvania, which involves similar action research to engage with large and
diverse communities of people. The Urban Health Partnership, located at the
King's Fund in London, has used 'future search' and similar conference
designs (Weisbord 1992, p. 1159; Weisbord and Janoff 1995) to engage large
numbers of people, drawn from different health care, social work and
community organizations, in explorations to improve the care of elders in UK
inner cities (Pratt 1999).

Bob Hudson and his colleagues move into a form of third-person research
when they engage with other organizations and a wider group of stakeholders
in the process of exploration which they have already started themselves. Note
how important it is that they don't seek to impose a solution, but to create a
situation in which continuing dialogue can take place.

Integrating first-, second- and third-person action research/practice

Third-person research represents in some ways the leading edge of action
research practice: it presents us with the challenge of creating large-scale
participative democracy and of dealing with some of the major issues which
confront our societies – issues of scale, of co-ordination between different
stakeholders and interest groups, of 'joined-up government' and so on. At the
same time these large-scale enterprises demand attention to first- and second-
person inquiry practices. For you cannot facilitate a large-scale inquiry
conference unless you have developed a quality of inquiry in your own practice,
so you exemplify inquiring behaviour and democratic dialogue, and are able to
navigate the complex choices that such an event presents with a reasonable
degree of comfort. You cannot do this unless you engage in mutual second-
person inquiry with peers, friends prepared to truly support and challenge you,
to engage with you on an in-depth journey of discovery. And of course, your
first- and second-person inquiry will in many ways be fruitless unless at least in
modest ways you are able to influence the wider third-person community to
explore the issues that have engaged you. A third, very different example, will
illustrate this.

> Carlis Douglas started her PhD [Douglas 1999] inquiries with the intention
> of exploring the application of equal opportunities policies and practices in
> British organizations. As she reflected on the project she had undertaken,
> she realized over time that a more pressing question was how black
> professional women like herself could thrive, rather than simply survive in
> their organizational lives – a phrase she took as inspiration from the black
> woman poet Maya Angelou. Her first-person inquiry processes included
> writing reflective autobiography, careful recording and reflection on day-to-

day professional activities, and experimentation with novel forms of behaviour. For her second-person inquiry processes she established a small co-operative inquiry group of black women, and used her professional consulting practices to develop inquiring dialogue with black and white members of the organizations with which she worked, in particular in training programmes for black women managers. Her third-person inquiry processes were more tacit, but clearly involved increasing the amount of discussion and dialogue about issues of race and gender in the organizations she worked with, and influencing the development of policy and practice.

The inquiry processes were increasingly challenging. In her first person inquiries, Carlis noticed how the ways she had learned to survive which were quite typical of black women – working very hard, not raising issues of race and gender, shielding herself emotionally from racist incidents and putting them down to ignorance – were also ways in which she stopped herself from thriving – she overworked and made herself ill, and by shielding herself shut herself down emotionally, and so on. The second-person inquiries both supported this observation and challenged it - the group members found they behaved in similar ways, but also realized that they shared a strong norm which made it a taboo to talk about these aspects of their experiences *even between themselves as black professional women*. As one of the participants noted as they struggled with these issues, 'If we hadn't had this inquiry group we wouldn't have even known what kinds of questions to be asking!' The second-person inquiry provided a space to explore both these experiences and the taboo against discussion of them under conditions of high and developing mutual love and trust. This provided Carlis with a deeper understanding of the issues involved in raising these questions in the wider, second- to third-person discussions with black women managers, and provided her with a wider range of options of action in these difficult discussions.

As Greenwood and Levin point out, action research lies at the very centre of human life (1998, p. 90). Action research is a family of approaches through which we can work to develop democratic dialogue in the service of mutual understanding and more informed action. It is an approach to living based on experience and engagement, on love and respect for the integrity of oneself and others. It depends on our willingness to rise above presupposition, to look, and to look again, to try out different behaviours, to risk security in the search for understanding and appropriate forms of action. All this in the service of opening possibilities for creative living.

References

Argyris, C. (1980). *Inner Contradictions of Rigorous Research*. New York: Academic Press.

Argyris, C., Putnam, R. and Smith, M. C. (1985) *Action Science: concepts, methods, and skills for research and intervention*. San Francisco: Jossey-Bass.

Argyris, C. and Schön, D. (1974) *Theory in Practice: increasing professional effectiveness*. San Francisco: Jossey-Bass.

Argyris, C. and Schön, D. (1978) *Organizational Learning*. Reading, MA: Addison-Wesley.

Argyris, C. and Schön, D. (1996) *Organizational Learning II*. Reading, MA: Addison-Wesley.

Bravette, G. (1997) *Towards Bicultural Competence: researching for personal and professional transformation*. Unpublished PhD, University of Bath.

Bunker, B. and Alban, B. (1997) *Large Group Interventions: engaging the whole system for rapid change*. San Francisco: Jossey-Bass.

Canter, R. J. (1998) *Clinical Decision Making in a Surgical Outpatients: relating the science of discovery with the science of implementation*. Unpublished PhD, University of Bath.

Chambers, R. (1997) *Whose reality counts? Putting the first last*. London: Intermediate Technology Publications.

Chisholm, R. F. (1998) *Developing Network Organizations: learning from practice and theory*. Reading, MA: Addison-Wesley.

Dickens, L. and Watkins, K. (1999) 'Action research: rethinking Lewin', in *Management Learning Special Issue: The Action Dimension in Management: Diverse Approaches to Research, Teaching and Development*, 30(2): 127–40.

Douglas, C. (1999) *From Surviving to Thriving; black women managers in Britain*. Unpublished PhD, University of Bath.

Fals-Borda, O. and Rahman, M. A. (Eds.) (1991) *Action and Knowledge: breaking the monopoly with participatory action research*. New York: IntermediateTechnology Pubs/Apex Press.

Fisher, D., Rooke, D. and Torbert, W.R. (2000) *Personal and Organizational Transformations through Action Inquiry*. Boston: Edge\Work Press.

Freire, P. (1970) *Pedagogy of the Oppressed*. New York: Herder & Herder.

Gaventa, J. (1991) 'Toward a knowledge democracy', in O. Fals-Borda and M. A. Rahman (Eds) *Action and Knowledge: breaking the monopoly with participatory action research*. New York: Intermediate Technology Pubs/Apex Press.

Greenwood, D. J. and Levin, M. (1998) *Introduction to Action Research: social research for social change*. Thousand Oaks, CA: Sage.

Hall, B. (1993) 'Participatory research', in *International Encyclopedia of Education*. London: Pergamon.

Heron, J. (1971) *Experience and Method: an inquiry into the concept of experiential research*. Human Potential Research Project, University of Surrey.

Heron, J. (1989) *The Facilitators Handbook*. London: Kogan Page.

Heron, J. (1992) *Feeling and Personhood: psychology in another key*. London: Sage.

Heron, J. (1993) *Group Facilitation: theories and models for practice*. London: Kogan Page.

Heron, J. (1996) *Co-operative Inquiry: research into the human condition*. London: Sage.

Heron, J. and Reason, P. (1997) 'A participatory inquiry paradigm', *Qualitative Inquiry* 3(3): 274–94.

Kolb, D. (1984) *Experiential Learning: experience as the source of learning and development*. London: Prentice Hall.

Marsick, V. J. and O'Neil, J. (1999) 'The many faces of action learning', in *Management Learning Special Issue: The Action Dimension in Management: Diverse Approaches to Research, Teaching and Development*, 30(2): 159–76.

Mies, M. (1993) 'Feminist research: science, violence and responsibility', in *Ecofeminism*. London: Zed Books, pp. 36–54.

Mitroff, I. I. (1998) 'On the fundamental importance of ethical management: why management is the most important of all human activities', *Journal of Management Inquiry* 7(1): 68–79.

New Economics Foundation. (1998) *Participation Works: 21 techniques of community participation for the 21st century*. London: New Economics Foundation.

Nonaka, I. and Takeuchi, H. (1995) *The Knowledge-Creating Company*. New York: Oxford University Press.

Park, P. (1999) 'People, knowledge, and change in participatory research', in *Management Learning Special Issue: The Action Dimension in Management: Diverse Approaches to Research, Teaching and Development*, 30(2): 141–58.

Park, P. (forthcoming) 'People, knowledge, and change in participatory research', *Management Learning*.

Payne, T. (1791) *Rights of Man and Common Sense* (1995 edition ed. by Mark Philip) Oxford: Oxford University Press.

Pratt, J., Gordon, P. and Plamping, D. (1999) *Working Whole Systems: putting theory into practice in organizations*. London: King's Fund.

Putman, R. (1999) 'Transforming social practice: an action science perspective', in *Management Learning Special Issue: The Action Dimension in Management: Diverse Approaches to Research, Teaching and Development*, 30(2): 177–88.

Raelin, J. (1999) 'Preface to Special Issue', *Management Learning* 30(2): 115–25.

Randall, R. and Southgate, J. (1980) *Co-operative and Community Group Dynamics, or your meetings needn't be so appalling*. London: Barefoot Books.

Reason, P. (Ed.) (1988) *Human Inquiry in Action: developments in new paradigm research*. London: Sage.

Reason, P. (Ed.) (1994) *Participation in Human Inquiry*. London: Sage.

Reason, P. (1998a) 'Co-operative inquiry as a discipline of professional practice', *Journal of Interprofessional Care* 12(4): 419–36.

Reason, P. (1998b) 'A participatory world', *Resurgence* 168: 42–4.

Reason, P. (1998c) 'Political, epistemological, ecological and spiritual dimensions of participation', *Studies in Cultures, Organizations and Societies* 4: 147–67.

Reason, P. (1999) 'Integrating action and reflection through co-operative inquiry', in *Management Learning Special Issue: The Action Dimension in Management: Diverse Approaches to Research, Teaching and Development* 30(2): 207–27.

Reason, P. and Bradbury, H. (Eds) (2000) *Handbook of Action Research: participative action and inquiry*. London: Sage

Reason, P. and Heron, J. (1996) 'A Layperson's Guide of Co-operative Inquiry', Centre for Action Research in Professional Practice, University of Bath. Published on World Wide Web http://www.bath.ac.uk/carpp/LAYGUIDE.htm.

Reason, P. and Marshall, J. (1987) 'Research as personal process', in D. Boud and V. Griffin (Eds) *Appreciating Adult Learning*. London: Kogan Page.

Reason, P. and Rowan, J. (Eds) (1981) *Human Inquiry: a sourcebook of new paradigm research*. Chichester: Wiley.

Reason, P. and Torbert, W. R. (in preparation) *Toward a Transformational Science: a further look at the scientific merits of action research*.

Revans, R.W. (1980) *Action Learning: new techniques for management*. Bromley: Chartwell-Bratt.

Schon, D.A. (1983) T*he Reflective Practitioner*. New York: Basic Books.

Selener, D. (1997) *Participatory Action Research and Social Change*. Cornell Participatory Action Research Network, Cornell University.

Senge, P. (1990) *The Fifth Discipline: the art and practice of the learning organization.* New York: Doubleday.

Shani, A. B. and Pasmore, W. A. (1985) 'Organizational inquiry: towards a new model of the action research process', in D. D. Warrick (Ed.), *Contemporary Organization Development: current thinking and applications.* Glenview, IL: Scott, Foresman and Co.

Susman, G. I. and Evered, R. D. (1978) 'An assessment of the scientific merits of action research', *Administrative Science Quarterly* 23: 582–602.

Torbert, W. R. (1976) *Creating a Community of Inquiry: conflict, collaboration, transformation.* New York: Wiley.

Torbert, W. R. (1981) 'Why educational research has been so uneducational: the case for a new model of social science based on collaborative inquiry', in P. Reason and J. Rowan (Eds) *Human Inquiry: a sourcebook of new paradigm research.* Chichester: Wiley, pp. 141–52.

Torbert, W. R. (1991) *The Power of Balance: transforming Self, Society, and Scientific Inquiry.* Newbury Park, CA: Sage.

Torbert, W. R. (1998) 'Developing wisdom and courage in organizing and sciencing', in S. Srivastva and D. Cooperrider (Eds) *Organizational Wisdom and Executive Courage.* San Francisco: New Lexington Press.

Torbert, W. R. (1999) 'The distinctive questions developmental action inquiry asks', in *Management Learning Special Issue: The Action Dimension in Management: Diverse Approaches to Research, Teaching and Development* 30(2): 189–206.

Toulmin, S. and Gustavsen, B. (Eds) (1996) *Beyond Theory: changing organizations through participation.* Amsterdam: John Benjamins.

Weisbord, M. R. (Ed.) (1992) *Discovering Common Ground – how future search conferences bring people together to achieve breakthrough innovation, empowerment, shared vision, and collaborative action.* San Francisco, CA: Berrett-Koehler Publishers, Inc.

Weisbord, M. R. and Janoff, S. (1995) *Future Search: an action guide to finding common ground in organizations and communities.* San Francisco: Berrett-Koehler.

15 Empowerment: The Emperor's New Clothes

Chris Argyris

Change programmes increase inner contradictions

Major change programmes are rife with inner contradictions. By this, I mean that even when these programmes and policies are implemented correctly, they do not – and cannot – foster the behaviour they are meant to inspire. If the inner contradictions are brought to the surface and addressed, they can be dealt with successfully; that is, they will not inhibit the kind of personal commitment that management says it wants. But if the contradictions remain buried and unacknowledged, as they usually do, they become a destructive force. Not only do they stifle the development of empowerment, they also sap the organization's efficiency by breeding frustration and mistrust.

To illustrate, consider the advice that currently represents best practice for implementing and promoting organizational change. That advice breaks the process down into four basic steps:

- Define a *vision*
- Define a competitive *strategy* consistent with the vision
- Define organizational *work processes* that, when executed, will implement the strategy
- Define individual *job requirements* so that employees can carry out the processes effectively

The underlying pattern of these instructions is consistent with what change researchers and practitioners have learned about effective implementation over the years. Start with a clear framework – a vision – and progressively make it operational so that it will come alive. So that no one will have any doubts about how to align the four parts of the process, management is advised to speak with one voice. This process makes sense. It is rational.

Yet the process is so riddled with inner contradictions that change programmes that follow it will only end up creating confusion, particularly at the implementation stage. Given that all the steps have been so precisely described through a set of instructions, the advice actually encourages more external than internal commitment (see Table 15.1). Clearly, when employees' actions are defined almost exclusively from the outside (as they are in most change programmes), the resulting behaviour cannot be empowering and liberating. One immediate consequence is that employees react to the change programme by quietly distancing themselves from it. Thus the change programme is successful in terms of improving performance because it helps reduce mistakes, as in the case of TQM, or because it helps employees embrace best practices. But at the same time, it undermines internal commitment. In short, the advice for implementing change simply does not provide the new source of energy that many executives want.

But the real danger is that change programmes end up poisoning the entire corporation with long-lasting mixed messages. Internally committed employees interpret these messages as 'do your own thing – the way we tell you'. They reluctantly toe the line. Employees who prefer external commitment will also pick up the mixed messages; however, these people will be relieved because they feel protected from having to take any personal responsibility. In this way, the very working habits that executives do not want to see continued in their organizations are strengthened and reinforced. The result is invariably more inner contradictions and more inefficiency and cynicism, all of which get in the way of real change.

Table 15.1 How commitment differs

External commitment	*Internal commitment*
Tasks are defined by others	Individuals define tasks
The behaviour required to perform tasks is defined by others	Individuals define the behaviour required
Performance goals are defined by management	Management and individuals jointly define performance goals that are challenging for the individual
The importance of the goal is defined by others	Individuals define the importance of the goal

CEOs undermine empowerment

CEOs work against empowerment both consciously and unconsciously. Surprisingly – at least to outsiders – executives do not always seem to want what they say they need. Consider a few typical remarks that I came across during my research. These remarks – excerpted from a roundtable discussion of executives from world-class companies – indicate very clearly the ambivalence of CEOs toward internal commitment and empowerment. The first CEO noted that with 'well-defined processes where the variances are small and the operating limits are well defined', you no longer need the old command-and-control approach. Workers are now empowered, 'provided they respect the process', he said. The second CEO agreed that these 'processes are liberating', while the third observed that many employees have a tough time understanding what it means for processes to be 'reliable, respectable, and in control'.

Let us stop a moment and ask ourselves how there can be empowerment when there is neither guesswork nor challenges – when the job requirements are pre-determined and the processes are controlled. For employees operating in such a world, the environment is not empowering; it is foolproof. This is not a milieu in which individuals can aspire to self-governance. On the contrary, as long as they buy in and follow the dictates of the processes, the employees in the companies just described will only become more externally motivated.

The enthusiastic use of champions in virtually all contemporary change programmes sends a similar mixed message from CEOs to employees. Top management is well aware of the dangers of piecemeal implementation and eventual fade-out in major change programmes. They strive to overcome those problems by anointing champions. The champions pursue performance objectives with tenacity, managing by decree. They have generous resources available to ensure compliance, and they monitor employees' progress frequently. Altogether, these behaviours reinforce the top–down control features of the external commitment model. The single voice of fervent champions leads employees to feel that management is in control, and it drives out the sense of internal responsibility and personal empowerment. How can employees feel empowered if someone is always 'selling' them or controlling them from the top down? Indeed, such champions would not be necessary if employees were internally committed.

The result of all these interventions is disarray. Managers and the change programmes they use undermine the empowerment they so desperately want to achieve. Why does this occur? Could it be that today's top-level managers don't truly want empowered employees? In truth, they are probably unsure. At the same time, employees do not hold executives to task for their behaviour. Employees have their own mixed feelings about empowerment.

Employees have their doubts

External commitment is a psychological survival mechanism for many employees – it is a form of adaptive behaviour that allows individuals to get by in most work environments. How that survival mechanism works is illustrated quite dramatically today in the former East Germany.

When the Berlin Wall came down, a routine way of life for East German workers came to an end. Most workers had learned to survive by complying. For 40 years, most plants were run in accordance with the dictates of central planners. If many East Germans had pushed for greater control over their destinies, their lives might have been endangered. As a result, East German workers over the years learned to define performance as doing the minimum of what was required of them.

After the fall of communism, I participated in many discussions with West German executives who were surprised and baffled by the lack of initiative and aspiration displayed by the East Germans. What those executives failed to understand is how bewildering – indeed, how threatening – it can be for people to take internal commitment seriously, especially those who have lived their entire lives by the rules of external commitment. As I listened to the West German executives who wanted to make East German employees more internally committed, I thought of several cases in the United States and elsewhere where similar problems exist. Again and again in my experience, prolonged external commitment made internal commitment extremely unlikely, because a sense of empowerment is not innate. It is something that must be learned, developed, and honed.

The question, then, is: how do you produce internal commitment? One thing for sure is that the incentive programmes executives have used – for instance, higher compensation, better career paths, 'employee of the month' recognition awards – simply do not work. On the contrary, in all my years as a change consultant, I have repeatedly witnessed how offering employees the 'right' rewards creates dependency rather than empowerment. Inevitably, the power of such methods wears off with use, and all that has been created is more external commitment.

Consider one company with substantial financial woes. In that case, the CEO decided at considerable personal sacrifice to raise his employees' salaries. But his own research later showed that the employees merely considered their raises to be in keeping with their equity in the labour market. Internal commitment had not increased. Employees continued to do only what was asked of them as long as the rewards were increased. They followed the rules, but they did not take any initiative. They did not take risks, nor did they show the sense of personal responsibility that management sought. The CEO was surprised, but I thought that these results were entirely predictable for two reasons. First, pay, like other popular incentive schemes, often advances external commitment. Second, and more fundamental, many employees do not embrace the idea of empowerment with any more gusto than management does. For a lot of people, empowerment is just too much work. Like the workers in East Germany, almost all employees have learned to survive by depending on external commitment.

When it comes to empowerment, executives and employees are engaged in shadowboxing. Management says it wants employees who participate more; employees say they want to be more involved. But it is difficult to know who means what. Is it just a charade? Employees push for greater autonomy; management says the right thing but tries to keep control through information systems, processes, and tools. Employees see vestiges of the old command-and-control model as confirming their worse suspicions – that superiors want unchallenged power. Management just wants to see better numbers. Thus the battle between autonomy and control rages on, and meanwhile, as companies make the transition into the next century, the potential for real empowerment is squandered.

Change professionals inhibit empowerment

During the past decade, I have had the opportunity to work with more than 300 change experts in different organizations. Such individuals differ in their practices and their effectiveness, of course, but more striking than the differences are the patterns that recur.

Caught in the middle of the battle between autonomy and control, the change professional has a tough assignment. The role of the change professional, whether internal or external, is ostensibly to facilitate organizational change and continuous learning. In their own way, however, the vast majority of change professionals actually inhibit empowerment in organizations.

To understand how that occurs, consider what happens as Tom, a change agent, tries to work with Jack, a line manager. (Both are composite figures typical of those I encountered in my research.) Jack is told by his boss to work with Tom, who is there to 'help' Jack empower his organization. The change programme begins with a series of meetings and discussions. Tom talks passionately about openness, honesty, and trust as the foundations of empowerment. Many employees leave these meetings feeling hopeful about the direction that the company is taking toward more open communication. A month into the programme, however, Tom observes that Jack has fallen back into his old style of management. He decides that he had better confront Jack:

Tom's unspoken thoughts	*What Tom and Jack say*
Tom:. *Things aren't going well.*	Tom: So how's everything going?
	Jack: Things are going pretty well. There's a lot of pressure from above, but we're meeting the numbers.
Tom: *Oh great. All Jack cares about is the numbers. Empowerment isn't even on his agenda.*	Tom: Great. Super. But I was also wondering how well we're doing at getting people more committed to their jobs. How empowered do you think people feel?
	Jack: Well, I think we're doing okay. If there are problems, people come to me and we work it out. Sure, some people are never satisfied. But that's just a few people, and we can handle them.

Tom: *Just what I feared. Jack's not 'walking the talk'. He just doesn't get it at all.*

Tom: *This is hopeless! There's got to be an easier way to make a living. I'll never get through to him. I wish I could tell Jack what I think, but I don't want to put him on the defensive. I've got to stay cool.*

Tom: Look, Jack, if you solve all their problems, how are we going to empower our employees?

Jack: Well, to be honest with you, Tom, the signal I'm getting from above is that my job is to produce the numbers without, you know, upsetting people. To be fair, I think I'm doing that.

What's happening here? The change programme that began with great enthusiasm is clearly in deep trouble. It's a pattern I've observed over and over again. After the initial excitement passes, reality inevitably settles in. Put aside the nice rhetoric of empowerment, employees *will* have problems. They *will* ask their managers for help, and their managers *will* tell them what to do. That is how most work gets done and how organizations meet their numbers. And in many cases, there's absolutely nothing wrong with this, except that it goes against the theory of empowerment.

What does Tom do when he observes Jack telling his employees what to do? Instead of figuring out whether Jack is doing the right thing in this situation, change experts like Tom will almost always be dismayed, because the managers aren't walking the talk of empowerment. Rarely have I seen a change professional help a manager deal effectively with being caught between a rock and a hard place. Even more uncommon is a change agent who offers practical advice to the manager about what to do.

Not only is Tom unwilling to acknowledge the real problem Jack is having, but he papers over his own thoughts. He tries to act as if he still believes the programme can be successful when, in fact, he has given up hope. Tom himself is guilty of not walking the talk of openness, honesty, and trust.

In my experience, line managers are far more willing to acknowledge the inner contradictions of change programmes – at least, in private. They will admit to distancing themselves from the soft stuff – two-way participation, internal commitment, and discontinuous thinking – to focus instead on the numbers. Managers like Jack often conclude – rightly, I'm afraid – that the change agent does not know how to help them. So Jack listens politely as Tom warns him about the dangers of backsliding and exhorts him to be more persistent. And then Jack goes on about his business.

In the end, everyone is frustrated. In theory, empowerment should make it easier for organizations to meet their numbers. But when change programmes are imposed without recognizing the limitations of empowerment and when managers and employees are not helped to deal effectively and openly with them, the organization ends up worse off than it was to begin with. Empowerment too often enters the realm of political correctness, which means that no one can say what he or she is thinking: this is just nonsense. In this scenario, if you challenge the change agent, you become an enemy of change.

So instead of feeling more empowered, people throughout the organization feel more trapped and less able to talk openly about what's really going on. Is it any wonder that change programmes don't succeed and that they actually undermine the credibility of top management?

Source: Extract from 'Empowerment: the emperor's new clothes', *Harvard Business Review*, 1998, May, pp. 98–105.

16 Informal Networks: The Company Behind the Chart

David Krackhardt and Jeffrey R. Hanson

The steps of network analysis

Much research has already established the influence of central figures in informal networks. Our studies of public and private companies showed that understanding these networks could increase the influence of managers outside the inner circle. If they learned who wielded power in networks and how various coalitions functioned, they could work with the informal organization to solve problems and improve performance.

Mapping advice networks, our research showed, can uncover the source of political conflicts and failure to achieve strategic objectives. Because these networks show the most influential players in the day-to-day operations of a company, they are useful to examine when a company is considering routine changes. Trust networks often reveal the causes of non-routine problems such as poor performance by temporary teams. Companies should examine trust networks when implementing a major change or experiencing a crisis. The communication network can help identify gaps in information flow, the inefficient use of resources, and the failure to generate new ideas. They should be examined when productivity is low.

Managers can analyse informal networks in three steps. Step one is conducting a network survey using employee questionnaires. The survey is designed to solicit responses about who talks to whom about work, who trusts whom, and who advises whom on technical matters. It is important to pretest the survey on a small group of employees to see if any questions are ambiguous or meet with resistance. In some companies, for example, employees are comfortable answering questions about friendship; in others, they deem such questions too personal and intrusive. The following are among the questions often asked:

- Whom do you talk to every day?
- Whom do you go to for help or advice at least once a week?
- With one day of training, whose job could you step into?
- Whom would you recruit to support a proposal of yours that could be unpopular?
- Whom would you trust to keep in confidence your concerns about a work-related issue?

Some companies also find it useful to conduct surveys to determine managers' *impressions* of informal networks so that these can be compared with the actual networks revealed by the employee questionnaires. In such surveys, questions are posed like this:

- Whom do you think Steve goes to for work-related advice?
- Whom would Susan trust to keep her confidence about work-related concerns?

The key to eliciting honest answers from employees is to earn their trust. They must be assured that managers will not use their answers against them or the employees mentioned in their responses and that their immediate colleagues will not have access to the information. In general, respondents are comfortable if upper-level managers not mentioned in the surveys see the results.

After the questionnaires are completed, the second step is cross-checking the answers. Some employees, worried about offending their colleagues, say they talk to *everyone* in the department on a daily basis. If Judy Smith says she regularly talks to Bill Johnson about work, make sure that Johnson says he talks to Smith. Managers should discount any answers not confirmed by both parties. The final map should not be based on the impressions of one employee but on the consensus of the group.

The third step is processing the information using one of the several commercially available computer programs that generate detailed network maps (drawing maps is a laborious process that tends to result in curved lines that are difficult to read). Maps in hand, a skilled manager can devise a strategy that plays on the strengths of the informal organization, as David Leers, the founder and CEO of a California-based computer company, found out.

		Leers (CEO)	
Software Applications	Field Design	Integrated Communications Technologies	Data Control Systems
O'Hara (SVP)	Calder (SVP)	Lang (SVP)	Stern (SVP)
—Bair	—Harris	—Muller	—Huttle
—Stewart	—Benson	—Jules	—Atkins
—Ruiz	—Fleming	—Baker	—Kibler
	—Church	—Daven	
	—Martin	—Thomas	
	—Lee	—Zanado	
	—Wilson		
	—Swinney		
	—Carlson		
	—Hoberman		
	—Fiola		

Figure 16.1 The formal chart shows who's on top

Whom do you trust?

David Leers thought he knew his employees well. In 15 years, the company had trained a cadre of loyal professionals who had built a strong regional reputation for delivering customized office information systems (see Figure 16.1). The field design group, responsible for designing and installing the systems, generated the largest block of revenues. For years it had been the linchpin of the operation, led by the company's technical superstars, with whom Leers kept in close contact.

But Leers feared that the company was losing its competitive edge by short-changing its other divisions, such as software applications and integrated communications technologies. When members of field design saw Leers start pumping more money into these divisions, they worried about losing their privileged position. Key employees started voicing dissatisfaction about their compensation, and Leers knew he had the makings of a morale problem that could result in defections.

To persuade employees to support a new direction for the company, Leers decided to involve them in the planning process. He formed a strategic task force composed of members of all divisions and led by a member of design to signal his continuing commitment to the group. He wanted a leader who had credibility with his peers and was a proven performer. Eight-year company veteran Tom Harris seemed obvious for the job.

Leers was optimistic after the first meeting. Members generated good discussion about key competitive dilemmas. A month later, however, he found that the group had made little progress. Within two months, the group was completely deadlocked by members championing their own agendas. Although a highly effective manager, Leers lacked the necessary distance to identify the source of his problem.

An analysis of the company's trust and advice networks helped him get a clearer picture of the dynamics at work in the task force. The trust map turned out to be most revealing. Task force leader Tom Harris held a central position in the advice network – meaning that many employees relied on him for technical advice (see Figure 16.2). But he had only *one* trust link with a colleague (see Figure 16.3). Leers concluded that Harris's weak position in the trust network was a main reason for the task force's inability to produce results.

In his job, Harris was able to leverage his position in the advice network to get work done quickly. As a task force leader, however, his technical expertise was less important than his ability to moderate conflicting views, focus the group's thinking, and win the commitment of task force members to mutually agreed-upon strategies. Because he was a loner who took more interest in computer games than in colleagues' opinions, task force members didn't trust him to take their ideas seriously or look out for their interests. So they focused instead on defending their turf.

With this critical piece of information, the CEO crafted a solution. He did not want to undermine the original rationale of the task force by declaring it a failure. Nor did he want to embarrass a valued employee by summarily removing him as task force head. Any response, he concluded, had to run with the natural grain of the informal organization.

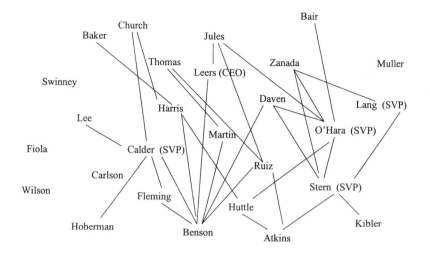

Figure 16.2 The advice network reveals the experts

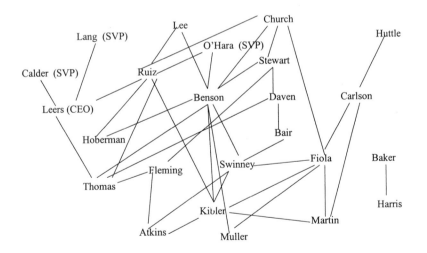

Figure 16.3 But when it comes to trust …

He decided to redesign the team to reflect the inherent strengths of the trust network. Referring to the map, Leers looked for someone in the trust network who could share responsibilities with Harris. He chose Bill Benson, a warm, amiable person who occupied a central position in the network and with whom Harris had already established a solid working relationship. He publicly justified his decision to name two task force heads as necessary, given the time pressures and scope of the problem.

Within three weeks, Leers could see changes in the group's dynamics. Because task force members trusted Benson to act in the best interest of the entire group, people talked more openly and let go of their fixed positions. During the next two months, the task force made significant progress in proposing a strategic direction for the company. And in the process of working together, the task force helped integrate the company's divisions.

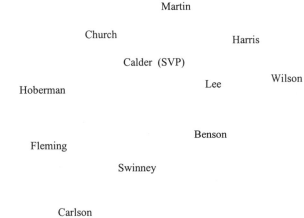

Figure 16.4 How the CEO views the trust network

Fleming   Hoberman

Figure 16.5 The trust network according to Calder

A further look at the company's advice and trust networks revealed another serious problem, this time with the head of field design Jim Calder. The CEO had appointed Calder manager because his colleagues respected him as the most technically accomplished person in the division. Leers thought Calder would have the professional credibility to lead a diverse group of very specialized design consultants. This is a common practice in professional service organizations: make your best producer the manager. Calder however turned out to be a very marginal figure in the trust network. His managerial ability and skills were sorely lacking, which proved to be a deficit that outweighed the positive effects derived from his technical expertise. He regularly told people they were stupid and paid little attention to their professional concerns.

Leers knew that Calder was no diplomat, but he had no idea to what extent the performance morale of the group was suffering as a result of Calder's tyrannical management style. In fact, a map based on Leers's initial perceptions of the trust network put Calder in a central position (see Figure 16.4). Leers took for granted that Calder had good personal relationships with the people on his team. His assumption was not unusual. Frequently, senior managers presume that formal work ties will yield good relationship ties over time, and they assume that if *they* trust someone, others will too.

The map of Calder's perceptions was also surprising (see Figure 16.5). He saw almost no trust links in his group at all. Calder was oblivious to *any* of the trust dependencies emerging around him – a worrisome characteristic for a manager.

The information in these maps helped Leers formulate a solution. Again, he concluded that he needed to change the formal organization to reflect the structure of the informal network. Rather than promoting or demoting Calder, Leers cross-promoted him to an elite 'special situation team', reporting directly to the CEO. His job involved working with highly sophisticated clients on specialized problems. The position took better advantage of Calder's technical skills and turned out to be good for him socially as well. Calder, Leers leaned, hated dealing with formal management responsibilities and the pressure of running a large group.

Leers was now free to promote John Fleming, a tactful, even-tempered employee, to the head of field design. A central player in the trust network, Fleming was also influential in the advice network. The field group's performance improved significantly over the next quarter, and the company was able to create a highly profitable revenue stream through the activities of Calder's new team.

Experienced network managers who can use maps to identify, leverage and revamp informal networks will become increasingly valuable as companies continue to flatten and rely on teams. As organizations abandon hierarchical structures, managers will have to rely less on overseeing employees 'below' them and more on managing people across functions and disciplines. Understanding relationships will be the key to managerial success.

Source: Extracted from *Harvard Business Review* 1993, July, pp. 104–11.

Part 3

Development

Section G   Culture

The changing business environment is leading to different organizational forms. Here Semler advocates the merits of self-organization and Fukuyama explains why networks need social capital.

Management control procedures risk stifling creative endeavour with red tape, but until recently most Western managers assumed the managerial paraphernalia of job descriptions, training, quality and planning departments were synonymous with good management. Semco is one of those companies demonstrating that a medium-sized organization can remove most of these monitoring devices to reveal a committed, motivated and responsible workforce. The chapter by Ricardo Semler, the majority shareholder in Semco, a Brazilian marine and food service equipment manufacturing company, champions the merits of a largely self-organizing workforce. Semler explains how Semco's practice of employee participation, profit sharing and open information systems have led to a highly entrepreneurial business where the distinction between employee and contractor has been well and truly blurred. He explains how this philosophy has seen them though serious recession in Brazil and how openness breeds motivation and responsibility and an entrepreneurial spirit.

Professor Francis Fukuyama has come to prominence through his exposition of the consequences of social capital for economic development. He has pointed out the correspondence between shared values, historical and economic development. For example familial societies with low trust between non-kin, such as China and France have experienced centralized state power, whereas societies with stronger non-familial links such as Japan, Germany or the UK built that trust through guilds, unions or religious sects, for example. These countries do not seem to have gone through a period of centralized state power and have maintained their social capital. The differing cultural values and degree of social capital a country possesses appear to have led to different forms of industrial structure, with countries like Japan and Germany, who possess strong non-kin institutions, developing large corporations and featuring strongly in sectors requiring these (such as automobiles, consumer electronics, semi-conductors). In countries where family ties are strong, and there is a lack of non-kin-based social institutions, trust between non-kin has remained low. China, Taiwan and Southern Italy possess few large corporations, instead they have developed a series of smaller but interrelated organizations, based round family networks, that have helped these countries feature strongly in areas where the flexibility afforded in such smaller ventures is advantageous, such as the clothing, design, machine tools and furniture industries. Fukuyama has also argued that countries with depleted social capital, such as Russia, are going to find it very difficult to rebuild economically until their social capital is restored.

In his most recent book he has suggested that there are some signs (the declining crime and divorce rate in the USA) that social capital might be beginning to regenerate. Though we might appear to be losing the art of association, our hi-tech societies still need hi-touch, and technology is generating new forms of informal social network that entail shared values and norms in a way that it is not dissimilar to the old craft guilds (Fukuyama 1999).

In his chapter he expounds on the idea that networks are not just structural entities but entail informally shared values and norms, qualities that define social capital. Further, that the information society requires sufficient social capital to generate high trust among its various human knowledge networks, if their members are going to be willing to share their intellectual ideas with each other.

Reference

Fukuyama, F, (1999) *The Great Disruption*. London: Profile.

17 Why my Former Employees Still Work for Me

Ricardo Semler[1]

I own a manufacturing company in Brazil called Semco, about which I can report the following curious fact: no one in the company really knows how many people we employ. When we walk through our manufacturing plants, we rarely know who works for us. Some of the people in the factory are full-time Semco employees; some work for us part-time; some work for themselves and supply Semco with components or services; some work for themselves under contract to outside companies (even Semco's competitors); and some of them work for each other. We could decide to find out which are which and who is who, but for two good reasons we never bother. First, the employment and contractual relationships are so complex that describing them all would take too much time and trouble. Second, we think it's all useless information.

Semco has long been a laboratory for unusual employment and management practices. What we're now engaged in might be called a radical experiment in unsupervised, in-house, company-supported satellite productions of goods and services for sale to Semco itself and to other manufacturers by employees, part-time employees, ex-employees, and people who have never been connected with Semco whatsoever (but who work on our premises and on our equipment). This is not at all the same thing as out-sourcing. This is a borderless system of short-term, non-contractual task assignment often using Semco's own fixed assets, some of it in Semco's own plants and some dispersed at a dozen sites that don't belong to the company.

This satellite programme, as we call it, sounds chaotic, can be frustrating, and is in some ways uncontrollable. It requires daily leaps of faith. It has serious implications for corporate security. And, for three years it has been working very well. Since 1990, 28% of Brazilian capital goods manufacturers have gone bankrupt. In 1990, 1991 and 1992, Brazilian gross industrial product fell by 14%, 11%, and 9%, respectively. Capital goods output has fallen back to what it was in 1977. But in this same period, Semco's overall sales and profits have remained intact, and I attribute the indifference first and foremost to our satellite production.

Ever since I took over the company 12 years ago, Semco has been unorthodox in a variety of ways. I believe in responsibility but not in pyramidal hierarchy. *I think that strategic planning and vision are often barriers to success.* I dispute the value of growth. I don't think a company's success can be measured in numbers, since numbers ignore what the end user really thinks of the product and what the people who produce it really think of the company.

I question the supremacy of talent, too much of which is as bad as too little. I'm not sure I believe that control is either expedient or desirable.

I don't govern Semco – I own the capital, not the company – but on taking over from my father, I did try to reconstruct the company so that Semco could govern itself on the basis of three values: employee participation, profit sharing, and open information systems. We've introduced idiosyncratic features like factory-floor flexitime, self-set salaries, a rotating CEOship, and, from the owner to the newest, greenest maintenance person-only three levels of hierarchy.

You might say that what we practise is an extreme form of common sense: 'common' because there's nothing we do that thousands of other people didn't think of ages ago, 'extreme' because we actually do it. Another way of looking at Semco is to say that we treat our employees like responsible adults. We never assume that they will take advantage of our rules (or our lack of rules); we always assume they will do their level best to achieve the results beneficial to the company, the customer, their colleagues, and themselves. As I put it in an earlier article in HBR, participation gives people control of their work, profit sharing gives them a reason to do it better, information tells them what's working and what isn't.

With rare exceptions, this approach has been successful. We've had two or three strikes, but they were quickly settled, especially once the strikers saw that we would neither lock them out of the plant nor suspend their benefits during work stoppage. (They were able to plan outgoing strike tactics while eating lunch in the company cafeteria.) We've had a few employees take wholesale advantage of our open stockrooms and trusting atmosphere, but we were lucky enough to find and prosecute then without putting in place a lot of insulting watchdog procedures for the nine out of ten who are honest. We've seen a few cases of greed when the people set their own salaries too high. We've tried a few experiments that we later backed away from. We've had to accept occasional democratic decisions that management disliked, but we learned to swallow hard and live with them.

On the whole, as I say, our approach has worked. Loyalty is high, quality is excellent, and sales and profits are surprisingly good for a manufacturing company in one of the worlds most lunatic business environments. But in Brazil no state of the economy is permanent. Few last long enough to be called temporary. Surviving the ups and downs of the Brazilian economy is a little like riding a Brahma bull. It is even more like riding a Brahma bull in an earthquake. Some of the worst jolts come not from the bull but the landscape.

In 1990, the jolt that sent us into our present experiment came from the minister of finance, who, believing Brazil's inflation was simply the result of too much money being used for too much speculation, seized 80% of the country's cash and introduced an extended period of economic bedlam. Employers could not meet payrolls. Consumer spending vanished. Business spending shuddered to a halt. Bankruptcies soared. Industrial output plummeted.

At Semco, we had several months of zero sales. After all, what company was going to buy machinery with a ten months delivery when it didn't know if it could last out the week? Worse yet, back orders were cancelled, or we found that our customers had gone out of business. Our marine division alone had $1.5 million of receivables that we couldn't hope to collect and $4 million worth of products that shipbuilders could no longer pay for. We had to rent warehouse space just to store all the unsold goods.

We cut costs. We organized workers into teams and sent them out to sell replacement parts directly to ships and restaurants. We cut down on coffee breaks, locked up the copiers, cancelled orders for new uniforms, and turned off the lights we all could find, scrimped on telephone calls. None of it was enough, and anyway, I don't really believe in cost cutting. I like to think we don't waste money when we've got it. *And who can say how many sales we lose when we play Scrooge with the travel money or penny pinch the phone calls?*

Finally, we called the workers together in groups of 100 and discussed what we should do. They came up with lots of ideas, and we tried them without success until we reached a point where no one had anything else to propose and neither did we – except for two unhappy alternatives: cut pay or cut workforce. We thought we could avoid layoffs by cutting salaries 30% across the board until business picked up again. But a lot of people were already struggling with bills and rents and mortgages and wanted us to start laying people off instead, so those who stayed could at least survive. We went on searching desperately for a third way out.

And then suddenly the shop-floor committee came to us and said, 'Okay, we will take a 30% pay cut, but on three conditions.' The first was that we increase their profit sharing by 15%, from just under 24% to just under 39%, until they got back up to their former salary levels. The second was that management takes a 40% pay cut. And the third was that a member of the union committee would co-sign every cheque we wrote. Because the workers wanted to be absolutely certain that their sacrifice would be worthwhile, they wanted to oversee each and every expenditure.

Well, at that moment, we *had* no profits to share, so there was nothing for us to lose and everything to gain. And by the second months, we were actually covering expenses. In their drive to save, the workers took on more and more of the former contract work. They did security and cleaning, drove trucks, even cooked the food in the cafeteria. No expense went unchallenged, and for four or five months, we made a small profit in the worst economic times any of us had ever seen.

But we kept on looking for a better solution.

In the first place, pure reduction has to be a temporary measure. What about training, research new product development, and all the seemingly peripheral activities that produce profits over the long haul? Those weren't responsibilities we could abdicate.

And what about those cheques? The dual-signature scheme was working at the moment, but management couldn't permanently yield its power of the purse to a person chosen by the union without management input or approval.

Yet the explosion of energy, inventiveness, and flexibility we'd been witnessing was hugely attractive. And when we then added in several other factors – the need to cut our standing labour costs, the demands of the Brazilian labour law, the dynamic example of our own peculiar Nucleus of Technological Innovation, which I'll come back to in a moment – what began taking shape was a radically new principle of organization.

The Thinkodrome at the Free-for-All corporation

Years ago, in the mid-1980s, three Semco engineers proposed a new kind of work unit. They wanted to take a small group of people raised in Semco's culture and familiar with its products and set them free. The new group would not have to worry about production problems, sales, inventory, equipment maintenance, delivery schedules or personnel. Instead they would invent new products, improve old ones, refine marketing strategies, uncover production inefficiencies, and dream up new lines of business. They would have no boss, no subordinates. They would pick their own focus, set their own agenda, and have complete freedom to change their minds. Twice a year they'd report to senior management, which would decide whether or not to keep them on for another six months.

The three engineers suggested we call the new unit the Nucleus of Technological Innovation (NTI) and somewhat predictably proposed themselves as its first three members. We bought their odd idea, and then we worked out an odd form of compensation to go along with it. Their guaranteed salaries went down sharply, but they would now share in the proceeds of their inventions, innovations, and improvements. They would received a percentage of any savings they introduced, royalties on new products they devised, a share of the profits on their inventions, and would also be free to sell consulting services on the open market. They might have done better as truly independent entrepreneurs, but as NTI members, Semco would cushion them against disaster and give them the support of an established and well-equipped manufacturing operation.

By the end of their first six months, NTI had 18 projects under way, and over the next few years they uncorked such an array of inventions, changes, and refinements (one of my favourites is a scale that weighs freight trains moving at full speed) that NTI's members began to prosper mightily and Semco became unthinkable without their constant innovation and reform.

By 1990, we'd begun to feel that we'd like to NTI the entire company, liberate more creativity, tie compensation even more specifically to performance, loosen the ties that bound us all together, and scramble our overall structure. The 30% pay-cut-and-cost-reductions scheme had given us breathing space of several months, but with the Brazilian economy in a bucket and no imminent prospect of recovery, we *had* to become permanently leaner and more flexible. At the same time, of course, we had a commitment to our workforce that was central to the way we did business, that commitment had been our principle reason for trying to avoid layoffs.

For most other companies, there was another reason as well: Brazilian labour law protects laid-off workers by granting them several different forms of special compensation. The largest of these comes from an individual fund for each worker to which the employer contributes 8% of wages every month. When people are fired (or retire early), they collect all this accumulated money, plus interest, in the form of a lump sum. Less substantial – not, unlike the 8% fund, a great problem for many employers – is severance pay itself, which is paid on the spot out of current income which can amount to two years' salary in the case of workers with many years' seniority. By the end of 1990, a lot of Brazilian companies drifted slowly into bankruptcy rather than lay people off and go bankrupt overnight. With our finances still more or less intact, this widespread problem proved in our case to be an opportunity.

Semco's sales had gradually increased again, and we were making enough money to restore salaries to where they had been before the 30% cut. We took back our cheque signing privileges. We were surviving in a crisis economy, but only just, and we began to face the facts that we had to cut out permanent staff and contract more of our work. We looked hard for a way of doing it without destroying the support system that Semco people lived on. It was here that NTI's free-form structure suggested solution.

Instead of giving contracts out to strangers, we decided we could just as well give the contracts to our own employees. We would encourage them to leave the Semco payroll and start their own satellite enterprises, doing work, at least initially for Semco. Like NTL, these satellites could stay under our larger umbrella by leasing our machines, even working in our plant. Like NTI, they could also do work for other companies, again on our machines and in our factories. Like NTI, their compensation would take a variety of forms – contract payments, royalties, commissions, profit sharing, piece-work, whatever they could think up that we could both live with. And like NTI, they could have some beginning guarantees. In particular, we would offer all of them some contract work to cut their teeth in, and would defer the lease payments on all equipment and space for two full years.

This satellite programme would have obvious advantages for Semco. We could reduce our payroll, cut inventory costs by spreading out raw materials and spare parts among our new suppliers, and yet enjoy the advantage of having subcontractors who knew our business and the idiosyncrasies of our company and our customers. Moreover, we would pick up the benefit of entrepreneurial motivation, because of our profit sharing, our employees already worked evenings and weekends when necessary, without any prompting from management, being in business for themselves ought to raise that sense of involvement higher still.

But what in heaven's name were the advantages for our workers, who'd be giving up a secure nest at Semco for the risks of small business? And in the midst of economic bedlam? To begin with, of course, they all had the chance to make many times what they could at Semco – if the economy straightened out. Of course that was a big *if*. And should the recession persist, they might make less. But only assuming they continued to have a job at Semco, which was becoming an even bigger *if* with every day that passed. The fact was, they had distressingly few choices. And so did we.

We eased the transition in every way we could. We created a team of executives to teach cost control, pricing, maintenance, inventory management. To provide seed money, we gave people layoff payments on top of severance pay and all the other legally required benefits. Many also made use of their 8% nest- egg funds. No one *had* to start a satellite. Some took their severance and left. Some managed to stay on the payroll for months or for good. But despite the difficulties, satellites sprang up quickly. White-collar workers were the first. Our tax accountants, human resources staffers, and computer programmers all went off on their own, then blue-collar workers in food services and refrigeration systems followed suit.

Today, about half the manufacturing we once did in-house has gone to satellites, and we think we can farm out another 10% to 20% in the coming years. Best of all, to this day only one satellite has failed. Some are expanding and looking for partners. The company has rehired some satellite workers, and a few had moved repeatedly back and forth between satellite and employee status as needs – theirs and ours – shifted. Some satellites have broadened their scope so greatly that most of their time – often right on our premises, remember – is spent with customers and production partners who have no other connection with Semco whatsoever.

In 1990, Semco had about 500 employees. Today, we have about 200, plus at least that many in our satellites, with another 50 or 60 people who work for a satellite and also work for us part-time. We have employees with fixed salaries. We have employees with variable salaries made up of royalties or bonuses based on self-set objectives like cash flow, sales, profits, production units, or any one of a dozen other measures. We have employees with both fixed and variable salaries. All our employees share in our profits.

On the satellite side, compensation may take the form of a fixed fee, an hourly stipend, a percentage of increased sales, a finder's fee, an honorarium, a retainer converting to an advance converting to a royalty, or even a simple win-or-lose commission. In one case, we had decided to kill a product-development project when one of our people picked it up from the table and said, 'I'll take it. If you give me $1,000 a month, which will just pay my expenses, plus a 7% royalty for the first five years if I can make it work – I'll take it.' So of course we gave it to him. The most we can lose is $1,000 a month, where we had been spending $10,000 to $15,000 a month and getting nowhere. The most he can make is something like half a million, I'd guess, with the other 93% coming to Semco.

Once we posted a job for one engineer and got 1,430 résumés. We took them home in packs of a hundred, and then we interviewed for five months. In the end, we invited several dozen final candidates to a one-day seminar where we walked them through the entire company, opened our files, showed them everything we did, then asked them for proposals. We wound up hiring 41 engineers – one salaried employee and 40 satellite workers whom we paid on various forms of percentage-based commission.

In one of our plants, we've set aside a large room full of desks and computers to give everyone within our company sphere and, for all we know, a variety of guests and visitors from well beyond it, a place to sit and plan and ask questions and solve problems. We call it the Thinkodrome, and it's a busy place, quiet place. That Semco survived at all we owe in large part to surrounding ourselves with people who look at everything we do and ask why we can't do it better or cheaper or faster or in some entirely novel way.

Hunting the free market

Our ancestors laid out the ground rules of human teamwork several thousand generations ago, they go like this: the woman with the keen eyesight is Chief Mammoth Finder, the guy with the strong arm and the long spear is Head Mammoth Killer, and the tribal elder with the special feel for herbs and spices gets to be Grand Mammoth Cook. For now. All these positions are temporary and to some extent self-selecting. If you want to be Chief Finder go find some mammoths and the job is probably yours. But since everyone's well being depends on your success, your status is also highly situational. Fail to find, and the job will pass swiftly and naturally to someone else.

Generally speaking, Semco's production process works along similar lines, both for satellite operations and for the work we do in-house. All work, including some aspects of management, goes to people with proven track records who want the jobs and can compete for them successfully. Satellite as well as in-house business units rise and fall on their merits alone – at least in theory.

This commitment to free-market principles was put to the test about a year into the satellite programme, when our marine division found itself with a good deal of idle capacity. Marine's strategy was built on quality, not price – low volume but high margins. A shipbuilder seeking the very best performance and dependability in, say, a propeller system, tended to come to us. But with the economy in a straightjacket, orders had nearly disappeared.

On the other hand, our biscuit division, which designs and builds turnkey cookie factories for global giants like Nabisco and Nestlé, had two fairly big contracts in hand, for about $2 million, another for $5.5 million, and was going to need a lot of skilled subcontracting. The portion of this work that marine could do would keep it occupied for four or five months, and marine's top manager (called a counsellor at Semco) went ahead and figured the contracts from the biscuit division into his budget. But biscuit's purchasing people did not award the contracts to the marine division, which took too long to deliver, they said, and which charged too high a price for its exaggerated quality. They gave the contracts instead to satellite producers and outside contractors, including one of the marine's archcompetitors. The fight that triggered was a bitter one, and the attempts of the interdepartmental management meeting to act as a go-between did not make things easier. We were of two minds ourselves.

On the one hand, we were going to pay marine employees to sit around on their hands while another division paid outsiders to do work the marine employees could have done. And on the other hand, how could we ask biscuit employees, who share in their division's profits, to subsidize a business in trouble? Moreover, wouldn't the subsidy just postpone marine's inevitable reckoning with its own strategic predicament? In the end, we let biscuit have its way and endorsed the need to be as unforgiving toward our own business units as we would to outsiders. It was the right decision, of course. We finished the cookie factories on schedule, and the marine division – which decided to stick with its high-quality, high-margin strategy but to eliminate a number of products whose quality and cost were too high for the market – cut its staff by 70%, began farming out a lot of its work to satellites, and recovered its profitability.

Control

At the centre of Semco are a group of six so-called counsellors, and all of us take a six-month turn as acting CEO. We also do six-month as opposed to yearly budgeting, because an annual budget tempts managers to postpone unpleasant decisions to the third and fourth quarters.

The budget cycles are January to June and July to December, but the CEO cycles begin in March and September. In other words, we avoid what other companies and shareholders think they want – responsibility nailed down to a single man or woman. Our CEOs don't wear themselves out trying to meet quarterly financial goals, and there's no one person to blame if the company goes down the drain. When financial performance is one person's problem then everyone else can relax. In our system, no one can relax. You get to pass on the baton, but it comes back again two and a half years later.

One consequence of this system is that we need to keep each other informed, which we do at regular divisional meetings and bi-weekly interdivisional meetings. All these meetings are open and optional, and those who attend make decisions that those who don't may simply have to live with.

This self-selecting element in decision making is another consequence of the deliberate fragmentation of responsibility. Like our predecessors the mammoth hunters, the people who get responsibility are the people who seek it out and meet it. In fact, the actual, ad hoc control structure we work with from day to day builds on this principle and on two others that, together, create a kind of invisible order from the apparent chaos that characterizes the Semco environment.

The first principle holds that information is the ultimate source of virtually all power. For this reason, we try to make all of it available to everyone. All meetings are open. Designs and specifications are shared. The company's books are open for inspections by employees and for auditing by their unions. In short, we try to undercut and so eliminate the process of filtering and negotiating information that goes on in so many corporations. The person who knows most about the subject under discussion rather than the person who has the highest declared status chairs meetings.

The second principle is that the responsibility for any task belongs to the person who claims it.

The third is that profit sharing for employees and success-orientated compensation for satellite enterprises will spread responsibility across the Semco map. With income and security at risk – and with information readily available – people try hard to stay aware of everyone else's performance.

To give an idea of how all of this works in practice, let's take a look of one of those turnkey cookie factories. The Big Cracker Company of Chicago wants a plant that will turn out a thousand tons a month of, say, butterscotch macaroons. To begin with, an independent agent will tell us of the project in return for a finder's fee. We will probably put in an initial customer interface in the hands of a satellite company – four men who used to be on our payroll and now work for themselves. They'll go through the specifications with the customer, then they'll share that information widely, announce a meeting (to which anyone can come and no one is summoned), and chair the discussion (which will cover several unexpected proposals from unanticipated participants like the guy from refrigeration with a special point of view about handling butter and coconut). Someone, a group of employees or satellites, will take on the job of costing the project, and with this estimate in hand, a Semco counsellor and biscuit-division co-ordinators will then set a margin and deliver the quote to Big Cracker.

(A couple of times, we have even communicated this margin to the customer, because we thought it would justify, for example, a 12% net margin than to play the disingenuous game of claiming pencil-thin profits and no room for compromise. Our chief argument has been our profit-sharing programme, since it seems so clear to us that people will work harder for more money and that a generous margin will therefore buy the customer much extra care and effort. But I'm afraid we've had only limited success with this approach.)

This margin-setting discussion often produces serious disagreements. In one case, we battled out the margin in a long, heated debate, and then the sales manager lowered it dramatically when he sat down with the customer.

By Semco rules, that kind of last-minute capitulation is perfectly legitimate. Battle or no battle, he was the customer, not we. Whoever holds the spear is completely in charge of bringing down the mammoth. Let's say Big

Cracker accepts our bid and the order comes in, 600 pages long. Let's say we choose a co-ordinator for the project from the outside company, and lets call him Bob. Bob will go through the contract and decide how he wants to divide it up. He may get help from engineering. He will certainly get help from all the meetings he holds to make decisions, which he will chair and where he will lobby for the people he wants to do each job. Next, the biscuit division's purchasing department will negotiate contracts with the dozens of suppliers chosen. In 1991, we did about 70% of such contracts in-house. Today, that's down to 35% of 40%.

When Bob has put together a completion schedule and time chart, everyone will go to work – each contractor, employee, and satellite responsible to no single authority but answerable to everyone. At most companies, when something goes wrong the real responsibility falls between the cracks. At Semco, the fact that Bob is not an employee makes everyone react much faster when there looks like trouble.

And lack of control

Semco needs to maintain in-house just a limited number of functions – top management, applications engineering, some R&D, and some high-tech, capital-intensive skills that we do exceptionally well. We don't care how everything else gets done, whether by contractors or subcontractors, satellites or nonsatellites, former employees or total strangers or by the very people who do the same thing for our competition. None of that matters.

When we started, people warned me that all sorts of information about our company would get into the wrong hands, that we had to protect ourselves. I heard the same argument when we started distributing profit-and-loss statements to our employees. But it's a waste of time to worry about leaks.

First of all, we no longer know whose the wrong hands are. The competition used to be a company a mile away that made the same products that we did, but now the competition comes from companies we've never even heard of in Taiwan and Finland. Second, I've never seen a company overtake another because it had its 10K or even the specifications for a valve. Third, we want to be a moving target. We don't care about yesterday's information or last year's oil pump, which in any case the competition can buy, take apart, and study to his heart's content.

Finally, we don't think people give out information anyway. I know, I've tried on numerous occasions to get a copy of, let's say, a pamphlet some company passed out to 1,000 employees, and nobody can lay their hands on one. The Chinese printed hundreds of millions of copies of Chairman Mao's *Little Red Book*, and still they're as rare as hen's teeth.

People also warned me about the loss of central goal setting and control. I admit that the lack of control is often hard to live with. But, let's not compare Semco's circumstances with some ideal world where managers actually get to decide what people will do and when and how they'll do it. We have limited control over the day-to-day behaviour of the people who make most of our components, but so do companies that do all their work in-house. At least none of our satellite people work nine to five and leave their problems at the plant when they go home at night – which means leaving them to management. We have motivation and responsibility working on our side. Our satellite workers are in business for themselves, so they'll work all night to complete an order to specification and in time. And if the order is later or fails to meet our quality standards, then we're free to give the next order to someone else. We can forget the witch-hunt and all the grief that goes into firing people or not promoting them.

As for planning and the control it presupposes, I think good planning is always situational. Thinking about the future is a useful, necessary exercise, but translating such conjecture into 'Strategic Planning' is worse than useless. It's an actual barrier to survival. Strategic planning leads us to *make* things happen that fly full in the face of reality and opportunity.

For example, Semco is today in the environmental consulting business, which I could not have imagined five years ago. Our gadfly NTI group was looking at one customer's need for an environmentally active pump – a pump that would shred and process the material it moved – and saw that the company could re-engineer its production line to do away with the pump altogether. Had we said, 'We're in the pump business, not the environmental business', we might never have pursued the problem. As it was, we addressed the company's overall need, jettisoned the pump, and when it was all over, we'd also acquired a small environmental consulting firm to flesh out our own limited expertise. More recently, we've also entered into a joint venture with one of the world's leading environmental groups. Today, the division represents about 14% to 15% of our total business and is growing at a rate of 30% to 40% a year.

The lesson this story teaches me is about the negative value of structure. Structure creates hierarchy, and hierarchy creates constraint. We have not utterly abandoned all control, but the old pyramidal hierarchy is simply unable to make leaps of insight, technology, and innovation. Within their own industries, pyramidal hierarchies can generate incremental change.

Take dishwashers, one of Semco's businesses. Dishwashers are expensive to operate and messy to use, but over the last 50 years, dishwashers have changed hardly at all. What the customer wants is machines that wash dishes silently, cheaply and without any mess at all, which probably means without water. I've recently seen indications that such a thing may be possible, but the idea could never come from a pyramid of Semco dishwashing executives. It was one of our satellites that brought us the idea. In fact, about two-thirds of our new products come from satellite companies.

What goes for planning goes equally for culture, vision, and responsibility. We find that fragmentation is strength in all these areas. Semco has no corporate credo, for example, and no mission statement. An articulation of company values or vision is just a photograph of the company as it is, or wants to be, at one given moment. Snapshots of this kind seem to hold some companies together, but they are terribly static devices. No one can impose corporate consciousness from above. It moves and shifts with every day and every worker. Like planning, vision at its best is dynamic and dispersed.

At Semco, so is responsibility. We have little control, even less organization, and no conventional discipline at all. People come and go whenever they like; many set their own compensation; divisions and units perpetuate themselves on however they can; satellite companies work on our machines in our factories for us and others in a great confusion of activity; the system tying it all together is painfully loose – and this is *manufacturing*, much of it assembly-line manufacturing.

When I describe Semco to other manufacturers, they laugh. 'What do you make,' they ask me 'beads?' And I say, 'no, among other things, we make rocket-fuel propellant mixers for satellites.' And they say, 'That's not possible.' And I say, 'Nevertheless…'

The point is simple but perhaps not obvious. Semco has abandoned a great many traditional business practices. Instead, we use minimal hierarchies, ad hoc structures, self-control, and the discipline of our own community marketplace of jobs and responsibilities to achieve high-quality, on-time performance. Does it make me feel that I have given up power and governance? You bet it does. But do I have more sleepless nights than the manufacturer who runs his business with an iron hand and whose employees leave their troubles in his lap every night? I think I probably sleep better. I know I sleep as well.

We delivered our last cookie factory with all its 16,000 components right on time. One of our competitors, a company with tight controls and hierarchies, delivered a similar factory to the same client a year and two months late.

Note

1. In 1990 and again in 1992, Ricardo Semler was elected business leader of the year by a poll of 52,000 Brazilian executives.

Source: *Harvard Business Review*, 1994, January, pp. 64–74.

18 Technology, Networks and Social Capital

Francis Fukuyama

The end of hierarchy

Max Weber argued that rational, hierarchical authority in the form of bureaucracy was the essence of modernity. What we find in the second half of the twentieth century, instead, is that bureaucratic hierarchy has gone into decline in both politics and the economy, to be replaced by informal, self-organized forms of co-ordination.

The political version of hierarchy was the authoritarian or, in an even more extreme form, totalitarian state, in which a dictator or small elite at the top had power over the whole society. Authoritarian states of all stripes, from Franco's Spain and Salazar's Portugal to East Germany and the Soviet Union, have collapsed since the 1970s. They have been replaced with, if not well-functioning democracies, at least states that aspire to permit a greater degree of political participation.

Democracies themselves are also organized hierarchically. A modern president of the United States in some respects has much more power than an oriental despot ever dreamed of, including the power to vaporize much of the world with nuclear weapons. The difference is less a matter of hierarchy than the fact that authority in a democracy is legitimized through popular consent and is limited in its power over individuals. Democratic hierarchies have produced inefficiencies just like their authoritarian counterparts, and so within virtually all contemporary democracies, there has been substantial pressure to decentralize, federalize, privatize and delegate authority.

Corporate hierarchies have also been under attack. There have been a number of setbacks to large, overly hierarchical and rigid companies – AT&T and IBM in the early 1980s were classic examples – which fell prey to smaller, quicker and more nimble competitors. Business school professors, management consultants and information technology gurus have all stressed the virtues of highly decentralized firms and some have argued that in the coming century, the large, hierarchical corporation will be replaced entirely by a new form of organization, the network.

Centralized, authoritarian corporations have been failing for the same reason that centralized, authoritarian states have failed: they cannot deal with the informational requirements of the increasingly complex world they inhabit. It is no accident that hierarchies have got into trouble precisely at the time that societies around the world have been making the transition from industrial to high-tech, information-based forms of production.

The problems that centralized hierarchies have in dealing with information were laid-out in a classic article by Friedrich von Hayek fifty years ago, which itself was based on a critique of socialism made earlier by Ludwig von Mises. To control everything in his domain, an authoritarian ruler needs to have the information and knowledge necessary to make decisions. In an agricultural society where lords rule over peasants, knowledge of horse-back riding, swordplay and some politics, as well as the blessing of the local bishop, were probably sufficient to ensure a monopoly of power. But as economies developed and became more complex, the informational requirements for ruling increased exponentially. Modern governance requires technological expertise, which no ruler can hope to master on his own, so he must rely on technical experts for everything from weapons design to fiscal management. Moreover, the overwhelming proportion of information generated in an economy is *local* in nature. If a supplier is providing low-quality rivets, it is the riveter who is more likely to know this than an economic bureaucrat in a centralized planning ministry or a corporate vice president in the company headquarters.

But the delegation of power downward, to either technical experts or those who generate and use local knowledge, begins to dilute the dictator's power. A process like this occurred in the Soviet Union and is one of the reasons that socialism collapsed on itself there. Stalin found himself relying on technical experts – the so-called Red directors – as well as a host of scientists, engineers and other specialists. Although he could control them through fear (the famed aircraft designer Tupolev created aeroplanes while in a jail cell), his successors found it increasingly difficult to do so. Technical experts could withhold knowledge and bargain with those holding political power. This brought them autonomy and thereby the freedom to start thinking for themselves. Further, despite the fact that all decisions concerning pricing and transfers of materials were in theory controlled by a ministry in Moscow, the centre had no way of keeping track of all the local knowledge being generated in the periphery. Consequently lower-level officials like provincial party secretaries and enterprise directors closer to local sources of knowledge began to accumulate substantial power. By the time Gorbachev came along in the 1980s, the totalitarian model of power had already failed.

The same process occurs within companies where CEOs enjoy similarly authoritarian powers over their employees. Certain CEOs, particularly first-generation entrepreneurs who have built companies from scratch, tend to want to control everything that goes on within their companies, and treat employees as if they were robots designed to carry out their orders. But as their companies grow larger and the problems they face become more complex, this type of decision making becomes too inflexible, and the boss becomes a bottleneck. Firms no less than governments need to devolve power to experts and to decision makers who are closer to local sources of information. Some present-day management experts talk as if the concepts of decentralization and employee empowerment are new, but as the business historian Alfred Chandler has shown, large firms have been devolving power to lower levels of their organizations steadily over at least the past hundred years. Large multidivisional firms like General Motors and Du Pont Chemical were hierarchically organized but still rather decentralized in terms of managerial authority when compared to, say, a small family business.

The problems afflicting large, hierarchical organizations are not trivial ones and it is reasonable to think that the devolution of power and authority within them will continue. But then a new problem emerges: co-ordinating the activities of all the players in a decentralized organization where low-level employees have newly acquired powers. One solution is the market, where decentralized buyers and sellers achieve efficient results without central control. The out-sourcing craze in American business during the 1990s is an effort to replace hierarchical control with market relationships. But market exchange generates transaction costs, and in any event firms can't organize their core functions as markets with everyone competing against everyone else.

The other solution to the problem of co-ordinating highly decentralized organizations is the network, a form of spontaneous order that emerges as the result of the interactions of decentralized actors, without being created by any centralized authority. If networks are to be truly productive of order, they necessarily depend on informal norms taking the place of formal organization – in other words, on social capital.

The rise of the network

The classic theory of the firm laid out by Ronald Coase in 1937 argues that hierarchies exist because of transaction costs. A complex activity like building cars could be done, in theory, by small, decentralized firms contracting with one another to produce all of the component parts, with separate companies providing design, systems integration and marketing. The reason cars are not made this way but by giant, vertically integrated firms is that the costs of all the negotiating, contracting and litigating required to out-source everything are much greater than the costs of bringing these activities in-house, where the firm can control the quality of all of the inputs and outputs by managerial fiat.

There is a substantial literature on the rise of the network as an intermediate form of organization between traditional markets and hierarchies, said to be better suited to the development of technologies than large, hierarchical organizations. Thomas Malone and Joanne Yates argued that the advent of cheap and ubiquitous information technology should reduce the transaction costs involved in market relationships and thereby reduce the incentive to create managerial hierarchies. Many apostles of the information revolution have seen the rise of the Internet not simply as a useful new communications technology, but as the harbinger of an entirely new, non-hierarchical form of organization uniquely adapted to the requirements of a complex, information-intensive economic world.

Much of the prevailing literature understands the shift that is going on in terms of formal organization. The classic hierarchical organization takes the shape of a pyramid, while Figure 18.1 shows the consequences of organizational flattening. The flat organization remains ultimately a centralized and hierarchical one; all that has been changed is the number of management layers intervening between the top and bottom. Flat organizations create enlarged spans of control; properly executed, they should not overburden senior manager with micromanagement responsibilities, but rather should push authority down to the lower levels of the organization.

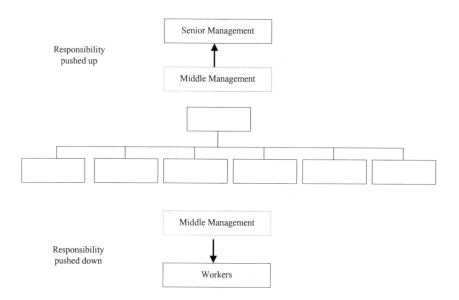

Figure 18.1 A flat organization

Sociologists have used the concept of networks for years, and at times express annoyance that business school professors are now reinventing the wheel. The definition of network commonly used by sociologists, however, is extremely broad and encompasses both markets and hierarchies, as they are understood by economists. There is a striking lack of precision in the use of the term network among the management specialists, however. Networks are commonly understood to be different from hierarchies but it is often not clear how they differ from markets. Indeed, Malone did not use the term network when he originally talked about the decline of hierarchies; co-ordination would be performed by classical market mechanisms. Some people treat the network as a category of formal organization in which there is no formal source of sovereign authority, while others understand it to be a set of informal relationships or alliances between organizations, each of which may be hierarchical but related to one another through vertical contractual relationships. Japanese *keiretsu* groups, alliances of small family firms in central Italy and Boeing's relationships with its suppliers are equally understood to be networks.

If we understand a network not as a type of formal organization, but as social capital, we will have much better insight into what a network's economic function really is. By this view, a network is a moral relationship of trust:

> A network is a group of individual agents who share informal norms or values beyond those necessary for ordinary market transactions

The norms and values encompassed under this definition can extend from the simple norm of reprocity shared between two friends to the complex value systems created by organized religions. Non-governmental organizations like Amnesty International and the National Organisation for Women achieve co-ordinated action on the basis of shared values. As in the case of friends or members of a religious denomination, the behaviour of the organization's individual members cannot be explained on the grounds of economic self-interest alone. A society like the United States is characterized by a dense, complex and overlapping set of networks (see Figure 18.2). The large ellipse may represent the United States as a whole, whose inhabitants share certain political values related to freedom and democracy. The overlapping ellipse may denote an immigrant group like Asian Americans, who partly share and partly stand outside mainstream American culture. The wholly enclosed ellipses could represent anything from religious sects to firms with particularly strong corporate cultures.

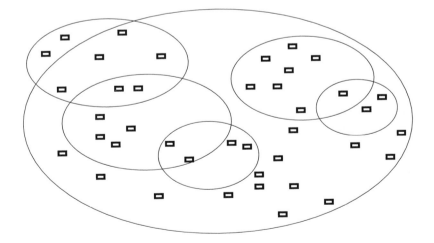

Figure 18.2 Multiple networks of trust

Note two features of this definition. A network is different from a market insofar as networks are defined by their shared norms and values. This means that economic exchange within a network will be conducted on a different basis from economic transactions in a market. A purist might argue that even market transactions require *some* shared norms (the willingness, for example, to engage in exchange rather than violence), but the norms required for economic exchange are relatively minimal. Exchange can occur between people who don't know or like one another, or who speak different languages; indeed, it can occur anonymously between agents who never know each other's identities. Exchange among members of a network is different. The shared norms give them a superordinate purpose that distorts the market relationship. Hence members of the same family, or the Sierra Club, or an ethnic rotating-credit association, sharing as they do certain common norms, do not deal with each other the way that anonymous individuals meeting in a marketplace do. They are much more willing to engage in reciprocal exchange in addition to market exchange – for example, conferring benefits without expecting immediate benefits in return. Although they may expect long-term individual returns, the exchange relationship is not simultaneous and is not dependent on a careful cost–benefit calculation as it is in a market transaction.

On the other hand, a network is different from a hierarchy because it is based on shared *informal* norms, not a formal authority relationship. A network understood in this sense can coexist with a formal hierarchy. Members of a formal hierarchy need not share norms or values with one another beyond the wage contracts that define their membership; formal organizations, however, can be overlaid with informal networks of various sorts, based on patronage, ethnicity or a common corporate culture.

When networks are overlaid on top of formal organizations, the results are not necessarily beneficial, and indeed can be the source of a good deal of organizational dysfunction. Everyone is familiar with old-boy and patronage networks, based on kinship, social class, friendship, love or some other factor. Members of such a network share important norms and values with one another (particularly reciprocity) that they do not share with other members of the organization. Within the patronage network, information passes readily, but these outer boundaries constitute a membrane through which information passes much less readily. Patronage networks are problematic in organizations because their structure is not obvious to those outside them, and they often subvert formal authority relationships. Common ethnicity may facilitate trust and exchange among members of the same ethnic group, but it inhibits exchange among members of different groups. When a boss is unwilling to criticize or fire an incompetent subordinate because the latter is a protégé, personal friend, or lover the networks reciprocity becomes a clear liability.

The other problem with informal networks is the inverse relationship between the strength of the values or norms linking the community (and therefore the degree of co-ordination they can achieve) and their openness to people, ideas and influences from outside the network. Being a member of the US Marine Corps or the Mormon Church involves much more than membership in a formal organization. Members are socialized into a strong and distinctive organizational culture that creates a high degree of internal solidarity and potential for co-ordinated activity. On the other hand, the cultural gap between Marine and civilian, or Mormon and non-Mormon, is much greater than for organizations with lesser degrees of moral relatedness. The impermeability of the communal walls around such groups can often make them intolerant, inbred, slow to adapt and oblivious to new ideas. Building on the work of sociologist Mark Granovetter, there has been a large literature on the importance of 'weak ties' to the effectiveness of information networks. It is the deviant individuals straddling different communities who are often responsible for bringing in heterodox ideas that are ultimately necessary if the group is to adapt successfully to changes in its environment.

Networks, understood as informal ethical relationships, are therefore associated with phenomena like nepotism, favouritism, intolerance, inbreeding and non-transparent, personalistic arrangements. Networks in this sense are as old as human communities themselves, and in many respects they were the dominant forms of social relationship in many pre-modern societies. In some sense, many of the institutions we associate with modern life, such as contracts, the rule of law, constitutionalism and the institutional separation of powers, were all designed to counter-act the defects of informal network relationships. That is why Max Weber and other interpreters of modernity argued that its essence is the replacement of informal authority with law and transparent institutions.

So why is it, then, that anyone should believe that human organizations in the future will rely less on formal hierarchies and more on informal networks? In fact, it is highly doubtful that formal hierarchies are about to go away anytime soon. To the extent that networks become important, they will exist in conjunction with formal hierarchies. But why should informal networks not wither away altogether? One answer has to do with the problems of co-ordination through hierarchies under conditions of increasing economic complexity.

Changing methods of co-ordination

The importance of social capital in a hierarchical organization can be understood in terms of the way information moves around in it. In a manufacturing firm, hierarchy exists in order to co-ordinate the flow of material resources in a production process. But although the flow of material product is determined by the formal structure of authority, the flow of information proceeds in a much different fashion. Information is a peculiar commodity. It can be extremely difficult and expensive to produce but once in existence, further copies are essentially free. This is all the more true in the digital age, when a mouse click can create endless copies of a computer file.

This means that any information generated within an organization in theory should optimally flow freely to all other parts of the organization where it can be of use. Since the organization in principle owns the rights to all information generated by its workers, there should be no cost to transferring information from one part of the organization to another.

Unfortunately, information never flows as freely within an organization as leaders at the top would like. The reason has to do with the fact that organizations have to delegate authority downward to lower levels of the hierarchy. This creates what economists call *principal–agent problems*, where the agent hired by the principal has his or her own agenda that is not always that of the boss or of the organization as a whole. Many managers think that the solution to the problem is to align individual incentives with organizational incentives so that the agents work in the principal's best interests. This is often easier said than done, however. Individual and organizational interests are at times in direct conflict. A middle manager who discovers a new application of information technology or a new plan for flattening the managerial structure that will eliminate his own job has no incentive to implement this discovery. In other cases where it is difficult to measure the quality of a worker's output, monitoring individual performance for the sake of individualized incentives becomes prohibitively expensive.

Thus, although it is in the organization's overall interest to promote the free flow of information, it is often not in the individual interests of the various people within the hierarchy to allow it to do so. Information, as the saying goes, is power and the granting or withholding of information becomes one important means by which various individuals within an organization seek to maximize their power relative to others. Everyone who has worked in a hierarchical organization knows that there is a constant struggle going on between superiors and subordinates, or between rival branches, to control information.

In addition to principal agent problems, hierarchical organizations suffer from other inefficiencies related to their internal processing of information. We are all familiar with bureaucracies in which Department X doesn't know what Department Y on the next floor is doing. Some decisions require higher-level monitoring and therefore generate internal transaction costs in order to carry out that monitoring. In other cases, organizations assign monitoring responsibilities unnecessarily, incorrectly or inefficiently.

The formality of hierarchies can also create problems in dealing with complex information. Management through a hierarchy usually entails the creation of a system of formal rules and standard operating procedures – the essence of Weberian bureaucracy. Formal rules become problematic when decisions have to be made on the basis of information that is complex or hard to measure and evaluate. In labour markets, advertising and listings of formal job requirements are used to match supply and demand for simple, low-skill jobs, informal networks take over when universities or firms need to hire hotshot economists or software engineers, because their skills and performance are much harder to define in formal terms. Tenure decisions in American universities are made on the basis not of detailed formal criteria but based on the fuzzier judgement of other tenured professors as to the quality of the candidates' work.

Finally, hierarchies can be less adaptive. Formalized systems of control are much less flexible than informal ones; when conditions in the outside world change, they are often more visible to lower levels of the organization than to higher-level ones. Hence over-centralization can be a particular liability in areas of rapid change in the external environment, such as the information technology industry.

The reason that networks, defined as groups sharing informal norms and values, are important is that they provide alternative conduits for the flow of information through and into an organization. Friends do not typically stand on their intellectual property rights when sharing information with each other and therefore do not incur transaction costs. Friendships thus facilitate the free flow of information within the organization. Nor do friends usually spend a lot of time strategizing over how to maximize their relative power positions in relation to each other. Someone in marketing knows someone in production and tells her over lunch about customer complaints concerning product quality, thereby bypassing the formal hierarchy and moving information to the place where it is most useful more quickly. A corporate culture ideally provides an individual worker with a group as well as an individual identity, encouraging effort toward group ends that again facilitate information flow within the organization.

Social capital is also critical to the management of highly-skilled workers manipulating complex, diffuse, tacit or hard-to-communicate knowledge and processes. Organizations from universities to engineering, accounting and architectural firms generally do not try to manage their professional staff through detailed bureaucratic work rules and standard operating procedures. Most software engineers know much more about their job than do the people who manage them; they alone can make informed judgements about their own productivity. Such workers are usually trusted to be self-managing on the basis of internalized professional standards. A doctor presumably will not do something unethical to a patient if someone pays him enough; he has taken an oath to serve the patient's interests rather than his own. Professional education is consequently a major source of social capital in any advanced information age society and provides the basis for decentralized, flat organizations.

Indeed social capital is important to certain sectors and certain forms of complex production precisely because exchange based on informal norms can avoid the internal transaction costs of large hierarchical organizations, as well as the external transaction costs of arms-length market transactions. The need for informal, norm-based exchange becomes more important as goods and services become more complex, difficult to evaluate, and differentiated. The increasing importance of social capital can be seen in the shift from low-trust to high-trust manufacturing, among other places.

From low-trust to high-trust production

The early twentieth-century workplace, exemplified by Henry Ford's huge factories, was a hierarchical organization characterized by a high degree of formality. That is, there was an extensive division of labour mandated and controlled through a centralized, bureaucratic hierarchy, which laid down a large number of formal rules for how individual members of the organization were to behave. The principles of scientific management as elucidated by industrial engineer Fredrick Winslow Taylor and implemented by Ford contained an implicit premise that there were economies of scale in managerial intelligence segregated in a white-collar managerial hierarchy rather than being distributed throughout the organization.

In such a system there was no need for trust, social capital, or informal social norms: every worker was told where to stand, how to move his arms and legs, and when to take breaks and generally was not expected to display the slightest degree of creativity or judgement. Workers were motivated by purely individual incentives, whether rewards or punishments and were readily interchangeable with one another. Reacting to this system through their unions, the blue-collar labour force demanded formal guarantees of their rights and the narrowest possible specification of duties – hence, the rise of job control unionism and labour contracts that were as thick as telephone books.

Taylorism was an effective means – perhaps the only means – of co-ordinating the activities of a low-skill industrial labour force. In the first two decades of the century, half of Ford's blue-collar workers were first-generation immigrants who could not speak English and as late as the 1950s 80% did not have a high school education. But Taylorism ran into all of the problems of large, hierarchical organizations, with slow decision making, inflexible workplace rules and an inability to adapt to new circumstances.

The move from a hierarchical Taylorite organization to a flat or networked one involves off-loading the co-ordination function from formal bureaucratic rules to informal social norms. Authority does not disappear in a flat or networked organization; rather, it is internalized in a way that permits self-organization and self-management. A lean or just-in-time automobile factory is an example of a flat, post-Fordist organization. In terms of formal authority, many of the functions previously assigned to assembly line workers who themselves are acting in teams. It is the factory floor workforce itself that manages day-to-day scheduling, machine set-up, work discipline and quality control.

The degree to which power has been moved down to the bottom layer of the organization is symbolized by the famous cord at each workstation in Toyota's Takaoka assembly plant, which allows individual workers to stop the entire assembly line if they see a problem in the production process. The cord constitutes what game theorists would call a unit veto, by which each actor can sabotage the entire group's effort. This kind of authority can be safely delegated only under certain conditions: the workforce has to be adequately trained to be able to undertake the management duties formerly performed by white-collar middle managers, and they have to have a sense of responsibility to use their power to further group ends rather than individual ones. Such authority cannot be implemented in a region with a history of poisonous labour–management relations. The post-Fordist factory requires, in other words, a higher degree of trust and social capital than the Taylorite workplace with its comprehensive workplace rules.

As any number of studies have indicated, lean manufacturing has succeeded in improving productivity in the automobile industry by substantial margins, at the same time that it has improved product quality. The reason is that local information is processed much closer to its source: if a door panel from a subcontractor doesn't fit properly, the worker assigned to bolt it to the chassis has both the authority and the incentive to see that the problem is fixed rather then letting the information get lost while travelling up and down a long managerial hierarchy.

Regions and social networks

There is one further example of where social capital is critical to implementing a flat or networked form of organization: the American information technology industry. Silicon Valley might at first glance seem to be a low-trust and low-social capital part of the American economy, where competition rather than co-operation is the norm and efficiency arises out of the workings of rational utility maximizes meeting in impersonal markets as described by neo-classical economics. Firms are numerous, small and constantly fissioning from one another, they bubble up and die as a result of cut-throat competition. Employment is insecure, lifetime employment and loyalty to a given company unheard of. The relatively unregulated nature of the information technology industry, combined with well-developed venture capital markets, permits a high degree of entrepreneurial individualism.

This picture of unbridled competitive individualism is belied, however, by a number of more detailed sociological studies of the actual nature of technological development in the valley, such as Annalee Saxenian's *Regional Advantage*. In modern economy, social capital does not have to exist only within the boundaries of individual companies, or be embodied in practices like lifetime employment. Saxenian contrasts the performance of Silicon Valley with Boston's Route 128, and notes that one important reason for Silicon Valley's success had to do with the different culture there. Saxenian makes clear that beneath the surface of apparently unbridled individualistic competition were a wide array of social networks linking individuals in different companies in the semiconductor and computer businesses. These social networks had a variety of sources, including common educational background (e.g., an electrical engineering degree from Berkeley or Stanford) and common employment histories (many key players in the semiconductor industry like Robert Noyce and Andy Grove worked closely with one another in the early days of the industry at Fairchild Semiconductor), or they arose out of the norms of the Bay Area counterculture of the late 1960s and 1970s.

Informal networks are critical to technology development for a number of reasons. A great deal of knowledge is tacit and cannot be easily reduced to a commodity that can be bought and sold in an intellectual property market. The enormous complexity of the underlying technologies and of the systems integration process means that even the largest firms will not be able to generate adequate technical knowledge in-house. While technology is transferred between firms through mergers, acquisitions, cross-licensing, and formal partnerships, the literature on technology development in Silicon Valley stresses the informal nature of a great deal of the R&D work there. According to Saxenian,

> The informal socialising that grew out of the quasi-familial relationships supported the ubiquitous practices of collaboration and sharing of information among local producers. The Wagon Wheel bar in Mountain View, a popular watering hole where engineers met to exchange ideas and gossip, has been termed the fountainhead of the semiconductor industry.....
>
> By all accounts, these informal conversations were pervasive and served as an important source of up-to-date information about competitors, customers, markets and technologies....In an industry characterised by rapid technological change and intense competition, such informal communication was often of more value than more conventional but less timely forums such as industry journals.

She argues that the proprietary attitudes of a Route 128 firm like Digital Equipment proved to be a liability. Unable ultimately to be a self-sufficient vertically integrated producer of technology, it lacked the informal links and trust necessary to share technology with rivals.

That these technology networks had an ethical and social dimension critical to their economic function is clear from the following comment: 'Local engineers recognise that the quality of the feedback and information obtained through their networks depends upon the credibility and trustworthiness of the information provider. This sort of quality is only assured with individuals with whom you share common backgrounds and work experiences.' These shared professional and personal norms thus constituted an important form of social capital.

Other writers have analysed the growth of so-called communities of practice in other areas of technology development. That is, individual engineers working on the development of a specific technology tend to share information with one another on the basis of mutual respect and trust. The communities that emerge are *sui generis*; while they may be based on common educational or employment backgrounds, they frequently span the boundaries of individual organizations and areas of professional specialization.

These informal networks are probably more important in the information technology industry than in other sectors. In the chemical-pharmaceutical industry, where a large revenue stream can rest on knowledge of a single molecule, companies are understandably more cautious about sharing their intellectual property. Information technology, by contrast, is much more complex, involving the integration of a large number of highly advanced product and process technologies. The likelihood that a given bit of proprietary knowledge shared with a potential competitor will lead to direct losses is relatively small.

The social capital produced but such informal social networks permits Silicon Valley to achieve scale economics in R&D not possible in large, vertically integrated firms. Much has been written about the co-operative character of Japanese firms and the way in which technology is shared among members of a *keiretsu* network. In a certain sense, the whole of Silicon Valley can be seen as a single large network organization that can tap expertise and specialized skills unavailable to even the largest vertically integrated Japanese electronics firm and their *keiretsu* partners.

The importance of social capital to technology development has some paradoxical results. One is that despite globalization, geographical proximity remains important – perhaps even more important – than previously. Michael Porter among other observers has noted that despite advances in communications and transportation technology, a number of industries, and particularly high-tech R&D, remain highly concentrated in particular geographical locations. If information can now be readily shared over electronic networks, why is there not further geographical dispersal of industries? It would appear that the impersonal sharing of data over electronic networks is not enough to create the kind of mutual trust and respect evident in places like Silicon Valley; for that, face-to-face contact and reciprocal engagement that comes about as a result of repeated social interaction are necessary. Thus, although the manufacture of commodity-like goods can be out-sourced to parts of the world with low labour costs, it is much more difficult to do this with sophisticated technology development.

The fact that regions remain important does not imply that the world is returning to some kind of small-town clubbiness. In a global economy, even large and technologically sophisticated regions like the area around Provo, Utah, home to a booming software industry that includes the now-failing Novell and WordPerfect, can find themselves lacking the scale they need to stay on the cutting edge. 'Weak' ties remain important; networks need to overlap one another if ideas and innovations are to flow freely. On the other hand, it is hard to turn ideas into wealth in the absence of social connectedness, which in the age of the Internet still requires something more than bandwidth and high-speed connectivity.

Source: Edited extract from Chapter 12 in *The Great Disruption*, 1999, London: Profile Books.

Section H   Responsibility

There is increasing attention being paid to the social responsibility of organizations. Here Handy argues for a new relationship between employer and employee that reflects this, and Kanter argues that social innovation partnerships between organizations and the community can be profitable for both parties.

Charles Handy, perhaps the foremost English business guru and social commentator, argues that it is time to redefine the relationship between the employer and employee in a more socially responsible direction, and that all staff are better seen as citizens of organizations which are largely facilitating mechanisms. He suggests this approach would facilitate trust among core members, a trust needed if staff are ever to bond enough to be willing to share their intellectual property.

Rosabeth Moss Kanter is known for her work on organizational transformation in innovative companies, but she began her working life in the public and not-for-profit sectors. Here she argues that socially responsible activities can offer more than good PR and a feel-good factor for the staff. Rather that social partnership with a community project in an area related to the organization's expertise can prove to be an excellent source of training, a useful R&D laboratory, a source of able and committed staff, and even offer new markets. In short, organizational involvement in social innovation seems to have the potential for knowledge and business performance payoff.

19 The Citizen Company

Charles Handy

Business and indeed all institutions, are communities not properties, and their inhabitants are to be more properly thought of as citizens rather then employees or human resources. What will this mean in practice?

Citizens in all democracies have the rights of residence, justice, free speech, a share of the wealth of society in some way, and a say, usually a vote, in the governance of their society. Most importantly, however, a citizen is entitled to life, liberty and the pursuit of happiness, as the Americans have it, in other words the right to make your own life, subject to the laws of the land. The essential freedom of the individual has been the driving force behind democracy down the ages. It is this force that organizations must now come to terms with as their individuals begin to expect from their work communities the same collection of freedoms, rights and responsibilities that they have in the wider society. People are property no more.

Translated into corporate terms, a citizen's right to residence means some guarantee of employment; not for life, because that would be unrealistic, but for a fixed period of years – a decade, for example. It is reasonable to substitute predictability for permanence in a more uncertain world, and few, anyway, of the citizen-calibre workers would want to sign a commitment for life. What is needed to restore commitment in the workplace is a rebalancing of power, so that those in control make commitments in order to win commitment. We will increasingly, I suggest, live our lives in five- to ten-year chunks, so that a ten-year commitment will be seen as a fair definition of guaranteed residence. Justice, free speech and a share of the wealth are all easy to translate into the corporate world, but not always delivered. A say in governance translates into a right to be consulted about major decisions affecting the future of the corporation.

This has all the feel of a trade union manifesto, and some unions are moving this way, wanting to make their members citizens of the employing organization. In 1997 two large British industrial groups agreed to a guarantee of four years' employment for their core workforce in return for a promise of flexible working. But citizenship is not just the outcome of negotiation or arbitration. It is more subtle than that, something that grows from a shared commitment, bits of which can be defined in writing, such as the length of residence and the share of the wealth, but much of which is more intangible. As long as trade unions have an adversarial relationship with the organization they will have little role in a citizen company, and the citizens will not want them.

Oddly, perhaps, the British are not citizens (except, by international convention, on their passports) but subjects, subjects of Her Majesty the Queen. Although this is an historical accident, the different words may have made a subconscious difference. There is no Bill of Rights in Britain and no written constitution. Citizens tend to expect these things, which are to be found in most other democracies. Citizen Companies will need written constitutions.

Partnership and associate are terms that fall more comfortably on British ears. They are also terms that are easier to apply to two other stakeholders – the suppliers and the customers. It is important for any company to win the trust and co-operation of the targets and most important of these groups, along with the most significant of their investors. Were citizenship to be formalized in any way, it would be appropriate to see these other stakeholders as associate citizens, with at least the right to be kept informed to be consulted whenever appropriate. This form of associate citizenship should help to bond these crucial players into the long-term aims of the organization and to build a degree of mutual trust by the sharing of information. To win trust you have first to give trust.

One way to give formal expression to the right of citizenship would be to resurrect the old idea of A shares and B shares – voting and non-voting shares. The A shares, with their votes, would be confined to the personal citizens of the business – the core employees, or a Trust representing their interests. To these could be added significant holders of the equity, being investors who could be presumed to have a long-term interest in the business. Citizen rights could also be extended to the larger suppliers if they held an equity stake (as suppliers tend to do in Japan). To involve the community it might be possible to create the equivalent of the 'golden share' which the British Government awarded themselves in some of the companies created by privatization. This would give the community a voice, and conceivably a veto, in specific areas to do with the environment.

The idea of non-voting shares has always been hotly contested by the investment community – for obvious reasons. The investors would lose much of their power. But it is this power that will have to be reduced if the real members of these wealth-creating communities, the people who work there, are to have more say over their destiny and if the business is going to be more than the property of its financiers. The change will not, however, be soon or sudden. It will happen as the newer businesses explore ways to enfranchise their important constituents. It is only when these new businesses become large in their turn that the stock markets of the world will notice that they have, in their turn, lost their power.

The emergence of completely new forms of organizations may, of course, make all the talk of ownership irrelevant. The Internet, probably the fastest growing organization of all time, is owned by no one. Visa, the credit card service, carries over 7 billion transactions a year, worth over $650 billion, but is 'owned', if that is the right word, by the financial institutions, well over 20,000 of them, who are its services. Organizations like the Internet and Visa are facilitating mechanisms rather than collections of assets. Few in number at the moment, they may set a pattern for the future as more and more independent operators look for Geoff Mulgan's mechanisms of connexity.

Federalism is an old idea for the combination of independents but one which, rethought for the information age, offers some clues to possible futures. The point of federalism is that too much power should never be in one place or in one function. The centre is the servant of the parts, a facilitating mechanism with powers delegated to it by those parts. In practical terms, ownership then resides with the parts even if the outside investors think that they own the whole. To equate federalism with a super-state ruled by a powerful centre is a uniquely British distortion, one that may come to haunt us in years to come if we turn our backs on what may well be the form of the future.

We recently installed a new kitchen in our home. The firm we went to implied that they would design, build and install the kitchen. In practice they did none of these things themselves. It was a hollow firm. All the functions were subcontracted. None of them worked as they should. There was little the original firm could do about it other than harass and cajole their subcontractors who held the real power. It would have worked better the other way round; if the subcontractors had owned the firm who first sold us the promise of the kitchen, because it was the subcontractors who had the real power, but needed help to deliver it.

It will happen that way, eventually. Effective ownership will gradually revert to those who hold the resources, who will employ those who previously employed them. Those on the outside who provide only one of the resources – finance – will inevitably see their effective power recede. It is called 'subsidiarity', the old idea that power should morally and rightly lie at the bottom not the top of things. Put more simply – stealing people's responsibilities is morally wrong and doesn't work in the end. It is a pleasing thought that, ultimately, the pressures of modern business will compel us to be moral.

Sometimes one has to wonder why we need the concept of ownership at all. Oxfam, that large non-governmental organization, was described to me as a community which belonged to no one and which was fuelled by belief. As business realizes that its best people are really volunteers, there because they want to be, not because they have to, the model of the voluntary agencies may become increasingly relevant.

The herding of cats

Citizenship is about autonomy, the freedom to run your own life. In return for this freedom, the corporate state can demand little, but hope for much. Citizens in a democracy are free to emigrate. You cannot stop anyone leaving. Nor can you demand commitment, only hope for it. Combining this freedom and these rights with the aim of the organization is the real challenge of the citizen company. Many managers would prefer not to accept the challenge, because organizing talented people is akin to the proverbial herding of cats – difficult by definition. We have to manage people whom we can't totally control. Instead we have to trust them, and they have to trust us. The principle is simple. The practicalities mean that it seldom happens.

For a start, organizations as well as individuals have to earn the right to be trusted. But in an atmosphere of downlayering and out-sourcing, loyalty to the organization is today a rare commodity. Which is odd, because loyalty is worth money. Frederick Reichfield has put numbers on the Loyalty Effect, suggesting that *dis*loyalty from employees, investors and customers can stunt performance and productivity by up to 50%.

Once established, however, an organization with mutual trust at its core can be both creative and efficient. People obviously work better if they are not looking over their shoulders for the next job. They work more creatively if they respect the people around them and believe in what they are doing. Where they trust the organization, where they are committed to its goals and share in some way in the results of the business, they are more likely to accept relocation, reassignments, even temporary across-the-board pay cuts.

Who are these citizens? States, nowadays, require proof of talent and good behaviour from those who would apply to be their citizens. Some states would like to apply similar tests to those born into their citizenship, were there only some place else that they could dump them. Organizations are privileged in this respect. They can choose all their citizens, and would be wise to do so very carefully. Citizenship will certainly not be granted to all. In changing times no organization can make even ten-year commitments to too many people, but will keep their citizenship core as small as possible.

There will also be the necessary mercenaries, who could always turn into citizens, and there will be probationer citizens, who have to prove their worth and earn trust. The citizen core will be the proven 'trusties'. For an example of how such an organization works we only have to look at professional partnerships, in law, accountancy, consulting or architecture. The partners in a professional partnership are the full citizens of that organization, so much so that all the outcomes belong to them, bad as well as good. A public company with limited liability does not have to ask so much of its citizens, but, proportionately, the rewards and the commitment are probably lower.

Businesses could also look at universities, who have long struggled with the dilemma of tenure, or life citizenship. This dilemma is nicely put in the jibe that those who need tenure don't deserve it and those who deserve it don't need it. Tenure, which was once the guarantee that you could speak your mind without fear of dismissal, is now a guarantee of a job for life, a protection that the best should not need. Unfortunately, the best are not guaranteed to remain that way. The universities fear that they may get lumbered with unworthy citizens who cannot be expelled. Indefinite tenure then becomes expensive and demoralizing to the rest.

To prevent this deterioration the stakes have been raised in the initial tenure decision. It is now much harder to be accepted as a full citizen after the necessary probationary period. Tenure is also becoming more conditional, subject to periodic review or, even, to termination after due process and proper notice. Citizenship, in other words, is now more clearly seen to have responsibilities as well as rights. In business it was often the other way round – citizens, if one could call them such, had more responsibilities than rights. The worlds of academia and commerce are meeting each other halfway.

The payoff for a citizen company should be a shared commitment and mutual trust. But the trust has to be in the bloodstream, no matter how well the bone structure or the nervous system have been designed. In a world where work is where you are – in the car or plane, at the office or at home, on the client's premises or in a hotel – you will increasingly have to work with people whom you do not see. Organizations are drowning in communications, in e-mail, voice mail, faxes and telephones, but you can tell lies on e-mail and not be noticed, and who knows whether your fax or your e-mail has actually been read, not crumpled, lost or deleted. More than ever before we have to trust those with whom we work.

Trust sounds like a nice motherhood term, something no one could be against, all warm and woolly. In practice, however, it is difficult and tough. Management by trust depends upon some clear rules and principles, which will have to become the guidebook for a citizen company. There are seven cardinal principles of trust:

1 Trust is not blind

It is unwise to trust people whom you do not know well, whom you have not observed in action over time, and who are not committed to the same goals. How many people do any of us know that well? In ordinary life there is seems to be a rule of twelve. When asked how many people's death would affect them personally, or how many telephone numbers they can remember it is seldom more than twelve. Work demands less stringent conditions. In practice, we can probably know a maximum of fifty people well enough to rely on them in ordinary circumstances. Those fifty can, in their turn, know another fifty, and so on.

Large organizations are not, therefore, incompatible with the principle of trust, but they have to be made up of relatively constant and smaller groupings. Impossible? Asea Brown Boveri (ABB) has 225,000 employees working in 5,000 business units which operate in 142 different countries. Each unit has an average of 45 people working in its citizen core. The larger factories manage with 300, which is stretching it. The units combine with each other in an infinitely flexible way to create a powerful and fast-growing complex corporation, but the building blocks conform to the rule of fifty.

Make the groups larger, or change them too frequently, and the organization starts to replace trust with systems of control, because the people do not know each other well enough to develop trust. My title, in one large organization, was MKR/32. In this capacity I wrote memos to FIN/41 or PRO/23. I often knew no names and met no people behind these titles. I had no reason to trust them and, frankly, no desire to. I was a 'temporary role occupant' in the jargon of the time, a role occupant in an organization of command and control, based on the premise that no one could really be trusted, only the system. I left after a year, for such places can truly be a prison for the human soul, and in those prisons people seldom grow because there is no space to explore the truth about yourself. Worse, these prisons, boring though they may be, suck up energy, leaving little over for explanation outside. Role underload, studies show, can be more crippling than role overload.

2   Trust needs boundaries

Unlimited trust is, in practice, unrealistic. We trust our friends in some respects of life but not in all. A neighbour may be a great help in emergencies, but hopelessly unreliable when it comes to money. 'I would trust him with everything – except for my wife' one man wrote in a reference for an applicant to the programme I was running. We manage our young on a loose rein, but the rein is always there, getting longer and looser as we trust them more. It is no different in organizations.

By trust, organizations really mean confidence, a confidence in someone's competence, and in their commitment to the goal. Define that goal, and the trusted individual or team can be left to get on with it. Control is then exercised after the event, by assessing the results, rather than before the event, by granting permission. This freedom within boundaries works best, of course, when the work-unit is self-contained, with the capability to solve its own problems.

Trust-based organizations are redesigning their work, pulling back from the old reductionist models of organization, whereby everything was divided into component parts or functions, where everybody only did bits of things and seldom saw the whole. The new, holistic designs for the units of the organization look, at first, to be more expensive that the old functional types, because they often duplicate functions, maintaining separate accounting sections, for instance. The hope is that the energy and effectiveness released by the new freedom within boundaries more than compensates. Where we are trusted to find our own means to some agreed results we have the room to explore, to put our own signature on the work.

Unfortunately, this redesigning was called 're-engineering' - a word from the old world of machines. Re-engineering became a euphemism for getting rid of people, the sign of a manipulative management, never to be trusted. This is sad, because the redesigning was intended to be an outward and visible sign of trust. It is interesting to reflect that very old organizations, such as the Catholic Church, were structured on the principle of the microcosm: that each part should be a microcosm, a smaller mirror image, of the whole, with the ability to organize its own destiny. Perversely, it was because the centre could not communicate with the parts that the parts had to be trusted to look after themselves, bonded together only by a common ethos and tradition. Trust was then essential. These days, the abundance of our communication gets in the way of trust. It is too easy to find out what is going on.

3   Trust requires constant learning

An organizational architecture made up of relatively independent and constant groupings, pushes the organization towards the sort of federal structure that is becoming more common everywhere. A necessary condition of constancy, however, is an ability to change. The constant groups must always be flexible enough to change when times, and customers, demand it. This, in turn, requires that the groups keep themselves abreast of change, forever exploring new options and new technologies, in order to create a real learning culture. The choice of people for these groups is, therefore, of crucial importance. Every individual has to be capable of self-renewal. The ability to search for oneself and to regard learning as a continuing part of life, which was the justification for trusting someone in the first place, becomes one of the keys to its success.

Learning, however, like trust, can be squashed by fear. No one will stick their neck out, or take the sort of initiatives which new situations require, if they are fearful of the consequences if they are wrong. Trust, like learning, requires unconditional support, and forgiveness for mistakes, provided always that the mistakes are learnt from.

4 Trust is tough

When trust proves to be misplaced, not necessarily because people are deceitful or malicious, but because they do not live up to expectations, or cannot be relied upon to do what is needed, then those people have, ultimately, to go, or have their boundaries severely curtailed. Trust is like glass: once broken it can never be the same again. Where you cannot trust, you have to check once more, with all the systems of control that involves. Therefore, for the sake of the bigger whole the individual must leave. Trust has to be ruthless. The pressures to perform, however, can be positive. Most of us need deadlines and targets to pull the best out of us. Where rules and checks predominate, on the other hand, satisficing, doing enough to get by, is the preferred behaviour. We settle for enough when enough, in the case of personal growth or creativity, is never enough.

5 Trust needs bonding

Self-contained units, responsible for delivering specified results, are the necessary building blocks of an organization based on trust, but long-lasting groups of trusties can create their problems, those of organizations within the organization. For the whole to work, the goals of the bits have to gel with the goals of the whole. The blossoming of Vision and Mission statements is one attempt to deal with this, as are campaigns for 'total quality' or 'excellence'. These well-meant initiatives can boomerang, however, if they are imposed from the top. They become the equivalent of the compulsory school song, more mocked than loved. In one organization where I worked, a memorandum was circulated from Head Office stating that with immediate effect the organization was committed to a Theory Y philosophy – a belief that individuals are self-motivating. The contrast between the medium and the message caused hilarity. Like morality, visions and missions are caught, not taught.

Anita Roddick holds her spreading Body Shop group together by what can best be called 'personal infection', pouring her energies into the reinforcement of her values and beliefs through every medium she can find. It is always a dangerous strategy to personalize a mission, in case the person themselves stumbles or falls, but organizations based on trust need this sort of personal statement from their leaders. Trust is not, and can never be, an impersonal commodity.

6 Trust needs touch

Visionary leaders, however, no matter how articulate, are not enough. A shared commitment still requires a personal contact to make the commitment feel real. Paradoxically, the more virtual an organization becomes the more people need to meet in person. The meetings, however, are different. They are more to do with process than task, more concerned that the people get to know each other than that they deliver. Video conferences are more task-focused, but they are easier and more productive if the individuals already know each other as persons, not just as images on the screen. Work and play, therefore, alternate in many of the corporate get togethers which now fill the conference resorts out of season.

These are not perks for the privileged. They are the necessary lubricants of virtuality, occasions for not only getting to know each other, and for meeting the leaders, but for reinforcing corporate goals and rethinking corporate strategies. As one who delivers the occasional 'cabaret' at such occasions, I am always surprised to find how few of the participants have met each other in person, even if they have worked together before. I am then further surprised by how a common mood develops. You can almost watch the culture grow and you wonder how anyone could have worked effectively without it.

7 Trust has to be earned

This principle is the most obvious and yet the most neglected. Organizations who expect their people to trust them, must first demonstrate that they are trustworthy. Organizations that break implied contracts through downsizing will find that those who are left will trust them even less. Individuals will not be trusted fully until they have proved they can deliver. Governments who promise to cut taxes but end up increasing them forfeit the trust of the voters.

These cultures of trust are easier to grow and to preserve within the bounds of a single organization. As organizations become semi-dismantled, as many more people find themselves outside the organization, then the issues become more difficult to deal with. Do you and your suppliers, or you and your clients, have the same goals? If not, then trust will be difficult because each will suspect the other of promoting their agenda rather then the joint one. Are the boundaries and the contracts clear and understood? How often have you met, and what sort of affinity is there between you? Are genuine mistakes acknowledged and forgiven? These questions are as important outside the organization as inside. If they can't be answered positively, business becomes adversarial, complicated and fun.

Stories to make a point

St Luke's Advertising Agency

At the end of 1996 there were fifty-five names on their notepaper, because that was the number of staff they had then. They were on the notepaper because the agency is owned by all members of the staff, from receptionist to chairman.

The ownership is handled through a British device called a 'Quest' – a qualifying employee share ownership trust. The Trust held all the shares initially, but then dispensed some of them to each employee. Every year there is another distribution so that those who stay longest get most shares. The company is valued every year and the Trust buys back, at full value, the shares of anyone who is leaving, although not many are expected to leave, says Andy Law, the chairman. In fact, unusually for the advertising industry, only two of the original thirty-five members in 1995 have since left, one to be a deep sea diver.

Although everyone is an equal citizen, as far as their ownership entitlement goes, the normal operational hierarchies do still exist, but they are as flat as can be. There are also pay differentials and annual performance reviews. The office is modelled on a university, in the sense that the place is a resource centre rather than a working-day apartment house. There is a refectory and a library, but no personal offices, and no one has a secretary, not even the chairman. Staff put their belongings in lockers and carry their work around in standard issue shoulder bags, borrowing an office or a desk when they need it. Each floor has computers where messages and diaries can be checked. The rooms are, in fact, allocated to clients rather than departments. Once a room has been allocated to a client, all meetings and data relevant to that client are held there. Andy Law tells clients, 'Here is a raw, boiling talent of creative people who are smart and have got the right resources. You tell us what you need and we'll change to fit the shape.'

Not to everyone's taste perhaps, but here is a new model of a citizenship company, where everyone is involved and committed to a common purpose, which is underlined by the physical layout. Why, after all, are we so fixated on having our private apartment at work? Most people work where the client is – teachers don't have private offices, nor do plumbers, electricians or almost anyone in the building trade. Shop assistants, restaurant staff, hairdressers, most journalists, actors, consultants most of the time, lorry drivers, gardeners and cooks, factory foremen and women – none of these feels the need for a private space which they can fill with their files and their family photographs. They find their privacy at home, if they need it.

More and more of us will be pressured into doing likewise as organizations begin to question the sense of having offices available for 168 hours a week but only used for 48 or so at most. We will turn the idea of the office upside down, as St Luke's have done, and make the office the client's room so that we work together where the client is, and on our own wherever we want to be.

Making magic

As an experiment in executive development, the Arts Business Forum in London invited ten leading companies to nominate one of their executives to join an experimental programme of learning from the theatre.

Six of them went to the circus, as one of their chosen shows. [Afterwards] they said that they had seldom seen such an example of teamwork, discipline and commitment to excellence – better, said one, than anything in our company. One of them summed it up: 'That night, we saw ordinary people making magic,' and he added, 'I bet they are paid peanuts, while my bank pays people fortunes and we don't get anything like that standard of work out of them. What are we missing?'

What they were missing, the group agreed, was a dedication to an art form which mattered more to them than money, plus the nightly applause which was a constant recognition of their expertise and their 'magic'. Large pay packets and an annual appraisal do not always compensate for that intensity of commitment or the nightly 'high' for the whole team.

The circus is one example of what businesses can learn from other organizations who have long experience of harnessing individual talent to common purposes. Professionalism, Projects, Passion and Pride seem to be the hallmarks of the organizations of talent. The theatre is another example, one where individuals become team members for a production, with a shared interest in its success. In like vein, the world of film and television is organized around projects and, at its best, draws on passion and pride as well as professionalism. Orchestras and jazz bands have also been cited as models for the new way of working. Few of these places would claim to be perfect, but they understand that at their best they are engaged in making magic.

The great game of business

This is the title of a book written by Jack Stack, describing his experience at Springfield Re-Manufacturing company in Missouri. This company has now become as much an exhibition as a manufacturing business. More than 2,500 people have paid $1,250 each to go and see what Jack Stack and his colleagues have been doing in this un-high-tech business, reconditioning engines. The concept which they gave birth to and called 'open book management' may be the most important of the new managerial gizmos of recent times, with the added value that it corresponds with common sense and a respect for the average human being's capacity for good work if he or she is treated as a citizen.

In 1983 Stack and others bought out a unit of International Harvester when that company was going through hard times. They started with no money and lots of debt, to be precise, an 89:1 debt:equity ratio with interest at 18%. Stack's only priority, he says, was 'don't run out of cash'. To help with that aim it was important to help all the 119 people working at Springfield Re-Manufacturing to understand the firm's cash situation, so the management started to share all the numbers with everyone, right down to the doorman, and to provide bonus systems and share incentives to reward their efforts. Over 30% of the company is now owned by the workers. All obvious, really, but more difficult than one might think to do in practice. You have to walk your talk, as they say.

The process begins by giving people information regularly, every week, on company performance, as if they were confidential analysts looking at the business. Job counts, inventory levels, sales, expense ratios, bank balances, nothing is held back. The company then puts a great deal of effort into educating people to understand all these numbers. There are what they call 'huddles' to share views and to help work out the implications of the financial figures, a network of 'player coaches' and a big emphasis on self-management. Stack called it The Great Game of Business, on the grounds that business can be fun and personally rewarding, like a good game, but that to play it everyone needs to know all the rules, they need to be able to follow the action, and they have to have a stake in winning.

Denise Bedfeld remembers her first experience. She worked on the line building pumps, valves and cylinders. Jack asked her one day if she thought that she was making the company money. 'Sure,' she replied. 'Prove it,' said Jack. 'Then he gave me a two-hour lecture on how to determine costs. I took two weeks and scrabbled around, digging up information. I didn't know anything. I had to learn as I went along. Finally I proved that our section was making money, but not as much as I thought. Transmissions were making more. They say numbers don't lie – and it was obvious from the numbers what we had to do. He armed us with the information we needed to make wise decisions.'

Some of the proof lies in the numbers. The share price rose from 10 cents to $18.60 in just ten years. The company now does over $100 million in sales, operates several different divisions, and employs nearly 800 people. Jack wrote his book about it all, and has now had more than 200 imitators. Treating people as responsible adults and citizens, trust and recognition, room to be yourself – it seems to work, for everyone.

The stories cited relate to relatively small organizations. At first sight it is hard to see how they might apply to the large supranationals discussed in the previous chapter. But, as ABB has proved, large organizations can be composed of flexible combinations of very small organizations, in each of which there can be a sense of partnership in a shared adventure, trust, recognition and a share in the rewards of success. The four Ps of Professionalism, Projects, Passion and Pride are not the exclusive property of new or creative businesses, but they seem to be the necessary elements of corporate citizenship. Given the mood of the times, and the hungry spirit which sits within each of us, there is no alternative but to give more space and more sense of partnership to the citizen core of any organization.

The practical implications are:

- a much greater emphasis on the selection of the citizens, to ensure that they are likely to be kindred spirits, as well as professionally competent;
- an explicit contract with each individual, laying down tenure limits and partnership rights, to demonstrate that the work is to the benefit of all and to make the commitment of the organization clear;
- a formal constitution which sets out rights and duties, so that the boundaries of trust are known;
- a clear understanding, not necessarily in writing, of the imperatives of the organization, what it stands for and what it seeks to achieve, above and beyond the monetary goals, to elicit some of that passion;
- control by results more than by procedures, as a demonstration of trust and a source of pride.

Those who qualify for the citizen core of any organization will no longer be content to be regarded as the instruments of that organization, no matter how well rewarded, because they will, mostly, be able to turn mercenary if they need to. The citizen company will, therefore, gradually become a necessary way to organize, difficult though it will always be to manage and to lead.

In *Organizing Genius*, Warren Bennis, philosopher of leadership and articulate observer of American organizations, has described the methods and the history of some of America's most famous creative groups, including the Manhattan Project which made the first atomic bomb, the Disney animation studio and Bill Clinton's campaign team for his first presidential election. As he analyses these Great Groups, Bennis finds they had much in common despite their variety. They were all grouped around a specific and prestigious project and their members were all recognized as experts in their field. Those members had a consuming passion for their cause. They were careless of money or material comfort, often working in makeshift quarters for long hours with little pay, they were young (mostly under thirty), had great camaraderie and were given as much space in their work as they could handle. Their pride in their membership and, eventually, their achievements was obvious. He doesn't call them citizens, but that is what, in effect, they were.

Source: Edited extract from *The Hungry Spirit*, 1997, New York: Random House, pp. 179–204.

20 From Spare Change to Real Change

Rosabeth Moss Kanter

Some companies are moving beyond corporate social responsibility to corporate social innovation. Companies are viewing community needs as opportunities to develop ideas and demonstrate business technologies; find and serve new markets; and solve long-standing business problems. Successful private–public partnerships share six characteristics: a clear business agenda, strong partners committed to change, investment by both parties, rootedness in the user community, links to other organizations, and a commitment to sustain and replicate the results.

Winning in business today demands innovation. Companies that innovate reap all the advantages of a first mover. They acquire a deep knowledge of new markets and develop strong relationships within them. Innovators also build a reputation of being able to solve the most challenging problems. That's why corporations spend billions of dollars each year trying to identify opportunities for innovation – unsolved problems or unmet needs, things that don't fit or don't work. They set up learning laboratories where they can stretch their thinking, extend their capabilities, experiment with new technologies, get feedback from early users about product potential, and gain experience working with underserved and emerging markets.

Today several leading companies are beginning to find inspiration in an unexpected place: the social sector – in public schools, welfare-to-work programmes, and the inner city. These companies have discovered that social problems are economic problems, whether it is the need for a trained workforce or the search for new markets in neglected parts of cities. They have learned that applying their energies to solving the chronic problems of the social sector powerfully stimulates their own business development. Today's better-educated children are tomorrow's knowledge workers. Lower unemployment in the inner city means higher consumption in the inner city. Indeed, a new paradigm for innovation is emerging: a partnership between private enterprise and public interest that produces profitable and sustainable change for both sides.

The new paradigm is long overdue. Traditional solutions to America's recalcitrant social ills amount to little more than Band-Aids. Consider the condition of public education. Despite an estimated 200,000 business partnerships with public schools, fundamental aspects of public education have barely changed in decades and performance is still weak. There are two reasons for this. First, traditional corporate volunteer activities only scratch the surface. And second, companies often just throw money at the problem, then walk away. The fact is, many recipients of business largesse often don't need charity; they need change. Not spare change, but real change-sustainable, replicable, institutionalized change that transforms their schools, their job prospects, and their neighborhoods. And that means getting business deeply involved in non-traditional ways.

Doing good by doing well

My team of researchers and I have found a number of companies that are breaking the mould – they are moving beyond corporate social responsibility to corporate social innovation. These companies are the vanguard of the new paradigm. They view community needs as opportunities to develop ideas and demonstrate business technologies, to find and serve new markets, and to solve long-standing business problems. They focus their efforts on inventing sophisticated solutions through a hands-on approach (see Box 20.1).

Tackling social sector problems forces companies to stretch their capabilities to produce innovations that have business as well as community payoffs. When companies approach social needs in this way, they have a stake in the problems, and they treat the effort the way they would treat any other project central to the company's operations. They use their best people and their core skills. This is not charity; it is R&D – a strategic business investment. Let's look at a few examples from the fields of education, welfare programmes, and inner-city development.

Public education

In 1991, Bell Atlantic began creating one of the first-ever models for using computer networks in public schools. Bell Atlantic's Project Explore, in Union City, New Jersey, enabled communication and learning to move beyond the classroom. In addition to installing computers in the schools, Bell Atlantic gave computers to 135 inner-city students and their teachers to use at home. Project Explore became a catalyst for increasing the use of technology to transform middle- and high-school classrooms, to improve students' skills, and to involve parents in their children's education. Union City's schools, once threatened with state takeover, have become national role models. Bell Atlantic has found new ways of handling data transmission. It refined its goals for video on demand and identified a new market in distance learning.

IBM began its Reinventing Education programme in 1994 under the personal leadership of CEO Louis V. Gerstner, Jr. Today the programme, designed to develop new tools and solutions for systemic change, operates in 2I U.S. sites and in four other countries. Many product innovations, which benefit both the schools and IBM, have resulted from this initiative. As part of the Wired for Learning programme in four new schools in Charlotte-Mecklenburg, North Carolina, for example, IBM created tools to connect parents to teachers digitally so that parents can view their children's schoolwork from home or a community centre and compare it with the district's academic standard. New tracking software is facilitating the introduction of flexible scheduling in Cincinnati, Ohio, including a new year-round high school. In Broward County, Florida – the fifth largest school district in the United States – IBM's data-warehousing technology gives teachers and administrators access to extensive information on students. In Philadelphia, Pennsylvania, IBM created a voice recognition tool to teach reading, which is based on children's high-pitched voices and speech patterns.

Box 20.1 Why America Needs Corporate Social Innovation

Despite its long economic boom, America's social problems abound. To ensure future economic success, the country needs dramatic improvement in public schools, more highly-skilled workers, jobs with a future for people coming off the welfare rolls, revitalized urban centres and inner cities, and healthy communities. Traditionally, businesses have supported the social sector in two ways: they contribute their employees' time for volunteer activities, and they support community initiatives with money and gifts in kind. Both accomplish good things and should be encouraged, but neither activity engages the unique skills and capabilities of business.

Consider the typical corporate volunteer program. It draws on the lowest common skills in a company by mobilizing people to do physical work – landscaping a school's grounds or painting walls in a community centre. Such projects are good for team building and may augment limited community budgets, even build new relationships, but they don't change the education system or strengthen economic prospects for community residents. In many cases, it is just as effective for the business simply to write a check to community residents or a small neighbourhood organization to do the work.

A great deal of business participation in social sector problems derives from the classic model of arm's-length charity – writing a check and leaving everything else to government and non-profit agencies. Businesses have little involvement in how these donations are used. This model discourages companies from taking an interest in results. Companies received their benefits up-front through tax write-offs and the public relations boost that accompanies the announcement of their largesse. There is little or no incentive to stay involved or to take responsibility for seeing that the contribution is used to reach a goal. However well meaning, many businesses treat the social sector as a charity case – a dumping ground for spare cash, obsolete equipment, and tired executives on their way out.

Such arm's-length models of corporate philanthropy have not produced fundamental solutions to America's most urgent domestic problems of public education, jobs for the disadvantaged, and neighbourhood revitalization. Traditional charity can't reach the root of the problems because it just treats the symptoms. Most business partnerships with schools, are limited in scope: they usually provide local resources to augment a school programme, such as scholarship funds, career days, sponsorship of an athletic team, or volunteer reading tutors. The criteria for involvement are minimal, often hinging only on geographic proximity to a company site. The 600 school principals I surveyed said they are grateful for any help. But what they really want are new ideas for systemic change that private enterprises are uniquely qualified to contribute.

As government downsizes and the public expects the private sector to step in to help solve community problems, it is important that businesses understand why the old models of corporate support don't create sustainable change. In partnership with government and non-profits, businesses need to go beyond the traditional models to tackle the much tougher task of innovation.

Welfare-to-work programmes

Since 1991, the hotel group Marriott International has been refining its pioneering training programme, Pathways to Independence. The programme, which currently runs in 13 US cities, hones the job skills, life skills, and work habits of welfare recipients, and Marriott guarantees participants a job offer when they complete the programme. The challenges of working with the unemployed has led the company to new insights about training, job placement, and supervision, which have helped Marriott reap the benefits of a more stable workforce and maintain unusually high standards of service. Pathways was a radical improvement on traditional programmes for the hard to employ, which were both bureaucratically cumbersome and often ineffective. The employee assistance innovations that Marriott has developed through the programme have also created new jobs in poor communities.

United Airlines is another company that derives business benefits from tapping a new workforce. Taking a leadership role in the Welfare-to-Work Partnership (a national coalition of 8,000 businesses that have pledged to hire people off the welfare rolls), CEO Gerald Greenwald seeks new ways to transport people from inner cities to suburban jobs. United has also created human resources innovations, such as a new mentoring programme. These innovations, developed in collaboration with workers, have become models for the new personnel practices United is now planning to roll out to its more than 10,000 new hires.

Inner-city development

BankBoston launched First Community Bank in 1990 as a way to target newcomers to the banking system – many of whom were located in the inner city. This initiative also responded to regulatory pressures on banks to increase investment in underserved urban neighborhoods. Thanks to First Community Bank, access to high-quality financial services for disadvantaged minorities and inner-city inhabitants has radically improved, which is helping to revitalize deteriorating neighborhoods. Since its inception, First Community Bank has been a laboratory for a stream of innovations that have been applied across BankBoston. From BankBoston's perspective, First Community Bank has been an undeniable success. The bank has grown from its initial 7 branches in Boston to 42 branches across New England. It offers a range of products and services that includes consumer lending, real estate, small-business loans, and venture capital. Today it is the anchor for all community banking services within BankBoston.

Making partnerships work

Making the new paradigm work isn't easy. In contrast to typical business-to-business relationships, there is an added layer of complexity. Government and non-profit organizations are driven by goals other than profitability, and they may even be suspicious of business motivations. Additionally, the institutional infrastructure of the social sector is undeveloped in business terms. For that reason, public schools and inner cities can be said to resemble emerging markets. Those difficulties, however, can be overcome. My research has identified six characteristics of successful private–public partnerships: a clear business agenda, strong partners committed to change, investment by both parties, rootedness in the user community, links to other community organizations, and a long-term commitment to sustain and replicate the results.

A clear business agenda

In the new paradigm, companies obviously want to make a social contribution. But a corporation has a better chance of making a real difference if it knows clearly, in advance, how its business agenda relates to specific social needs. A company that wants to develop new data analysis technology, for example, might target a large and complex education system as its beta site. Finding test users in the public schools would clearly benefit both the community and the company. Indeed, apart from the social benefits, there are two distinct business advantages. The first is the opportunity to test the new technology, and the second is the chance to build political capital – for instance, to influence regulations, to re-shape public institutions on which the company depends, to augment a public image as a leader, or to build closer relationships with government officials.

This coincidence of social needs with business and political goals is precisely illustrated by Bell Atlantic's Project Explore. Bell Atlantic was developing intelligent network technologies, video on demand, and other communications ideas. By the early 1990s, Bell Atlantic was ready to test Highbit-rate Digital Subscriber Line (HDSL) technologies with personal computers. Bell Communications Research, then the R&D laboratory shared by the Baby Bells after their divestiture from AT&T, sent Bell Atlantic a proposal to equip schools with computers. That would get the technology out into the field and allow the company to test the services that could be delivered over high-capacity lines into schools and homes.

Working with schools also fit the company's political agenda. In New Jersey, Bell Atlantic leaders hoped to win the support of legislators and regulators for the Opportunity New Jersey project, Bell Atlantic's proposed statewide technology communications plan. To garner support, they needed a demonstration site to showcase their communications networks. Bell Atlantic saw that testing its transmission technology in special-needs school districts could benefit both the company and the schools. Bell Atlantic's new technology, however, could work only for distances of about 9,000 feet on copper telephone wires, which in New Jersey had not yet been replaced with fibre-optic lines. The density of Union City's population and Union City's proximity to Bell Atlantic's central switching office made it an ideal site for testing and developing the company's innovations.

Marriott International also had a clear business agenda that addressed a social need. Over two-thirds of the company's 131,000 employees are entry level, lower-wage workers in housekeeping, engineering, security, maintenance, food service, and reservations. Developing an effective method to recruit, train, and retain workers in these positions has always been a critical concern. Throughout the 1980s, Marriott had reached out to untapped pockets of the labour market, such as Vietnam veterans, ex-offenders, the disabled, recent immigrants, and welfare mothers. Although the company received tax credits as a financial incentive, Marriott continued to be plagued by a high level of turnover and poor job performance. By the beginning of the 1990s, the company badly needed new sources of reliable labor. After some experimentation, the first viable Pathways program was launched in Atlanta, Georgia, in 1991. Since then, Marriott has not only reduced turnover rates but also improved job prospects in inner cities.

Strong partners committed to change

A critical feature of the new paradigm is the presence of committed social sector organizations and leaders who are already working on change. These can include public servants and community figures such as mayors, governors, school superintendents, and civic activists. Companies need such partners to bring together diverse constituencies and to provide political legitimacy. Strong support helps ensure that new solutions will create systemic change, not languish in isolated projects. Committed social partners can also help businesses win access to underserved markets – for example, the inner city – and they can build widespread support for other new ventures.

Consider how IBM chose partners for its Reinventing Education initiative. The company singled out school districts where leaders were thinking in new and creative ways. When evaluating grant proposals, IBM looked for widely communicated education reform goals and strategic plans that clearly identified where projects could add value. The backing of strong mayors who were personally committed to education reform was considered vital. Mayor Edward Rendell, for example, supported superintendent David Hornbeck's programme, Children Achieving in Philadelphia. The programme showed how business involvement could contribute and was a major factor behind IBM's decision to invest there. Similarly, in Florida, Broward County's nine-point vision statement and five-year information technology plan were crucial in convincing IBM to get involved. By seizing on local agendas, IBM ensured that its projects would command the personal attention of superintendents and other key figures.

Bell Atlantic also found willing partners already working on major change. A key factor in getting Project Explore started was the commitment of Thomas Highton, superintendent of schools, and Congressman Robert Menendez, then state senator and mayor of Union City. When Highton was promoted to superintendent in 1988, Union City schools were failing on almost all scores. There was very little teacher involvement in decision making or parent involvement in their children's education; facilities were in poor shape; the curriculum was outdated; there was little to no technology. Highton proposed to turn an abandoned parochial school into a technology school, an action that required state approval. For his part, Menendez wanted to get fibre-optic networks throughout New Jersey to improve education and health services. Bell Atlantic's proposal was timely. The company's commitment to Union City, brokered by Menendez, gave Highton the credibility he needed to get approval to buy the abandoned parochial school. The school was renamed after Christopher Columbus to reflect the journey of discovery ahead in the trial called Project Explore.

Partners for educational projects are easily identifiable because schools are large and highly organized. Companies confronting other social needs, however, may encounter many small nonprofit organizations, each of which works on a different piece of the problem. Marriott worked with various government and non-profit partners in each of its Pathways to Independence programmes – organizations such as Goodwill Industries, the Jewish Vocational Service, Private Industry Councils, and Workforce Development Boards. Marriott chose the strongest partner in each community.

United Airlines was also confronted with a patchwork of small community organizations working with welfare recipients. In launching its welfare-to-work efforts in San Francisco, United chose one strong non-profit placement organization to be its lead partner and urged other groups to work through that agency. The details differ, but in all cases, strong partnerships are a crucial aspect of the new paradigm.

Investment by both parties

The best way to ensure full commitment is to have both partners – not just the corporate but the community partner – put their resources on the line. Investment by both partners builds mutuality. It also ensures that the community partner will sustain the activities when contributions from business taper off.

In all of IBM's Reinventing Education initiatives, both partners put their hands in their pockets. IBM gave each school system a $2 million grant – up to 25% in cash and 75% or more in technical equipment, software, research, and consulting time. The team at each site determined the mix. Almost all of IBM's grant to Broward County, for example, went toward consulting time.

The schools also contributed financially to the projects, both in the development phase and when full rollout took place after the money ran out. The Philadelphia school system, for example, bought at least 100 computers in addition to the 36 PCs and 8 ThinkPads provided by IBM. Individual school principals also supplemented IBM and central office funds from their own budgets. To help manage the transition to internal leadership in Broward County, for instance, the schools paid for an IBM project manager and systems architect to remain for several months after grant funds were expended. Each school district also used considerable funds on staff time for planning and training, in addition to major technology investments.

BankBoston and its community partners sometimes share the costs of First Community Bank's projects. In Hartford, Connecticut, First Community Bank worked with the South Hartford Initiative, a community development organization, to establish a unique small-business lending programme in 1997. That innovation took many months to structure and negotiate. First Community Bank funds an average of 46% of each loan in South Hartford Initiatives' neighbourhoods; SHI funds the balance on a fully subordinated basis. First Community Bank reduces its normal commitment fee and interest rate, and SHI agrees to collect only interest for the term of the loan, until the principal amount is due. SHI has the option to underwrite loans declined by the bank, and First Community then services those loans.

Investment by both parties means more than just financial investments. Consider the Pathways to Independence programme. Some of Marriott's partners make direct financial contributions: Goodwill Industries reimburses over half of the programme's costs of approximately $5,000 per student in those cities in which it is Marriott's partner. But even partners that don't contribute financially commit resources. For example, while Marriott provides uniforms, lunches, training sites, programme management, on-the-job training, and mentoring, its partners help locate and screen candidates and assist them with housing, child care, and transportation.

During the life of an innovation project, the balance of investments can shift. Bell Atlantic bore the bulk of the costs for Project Explore when it was launched in 1993, after two years of planning. The company wired the new Columbus Middle School; trained the teachers; and gave 135 seventh graders and their teachers computers in their homes, along with printers and access to the Internet. Once involved, Bell Atlantic found its commitment growing. Even when the project had moved beyond a trial phase and had to compete for company resources every year, Bell Atlantic kept a project team on board to follow the group through seventh and eighth grades and into Emerson High. By 1995, Union City began to pick up the bills. The school system received a National Science Foundation grant to wire Emerson High School and buy most of the computers. By 1997, Union City was picking up 100% of the cost, although a part-time project manager from Bell Atlantic's Opportunity New Jersey remained to maintain the relationship.

Both partners also need to make strong staff commitments
IBM ensures that responsibilities in this area are balanced: a school-district project sponsor is matched with an IBM project executive, and a school-district project manager with an IBM on-site project manager. IBM does not rely on volunteers or part-time staff. It recruits the best talent it can for assignments, which are considered challenging as well as personally rewarding. Participants in the programmes must report their monthly costs and expenses – just as they

would report them to the CEO of a client company. Says an IBM official, 'We treat our school partners the way we treat our best customers.'

The experience of working so closely with businesses has had a deep impact on organizations in the social sector. Schools involved in the Bell Atlantic and IBM experiments, for example, have found that they have had to become more efficient and market-oriented in selecting staff for the projects.

Rootedness in the user community

Innovation is facilitated when developers learn directly from user experience. Therefore, IBM's projects were designed to bring technologists close to the schools. In Broward County, the initial IBM office was housed in the computer lab at Sunrise Middle School. This location enabled constant interaction between IBM staff and teachers who evaluated the software. Moreover, becoming part of the school environment fostered rapid acceptance of the IBM team. 'They even ate cafeteria food,' an administrator exclaimed.

Yet even when a company goes on-site, there can be cultural obstacles. IBM employees tended to see school procedures as bureaucratic, while teachers had negative stereotypes of people working in large corporations. 'We move at different speeds,' one IBM team member explained. Cultural differences were also apparent in language – jargon was a significant barrier to communication. According to one IBM employee, the 'educational world has even more acronyms than the IBM world, which surprised everybody.' But over time, the presence of IBM people in the schools, and their openness to learn from educators, helped bridge the differences and allayed many of the schools' concerns that they would be taken over by business people.

In the inner-city neighbourhoods in which it operates, BankBoston's First Community Bank takes great care in staffing its branches to ensure that the employees understand the community. First Community Bank founder and president Gail Snowden, for example, grew up in the bank's core neighbourhood, where her parents ran a well-regarded community service organization. First Community Bank managers are expected to attend community events as part of their job. The bank has created new functions – such as community development officers who act as liaisons with customers in specific ethnic populations – to further embed it in its communities. The bank also offers customized technical assistance – for example, document translation or explanation of customs to new immigrants. Although these service innovations increase the time spent per transaction, they make First Community Bank branches part of the fabric of the neighborhood. That helps make parent BankBoston a leader in the urban market.

Links to other organizations

For projects to succeed, the business partner must call on the expertise of key players in the broader community. Bell Atlantic, for example, brought in the Stevens Institute of Technology – which had expertise in Internet capabilities and equipment configurations – to help build a curriculum for teachers around

Internet access. Similarly, IBM nurtured connections with the school districts' other partners, some of which already had a deep local presence. In Philadelphia, IBM relied on the Philadelphia Education Fund - an offshoot of Greater Philadelphia First, a coalition of the city's 35 largest corporations – as a source of local knowledge. In Cincinnati, IBM convened businesses and funders such as Procter & Gamble and General Electric to ensure that everyone worked toward the same ends in the schools.

BankBoston, too, finds its broader community and government contacts to be useful sources of additional ideas and finance for riskier deals and start-up businesses. First Community Bank's community development group, for instance, worked with about eight other banks and the US Small Business Administration to create a new 'fast track' SBA loan approval. Without external collaboration, no business innovation partnership can expect to enact lasting change.

A long-term commitment to sustain and replicate the solution

Like any RSD project, new-paradigm partnerships require sustained commitment. The inherent uncertainty of innovation – trying something that has never been done before in that particular setting – means that initial project plans are best guesses, not firm forecasts. Events beyond the company's control, unexpected obstacles in technology, political complexities, new opportunities or technologies unknown at the time plans were made – all of these can derail the best-laid plans. First Community Bank took five years to show a profit, but last year it was number one in sales out of all of BankBoston's retail operations. Investments in the social sector, just as in any start-up, require patient capital.

Each of the new-paradigm companies described wanted to create a successful prototype or demonstration project in the test site. But test sites, by nature, receive concentrated attention and resources. The real challenge is not sustaining an individual project but replicating it elsewhere. The best innovations can be mass-produced, adopted by users in other settings, and supported by additional investors. That is why replication and extension were explicit parts of IBM's strategy.

The Reinventing Education project began in ten school districts. First-round grants from IBM covered a three- to five-year period, and IBM wanted most of the money disbursed in the first two years so that the next three could be spent diffusing the innovation and examining the project's impact. Tools developed in the first round of innovations were then introduced through an additional IT project. To help the sites complete their individual rollouts, IBM staff continue to monitor sites for five years. IBM encourages cross-fertilization of ideas among all the Reinventing Education project sites. Broward County, for example, hosts officials from other school districts on a quarterly basis. Charlotte Mecklenburg's Wired for Learning prototype is spreading throughout North Carolina. And an IBM Web site discussion forum also helps spread ideas among the project sites – an arrangement that is beneficial both to schools and to IBM.

How business benefits

Sometimes business attempts to find innovation in the social sector are discounted by critics as public relations ploys. But as the depth and breadth of each company's commitment should make clear, that would be an extremely costly and risky way to get favourable press. The extensive efforts described here, with their goal of creating systemic change, also cannot be justified only on the grounds that they make employees or the community feel good even though that obviously motivates people to work hard. In reality, the primary business justification for the sustained commitment of resources is the new knowledge and capabilities that will stem from innovation.

Bell Atlantic's Project Explore was expensive, and it was not philanthropy. It was funded out of operating and technology-development budgets. Certainly, Bell Atlantic people felt good about helping inner-city schoolchildren succeed. And the company generates a continuing and growing revenue stream from selling network services to the education market, which it learned how to approach from its extensive experience in Union City. But the ultimate business justification for Project Explore was the know-how Bell Atlantic developed about networking technologies. As John Grady, now HDSL product manager but then the first Union City project manager, puts it, 'The Union City trial provided the first evidence that HDSL technology could work.' In April 1997, Grady and three other Bell Atlantic employees received a patent for a public-switch telephone network for multimedia transmission – a direct consequence of the innovations developed in Union City. That patent ultimately led to the introduction of Bell Atlantic's new Infospeed DSL product line in 1999.

IBM, too, stretches its technical capabilities by tackling the difficult problems in public schools. IBM employees experimented with new technology that has commercial applications. For the Reinventing Education project in Cincinnati, for example, IBM researchers developed new drag-and-drop technology for the Internet, which uses the latest features of Java and HTML and can be leveraged throughout IBM. As a systems architect in Cincinnati remarked, 'The group that I'm working with and I have learned more on this project than any other that we've worked on previously. We're working with people from the ground up. When we started, there was absolutely nothing except an idea about new Internet technology.' And the Broward County project extended IBM's data-warehousing know-how from small groups of users in retailing and related industries to very large groups of users with complicated data requirements – over 10,000 teachers and administrators in a school system.

Marriott's Pathways to Independence has produced tangible benefits for the company. About 70% of Pathways' graduates are still employed by Marriott after a year, compared with only 45% of the welfare hires who did not participate in Pathways and only 50% of other new hires. Marriott estimates that programme costs are recovered if graduates are retained 2.5 times longer than the average new hire. In fact, Pathways is considered to be such a source of competitive advantage for Marriott that the company shares only the general outlines of the programme with other companies and keeps the details proprietary. And success in the Pathways to Independence programme has encouraged Marriott to undertake other initiatives, such as the Associate Resource Line, a hot line that provides assistance with housing, transportation, immigration, financial and legal issues, even pet care. It cost Marriott $2 million to set up the hot line; it now saves $4 for every dollar spent, through lower turnover and reduced absenteeism.

BankBoston, too, has found business benefits from its social initiative. Its First Community Bank has become both a profitable operating unit and a source of product and service innovations that have been applied across all of BankBoston. These include First Step products for newcomers to banking; multilingual ATMs; a new venture-capital unit for equity investments in inner-city businesses; and community development officers, who help create lending opportunities. In fact, First Community bank has been so successful that BankBoston is refocusing its retail strategy toward community banking.

Employees' opinions of the initiative have also been transformed. Far from being a dead-end assignment, a position at First Community Bank is highly desirable because it offers the challenge and excitement of innovation. In January 1999, founding president Gail Snowden was promoted to head up the regional leadership group for all of BankBoston's retail banking. And in March 1999, President Clinton presented BankBoston with the Ron Brown Award for Corporate Leadership (for which I was a judge) in recognition of its community-banking activities. Clearly, businesses that partake in these new-paradigm partnerships reap tangible benefits.

Spreading the new paradigm

This article describes a new way for companies to approach the social sector: not as an object of charity but as an opportunity for learning and business development, supported by R&D and operating funds rather than philanthropy. Traditional charity and volunteerism have an important role in society, but they are often not the best or fastest way to produce innovation or transformation.

High-impact business contributions to the social sector use the core competencies of a business – the things it does best. For Bell Atlantic, it is communications technology; for IBM, it is information technology solutions; for Marriott, it is service strategies. In this new paradigm, the activities are focused on results, seeking measurable outcomes and demonstrated changes. The effort can be sustained and replicated in other places. The community gets new approaches that build capabilities and point the way to permanent improvements. The business gets bottom-line benefits: new products, new solutions to critical problems, and new market opportunities.

New-paradigm partnerships could reinvent American institutions. They open new possibilities for solving recalcitrant social and educational problems. They give businesses a new way to innovate. Today these examples are still works in progress. But tomorrow they could be the way business is done everywhere.

Source: Harvard Business Review; 1999, May, pp. 122–32.

Section I Sustainability

The threat to the Earth's eco-systems posed by economic activity is placing organizations under increasing pressure to operate in a more sustainable manner. Here Lovins argues that a change in business values can help businesses operate both sustainably and profitably, and Shiva shows how fragmented Western thinking has led to the dominance of unsustainable Western patterns of cultivation and the neglect of traditional local knowledge that offers sustainable alternatives.

Hunter and Amory Lovins have been arguing the merits of what they term Natural Capitalism for some time. The idea here is that the way forward for industry is to mimic nature in manufacturing though systems of closed-loop manufacturing, and by so doing to make money. Their diagnosis of the problem is that our current habits of thought and accounting lead us to make non-optimum decisions, a problem for which they advocate a switch to whole systems thinking, for example basing purchasing decisions on the life cycle cost, not purchase price. Also improved incentives, for example a system that compensates you for what you save rather than what you spend. One telling example they offer is the idea of a redefinition of business purpose around value rather than output (such as selling illumination rather than light bulbs) which they argue is both environmentally and business friendly. They quote carpet and elevator companies who have begun to lease their products rather than sell them; with this the business incentives shift towards manufacturing fewer longer lasting products rather than cheaper and more wasteful ones, an environmentally desirable goal.

Vandana Shiva is an Indian environmentalist and recent BBC Reith lecturer. She explains how Western patterns of thought lead to particular ways of being in the world which lead to the West exporting its approaches and assuming that this knowledge is appropriate in other settings, aptly summarized in her title 'Monocultures of the mind'. Shiva argues that the fragmented nature of Western thought leads Westerners to ignore the holistic aspects of problems in a way which would be unthinkable in a traditional society, and that imposing Western accounting and agricultural systems discounts important local knowledge to the detriment of the local inhabitants and their environment.

21 A Road Map for Natural Capitalism

Amory B. Lovins, L. Hunter Lovins and Paul Hawken

Business strategies built around the radically more productive use of natural resources can solve many environmental problems at a profit.

The earth's ability to sustain life, and therefore economic activity, is threatened by the way we extract, process, transport, and dispose of a vast flow of resources – some 220 billion tons a year, or more than 20 times the average American's body weight every day. With dangerously narrow focus, our industries look only at the exploitable resources of the earth's ecosystems – its oceans, forests, and plains – and not at the larger services that those systems provide for free. Resources and ecosystem services both come from the earth – even from the same biological systems – but they're two different things. Forests, for instance, not only produce the resource of wood fibre but also provide such ecosystem services as water storage, habitat, and regulation of the atmosphere and climate. Yet companies that earn income from harvesting the wood fibre resource often do so in ways that damage the forest's ability to carry out its other vital tasks.

Unfortunately, the cost of destroying ecosystem services becomes apparent only when the services start to break down. In China's Yangtze basin in 1998, for example, deforestation triggered flooding that killed 3,700 people, dislocated 223 million, and inundated 60 million acres of cropland. That £30 billion disaster forced a logging moratorium and a $12 billion crash programme of reforestation.

The reason companies (and governments) are so prodigal with ecosystem services is that the value of those services doesn't appear on the business balance sheet. But that's a staggering omission. The economy, after all, is embedded in the environment. Recent calculations published in the journal *Nature* conservatively estimate the value of all the earth's ecosystem services to be at least £33 trillion a year. That's close to the gross world product, and it implies a capitalized book value on the order of half a quadrillion dollars. What's more, for most of these services, there is no known substitute at any price, and we can't live without them.

This article puts forward a new approach not only for protecting the biosphere but also improving profits and competitiveness. Some very simple changes to the way we run our businesses, built on advanced techniques for making resources more productive, can yield startling benefits both for today's shareholders and for future generations.

This approach is called *natural capitalism* because it's what capitalism might become if its largest category of capital – the 'natural capital' of ecosystems services – were properly valued. The journey to natural capitalism involves four major shifts in business practices, all virtually interlinked:

- *Dramatically increase the productivity of natural resources.* Reducing the wasteful and destructive flow of resources from depletion to pollution represents a major business opportunity. Through fundamental changes in both production design and technology, far-sighted companies are developing ways to make natural resources – energy, minerals, water, forests – stretch 5, 10, even 100 times further than they do today. These major resource savings often yield higher profits than small resource savings do – or even saving no resource at all would – and not only pay for themselves over time bit in many cases reduce the initial capital investments.
- *Shift to biologically inspired production models.* Natural capitalism seeks not merely to reduce waste but to eliminate the very concept of waste. In closed-loop production systems, modelled on nature's designs, every output either is returned harmlessly to the ecosystem as a nutrient, like compost, or becomes an input for manufacturing another product. Such systems can often be designed to eliminate the use of toxic materials, which can hamper nature's ability to reprocess the materials.
- *Move to a solutions-based business model.* The business model of traditional manufacturing rests on the sale of goods. In the new model, value is instead delivered as a flow of services – providing illumination, for example, rather than selling lightbulbs. This model entails a new perception of value, a move from the acquisition of goods as a measure of affluence to one where well-being is measured by the continuous satisfaction of changing expectations for quality, utility, and performance. The new relationship aligns the interests of providers and customers in ways that reward them for implementing the first two innovations and closed-loop manufacturing.
- *Reinvest in natural capital.* Ultimately, business must restore, sustain, and expand the planet's ecosystems so that they can produce their vital services and biological resources even more abundantly. Pressures to do so are mounting, as human needs expand, the costs endangered by deteriorating ecosystems rise, and the environmental awareness of consumers increases. Fortunately, these pressures all create business value.

Natural capitalism is not motivated by a current scarcity of natural resources. Indeed, although many biological resources, like fish, are becoming scarce, most mined resources, such as copper and oil, seem ever more abundant. Indices of average commodity prices are at 28-year lows; thanks partly to powerful extractive technologies, which are often subsidized and whose damage to natural capital remains unaccounted for. Yet even despite these artificially low prices, using resources manifold more productively can now be so profitable that pioneering companies – large and small – have already embarked on the journey toward natural capitalism.

Still the question arises – if large resource savings are available and profitable, why haven't they all been captured already? The answer is simple: scores of common practices in both the private and public sectors systematically reward companies for wasting natural resources and penalize them for boosting resource productivity. For example, most companies expense their consumption of raw materials through the income statement but pass the resource-saving investment through the balance sheet. That distortion makes it more tax efficient to waste fuel than to invest in improving fuel efficiency. In short, even though the road seems clear, the compass that companies use to direct their journey is broken. Later we'll look in more detail at some of the obstacles to resource productivity of the important business opportunities they reveal. But first, let's map the route toward the natural capitalism.

Dramatically increase the productivity of natural resources

In the first stage of a company's journey toward natural capitalism, it strives to wring out the waste of energy, water, materials, and other resources throughout its productions systems and other operations. There are two main ways companies can do this at a profit. First, they can adopt a fresh approach to design that considers industrial systems as a whole rather than part by part. Second, companies can replace old industrial technologies with new ones, particularly with those based on natural processes and materials.

Implementing whole-system design

Inventor Edwin Land once remarked that 'people who seem to have had a new idea have often simply stopped having an old idea.' This is particularly true when designing for resource savings. The old idea is one of diminishing returns – the greater the resource saving the higher the cost. But that old idea is giving way to the new idea that bigger savings can cost less – that saving a large fraction of resources can actually cost less than saving a small fraction of resources. This is the concept of expanding returns, and it governs much of the revolutionary thinking behind the whole-system design. Lean manufacturing is an example of whole-system thinking that has helped many companies dramatically reduce such forms of waste as lead times, defect rates, and inventory. Applying whole-system thinking to the productivity of natural resources can achieve even more.

Consider Interface Corporation, a leading maker of materials for commercial interiors. In its new Shanghai carpet factory, a liquid had to be circulated through a standard pumping loop similar to those used in nearly all industries. A top European company designed the system to use pumps requiring a total of 95 horsepower. But before construction began, Interface's engineer, Jan Schilham, realized that two embarrassingly simple design changes would cut that power requirement to only 7 horsepower – a 92% reduction. His redesigned system cost less to build, involved no new technology, and worked better in all respects.

What two design changes achieved this 12-fold saving in pumping power? First, Schilham chose fatter-than-usual pipes, which create much less friction than thin pipes do and therefore need far less pumping energy. The original designer had chosen thin pipes because, according to the textbook method, the extra cost of fatter ones wouldn't be justified by the pumping energy that they would save. This standard design trade-off optimizes the pipes by themselves but 'pessimizes' the larger system. Schilham optimized the *whole* system by counting not only the higher capital cost of the fatter pipes but also the *lower* capital cost of the smaller pumping equipment that would be needed. The pumps, motors, motor controls, and electrical components could all be much smaller because there'd be less friction to overcome. Capital cost would fall far more for the smaller equipment than it would rise for the fatter pipe. Choosing big pipes and small pumps – rather than small pipes and big pumps – would therefore make the whole system cost less to build, even before counting its future energy savings.

Schilham's second innovation was to reduce the friction even more by making the pipes short and straight rather than long and crooked. He did this by laying out the pipes first, *then* positioning the various tanks, boilers, and other equipment that they connected. Designers normally locate the production equipment in arbitrary positions and then have a pipe fitter connect everything. Awkward placement forces the pipes to make numerous bends that greatly increase friction. The pipe fitters don't mind: they're paid by the hour, they profit from the extra pipes and fittings, and they don't pay for the oversized pumps or inflated electric bills. In addition to reducing those four kinds of costs, Schilham's short, straight pipes were easier to insulate, saving an extra 70% kilowatts of heat loss and repaying the insulation's cost in three months.

This small example has big implications for two reasons. First, pumping is the largest application of motors, and motors use three-quarters of all industrial electricity. Second, the lessons are very widely relevant. Interface's pumping loop shows how simple changes in design mentality can yield huge resource savings and returns on investment. This isn't rocket science, often it's just a rediscovery of good Victorian-engineering principles that have been lost because of specialization.

Whole-system thinking can help managers find small changes that lead to big savings that are cheap, free, or even better than free (because they make the whole system cheaper to build). They can do this because often the right investment in one part of the system can produce multiple benefits throughout the system. For example, companies would gain 18 distinct economic benefits – of which direct energy savings is the only one – if they switched from ordinary motors to premium – efficiency motors or from ordinary lighting to ballasts that automatically dim the lamps to match available daylight. If everyone in America integrated these and other selected technologies into all existing motor and lighting systems in an optimal way, the nation's $220-billion-a-year electric bill would be cut in half. The after-tax return on investing in these changes would in most cases exceed 100% per year.

The profits from saving electricity could be increased even further if companies also incorporated the best off-the-shelf improvements into their building structure and their office, heating, cooling, and other equipment. Overall, such changes could cut national electricity consumption by at least 75% and produce returns of around 100% a year on investments made. More important, because workers would be more comfortable, better able to see, and less fatigued by noise, their productivity and the quality of their output would rise. Eight recent case studies of people working in well-designed, energy efficient buildings measured labour productivity gains of 6% to 16%. Since a typical office pays about 100 times as much for people as it does for energy, this increased productivity in people is worth about 6 to 16 times as much as eliminating the entire energy bill.

Energy-saving, productivity-enhancing improvements can often be achieved at even lower cost by piggybacking them onto the periodic renovations that all buildings and factories need. A recent proposal for reallocating the normal 20-year renovation budget for a standard 200,000-square-foot glass-clad office tower near Chicago, Illinois shows the potential of whole-system design. The proposal suggested replacing the ageing glazing system with a new kind of window that lets in nearly six times more daylight than the old sun-blocking glass units. The new windows would reduce the flow of heat and noise four times better than traditional windows do. So even though the glass costs slightly more, the overall cost of the renovation would be reduced because the windows would let in cool, glare-free daylight that, when combined with more efficient lighting and office equipment, would reduce the need for air-conditioning by 75%. Installing a fourfold more efficient, but fourfold smaller, air conditioning system would cost $200,000 less than giving the old system its normal 20-year renovation. The $200,000 saved would, in turn, pay for the extra cost of the new windows and other improvements. This whole-system approach to renovation would not only save 75% of the building's total energy use, it would also greatly improve the building's comfort and marketability. Yet it would cost essentially the same as the normal renovation. There are about 100,000 twenty-year-old glass office towers in the United States that are ripe for such improvement.

Major gains in resource productivity require that the right steps be taken in the right order. Small changes made at the downstream end of a process often create far larger savings further upstream. In almost any industry that uses a pumping system, for example, saving one unit of liquid flow or friction in an exit pipe saves about ten units of fuel, cost, and pollution at the power station.

Of course, the original reduction in flow itself can being direct benefits, which are often the reason changes are made in the first place. In the 1980s, while California's industry grew 30%, for example, its water use was cut by 30%, largely to avoid increased wastewater fees. But the resulting reduction in pumping energy (and the roughly tenfold larger saving in power-plant fuel and pollution) delivered bonus savings that were at the time largely unanticipated.

To see how downstream cuts in resource consumption can create huge savings upstream, consider how reducing the use of wood fibre disproportionately reduces the pressure to cut down forests. In round numbers, half of all harvested wood fibre is used for such structural products as lumber; the other half is used for paper and cardboard. In both cases, the biggest leverage comes from reducing the amount of the retail product used. If it takes, for example, three pounds of harvested trees to produce one pound of product, then saving one pound of all product will save three pounds of trees – plus all the environmental damage avoided by not having to cut them down in the first place.

The easiest savings come from not using paper that's unwanted or unneeded. In an experiment at its Swiss headquarters, for example, Dow Europe cut office paper flow by about 30% in six weeks simply by discouraging unneeded information. For instance, mailing lists were eliminated and senders of memos got back receipts indicating whether each recipient had wanted the information. Taking those and other small steps, Dow was also able to increase labour productivity by a similar proportion because people could focus on what they really needed to read. Similarly, Danish hearing-aid maker Oticon saved upwards of 30% of its paper as a by-product of redesigning its business processes to produce better decisions faster. Setting the default on office printers and copiers to double-sided mode reduced AT&T's paper costs by about 15%. Recently developed copiers and printers can even strip off old toner and ink, permitting each sheet to be reused about ten times.

Further savings can come from using thinner but stronger and more opaque paper, and from designing packaging more thoughtfully. In a 30-month effort at reducing such waste, Johnson & Johnson saved 2,750 tons of packaging, 1,600 tons of paper, $2.8 million, and at least 330 acres of forest annually. The downstream savings in paper in use are multiplied by the savings further upstream, as less need for paper products (or less need for fibre to make each product) translates into less raw paper, less raw paper means less pulp, and less pulp requires fewer trees to be harvested from the forest. Recycling paper and substituting alternative fibres such as wheat straw will save even more.

Comparable savings can be achieved for the wood fibre used in structural products. Pacific Gas and Electric, for example, sponsored an innovative design developed by Davis Energy Group that used engineered wood products to reduce the amount of wood needed in a stud wall for a typical tract house by more than 70%. These walls were stronger, cheaper, more stable, and insulated twice as well. Using them enabled the designers to eliminate heating and cooling equipment in a climate where temperatures range from freezing to 113° F. Eliminating the equipment made the whole house much less expensive both to build and to run while still maintaining high levels of comfort. Taken together, these and many other savings in the paper and construction industries could make our use of wood fibre so much more productive that, in principle the entire world's present wood fibre needs could probably be met by an intensive tree farm about the size of Iowa.

Adopting Innovative Technologies

Implementing whole-system design goes hand in hand with introducing alternative, environmentally friendly technologies. Many of these are already available and profitable but not widely known. Some, like the 'designer catalysts' that are transforming the chemical industry, are already runaway successes. Others are still making their way to market, delayed by cultural rather than by economic or technical barriers.

The automobile industry is particularly ripe for technological change. After a century of development, motorcar technology is showing signs of age. Only 1% of the energy consumed by today's cars is actually used to move the driver: only 15% to 20% of the power generated by burning gasoline reaches the wheels (the rest is lost in the engine and drive-train) and 95% of the resulting propulsion moves the car, not the driver. The industry's infrastructure is hugely expensive and inefficient. Its convergent products compete for narrow niches in saturated core markets at commodity-like prices. Auto making is capital intensive, and product cycles are long. It is profitable in good years but subject to large losses in bad years. Like the typewriter industry just before the advent of personal computers, it is vulnerable to displacement by something completely different.

The Hypercar

Enter the Hypercar. Since 1993, when Rocky Mountain Institute places this automotive concept in the public domain, several dozen current and potential auto manufacturers have committed billions of dollars to its development and commercialization. The Hypercar integrates the best existing technologies to reduce the consumption of fuel as much as 85% and the amount of materials used up to 90% by introducing four main innovations.

First, making the vehicle out of advance polymer composites, chiefly carbon fibre, reduces its weight by two-thirds while maintaining crash-worthiness. Second, aerodynamic design and better tires reduce air resistance by as much as 70% and rolling resistance by up to 80%. Together, these innovations save about two-thirds of the fuel. Third, 30% to 50% of the remaining fuel is saved by using a 'hybrid-electric' drive. In such a system, the wheels are turned by electric motors whose power is made onboard by a small engine or turbine, or even more efficiently by a fuel cell. The fuel cell generates electricity directly by chemically combining stored hydrogen with oxygen, producing pure hot water as its only by-product. Interactions between the small, clean, efficient power source and the ultralight, low-drag auto body then further reduces the weight, cost, and complexity of both. Fourth, much of the traditional hardware – from transmissions and differentials to gauges and certain parts of the suspension – can be replaced by electronics controlled with highly integrated, customizable, and upgradable software.

These technologies make it feasible to manufacture pollution-free, high-performance cars, sport utilities, pickup trucks, and vans that get 80 to 200 miles per gallon (or its energy equivalent in other fuels). These improvements will not require any compromise in quality or utility. Fuel savings will not come from making vehicles small, sluggish, unsafe, or unaffordable, nor will they depend on government fuel taxes, mandates, or subsidies. Rather, Hypercars will succeed for the same reason that people buy compact discs instead of phonograph records: the CD is a superior product that redefines marker expectations. From the manufacturers' perspective, Hypercars will cut cycle times, capital needs, body part counts, and assembly effort and space by as much as tenfold. Early adopters will have a huge competitive advantage – which is why dozens of corporations, including most automakers, are now racing to bring Hypercar-like products to market.[1]

In the long term, the Hypercar will transform industries other than automobiles. It will displace about an eighth of the steel market directly and most of the rest eventually, as carbon fibre becomes far cheaper. Hypercars and their cousins could ultimately save as much oil as OPEC now sells. Indeed, oil may well become uncompetitive as a fuel long before it becomes scarce and costly. Similar challenges face the coal and electricity industries because the development of the Hypercar is likely to accelerate greatly the commercialization of inexpensive hydrogen fuels. These fuel cells will help shift power production from centralized coal-fired and nuclear power stations to networks of decentralized, small-scale generators. In fact, fuel-cell-powered Hypercars could themselves be part of these networks. They'd be, in effect, 20-kilowatt power plants on wheels. Given that cars are left parked – that is, unused – more than 95% of the time, these Hypercars could be plugged into the grid and could then sell back enough electricity to repay as much as half the predicted cost of leasing them. A national Hypercar fleet could ultimately have five to ten times the generating capacity of the national electric grid.

As radical as it sounds, the Hypercar is not an isolated case. Similar ideas are emerging in such industries as chemicals, semiconductors, general manufacturing, transportation, water and wastewater treatment, agriculture, forestry, energy, real estate, and urban design. For example, the amount of carbon dioxide released for each microchip manufactured can be reduced almost 100-fold through improvements that are now profitable or soon will be.

Some of the most striking developments come from emulating nature's techniques. In her book, *Biomimicry*, Janine Benyus points out that spiders convert digested crickets and flies into silk that's as strong as Kelvar without the need for boiling sulfuric acid and high-temperature extruders. Using no furnaces, abalone can convert seawater into an inner shell twice as tough as out best ceramics. Trees turn sunlight, water, soil, and air into cellulose, a sugar stronger than nylon but one-fourth as dense. They then bind it into wood, a natural composite with a higher bending strength than concrete, aluminum alloy, of steel. We may never become as skilful as spiders, abalone, or trees, but smart designers are already realizing that nature's environmentally benign chemistry offers attractive alternatives to industrial brute force.

Whether through better design or through new technologies, reducing waste represents a vast business opportunity. The US economy is not even 10% as energy efficient as the laws of physics allow. Just the energy thrown off as waste heat by US power stations equals the total energy use of Japan. Materials efficiency is even worse: only about 1% of all materials mobilized to serve America is actually made into products and still in use six months after sale. In every sector, there are opportunities for reducing the amount of resources that go into a production process, the steps required to run that process, and the amount of pollution generated and by-products discarded at the end. These all represent avoidable costs and hence profits to be won.

Redesign production according to biological models

In the second stage on the journey to natural capitalism, companies use closed-loop manufacturing to create new products and processes that can totally prevent waste. This plus more efficient production processes could cut companies' long-term materials requirements by more than 90% in most sectors.

The central principle of closed-loop manufacturing, as architect Paul Bierman-Lytle of the engineering firm CH2M Hill puts it, is 'waste equals food.' Every output of manufacturing should be either composted into natural nutrients or re-manufactured into technical nutrients – that is, it should be returned to the ecosystem or recycled for further production. Closed-loop production systems are designed to eliminate any materials that incur disposal costs, especially toxic ones, because the alternative – isolating them to prevent harm to natural systems – tends to be costly and risky. Indeed, meeting EPA and OSHA standards by eliminating harmful materials often makes a manufacturing process cost less than the hazardous process it replaced. Motorola, for example, formerly used chlorofluorocarbons for cleaning printed circuit boards after soldering. When CFCs were outlawed because they destroy stratospheric ozone, Motorola at first explored such alternatives as orange-peel terpenes. But it turned out to be even cheaper – and to produce a better product – to redesign the whole soldering process so that it needed no cleaning operations or cleaning materials at all.

Closed-loop manufacturing is more than just a theory. The US re-manufacturing industry in 1996 reported revenues of $53 billion – more than consumer-durables manufacturing (appliances; furniture; audio, video, farm, and garden equipment). Xerox, whose bottom line has swelled by $700 million from remanufacturing, expects to save another $1 billion just by manufacturing its new, entirely reusable or recyclable line of 'green' photocopiers. What's more, policy makers in some countries are already taking steps to encourage industry to think along these lines. German law, for example, makes many manufacturers responsible for their products forever, and Japan is following suit.

Combining closed-loop manufacturing with resource efficiency is especially powerful. Dupont, for example, now makes much of its polyester film ever stronger and thinner so it uses less material and costs less to make. Yet because the film performs better, customers are willing to pay more for it. As DuPont chairman Jack Krol noted in 1997, `Our ability to continually improve the inherent properties [of our films] enables this process [of developing more productive materials, at lower cost, and higher profits] to go on indefinitely.'

Interface is leading the way to this next frontier of industrial ecology. While its competitors are 'down cycling' nylon-and-PVC-based carpet into less valuable carpet backing, Interface has invented a new floor covering material called Solenium, which can be completely remanufactured into identical new product. This fundamental innovation emerged from a clean-sheet redesign. Executives at Interface didn't ask how they could sell more carpet of the familiar kind; they asked how they could create a dream product that would best meet their customers' needs while protecting and nourishing natural capital.

Solenium lasts four times longer and uses 40% less material than ordinary carpets – an 86% reduction in materials intensity. What's more, Solenium is free of chlorine and other toxic materials, is virtually stainproof, doesn't grow mildew, can easily be cleaned with water, and offers aesthetic advantages over traditional carpets. It's so superior in every respect that Interface doesn't market it as en environmental product – just a better one.

Solenium is only one part of Interface's drive to eliminate every form of waste. Chairman Ray C. Anderson defines waste as 'any measurable input that does not produce customer value,' and he considers all inputs to be waste until shown otherwise. Between 1994 and 1998, this zero-waste approach led to a systematic treasure hunt that helped to keep resource inputs constant while revenues rose by $200 million. Indeed, $67 million of the revenue increase can be directly attributed to the company's 60% reduction in landfill waste.

Subsequently, president Charlie Eitel expanded the definition of waste to include all fossil fuel inputs, and now many customers are eager to buy products from the company's recently opened solar-powered carpet factory. Interface's green strategy has not only won plaudits from environmentalists, it has also proved a remarkably successful business strategy. Between 1993 and 1998, revenue has more than doubled, profits have more than tripled, and the number of employees has increased by 73%.

Change the business model

In addition to its drive to eliminate waste, Interface has made a fundamental shift in its business model – the third stage on the journey toward natural capitalism. The company has realized that clients want to walk on and look at carpets – but not necessarily to own them. Traditionally, broadloom carpets in office buildings are replaced every decade because some portions look worn out. When that happens, companies suffer the disruption of shutting down their offices and removing their furniture. Billions of pounds of carpets are removed each year and sent to landfills, where they will last up to 20,000 years. To escape this unproductive and wasteful cycle, Interface is transforming itself from a company that sells and fits carpets into one that provides floor-covering services.

Under its Evergreen Lease, Interface no longer sells carpets but rather leases a floor-covering service for a monthly fee, accepting responsibility for keeping the carpet fresh and clean. Monthly inspections detect and replace worn carpet tiles. Since at most 20% of an area typically shows at least 80% of the wear, replacing only the worn parts reduces the consumption of carpeting material by about 80%. It also minimizes the disruption that customers experience – worn tiles are seldom found under furniture. Finally, for the customer, leasing carpets can provide a tax advantage by turning a capital expenditure into a tax-deductible expense. The result: the customer gets cheaper and better services that cost the supplier far less to produce. Indeed, the energy saved from not producing a whole new carpet is in itself enough to produce all the carpeting that the new business model requires. Taken together, the 5-fold savings in carpeting material that Interface achieves through the Evergreen Lease and the 7-fold materials savings achieved through the use of Solenium deliver a stunning 35-fold reduction in the flow of materials needed to sustain a superior floor-covering service. Remanufacturing, and even making carpet initially from renewable materials, can reduce the extraction of virgin resources essentially to the company's goal of zero.

Interface's shift to a service-leasing business reflects a fundamental change from the basic model of most manufacturing companies, which still look on their businesses as machines for producing selling products. The more products sold, the better – at least for the company, if not always for the customer or the earth. But any model that wastes natural resources also wastes money. Ultimately, that model will be unable to compete with a service model that emphasizes solving problems and building long-term relationships with customers rather than making and selling products. The shift to what James Womack of the Lean Enterprise Institute calls a 'solutions economy' will almost always improve customer value *and* providers' bottom lines because it aligns both parties' interests, offering rewards for doing more and better with less.

Interface is not alone. Elevator giant Schindler, for example, prefers leasing vertical transportation services to selling elevators because leasing lets it capture the savings from its elevators' lower energy and maintenance costs. Dow Chemical and Safety Kleen prefer leasing dissolving services to selling solvents because they can reuse the same solvent scores of times, reducing costs. United Technologies' Carrier division, the world's largest manufacturer of air-conditioners, is shifting its mission from selling air conditioners to leasing comfort. Making its air conditioners more durable and efficient may compromise future equipment dales, but it provides what customers want and will pay for – better comfort at lower cost. But Carrier is going even further. It's starting to team up with other companies to make buildings more efficient so that they need less air-conditioning, or even none at all, to yield the same level of comfort. Carrier will get paid to provide the agreed-upon level of comfort, however, that's delivered. Higher profits will come from providing better solutions rather than from selling more equipment. Since comfort with little or no air-conditioning (via better building designs) works better and costs less than comfort with copious air-conditioning, Carrier is smart to capture this opportunity itself before its competitors do. As they say at 3M: 'We'd rather eat our *own* lunch, thank you.'

The shift to a service business model promises benefits not just to participating businesses but to the entire economy as well. Womack points out that by helping customers reduce their need for capital goods such as carpets or elevators, and by rewarding suppliers for extending and maximizing asset values rather than for churning them, adoption of the service model will reduce the volatility in the turnover of capital goods that lies at the heart of the business cycle. That would significantly reduce the overall volatility of the world's economy. At present, the producers of capital goods face feast or famine because the buying decisions of households and corporations are extremely sensitive to fluctuating income. But in a continuous flow-of-services economy, those swings would be greatly reduced, bringing a welcome stability to businesses. Excess capacity – another form of waste and source of risk – need no longer be retained for meeting peak demand. The result of adopting the new model would be an economy in which we grow and get richer by using less and become stronger by being leaner and more stable.

Reinvest in natural capital

The foundation of textbook capitalism is the prudent reinvestment of earnings in productive capital. Natural capitalists who have dramatically raised their resource productivity, closed their loops, and shifted to a solutions-based business model have one key task remaining. They must reinvest in restoring, sustaining, and expanding the most important form of capital – their own natural habitat and biological resource base.

This was not always so important. Until recently, business could ignore damage to the ecosystem because it didn't affect production and didn't increase costs. But that situation is changing. In 1998 alone, violent weather displaced 300 million people and caused upwards of $90 billion worth of damage, representing more weather-related destruction than was reported through the entire decade of the 1980s. The increase in damage is strongly linked to deforestation and climate change, factors that accelerate the frequency and severity of natural disasters and are the consequences of inefficient industrialization. If the flow of services from industrial systems is to be sustained or increased in the future for a growing population, the vital flow of services from living systems will have to be maintained or increased as well. Without reinvestment in natural capital, shortages of ecosystem services are likely to become the limiting factor to prosperity in the next century. When a manufacturer realizes that a supplier of key components is overextended and running behind on deliveries, it takes immediate action lest its own production lines come to a halt. The ecosystem is a supplier of key components for the life of the planet, and it is now falling behind on its orders.

Failure to protect and reinvest in natural capital can also hit a company's revenues indirectly. Many companies are discovering that public perceptions of environmental responsibility, or its lack thereof, affect sales. MacMillan Bloedel, targeted by environmental activists as an emblematic clear-cutter and chlorine user, lost 5% of its sales almost overnight when dropped as a UK supplier by Scott Paper and Kimberly-Clark. Numerous case studies show that companies leading the way in implementing changes that help protect the environment tend to gain disproportionate advantage, while companies perceived as irresponsible lose their franchise, their legitimacy, and their shirts. Even businesses that claim to be committed to the concept of sustainable development but whose strategy is seen as mistaken, like Monsanto, are encountering stiffening public resistance to their products. Not surprisingly, University of Oregon business professor Michael Russo, along with many other analysts, has found that a strong environmental rating is 'a consistent predictor of profitability.'

The pioneering corporations that have made reinvestments in natural capital are starting to see some interesting paybacks. The independent power producer AES, for example, has long pursued a policy of planting trees to offset the carbon emissions of its power plants. The ethical stance, once thought quixotic, now looks like a smart investment because a dozen brokers are now starting to create markets in carbon reduction. Similarly, certification by the Forest Stewardship Council of certain sustainably grown and harvested products has given Collins Pine the extra profit margins that enabled its US manufacturing operations to survive brutal competition. Taking an even longer view, Swiss Re and other European reinsurers are seeking to cut their storm-damage losses by pressing for international public policy to protect the climate and by investing in climate-safe technologies that also promise good profits. Yet most companies still do not realize that a vibrant ecological web underpins their survival and their business success. Enriching natural capital is not just a public good – it is vital to every company's longevity.

It turns out that changing industrial processes so that they actually replenish and magnify the stock of natural capital can prove especially profitable because nature does the production; people need just to step back and let life flourish. Industries that directly harvest living resources, such as forestry, farming, and fishing, offer the most suggestive examples. Here are three:

- Allan Savory of the Center for Holistic Management in Albuquerque, New Mexico, has redesigned cattle ranching to raise the carrying capacity of rangelands, which have often been degraded not by overgrazing but by undergrazing and grazing the wrong way. Savory's solution is to keep the cattle moving from place to place, grazing intensively but briefly at each site, so that they mimic the dense but constantly moving herds of native grazing animals that coevolved with grasslands. Thousands of ranchers are estimated to be applying this approach, improving both their range and their profits. This 'management-intensive rotational grazing' method, long standard in New Zealand, yields such clearly superior returns that over 15% of Wisconsin's dairy farms have adopted it in the past few years.

- The California Rice Industry Association has discovered that letting nature's diversity flourish can be more profitable than forcing it to produce a single product. By flooding 150,000 to 200,000 acres of Sacramento valley rice fields – about 30% of California's rice-growing area – after harvest, farmers are able to create seasonal wetlands, replenish groundwater, improve fertility, and yield other valuable benefits. In addition, the farmers bale and sell the rice and straw, whose high silica content – formerly an air-pollution hazard when the straw was burned – adds insect resistance and hence value as a construction material when it's resold instead.

- John Todd of Living Technologies in Burlington, Vermont, has used biological Living Machines – linked tanks of bacteria, algae, plants, and other organisms – to turn sewage into clean water. That not only yields cleaner water at a reduced cost, with no toxicity or odour, but it also produces commercially valuable flowers and makes the plant compatible with its residential neighbourhood. A similar plant at the Ethel M Chocolates factory in Las Vegas, Nevada, not only handles difficult industrial wastes effectively but is showcased in its public tours.

Although such practices are still evolving, the broad lessons they teach are clear. In almost all climates, soils, and societies, working with nature is more productive than working against it. Reinvesting in nature allows farmers, fishermen, and forest, managers to match or exceed the high yields and profits sustained by traditional input-intensive, chemically-driven practices. Although much of mainstream business is still headed the other way, the profitability of sustainable, nature-emulating practices is already being proven. In the future, many industries that don't now consider themselves dependent on a biological resource base will become more so as they shift their raw materials and production processes more to biological ones. There is evidence that many business leaders are starting to think this way. The consulting firm Arthur D. Little surveyed a group of North American and European business leaders and found that 83% of them already believe that they can derive 'real business value [from implementing a] sustainable-development approach to strategy and operations.'

A broken compass?

If the road ahead is clear, why are so many companies straying or falling by the wayside? We believe the reason is that the instruments companies use to set their targets, measure their performance, and hand out rewards are faulty. In other words, the markets are full of distortions and perverse incentives. Of the more than 60 specific forms of misdirection that we have identified,[2] the most obvious involve the ways companies allocate capital and the way governments set policy and impose taxes. Merely correcting these defective practices would uncover huge opportunities for profit.

Consider how many companies make purchasing decisions. Decisions to buy small items are typically based on their initial cost rather than their full life-cycle cost, a practice that could add up to major wastage. Distribution transformers that supply electricity to buildings and factories, for example, are a minor item at just $320 apiece, and most companies try to save a quick buck by buying the lowest price models. Yet nearly all the nation's electricity must flow through transformers, and using cheaper but less efficient models wastes $1 billion a year. Such examples are legion. Equipping standard new office-lighting circuits with fatter wire that reduces electrical resistance could generate after-tax returns of 193% a year. Instead, wire as thin as the National Electrical Code permits is usually selected because it costs less up-front. But the code is meant only to prevent fires from overheated wiring, not to save money. Ironically, an electrician who chooses fatter wire – thereby reducing long-term electricity bills – doesn't get the job. After paying for the extra copper, he's no longer the low bidder.

Some companies do consider more than just the initial price in their purchasing decisions but still don't go far enough. Most of them use a crude payback estimate rather than more accurate metrics like discounted cash flow. A few years ago, the median simple payback these companies were demanding from energy efficiency was 1.9 years. That's equivalent to requiring an after-tax return of around 71% per year – about six times the marginal cost of capital.

Most companies also miss major opportunities by treating their facilities costs as an overhead to be minimized, typically by laying off engineers, rather than as profit centre to be optimized – by using those engineers to save resources. Deficient measurement and accounting practices also prevent companies from allocating costs – and waste – with any accuracy. For example, only a few semiconductor plants worldwide regularly and accurately measure how much energy they're using to produce a unit of chilled water or clean air for their clean-room production facilities. That makes it hard for them to improve efficiency. In fact, in an effort to save time, semiconductor makers frequently build new plants as exact copies of previous ones – a design method nicknamed 'infectious repetitis.'

Many executives pay too little attention to saving resources because they are often a small percentage of total costs (energy costs run to about 2% in most industries). But those resource savings drop straight to the bottom line and so represent a far greater percentage of profits. Many executives also think they already 'did' efficiency in the 1970s, when the oil shock forced them to rethink old habits. They're forgetting that with today's far better technologies, it's profitable to start all over again. Malden Mills, the Massachusetts maker of such products as Polartec, was already using 'efficient' metal-halide lamps in the mid-1990s. But a recent warehouse retrofit reduced the energy used for lighting by another 93%, improved visibility, and paid for itself in 18 months.

The way people are rewarded often creates perverse incentives. Architects and engineers, for example, are traditionally compensated for what they spend, not for what they save. Even the striking economics of the retrofit design for the Chicago office tower described earlier wasn't incentive enough actually to implement it. The property was controlled by a leasing agent who earned a commission every time she leased space, so she didn't want to wait the few extra months needed to refit the building. Her decision to reject the efficiency-quadrupling renovation proved costly for both her and her client. The building was so uncomfortable and expensive to occupy that it didn't lease, so ultimately the owner had to unload it at a firesale price. Moreover, the new owner will for the next 20 years be deprived of the opportunity to save capital cost.

If corporate practices obscure the benefits of natural capitalism, government policy positively undermines it. In nearly every country on the planet, tax laws penalize what we want more of – jobs and income – while subsidizing what we want less of – resource depletion and pollution. In every state but Oregon, regulated utilities are rewarded for selling more energy, water, and other resources, and penalized for selling less, even if increased production would cost more then improved customer efficiency. In most of America's arid western states, use-it-or-lose-it water laws encourage inefficient water consumption. Additionally, in many towns, inefficient use of land is enforced though outdated regulations, such as guidelines for ultrawide suburban streets recommended by 1950s civil-defence planners to accommodate the heavy equipment needed to clear up rubble after a nuclear attack.

The costs of these perverse incentives are staggering: $300 billion in annual energy wasted in the United States, and £1 trillion already misallocated to unnecessary air-conditioning equipment and the power supplies to run it (about 40% of the nation's peak electric load). Across the entire economy, unneeded expenditures to subsidize, encourage, and try to remedy inefficiency and damage that should not have occurred in the first place probably account for most, if not all, of the GDP growth of the past two decades. Indeed, according to former World Bank economist Herman Daly and his colleague John Cobb (along with many other analysts), Americans are hardly better off than they were in 1980. But if the US government and private industry could redirect the dollars currently earmarked for remedial costs toward reinvestment in natural and human capital, they could bring abut a genuine improvement in the nation's welfare. Companies, too, are finding that wasting resources also means wasting money and people. These intertwined forms of waste have equally intertwined solutions. Firing the unproductive tons, gallons, and kilowatt-hours often makes it possible to keep the people, who will have more and better work to do.

Recognizing the scarcity shift

In the end, the real trouble with our economic compass is that it points in exactly the wrong direction. Most businesses are behaving as if people were scarce and nature still abundant – the conditions that helped to fuel the first Industrial Revolution. At that time, people were relatively scarce compared with the present-day population. The repaid mechanization of the textile industries caused explosive economic growth that created labour shortages in the factory and the field. The Industrial Revolution, responding to those shortages and mechanizing one industry after another, made people a hundred times more productive than they had ever been.

The logic of economizing on the scarcest resource, because it limits progress, remains correct. But the pattern of scarcity is shifting: now people aren't scarce but nature is. This shows up first in industries that depend directly on ecological health. Here, production is increasingly constrained by fish rather than by boats and nets, by forests rather than by chain saws, by fertile topsoil rather than by plows. Moreover, unlike the traditional factors of industrial production – capital and labour – the biological limiting factors cannot be substituted for one other. In the industrial system, we can easily exchange machines for labour. But no technology or amount of money can substitute for a stable climate and a productive biosphere. Even proper pricing can't replace the priceless.

Natural capitalism addresses those problems reintegrating ecological with economic goals. Because it is both necessary and profitable, it will subsume traditional industrialism previously subsumed agrarianism. The companies that first make the changes we have described will have a competitive edge. Those that don't make the effort won't be a problem because ultimately they won't be around. In making the choice, as Henry Ford said, 'Whether you believe you can, or whether you believe you can't you're absolutely right.'

Notes

1. Non-proprietary details are posted at http://www.hypercar.com.
2. Summarized in the report 'Climate: making sense *and* making money' at http://www.rmi.org/catalog/climate.htm.

Source: Extract from *Harvard Business Review*, 1999, May, pp. 145–58.

22   Monocultures of the Mind

Vandana Shiva

The 'disappeared' knowledge systems

The disappearance of local knowledge through its interaction with the dominant Western knowledge takes place at many levels, through many steps. First, local knowledge is made to disappear by simply not seeing it, by negating its very existence. The Western systems of knowledge have generally been viewed as universal. However, the dominant system is also a local system, with its social basis in a particular culture, class and gender. It is the globalized version of a very local and parochial tradition.

Emerging from a dominating and colonizing culture, modern knowledge systems are themselves colonizing. [They are] associated with a set of values based on power which emerged with the rise of commercial capitalism. Power is also built into the perspective which views the dominant system not as a globalized local tradition, but as a universal tradition, inherently superior to local systems. When local knowledge does appear in the field of globalizing visions, it is made to disappear by denying it the status of a systematic knowledge, and assigning it the adjectives 'primitive' and 'unscientific'. Correspondingly, the Western system is assumed to be uniquely 'scientific' and universal. Scientists, in accordance with an abstract scientific method, were viewed as putting forward statements corresponding to the realities of a directly observable world. The theoretical concepts in their discourse were in principle seen as reducible to directly verifiable observational claims. New trends in the philosophy and sociology of science challenged the positivist assumptions, but did not challenge the assumed superiority of Western systems.

However, the historical experience of non-Western culture suggests that it is the Western systems knowledge which is blind to alternatives. The 'scientific' label assigns a kind a sacredness or social immunity to the Western system. By elevating itself *above* society and other knowledge systems and by simultaneously excluding other knowledge systems from the domain of reliable and systematic knowledge, the dominant system creates its exclusive monopoly. Paradoxically, it is the knowledge systems which are considered most open, that are, in reality, closed to scrutiny and evaluation. Modern Western science is not to be evaluated, it is merely to be accepted.

The cracks of fragmentation

The dominant system also makes alternatives disappear by erasing and destroying the reality which they attempt to represent. The fragmented linearity of the dominant knowledge disrupts the integrations between systems. Local knowledge slips through the cracks of fragmentation. Dominant scientific knowledge breeds a monoculture of the mind by making space for local alternatives to disappear, very much like monocultures of introduced plant varieties leading to the displacement and destruction of local diversity. Dominant knowledge also destroys the very *conditions* for alternatives to exist, very much like the introduction of monocultures destroying the very conditions for diverse species to exist.

As a metaphor, the monoculture of the mind is best illustrated in the knowledge and practice of forestry and agriculture. 'Scientific' forestry and 'scientific' agriculture, split the plant artificially into separate, non-overlapping domains, on the basis of separate commodity markets to which they supply raw materials and resources. In local knowledge systems, the plant world is not artificially separated between a forest supplying commercial wood and agricultural land supplying food commodities. The forest and the field are in ecological continuum, and activities in the forest contribute to the food needs of the local community, while agriculture itself is modelled on the ecology of the tropical forest. Some forest dwellers gather food directly from the forest, while many communities practise agriculture outside the forest, but depend on the fertility of the forest for the fertility of agricultural land.

In the 'scientific' system which splits forestry from agriculture and reduces forestry to timber and wood supply, food is no longer a category related to forestry. The cognitive space that relates forestry to food production, either directly, or through fertility links, is therefore erased with the split. Knowledge systems which have emerged from the food giving capacities of the forest are therefore eclipsed and finally destroyed (see Figure 22.1).

Most local knowledge systems have been based on the life support capacities of tropical forests, not on their commercial timber value. These systems fall in the blind spot of a forestry perspective that is based exclusively on the commercial exploitation of forests. Food systems based on the forest, are therefore non-existent in the field of vision of a reductionist forestry and a reductionist agriculture even though they have been and still are the sustenance base for many communities of the world. Famine has never been a problem in Bastar as tribes have always been able to draw half of their food from the innumerable edible forest products.

In non-tribal areas, too, forests provide food and livelihood through critical inputs to agriculture, through soil and water conservation, and through inputs of fodder and organic fertilizer. Indigenous silvicultural knowledge is passed on from generation to generation, through participation in the processes of forest renewal and of drawing sustenance from the forest ecosystems.

In countries like India, the forest has been the source of fertility renewal of agriculture, a source of fodder and fertilizer and a significant part of the agricultural ecosystem. In the Himalayas, the oak forests have been central to sustainability of agriculture. Estimates show that over 50% of the total fodder supply for peasant communities in the Himalayas comes from forest sources, with forest trees supplying 20%. Forests also make an important contribution to hill farming in the use of plant biomass as bedding for animals. Forests are the principal source of fallen dry leaf-litter, and lopped green foliage of trees and herbaceous species which are used for animal bedding and composting. Forest biomass, when mixed with animal dung, forms the principal source of soil nutrients for hill agriculture. As the input declines, agricultural yields go down.

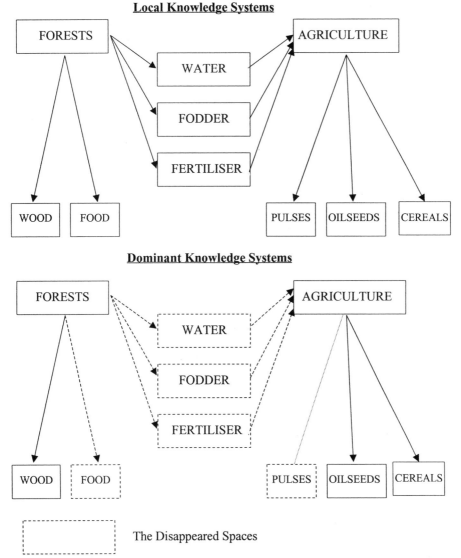

Figure 22.1 Dominant knowledge and the disappearance of alternatives

The diverse knowledge systems which have evolved with the diverse uses of the forest for food and agriculture were eclipsed with the introduction of 'scientific' forestry, which treated the forest only as a source of industrial and commercial timber. The linkages between forests and agriculture, were broken and the function of the forest as a source of food was no longer perceived.

When the West colonized Asia, it colonized her forests. It brought with it the ideas of nature and culture as derived from the model of the industrial factory. The forest was no longer viewed as having a value itself, in all its diversity. Its value was reduced to the value of commercially exploitable industrial timber. Having depleted their forests at home, European countries started the destruction of Asia's forests. England searched in the colonies for timber for its navy because the oak forests in England were depleted.

'Scientific forestry' was the false universalization of a local tradition of forestry which emerged from the narrow commercial interest which viewed the forest only in terms of commercially valuable wood. It first reduced the value of diversity of life in the forest to the value of a few commercially valuable species, and further reduced the value of these species to the value of their dead product – wood. The reductionism of the scientific forestry paradigm created by commercial industrial interests violates the integrity of the forests and the integrity of forest cultures who need the forest in its diversity to satisfy their needs for food, fibre and shelter.

The existing principles of scientific forest management lead to the destruction of the tropical forest ecosystem because it is based on the objective of modelling the diversity of the living forest on the uniformity of the assembly line. The system of 'scientific management', as it has been practised over a century, is thus a system of tropical deforestation, which transforms the forest from a renewable to a non-renewable resource. Tropical timber exploitation thus becomes like mining, and tropical forests become a timber mine.

The tropical forests, when modelled on the factory and used as a timber mine, become a non-renewable resource. Tropical peoples also become a dispensable and historical waste. In place of cultural and biological pluralism, the factory produces non-sustainable monocultures in nature and society. There is no place for the small, no value for the insignificant. Organic diversity gives way to fragmented atomism and uniformity. The diversity must be weeded out, and the uniform monocultures – of plants and people – must now be externally managed because they are no longer self-regulated and self-governed. Those that do not fit into the uniformity must be declared unfit. Symbiosis must give way to competition, domination and dispensability. There is no survival possible for the forest of its people when they become feedstock for industry. The survival of the tropical forest depends on the survival of human societies modelled on the principles of the forest. These lessons for survival do not come from text of 'scientific forestry'. They lie hidden in the lives and beliefs of the forest peoples of the world.

There are in Asia today two paradigms of forestry – one life enhancing, the other life destroying. The life-enhancing paradigm emerges from the forest and forest communities – the life destroying from the market. The life-enhancing paradigm creates a sustainable, renewable forest system, supporting and renewing food and water systems. *The maintenance of conditions for renewability is the primary management objective of the former.* The maximizing of profits through commercial extraction is the primary management objective of the latter. Since maximizing profits is consequent upon destruction of conditions of renewability, the two paradigms are cognitively and ecologically incommensurate. Today, in the forests of Asia the two paradigms are struggling against each other. This struggle is very clear in the two slogans on the utility of the Himalayan forests, one emanating from the ecological concepts of Garhwali women, the other from the sectoral concepts of those associated with trade in forest products. When Chipko became an ecological movement in 1977, the spirit of local science was captured in the slogan:

> What do forests bear?
> Soil, water and pure air.

This was the response to the commonly accepted slogan of the dominant science:

> What do the forests bear?
> Profit on resin and timber.

The Chipko movement was transformed qualitatively from being based merely on conflicts over resources to involving conflicts over scientific perceptions and philosophical approaches to nature. The slogan has become the scientific and philosophical message of the movement, and has laid the foundations of an alternative forestry science, oriented to the public interest and ecological in nature.

The destruction of diversity as 'weeds'

The destruction of biological diversity is intrinsic to the very manner in which the reductionist forestry paradigm conceives of the forest. The forest is defined as 'normal' according to the objective of managing the forest for maximizing production of marketable timber. Since the natural tropical forest is characterized by richness in diversity, including the diversity of non-marketable, non-industrial species, the 'scientific forestry' paradigm declares the natural forest as 'abnormal'. In Sclich's words, forest management implies that 'the abnormal conditions are to be removed'.

The natural forest, in its diversity, is thus seen as 'chaos'. The man-made forest is 'order'. 'Scientific' management of forests therefore has a clear anti-nature bias, and a bias for industrial and commercial objectives, for which the natural forest must be sacrificed. Diversity thus gives way to the uniformity of even-aged, single species stands, and this uniformity is the ideal of the normal forestry towards which all silvicultural systems aim. The destruction and dispensability of diversity are intrinsic to forest management guided by the objective of maximizing commercial wood production, which sees non-commercial parts and relationships of a forest ecosystem as valueless – as weeds to be destroyed. Nature's wealth characterized by diversity is destroyed to create commercial wealth characterized by uniformity.

In biological terms, tropical forests are the most productive biological systems on our planet. However, in the reductionist commercial forestry, the overall productivity is not important, nor are the functions of tropical forests in the survival of tropical peoples.

The industrial materials standpoint is the capitalist reductionist forestry which splits the living diversity and democracy of the forest into commercially valuable dead wood and destroys the rest as 'weeds' and 'waste'. This 'waste' however is the wealth of biomass that maintains nature's water and nutrient cycles and satisfies needs of food, fuel, fodder, fertilizer, fibre and medicine of agricultural communities.

Just as 'scientific' forestry excludes the food producing functions of the forest, and destroys the forest diversity as 'weeds', 'scientific' agriculture too destroys species which are useful as food, even though they may not be useful on the market.

The Green Revolution has displaced not just seed varieties but entire crops in the Third World. What have usually been called 'marginal crops' or 'coarse grains' are nature's most productive crops in terms of nutrition. That is why women in Garhwal continue to cultivate mandua and women in Karnataka cultivate ragi inspite of all attempts by state policy to shift to cash crops and commercial foodgrains, to which all financial incentives of agricultural 'development' are tied. What the Green Revolution has declared 'inferior' grains are actually superior in nutritive content to the so-called 'superior' grains, rice and wheat.

Not being commercially useful, people's crops are treated as 'weeds' and destroyed with poisons. The most extreme example of this destruction is that of bathua, an important green leafy vegetable, with a very high nutritive value and rich in Vitamin A, which grows as an associate of wheat. However, with intensive chemical fertilizer use bathua becomes a major competitor of wheat and has been declared a 'weed' that is killed with herbicides. Forty thousand children in India go blind each year for lack of Vitamin A, and herbicides contribute to this tragedy by destroying the freely available sources of vitamin A. Thousands of rural women who make their living by basket and mat-making, with wild reeds and grasses, are also losing their livelihoods because the increased use of herbicide is killing the reeds and grasses. The introduction of herbicide-resistant crops will increase herbicide use and thus increase the damage to economically and ecologically useful plant species. Herbicide resistance also excludes the possibility of rotational and mixed-cropping, which are essential for a sustainable and ecologically balanced agriculture, since the other crops would be destroyed by the herbicide. US estimates now show a loss of US $4 billion per annum due to loss as a result of herbicide spraying. The destruction in India will be far greater because of higher plant diversity, and the prevalence of diverse occupations based on plants and biomass.

Strategies for genetic engineering resistance which are destroying useful species of plants can also end up creating superweeds. There is an intimate relationship between weeds and crops, especially in the tropics where weedy and cultivated varieties have genetically interacted over the centuries and hybridize freely to produce new varieties. Genes for herbicides tolerance, that genetic engineers are striving to introduce into crop plants may be transferred to neighbouring weeds as a result of naturally, occurring gene transfer.

Scarcities of locally useful plant varieties have been created because the dominant knowledge systems discount the value of local knowledge and declares locally useful plants to be 'weeds'. Diversity is thus destroyed in plant communities and forest and peasant communities, because in commercial logic it is not 'useful'. When what is useful and what is not is determined one-sidedly, all other systems of determining value are displaced.

'Miracle trees' and 'miracle seeds'

The one-dimensional perspective of dominant knowledge is rooted in the intimate links of modern science with the market. As multidimensional integrations between agriculture and forestry at the local level are broken, new integrations between non-local markets and local resources are established. Since economic power is concentrated in these remote centres of exploitation, knowledge develops according to the linear logic of maximizing flow at the local level. The integrated forest and farm gives way to the separate spheres of forestry and agriculture. The diverse forest and agricultural ecosystems are reduced to 'preferred' species by selective annihilation of species diversity which is not 'useful' from the market perspective. Finally, the 'preferred' species themselves have to be engineered and introduced on the basis of 'preferred' traits. The natural, native diversity is displaced by introduced monocultures of trees and crops.

In forestry, as the paper and pulp industry rose in prominence, pulp species became the 'preferred' species by the dominant knowledge system. Natural forests were clear-felled and replaced by monocultures of the exotic Eucalyptus species which were good for pulping. However, 'scientific' forestry did not project its practice as a particular response to the particular interest of the pulp industry. It projected its choice as based on a universal and objective criteria of 'fast growth' and 'high yields'. In the 1980s, when the concern about deforestation and its impact on local communities and ecological stability created the imperative for afforestation programmes, the eucalyptus was proposed worldwide as a 'miracle' tree. However, local communities everywhere seemed to think otherwise.

The main thrust of conservation struggles like Chipko is that forests and trees are life support systems, and should be protected and regenerated for their biospheric functions. The monoculture mind on the other hand sees the natural forest and trees as 'weeds' and converts even afforestation into deforestation and desertification. From life support systems, trees are converted into green gold – all planting is motivated by the slogan, 'Money grows on trees'. Whether it is schemes like social forestry or wasteland development, afforestation programmes are conceived at the international level by 'experts' whose philosophy of tree planting falls within the reductionist paradigm of producing wood for the market, not biomass for maintaining ecological cycles or satisfying local needs of food, fodder and fertilizer. All official programmes of afforestation, based on heavy funding and centralized decision making, act in two ways against the local knowledge systems – they destroy the forest as a diverse and self-producing system, and destroy it as commons, shared by a diversity of social groups with even the smallest having rights, access and entitlements.

'Social' forestry and the 'miracle' tree

Social forestry projects are a good example of single species, single commodity production plantations, based on reductionist models which divorce forestry from agriculture and water management, and seeds from markets.

A case study of World Bank-sponsored social forestry in the Kolar district of Karnataka (Shiva 1981) is an illustration of reductionism and maldevelopment in forestry being extended to farmland. Decentred agro-forestry, based on multiple species and private and common tree stands, has been India's age-old strategy for maintaining farm productivity in arid and semi-arid zones. The honge, tamarind, jackfruit and mango, the jola, gobli, kagli and bamboo traditionally provided food and fodder, fertilizer and pesticide, fuel and small timber. The invisible, decentred agro-forestry model was significant because the humblest of species and the smallest of people could participate in it, and with space for the small, everyone was involved in protecting and planting.

The reductionist mind took over tree planting with 'social forestry'. Plans were made in national and international capitals by people who could not know the purpose of the honge and the neem, and saw them as weeds. The experts decided that indigenous knowledge was worthless and 'unscientific', and proceeded to destroy the diversity of indigenous species by replacing them with row after row of eucalyptus seedlings in polythene bags, in government nurseries. Nature's locally available seeds were laid waste; people's locally available knowledge and energies were laid waste. With imported seeds and expertise came the import of loans and debt and the export of wood, soils and people. Trees, as a living resource, maintaining the life of the soil and water and of local people, were replaced by trees whose dead wood went straight to a pulp factory hundreds of miles away. The smallest farm became a supplier of raw material to industry and ceased to supply food to local people. Local work, linking the trees to the crops, disappeared and was replaced by the work of brokers and middlemen who brought the eucalyptus trees on behalf of industry.

Industrialists, foresters and bureaucrats loved the eucalyptus because it grows straight and is excellent pulpwood, unlike the honge which shelters the soil with its profuse branches and dense canopy and whose real worth is as a living tree on a farm.

The honge could be nature's idea of the perfect tree for arid Karnataka. It has rapid growth of precisely those parts of the tree, the leaves and small branches, which go back to the earth, enriching and protecting it, conserving its moisture and fertility. The eucalyptus on the other hand, when perceived ecologically, is unproductive, even negative, because this perception assesses the 'growth' and 'productivity' of trees in relation to soil fertility and in relation to human needs for food and food production. The eucalyptus has destroyed the water cycle in arid regions due to its high water demand and its failure to produce humus, which is nature's mechanism for conserving water.

Most indigenous species have a much higher biological productivity than the eucalyptus, when one considers water yields and water conservation. The non-woody biomass of trees has never been assessed by forest measurements, yet it is this very biomass that functions in conserving water and building soils.

Eucalyptus

The most powerful argument in favour of the expansion of Eucalyptus is that it is faster growing than all indigenous alternatives. Even where biotic and climatic factors are conducive to good growth, Eucalyptus cannot compete with a number of indigenous fast growing species.

The points that emerge are:

1. In terms of yields measured as mean annual increment (MAI) Eucalyptus is a slow producer of woody biomass even under very good soil conditions and water availability.
2. When the site is of poor quality such as eroded soils or barren land Eucalyptus yields are insignificant.
3. The growth rate of Eucalyptus under the best conditions is not uniform for different age groups. It falls very drastically after 5 or 6 years.

The Eucalyptus, quite clearly, will not fill the gap in the demand of woody biomass more effectively than other faster growing species which are also better adapted to Indian conditions.

The assessment of yields in social forestry must include the diverse types of biomass which provides inputs to the agro-ecosystem. When the objective for tree planting is the production of fodder or green fertilizer, it is relevant to measure crown biomass productivity. India, with its rich genetic diversity in plants and animals, is richly endowed with various types of fodder tree which have annual yields of crown biomass that is much higher than the total biomass produced by Eucalyptus plantations.

An important biomass output of trees that is never assessed by foresters who look for timber and wood is the yield of seeds and fruits. Fruit trees such as jack, jaman, mango, tamarind, etc. have been important components of indigenous forms of social forestry as practised over centuries in India. Tamarind trees yield fruits for over two centuries. Other trees, such as neem, pongamia and sal, provide an annual harvest of seeds which yield valuable non-edible oils. In contrast, the biomass of the Eucalyptus is useful only after the tree is felled.

Figures 22.2 and 22.3 describe the comparative biomass contribution of indigenous trees and Eucalyptus. Afforestation strategies based dominantly on Eucalyptus are not therefore the most effective mechanism for tiding over the serious biomass crisis facing the country. The benefits of Eucalyptus have often been unduly exaggerated through the myth of its fast growth and high yields. The myth has become pervasive because of the unscientific and unjustified advertisement of the species. It has also been aided by the linear growth of Eucalyptus in one dimension while most indigenous trees have broad crowns that grow in three dimensions.

The Green Revolution and 'miracle' seeds

In agriculture, too, the monoculture mind creates the monoculture crop. The miracle of the new seeds has most often been communicated through the term 'high-yielding varieties' (HYV) – a central category of the Green Revolutionparadigm. Unlike what the term suggests, there is no neutral or objective measure of 'yield' on the basis of which the cropping systems based on miracle seeds can be established to be higher yielding than the cropping systems they replace.

Cropping systems, in general, involve an interaction between soil, water and plant genetic resources. In indigenous agriculture, for example, cropping systems include a. Crop components of one system are then measured with crop components symbiotic relationship between soil, water, farm animals and plants. Green Revolution agriculture replaces this integration at the level of the farm with the integration of inputs such as seeds and chemicals. The seed/chemical package sets up its own interactions with soils and water systems, which are, however, not taken into account on the assessment of yields.

Modern plant breeding concepts like HYVs reduce farming systems to individual crops and part cropsof another. Since the Green Revolution strategy is aimed at increasing the output of a single component of a farm, at the cost of decreasing other components and increasing external inputs, such a partial comparison is by definition biased to make the new varieties 'high yielding' although at the systems level, they may not be.

Traditional farming systems are based on mixed rotational cropping systems of cereals, pulses, oilseeds with diverse varieties of each crop, while the Green Revolution package is based on genetically uniform monocultures. No realistic assessments are ever made of the yield of the diverse crop outputs in the mixed and rotational systems. Usually the yield of a single crop like wheat or maize is singled out and compared to yields of new varieties. Even if the yields of all the crops were included, it is difficult to convert a measure of pulse

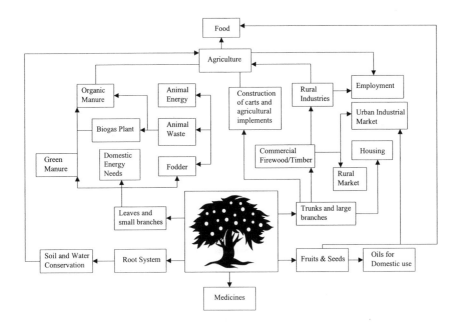

Fig 22.2 The contribution of traditional tree species to the rural life-support system

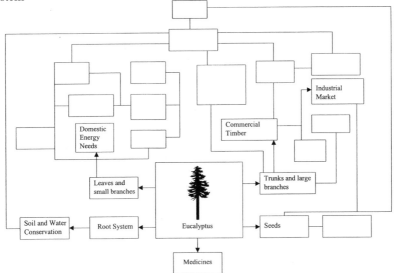

Fig 22.3 The comparative contribution of Eucalyptus to the rural life-support system

into an equivalent measure of wheat, for example, because in the diet and in the ecosystem, they have distinctive functions (see Figure 22.4).

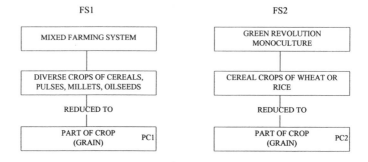

> The real scientific comparison should be between two farming systems - FS1 and FS2, with the full range of inputs and outputs included.
> This would be the comparison if FS2 was not given immunity from an ecological evaluation
> In the Green Revolution strategy, a false comparison is made between PC1 and PC2.
> So while PC2 > PC1, generally FS1 > FS2.

Figure 22.4 How the Green Revolution makes unfair comparisons

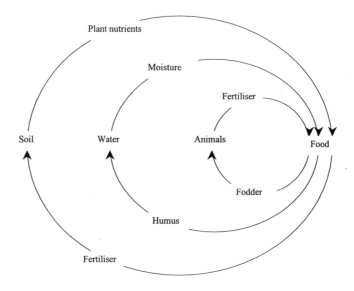

Figure 22.5 Internal input farming system

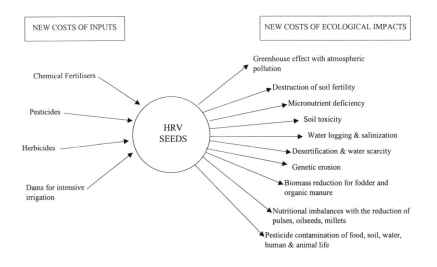

Figure 22.6 External input farming system

The protein value of pulses and the calorie value of cereals are both essential for a balanced diet, but in different ways and one cannot replace the other. Similarly, the nitrogen fixing capacity of pulses is an invisible ecological contribution to the yield of associated cereals. The complex and diverse cropping systems based on indigenous varieties are therefore not easy to compare to the simplified monocultures of HYV seeds. Such a comparison has to involve entire systems and cannot be reduced to a comparison of a fragment of the farm system. In traditional farming systems, production has also involved maintaining the conditions of productivity. The measurement of yields and productivity in the Green Revolution paradigm is divorced from seeing how the processes of increasing output affect the processes that sustain the condition for agricultural production. While these reductionist categories of yield and productivity allow a higher destruction that affects future yields, they also exclude the higher perception of how the two systems differ dramatically in terms of inputs (Figure 22.5).

The indigenous cropping systems are based only on internal organic inputs. Seeds come from the farm, soil fertility comes from the farm and pest control is built into the crop mixtures. In the Green Revolution package, yields are intimately tied to purchased inputs of seeds, chemical fertilizers, pesticides, petroleum and to intensive and accurate irrigation. High yields are not intrinsic to the seeds, but are a function of the availability of required inputs, which in turn have ecologically destructive impacts (Figure 22.6).

The distinguishing feature of the seeds is that they are highly responsive to certain key inputs such as fertilizers and irrigation. Palmer therefore suggested the term 'high-responsive-varieties' (HRVs) in place of 'high yielding varieties' (Lappe and Collins 1982). In the absence of additional inputs of fertilizers and irrigation, the new seeds perform worse than the indigenous varieties. With the additional inputs, the gain in output is insignificant compared to the increase in inputs. The measurement of output is also biased by restricting it to the marketable part of crops.

The Green Revolution package was built on the displacement of genetic diversity at two levels. Firstly, mixtures and rotation of diverse crops like wheat, maize, millets, pulses, and oilseeds were replaced by monocultures of wheat and rice. Secondly, the introduced wheat and rice varieties reproduced over a large scale as monocultures came from a very narrow genetic base, compared to the high genetic variability in the population of traditional wheat or rice plants. When 'HYV' seeds replace native cropping systems diversity is lost and irreplaceable.

The destruction of diversity and the creation of uniformity simultaneously involve the destruction of stability and the creation of vulnerability. Local knowledge on the other hand, focuses on multiple use of diversity. Rice is not just grain, it provides straw for thatching and mat-making, fodder for livestock, bran for fishponds, husk for fuel. Local varieties of crops are selected to satisfy these multiple uses. The so-called HYV varieties increase grain production, by decreasing all other outputs, increasing external inputs, and introducing ecologically destructive impacts.

There is, moreover, a cultural bias, which favours the modern system, a bias which becomes evident in the naming of plant varieties. The indigenous varieties, evolved through both natural and human selection produced and used by Third World farmers worldwide, are called 'primitive cultivar'. Those varieties created by modern plant breeders in international agricultural research centres of by transnational seed corporations are called 'advanced' or 'elite'.

The non-sustainability of monocultures

The crucial characteristic of monocultures is that they do not merely displace alternatives they destroy their own basis. They are neither tolerant of other systems, nor are they able to reproduce themselves sustainably. The uniformity of the 'normal' forest that 'scientific' forestry attempts to create becomes a prescription for non-sustainability.

Since the biological productivity of the forest is ecologically based on its diversity, the destruction of local knowledge, and with it of plant diversity, leads to a degradation of the forest and an undermining of its sustainability. The increase in productivity from the commercial point of view destroys productivity from the perspective of local communities. The uniformity of the managed forest is meant to generate 'sustained yields'. However, uniformity destroys the conditions of renewability of forest eco-systems, and is ecologically non-sustainable.

In the commercial forestry paradigm 'sustainability' is a matter of supply to the market, not the production of an eco-system in its biological diversity or hydrological and climatic stability. Sustained yield management is aimed at producing 'the best financial results, or the greatest volume', or the 'most suitable class of produce'.

Uniformity in the forest is the demand of centralized markets and centralized industry. However, uniformity acts against nature's processes. The transformation of mixed natural forests into uniform monocultures allows the direct entry of tropical sun and rain, baking the forest soils dry in the heat, washing the soils off in the rain. Less humid conditions are the reason for rapid retrogression of forest regions. The fires of Kalimantan are largely related to the aridization caused by the conversion of rainforests into plantations of Eucalyptus and Acacias. Floods and drought are created where the tropical forest has earlier cushioned the discharge of water.

This paradigm which destroys the diversity of the forest community either by clear felling or selective felling simultaneously destroys the very *conditions* for the renewal of the forest community. While species diversity is what makes the tropical forest biologically rich, and sustainable, this same diversity leads to allow density of individual species. The reductionist paradigm thus converts a biologically rich system into an impoverished resource and hence a non-renewable one.

In the dominant system, financial survival strategies determine the concept of 'sustained yield', which are in total violation of the principles of sustaining biological productivity. Sustained yields based on continuously reducing exploitable diameter classes lead to biological suicide, and a total destruction of forests.

Where the local knowledge is not totally extinct, communities resist the ecological destruction of introduced monocultures. 'Greening' with eucalyptus works against nature and its cycles, and it is being resisted by communities who depend on the stability of nature's cycles to provide sustenance in the form of food and water. The Eucalyptus guzzles nutrients and water and, in the specific conditions of low rainfall zones, gives nothing back but terpenes to the soil. These inhibit the growth of other plants and are toxic to soil organisms which are responsible for building soil fertility and improving soil structure. The eucalyptus certainly increased cash and commodity flows, but it resulted in a disastrous interruption of organic matter and water flows within the local ecosystem. Its proponents failed to calculate the costs in terms of the destruction of life in the soil, the depletion of water resources and the scarcity of food and fodder that eucalyptus cultivation creates. Nor did they, while trying to shorten rotations for harvesting, see that tamarind, jackfruit and honge have very short rotations of one year in which the biomass harvested is far higher than that of eucalyptus, which they nevertheless declared a 'miracle' tree. People everywhere have resisted the expansion of eucalyptus because of its destruction of water, soil and food systems.

The destruction of diversity in agriculture has also been a source of non-sustainability. The 'miracle' varieties displaced the traditionally grown crops and through the erosion of diversity, the new seeds became a mechanism for introducing and fostering pests. Indigenous varieties, or land races are resistant to locally occurring pests and diseases. Even if certain diseases occur, some of the strains may be susceptible, while others will have the resistance to survive. Crop rotations also help in pest control. Since many pests are specific in particular plants, planting crops in different seasons and different years causes large reductions in pest population. On the other hand, planting the same crop over large areas year after year encourages pest build-ups. Cropping systems based on diversity thus have a built-in protection.

Having destroyed nature's mechanisms for controlling pests through the destruction of diversity, the only miracle that seems to have been achieved with the breeding strategy of the Green Revolution is the creation of new pest and diseases, and with them the ever-increasing demand for pesticides. Yet the new costs of new pests and poisonous pesticides were never counted as part of the 'miracle' of the new seeds that modern plant breeders had given the world in the name of increasing 'food security'.

The 'miracle seeds' of the Green Revolution were meant to free the Indian farmer from constraints imposed by nature. Instead, large-scale monocultures of exotic varieties generated a new ecological vulnerability by reducing genetic diversity and destabling soil and water systems. The Green Revolution led to a shift from earlier rotations of cereals, oilseeds, and pulses to a paddy-wheat rotation with intensive inputs of irrigation and chemicals. The paddy-wheat rotation has created an ecological backlash with serious problems of waterlogging in canal irrigated regions and groundwater mining in tubewell irrigated regions. Further, the high yielding varieties have led to large-scale micronutrient deficiencies in soils, particularly iron in paddy cultivation and manganese in wheat.

These problems were built into the ecology of the HYV's even through they were not anticipated. The high water demands of these seeds necessitated high water inputs, and hence the hazards of desertification through water logging in some regions and desertification and aridization in others. The high nutrient demands caused micronutrient deficiencies on the one hand, but were also unsustainable because increased applications of chemical fertilizers were needed to maintain yields, thus increasing costs without increasing returns. The demand of the HYV seeds for intensive and uniform inputs of water and chemicals also made large-scale monocultures an imperative, and with monocultures being highly vulnerable to pests and diseases, a new cost was created for pesticide applications. The ecological instability inherent in HYV seeds was thus translated into economic non-viability. The miracle seeds were not such a miracle after all.

Sustainable agriculture is based on the recycling of soil nutrients. This involves returning to the soil part of the nutrients that come from the soil either directly as organic fertilizer or indirectly through the manure from farm animals. Maintenance of the nutrient cycle, and through it the fertility of the soil, is based on this inviolable law of return, which is a timeless, essential element of sustainable agriculture.

The Green Revolution paradigm substituted the nutrient cycle with linear flows of purchased inputs of chemical fertilizers from factories and marketed outputs of agricultural commodities.

The Green Revolution created the perception that soil fertility is produced in chemical factories, and agricultural yields are measured only through marketed commodities. Nitrogen fixing crops like pulses were therefore displaced. Millets which have high yields from the perspective of returning organic matter to the soil, were rejected as 'marginal' crops. Biological products not sold on the market but used as internal inputs for maintaining soil fertility were totally ignored in the cost-benefit equations of the Green Revolution miracle. They did not appear in the list of inputs because they were not purchased, and they did not appear as outputs because they were not sold.

Yet what is 'unproductive' and 'waste' in the commercial context of the Green Revolution is now emerging as productive in the ecological context and as the only route to sustainable agriculture. By treating essential organic inputs that maintain the integrity of nature as 'waste', the Green Revolution strategy ensured that fertile and productive soils are actually laid waste. The 'land augmenting' technology has proved to be a land-degrading and land-destroying technology. With the greenhouse effect and global warming, a new dimension has been added to the ecologically destructive effect of chemical fertilizers. Nitrogen-based fertilizers release nitrous oxide to the atmosphere which is one of the greenhouse gases causing global warming. Chemical farming has thus contributed to the erosion of food security through the pollution of land, water and the atmosphere (Shiva 1989).

Democratizing knowledge

Modern silviculture as an exclusivist knowledge system, which focuses exclusively on industrial wood production, displaces local knowledge systems which view the forest in the perspective of food production, fodder production and water production. The exclusive focus on industrial wood destroys the food, fodder and water production capacities of the forest. It disrupts links between forestry agriculture and, in attempting to increase commercial/industrial wood, it creates a monoculture of tree species. The eucalyptus has become a symbol of this monoculture (see Table 22.1).

Modern agriculture focuses exclusively on agricultural commodity production. It displaces local knowledge systems which view agriculture as the production of diverse food crops with internal inputs, and replaces it with monocultures of introduced varieties needing external industrial inputs. The exclusive focus on external inputs and commercial outputs, destroys diverse food crops such as pulses, oilseeds and millets, and disrupts the local ecological cycles; and in attempting to increase single crop output, it creates monocultures of crop varieties. The HYV becomes a symbol of monoculture.

The crisis of the dominant knowledge systems has many facets:

1. Since dominant knowledge is deeply wedded to economism, it is unrelated to human needs. Ninety percent of such production of knowledge could be stopped without any risk to human deprivation. On the contrary, since a large part of such knowledge is a source of hazards, and threats to human life (Bhopal, Chernobyl, Sandoz).
2. The political implications of the dominant knowledge system are inconsistent with equality and justice. It is disrupting of cohesion within local communities and polarizes society into those with access and those without it, both in respect to the knowledge systems and the power system.
3. Being inherently fragmenting and having built in obsolescence, dominant knowledge creates an alienation of wisdom from knowledge and dispenses with the former.
4. It is inherently colonizing.
5. It breaks away from concrete contexts, disqualifying as inadequate the local and concrete knowledge.
6. It closes access and participation to a plurality of actors.
7. It leaves out a plurality of paths to knowing nature and the universe. It is a monoculture of the mind.

Modern Western knowledge is a particular cultural system with a particular relationship to power. It has, however, been projected as above and beyond culture and politics. Its relationship with the project of economic development has been invisible; and therefore it has become a more effective legitimizer for the homogenization of the world and the erosion of its ecological and cultural richness. The tyranny and hierarchy privileges that are part of the development paradigm is rooted and from which it derives its rationalization and legitimisation. The power by which the dominant knowledge system has subjugated all others makes it exclusive and undemocratic.

Democratizing of knowledge becomes a central precondition for human liberation because the contemporary knowledge system excludes the humane by its very structure. Such a process of democratization would involve a redefining of knowledge such that the local and diverse become legitimate as knowledge, and they are viewed as indispensable knowledge because concreteness is the reality, and globalization and universalization are abstractions which have violated the concrete and hence the real. Such a shift from the globalizing to the local knowledge is important to the project of human freedom because it frees knowledge from the dependency on established regimes of thought, making it simultaneously more autonomous and more authentic.

Democratization based on such an 'insurrection of subjugated knowledge' is both a desirable and necessary component of the larger processes of democratization because the earlier paradigm is in crisis and in spite of its power to manipulate, is unable to protect both nature and human survival.

Table 22.1 Comparison of local and dominant knowledge systems

Local System	*Dominant System*
Forestry and agriculture integrated	Forestry separate from agriculture
Integrated systems have multidimensional outputs. Forests produce wood, food, fodder, water etc. Agriculture produces diversity of food crops	Each separate system made one dimensional. Forests produce only commercial wood. Agriculture produces only commercial crops with industrial inputs
Productivity in local system is a multidimensional measure, which has a conservation aspect	Productivity is a one-dimensional measure which is unrelated to conservation
Increasing productivity in these knowledge systems involves increasing the multidimensional outputs, and strengthening the integration.	Increasing productivity in these knowledge systems involves increasing one-dimensional output by breaking up integrations and displacing diverse outputs
Productivity based on conservation of diversity	Productivity based on creation of monocultures and destruction of diversity
Sustainable system	Non-sustainable system

References and further reading

Chin, S.C. (1989) *The Sustainability of Shifting Cultivation.* Penang: World Rainforest Movement.

Horton, R. (1967) 'African traditional thought and Western science', *Africa* 37: 2.

Lappe, F. and Collins, J. (1982) *Food First.* Abacus, p. 114.

Richaria, R H. (1986) Paper presented at Seminar on Crisis in Modern Science, Penang

Shiva, V. (1981) *Ecology and the Politics of Survival.* New Delhi: Sage.

Shiva, V. (1989) *Staying Alive.* London: Zed Books, p. 59.

Shiva, V. (1989) *The Violence of the Green Revolution.* Dehra Dun: Research Foundation of Science and Ecology.

Shiva, V., Bandyopadhyay, J. and Sharatchandra, H.C. (1981) *The Social, Ecological and Economic Impact of Social Forestry in Kolar.* Bangalore: IIM.

Troup, R S. (1916) *Silviculture Systems.* Oxford: Oxford University Press.

Source: Edited from Chapter 1, *Monocultures of the Mind*, 1993, London: Zed Books.

Author Index

Subject Index